Published in Paris

PUBLISHED IN PARIS

A Literary Chronicle of Paris in the 1920s and 1930s

HUGH FORD

With a Foreword by
Janet Flanner

COLLIER BOOKS
MACMILLAN PUBLISHING COMPANY
NEW YORK

The Acknowledgments on pages 418–20 are an extension of the
copyright page.

Collier Books
Macmillan Publishing Company
866 Third Avenue, New York, NY 10022
Collier Macmillan Canada, Inc.

Library of Congress Cataloging-in-Publication Data

Ford, Hugh D., 1925–
Published in Paris: American and British writers, printers, and
publishers in Paris, 1920–1939 / Hugh Ford; with a foreword by
Janet Flanner.—1st Collier Books ed.
p. cm.
Bibliography: p.
Includes index.
1. Publishers and publishing—France—Paris—History—
20th century. 2. Authors, American—20th century—
Biography. 3. Authors, English—20th century—
Biography. 4. Americans—France—Paris—
Biography. 5. British—France—Paris—Biography. 6. American
literature—France—Paris—History and criticism. 7. English
literature—France—Paris—History and criticism. 8. Paris
(France)—Intellectual life—20th century. I. Title.
Z310.6.P37F67 1988
820'.9'94436—dc19   87-32024
                                                                    CIP
ISBN 0-02-032550-9

Macmillan books are available at special discounts for bulk purchases
for sales promotions, premiums, fund-raising, or educational use.
For details, contact:
Special Sales Director
Macmillan Publishing Company
866 Third Avenue
New York, NY 10022

First Collier Books Edition 1988

10 9 8 7 6 5 4 3 2 1

PRINTED IN THE UNITED STATES OF AMERICA

This book is for MY MOTHER *and* FATHER

for THERESE

for MARTITA and JOHN

CONTENTS

Preface

ix

A Foreword: Three Amateur Publishers by Janet Flanner

xi

I   From Princeton to Paris: Sylvia Beach

3

II   Robert McAlmon's Contact Publishing Company

34

III   Bill Bird and the Three Mountains

95

IV   Edward Titus at the Sign of the Black Manikin

117

V   Harry and Caresse Crosby and the Black Sun

168

VI   Gertrude Stein's Plain Editions

231

VII   Nancy Cunard's Twenty-four Hours

253

VIII   Four New Directions

The Need for Anonymity: Carrefour

290

Fourth-Dimensional Writing: The Roving Eye

302

The Revolution of the Word: Servire

311

Content over Form: New Review

318

CONTENTS

IX   Harrison of Paris
323
X   Jack Kahane and the Guardian Obelisk
345
Appendix 1: The Seizin Press by Hugh Ford
385
Appendix 2: List of Press Publications, Periodicals, and Newspapers
404
Acknowledgments
418
Bibliography
421
Index
427

PREFACE

FOR THEIR CONTINUOUS and generous support and cooperation, I express my warm and lasting gratitude to the following: the late Miss Margaret Anderson, Miss Djuna Barnes, Mr. Oswell Blakeston, Mrs. William A. Bradley, Miss Kay Boyle, Mr. Morley Callaghan, Mr. Malcolm Cowley, Mr. Beresford Egan, Mrs. Solon R. Featherstone, Mr. John Ford, Mrs. William Friedman, Miss Florence Gilliam, Mr. Maurice Girodias, Mrs. Wyn Henderson, the late Mr. Hilaire Hiler, Mrs. Laura Riding Jackson, Mr. Phil Kaplan, Mr. Manuel Komroff, Mr. Edwin Lanham, Miss Jane Lidderdale, Mr. Walter Lowenfels, Mr. Len Lye, Mr. Ian MacNiven, Sir Francis Meynell, Mrs. Curtis Moffat, Mr. Ivan Moffat, Mr. James Moran, Mrs. Anna Neagoe, Miss Anais Nin, Mr. Patrick O'Higgins, Mr. Alfred Perlès, Mr. George Reavey, Mr. W. G. Rogers, Mr. Waverley Root, Mr. John Ryder, Mr. Jacob Schwartz, the late Mr. Roger Senhouse, Mr. Howard Simon, Mr. Allen Tanner, Mr. Mark Turbyfill, Mr. Parker Tyler, Mr. Edward Weeks, Mr. Robert Wilson, Mr. Glenway Wescott, Mr. Lloyd B. Wescott, Mr. Monroe Wheeler.

Of the many librarians who took a lively interest in this project and provided services far beyond my expectations, I extend my deepest thanks to Miss Joyce Brodowski, Roscoe L. West Library, Trenton State College, Trenton, New Jersey; Mr. Donald C. Gallup, Beinecke Library, Yale University, New Haven, Conn.; Mr. C. E. Greene, Harvey S. Firestone Library, Princeton University, Princeton, New Jersey; Mr. David Koch, Morris Library, Southern Illinois University, Carbondale, Illinois; Mr. John Mayfield, George Arents Research Library, Syracuse University, Syracuse, New York.

To the National Endowment for the Humanities I am greatly indebted for a Senior Fellowship, which enabled me to devote a full year's work to this project. In addition I owe thanks to the American Philosophical Society and to the Research Committee of Trenton State College for generous allowances of money and time.

I am in special debt to Miss Janet Flanner for her friendship and unfailing encouragement, and to Mr. Ray Roberts, my editor, for his firm support and patience during the preparation of this book.

A FOREWORD
Three Amateur Publishers

I

IN THE EVOLUTION of literature the book publisher has undeniably been the second main essential. Yet individually he has rarely been famed as this necessary major element connected with the appearance of a new great book or even much thanked by its readers. He has been literature's common carrier, like a donkey, with the authors and occasionally their weight of genius loaded on his back. As the original publisher of *Ulysses*, the late Miss Sylvia Beach escaped one or two of these constrictive categories. She became famous for having published only this one enormous magnum opus of James Joyce, so difficult to read and fathom that readers and many critics had at first to take their time about it to appreciate it. At the beginning she was mostly thanked merely by the very commotion it increasingly provoked in the whole Western literary world of the opening nineteen-twenties. Then as the years proceeded, for her service to literature she was thanked in person by literally the thousands of tourists and readers and writers from both sides of the Atlantic who came to her little Shakespeare bookshop in the rue de l'Odéon, which had become an incalculably large radiating center of literary influence and illumination over which she modestly presided, as small in her person as in her premises— adolescent in her size, with a schoolgirl cut of bobbed hair and white low collars, and economical steel-rimmed glasses. Where she did not escape the publisher's fate was as the beast of burden struggling beneath the crushing load of a singular author's genius and egotisms, heavy as stones or marble in the case of the Dubliner Joyce. There is no record of any other great writer of English prose in our time inhabited by so monumental a personality as he possessed or with a character so deeply inscribed and carved by his own ego. He was like a thin dapper granite column set up in his own honor.

A part of her fame came from her being an amateur woman publisher with the courage to publish so daring a modern masculine classic as *Ulysses*. All of Joyce's gratitude, largely unexpressed, should have been addressed to her as a woman. For the patience she gave to him was female, was even quasi-maternal in relation to his book. In one of those British obituaries so often remarkable for their mixture of justice, candor, and dry humor, Mr. Darsie Gillie, the Paris correspondent of the *Guardian* wrote after her death to signal her as "a woman who has left a mark on literature that has very few parallels. That *Ulysses* became the sort of book it is is largely due to her, for it was she in this, her one publishing venture, who decided to allow Joyce an indefinite right to correct his proofs. It was in the exercise of this right that the peculiarities of Joyce's prose reached their novel flowering. Sylvia Beach was brave to risk the publication of this strange book so soon after opening her bookshop, Shakespeare and Company, and with her slender means, but she was still braver to give Joyce this incomparable freedom for expanding and entangling his sentences."

She was a sufferer from migraine headaches and her eyesight was not strong. The seemingly endless entanglements of his interwritten or rewritten or newly written sentences on his *Ulysses* page proofs sent from the Dijon printer were a tiring trial even to that loyal volunteer company of her friends and his admirers—a handful of Americans, English, and bilingual literary French—who struggled to decipher his cryptic handwriting as his own sight worsened and was not redeemed by surgery. For Sylvia the never-ceasing proofreading was a nightmare. But the strain of responsibility for the welter of his scrawled additional phrases had to be hers alone, as the swelling book of genius progressed into gigantism. The two years of labor and of collaboration, of financial worries and of eye troubles shared by the author and publisher until the book was finally printed, were probably sustained by the ideal formality of their relations. In his notes to her he invariably wrote to her as Miss Beach and in conversation she always addressed him as Mr. Joyce. Even the irrepressive Ernest Hemingway did not call him by his first name; apparently the outstanding Left Bank exception to this respectful practice was the gifted and intrepid Djuna Barnes, who feared no man. She called Mr. Joyce Jim.

Sylvia's forebears had included nine Presbyterian ministers, counting her father, and her mother was born in India where her own father was a medical Protestant missionary. Sylvia had inherited morality and you could feel it in her and actually enjoy it, too, in her bookshop, which she dominated with her cheerfulness, her trust in other human beings, and her own trustworthiness for good things like generosity, sympathy, integrity, humor, kind acts, and an invariably polite *démodé* vocabulary. She was no renegade. A coarsening of the American language, spoken and written, was just coming in with the nineteen-twenties as a form of realism following World War One, as a form of rebellion, too, against our Puritanism, our hypocrisy, against Prohibition, against our anti-hedonism generally. By a coincidence in expatriation, a half-dozen of what turned out to be indubitably the most talented young American writers—Hemingway, Dos Passos, and Fitzgerald were the leaders—were all collected on the Paris Left Bank. Their talent was like a form of colonial energy that had come back to Europe in the brains of these few expatriate writing outlanders. They all used Sylvia's bookshop as their club and parliament. Sylvia herself did not have a literary mind or much literary taste, though in time a certain sense of literature rubbed off onto her from the people around her. What she instinctively recognized and was attracted to was merely literary genius or flashes and fractions of it, or of tremendous great talent—men like Joyce, Hemingway, and T. S. Eliot, or Gide and Valéry, Frenchmen whom she knew through her French friend Mademoiselle Adrienne Monnier, who ran La Maison des Amis des Livres bookshop across the street. Sylvia had a vigorous clear mind, an excellent memory, a tremendous respect for books as civilizing objects, and was a really remarkable librarian. She loved the printed word and books in long rows. She exerted an enormous transatlantic influence without recognizing it.

II

Another important event was the entry in Paris into book writing by Gertrude Stein and the collecting of contemporary friends' art by the Stein households. The first picture Leo Stein bought in Paris was by Cézanne, whom he had heard of when he lived in Florence. It was a lovely green landscape, though what Leo had wanted was a yellowish landscape from the region around Aix. It was his first purchase from the moody art dealer Vollard, from whom he and Gertrude subsequently bought a tiny Daumier head of an old woman, then bought a very small black Manet, then two little Renoirs, and several Cézanne portraits because they were not dear, including finally one large one. Thus the famous Stein collection of contemporary French art started in a neighborly relation with one Cézanne and one Picasso. It culminated later as a purchase for the New York Museum of Modern Art to serve as its great modern-art nucleus, which today remains the most complete of any in America.

In the early years of the First World War came the great innovation which changed contemporary French art and became of worldwide historical importance. It was a type and style of a new art being talked of privately by Picasso and Braque and even being tentatively tried out by them on canvas in their studios, a new style in painting never yet seen on earth before, which would be known as Cubism. The well-educated German art dealer Daniel-Henry Kahnweiler, who was their picture merchant, wrote a booklet in 1908, unfortunately published only in German and in Munich, called "Der Weg zun Cubismus," which described the "new art style as a pictorial preview [years in advance and in stylized geometric terms] of the space-time continuum that the century later discussed as a commonplace of scientific and metaphysical thought." What Cubism was supposed to be at the time it was being fumbled for by its creators is less clear. Picasso and Braque were apparently able to paint its beginning but not to explain it. Years later, Braque finally said that Cubism's main aim had been "the materialization of space," though as early as 1910 Miss Stein with her hearty curiosity for explanations had asked Picasso to put Cubism into words, to which he had replied, "You paint not what you see but what you know is there." It was Kahnweiler who put down in writing the first authoritative account of the early intentions of Picasso and Braque. "Their ideas," Kahnweiler wrote, "were no doubt clear in their minds yet were mentioned in their conversations rarely and only casually. The general goal seemed to be the representation of the three dimensional and its position in space on a two-dimensional surface." It is astonishing that today in the 1970s, with the preserved popularity of old Cubism in pictures which are treated as twentieth-century classics, that few of its admirers can define it. Looking back on those early Cubist years of creation, Braque, who had an excellent memory, later recalled in a famous interview published in 1954 in the Paris *Cahiers d'Art*, "Picasso and I both lived in Montmartre. We saw each other every day. We talked. During those years we said things that nobody will say again, things that nobody would understand anymore, things that would be incomprehensible and that gave us enormous pleasure." As Gertrude Stein herself later said, 1914 marked the end of an epoch even before the war began, and the war only made its ending official.

xiv

Gertrude Stein was the handsomest and most dominant of the women in the various Stein family units and the most watchful of what was going on in Paris in modern art. Negro sculpture had just been introduced to Picasso by Matisse who, to earn money, also began to teach art in one of the emptied Catholic convents made publicly available through the separation of church and state which legally took place in France at this time. All these changes led to infinite items of gossip enjoyed and privately recorded between Gertrude and the Matisses. Another change was the publishing of Gertrude's first book of short stories, *Three Lives*, which contained the story of the Negress Melanctha, the most popular that she ever wrote. The Indiana publisher Bobbs-Merrill had first been interested in publishing it and then changed its mind, so Gertrude had recourse to a grace-and-favor publisher, the Grafton Press of New York, that specialized in publishing manuscripts which clients wished to have put in book form at their own expense. Soon a young man called to see Gertrude and hesitantly said he was from the Grafton Press, and with embarrassment added that the Grafton people thought Miss Stein's knowledge of English seemed faulty, which she indignantly denied. She explained that her book was to be published exactly as it was typed on the manuscript, which with further embarrassment the young man declared would be done. In print it even elicited some reviewers' literary appreciation, which so surprised the Grafton Press that they wrote Gertrude a note declaring they were gratified they had printed her manuscript in the first place.

Janet Flanner, Orgeval,
France, 1930s.
COURTESY OF MISS SOLITA
SOLANO

Her next opus ready for book form was the thousand-page-long *The Making of Americans*. In it she made three important personal statements. The first was, "I like living with so many people," meaning the French; the second, "I like being alone with English and myself." The third was a chapter opening which began, "I write for myself and strangers." As a foreign literary figure Gertrude Stein was thus launched by herself in France. Though Gertrude was the accepted literary member of the Stein complex, her handwriting was so difficult to decipher that a new Californian named Alice B. Toklas, who had lately moved into the rue de Fleurus as Gertrude's best friend, became also her amanuensis and typist. The initial "B." in her signature stood for Babette, the name of Alice's mother's favorite girlhood friend. Immediately, Miss Toklas became as influential a figure in the Stein group as if she had become a member by marriage.

In 1932 an abridged version of Gertrude Stein's *The Autobiography of Alice B. Toklas* appeared in the *Atlantic Monthly* and was later published as part of the full book by Random House in 1962, edited by Carl Van Vechten. In the little preface to the 1933 edition, Gertrude intimately wrote, "Well, it was a beautiful autumn and in six weeks I wrote *The Autobiography of Alice B. Toklas* and it was published and I became a best seller. . . . I bought myself a new eight-cylinder Ford car and the most expensive coat made to order by Hermes and fitted by the man who makes horse covers for race horses for Basket the white poodle and two studded collars for Basket. I had never made any money before in my life and I was most excited."

III

The only press I myself knew from seeing it being worked in the making of some books was the Hours Press of Nancy Cunard which had previously operated in Paris as Bill Bird's Three Mountains Press. When Nancy Cunard bought it she had it shipped to her country house in Chapelle-Réanville in the Department of the Eure, where the machinery was with considerable difficulty set up and assembled in what had become the buttery of her farm buildings, which were chill and damp owing to the stream of spring water that constantly flowed into several lavabos. One night of a weekend that I spent at Réanville I heard someone fiddling with loose type until long after midnight. The next morning Louis Aragon, who was also a weekend guest, proudly appeared with the typeset ready for printing *The Hunting of the Snark*, by Lewis Carroll, as a small book. Its outside cover was of extreme interest for the decoration he had created for it, composed of all the symbols for punctuation that the old press type boxes had preserved—exclamation points, commas, paragraph markers, brackets, parentheses, ampersands, and semicolons, quotation marks, foreign accents for both French and German, and periods, or full stops, in plethora, the whole lot arranged like a frame of differing thicknesses around the edge of the outside page, forming a decoration of grace and oddity. For some reason, perhaps because he regarded Carroll as a surrealist, Aragon chose to view this cover decoration as a form of what he called surrealism. It was very gay, pretty, inventive, and innocently childlike.

There was an old-fashioned deep well at the top of the little rise, or hill, below which the buttery had been installed. It was at the end closest to her house that a short field had been planted with potatoes in rows. They had attracted an elderly and vicious old sow boar habitually to come there at night with her three young piglets to feast. I saw her only once, by moonlight. Her tusks were sinister in length. She had literally ploughed up the hills of new potatoes with them, apparently using the tusks like forks to lift the potatoes out of the ground. After the war, when for the first time I revisited Réanville with Nancy Cunard on a tour of inspection, she found the well crammed almost to the top of the wellhead with some of the finest volumes from her library—books bound in vellum, in tooled leather, and some in silk—which had been tossed into it in a destructive fury of hate by the local peasants who were many of them communists and regarded her as a rich fascist. What was even worse, they had completed this project of defiling the well by adding the carcass of some small beast, a squirrel or rabbit probably, whose rotting stench added the last horror that the peasant's hatred of her had utilized to make her homecoming express their political enmity, which was such a commonplace in that district when the war came to a close and the Nazis who had occupied the village were driven out by the French army. Nancy Cunard lived for the rest of her life alternating between her country house and modest Left Bank hotels in Paris. She died mourned, loved, and appreciated by her friends.

It was a rich if incoherent period in writing and publishing but continuous in the interest it roused in the scattered readers of this stream of original literary material that flowed from the pens, pencils, and brains of the small group of American tyros writing in English in Paris at this early date just after the end of the first war.

Janet Flanner
New York, 1973

Published in Paris

I

FROM PRINCETON TO PARIS:
Sylvia Beach

I

THE STORY of how the proprietor of an obscure little bookstore in Paris
became the publisher of what is widely considered to be the most important novel of this century will probably always provoke a few incredu-
lous gasps, if only because so audacious an undertaking was accomplished
by a slight, brisk, quick-tongued American woman whose knowledge of
publishing, a business at least as circuitous in France as in America, was
practically nil. Her triumph—destined to be indissolubly linked forever
with the author's—brought her immediate and lasting fame. Sylvia Beach
"is probably the best known woman in Paris," the literary critic Eugene
Jolas wrote in 1925, and "certainly one of the important figures in contemporary letters." By then others were bestowing similar encomiums on
her bookshop, which she had diplomatically named Shakespeare and
Company ("it was a peace-inducing choice"), and confidently predicting
the time would come when it would be recognized as America's single
most important literary outpost in Europe. Morrill Cody prophesied, with
impressive accuracy, that its distinction would arise from the "aid and
encouragement" it would offer writers who perhaps otherwise would be
lost in the shuffle, and from giving readers a new angle on the personality
and intimacy of books and their authors. Even before the accomplishment
of the publishing feat that made it the most famous American cultural
landmark in pre-World War II Paris—and for nearly twenty years the best-
known bookshop in the world—Sylvia Beach's Shakespeare and Company
had gone far toward fulfilling Cody's predictions.

From her own telling, the adventure that so splendidly and permanently transformed her life she herself had initiated in a way so natural

3

Sylvia Beach in front of Shakespeare and Company,
8 rue Dupuytren, Paris, 1920.

that, in retrospect, it almost assumes the simple dimensions of a fable. One day in the summer of 1921, barely a year after she had opened Shakespeare and Company, a grumpy, disconsolate James Joyce came to the shop and told the young proprietor the grim news that the prospects of having *Ulysses* published in the United States had just vanished with the suppression in New York of the *Little Review* for printing installments of his novel. The editors, Margaret Anderson and Jane Heap, although brilliantly defended in court by Joyce's friend, the lawyer and bibliophile John Quinn, had nonetheless been found guilty of printing obscenity (i.e., *Ulysses*) and fined a hundred dollars. Depressed as much by the charge as by the abrupt loss of all expectations of seeing *Ulysses* published in America, Joyce had cabled his New York publisher, Ben Huebsch, to withdraw the book. Bad news had also come from his English publisher and benefactress, Harriet Weaver, who reported that the five installments from *Ulysses* that had appeared in her magazine, *The Egoist*, had provoked similar charges in England. She was certain British printers would never consent to set type for a book which authorities would undoubtedly find objectionable, and for which the law would hold them accountable. Crushed, Joyce had resigned all hope of seeing *Ulysses* appear in either country, a sad prospect, since he had already labored on it for seven years and presumably would now have to finish without the assurance of publication. In a tone of "complete discouragement" he told Miss Beach that *Ulysses* would "never come out now."

Was it Joyce's plaint, the example of the *Little Review*, her own feeling that the author's pride had been hurt, or all three, that inspired Miss Beach to do something about the situation? Whatever the answer, she did what she must have intuitively believed would at least relieve the gloom and repair Joyce's injured pride. "It occurred to me that something might be done, and I asked, 'Would you let Shakespeare and Company have the honor of bringing out your Ulysses?' " The question, coming from one who at that time was hardly more than an acquaintance, must have startled Joyce, and although her offer contained a promise to rescue his book, he had no reason to believe that she, an inexperienced bookseller, could assume the complicated and challenging responsibilities of publishing *Ulysses*. Joyce, however, had few, if any, alternatives, and he could not have regarded with any equanimity the prospect of waiting for restrictions to be lifted in England and America. His response, recalled Miss Beach, was immediate and joyful acceptance of her proposal, a response apparently so unexpected that, despite the pleasure it brought,

5

she herself regarded as slightly incautious. It seemed rash "to entrust his great *Ulysses* to such a funny little publisher." Joyce nonetheless "seemed delighted," no doubt feeling that at last his misfortune had been reversed. Sylvia Beach was delighted, too, and they parted "very much moved."*

The rhetorical question, "Who is Sylvia?" provided a Paris *Times* reporter with the opening line for his column on Miss Beach, one of many to appear in the city's English-language dailies before and after the appearance of *Ulysses*. Invariably reporters asked her the same questions, and Miss Beach, invariably—and patiently—repeated the facts of her life. "Well," she would begin, "I come from Princeton. My father was pastor to Woodrow Wilson. My grandfather was pastor to Grover Cleveland. I came here [Paris] during the war—in 1915—to study French books. I worked for a while as a *volontaire agricole* in Serbia." Facts like these and others, such as having nine ministers among her ancestors, added a tantalizing piquancy to her character, and many openly wondered how she had ever come to publish a book that was reputedly as erotic as *Ulysses*. What Miss Beach was, and what to many she may have seemed to be, created complications and confusion from the start. For those who assumed she intended to make erotica a specialty—and who sometimes mistakenly brought such work to her for consideration—there awaited a revelation that was "too funny." And for those who came to Shakespeare and Company expecting to find a renegade with advanced prurient tastes there was bound to be a sudden reversal of expectation. Even her attire suggested restraint and a no-nonsense approach to things. Removed from her bibliophilistic surroundings she might have passed for a corporation secretary, or a schoolmistress, prim, forceful, formidable. She preferred mannish clothing: a tailor-made velvet jacket, a bow tie set in a low white collar, a felt hat, a shirt of nondescript dark cloth, and sensible American

---

* Both Miss Beach and Joyce have contributed to the confusion that still surrounds the matter of whether it was Miss Beach who first proposed to Joyce that she publish *Ulysses*, or whether it was Joyce himself who first asked her to do it. In a letter he wrote to Harriet Weaver at the time Joyce mentioned that he had "arranged for a Paris publication to replace the American one." Later in the same letter, however, he qualified his statement, saying that he had "accepted a proposal" made him by Shakespeare and Company "at the instance of Mr. Valery Larbaud." According to Miss Beach, Larbaud had nothing to do with the transaction; in fact, he became interested in Joyce's work only around the time *Ulysses* went to press. Miss Beach is also the source of two conflicting versions. In one of the several drafts of *Shakespeare and Company*, her memoir, she wrote: "I accepted with enthusiasm Joyce's suggestion that I publish his book. I felt that my little bookshop was immensely honored." In later drafts, however, and of course in her published memoir, she stated that it was she who asked Joyce to let Shakespeare and Company publish *Ulysses*.

shoes. She did not believe she looked any better this way, she once told a curious reporter; it was simply a matter of being "too busy to wear anything but a uniform." Her hair she kept neatly crimped. A sufferer all her life from poor eyesight (an affinity with Joyce that many noticed), she wore steel-rimmed glasses that gave her features a touch of severity. Direct and cheerful and endowed with a lively and curious mind and a retentive memory, she radiated a passion and a respect for literature and a near-adoration for those whose "literary genius or flashes and fractions of it" she had instinctively recognized. As Archibald MacLeish observed, Sylvia "cared less for books than for the men who wrote them," foremost of whom, of course, was James Joyce.

Ulysses brought Miss Beach exactly what she wanted and needed to survive: customers. By the mid-twenties, flocks of tourists, mostly English and American, their curiosity divided between sampling the contents of Joyce's banned book and seeing the woman responsible for its existence, began finding her shop, relocated by then in larger and more comfortable quarters in the rue de l'Odéon. Across the street stood its French pendant, La Maison des Amis des Livres, a bookshop-salon owned and presided over by Adrienne Monnier, a stoutish, animated Frenchwoman with a Whistlerian penchant for grey and white. Like others in the Quarter Miss Monnier had fashioned her own costume, a cross between a peasant's and a nun's habit, consisting of a white silk blouse with an ample white collarette, a velvet waistcoat, and a long full skirt of grey wool. Looking "extremely alive," she was easily the "most striking-looking person" Miss Beach had ever seen; and years later, when describing the circumstances that led to their first meeting in 1918, she hardly bothered to disguise the belief that it just might have been foreordained:

> One day at the Bibliothèque National, I noticed that one of the reviews . . . could be purchased at A. Monnier's bookshop, 7 rue de l'Odéon, Paris VI. I had not heard the name before, nor was the Odéon quarter familiar to me, but suddenly something drew me irresistibly to the spot where such important things in my life were to happen.

Around Miss Monnier at that time thronged congeries of young French writers (some of them like Louis Aragon and André Breton on leave from the front) who responded, with touching gratitude, to her almost maternal interest in them and their work. With nunlike devotion she labored to make her little place the most advanced bookshop in Paris, stocking all the avant-garde publications and maintaining the first circulating library in Paris to offer subscribers translations of American and British books. To keep the "friends of books" informed, she published the monthly *Le Bulletin des Amis des Livres*, containing short literary notices and announcements of coming events; and a review, *Le Navire d'Argent*, in which she printed French translations of stories by Hemingway and Robert McAlmon, poems by E. E. Cummings and William Carlos Williams, and Eliot's *The Love Song of J. Alfred Prufrock*. As a salon La Maison des Amis des Livres had no rivals. To Miss Monnier's weekly gatherings came special friends like André Gide, Paul Valéry, Léon-Paul Fargue, Paul Claudel, Sorbonne professors and students, poets and novelists and critics, and of course all the "friends of books." The programs included poetry readings (Jules Romains read his peace poem, "Europe"), lectures (Paul Valéry discussed Poe's "Eureka"), and tryouts, when authors would read from their work in progress. Perhaps the most memorable of Miss Monnier's "seances" occurred one evening in December 1921, when Valéry Larbaud and Jimmy Light each read selections from *Ulysses* in French. Joyce, who was present but unseen during the program, received an enthusiastic ovation at the conclusion. Miss Monnier later published the first French translation of *Ulysses* by Auguste Morel. The whole atmosphere of La Maison des Amis des Livres, Sisley Huddleston described as one "laden with an indefinable emanation of the intellect"; the place was a forum for theories and ideas, ideally suited for writers "planning, confiding their intentions, their hopes, their ambitions to each other."

That sampling of French *haute littérature* at Miss Monnier's turned what had long been Miss Beach's cherished dream to operate a bookstore into an obsession, one which, with her friend's blessing, she came close to satisfying after the war when she traveled to New York intending to open an American branch of La Maison des Amis des Livres, which the two women agreed might perform the commendable function of acquainting Americans with modern French literature. But when she discovered that real-estate costs and other expenses would be more than she could afford, all the plans to bring the "friends of books" to America had to be abandoned. Next, she wondered if a French bookshop could succeed in London, and the answer she obtained from Harold Munro, who at his Poetry Bookshop in Great Russell Street performed the functions she would later assume in Paris, was a firm no; there simply was not enough demand in London for French books, old or new. Still undaunted and still "juggling many ideas as to how [she could] be the most useful to Americans," she went back to Paris, where Miss Monnier, instead of offering condolences, suggested that she reverse things and open an American bookshop in the Quarter. Besides the practical advantages that Paris offered of lower rents and cheaper living expenses, the services that an American bookstore with a large circulating library of English-language books could provide would be immensely valuable to French as well as English-speaking customers. She reminded Sylvia that the demand at her shop for contemporary American writing had always exceeded the supply, that she had often herself said that the French should know about Eliot, Anderson, and Dreiser, and that something had to be done to get them out of the rut of reading Twain, Galsworthy, Kipling, and London. Moreover, Miss Monnier promised to guide her friend's "first steps" and to send her "lots of customers." Persuasive arguments they were for one already resolved to have her own shop. And for a fervent Francophile, what better reason than business could she possibly have for staying in Paris, perhaps forever?

In November 1919 Shakespeare and Company opened for business in a converted laundry which, at a cost of three thousand dollars (supplied by members of the Beach family), had been attractively renovated and stocked with books hastily collected from shops in London and Paris. Although it was auspiciously launched by the indefatigable Miss Monnier and god-fathered by Valéry Larbaud, who announced that his influence and support would have to take the place of the traditional gift of a silver cup, Shakespeare and Company from the start needed and, as expected, received the support of friends to remain afloat. The important thing for anyone opening a bookshop in France to remember, Sylvia Beach once remarked, is to get adopted by the French. That way you avoid being regarded as a tourist and "are in the home of your adoption." Managing to be adopted by many of her adopted country's literary figures had been, with Miss Monnier's help, an easy accomplishment for her, and for a time they outnumbered her American supporters, among the first of whom were Gertrude Stein and Alice B. Toklas, who drove up one day in their war-seasoned Ford to look over the new American outpost. Miss Stein subscribed to the lending library but remarked that it had "nothing amusing, none of the works that had formed the foundation of American literature—for instance, *The Girl of the Limberlost* and *The Trail of the Lonesome Pine*," two of her favorites. True enough, Miss Beach replied, but then no other library in Paris offered the works of Gertrude Stein either, and certainly none had two copies of *Tender Buttons* in circulation.

Miss Stein may have wanted to compensate for that "unjust criticism" when she later donated copies of *The Portrait of Mable Dodge at the Villa Curonia* and *Have They Attacked Mary: He Giggled: A Political Caricature* to Miss Beach's library. Dorothy Shakespear Pound, another early visitor, turned out to be more constructive than Gertrude Stein. While appreciative of the quaintness of the location Miss Beach had chosen for her shop, she nonetheless feared that its very remoteness would deter more customers than it would attract. Not only did taxi drivers have trouble finding it, but few Americans could pronounce the street on which the shop stood. Mrs. Pound's remedy was a map of the Quarter, with the location of Shakespeare and Company well indicated, which Miss Beach afterward never failed to print on all her trade circulars.

For those who found Shakespeare and Company, with or without a map, there were pleasant rewards. The lending library contained several hundred classic and modern British and American books, many of them gleaned from second-hand bookstores in Paris. Subscribers, nearly two hundred of them in 1919, included, from the English contingent, Ronald Firbank, Nancy Cunard, Roger Fry, Aldous Huxley, Edith Sitwell, and Walter de la Mare; from the French, André Gide, Georges Duhamel, Jules Romains, Louis Aragon, and Paul Valéry; and a handful of Americans. The purchases made on a hasty expedition to London a few months before the opening consisted of a small but good selection of English poetry. From New York had come some recent American books, and from Elkin Mathews (London) a few volumes of Yeats, Pound, and Joyce. American and British periodicals—*Nation, Dial, New Republic, New Masses, Egoist*, and the *New English Review*—hung side by side on a review rack. Two Blake drawings, photographs of Oscar Wilde, portraits of Emerson, Whitman, and Poe—the beginnings of an ever-expanding gallery which would eventually include most of the writers and artists who passed through Paris—shared wall space with black-and-white hangings from Serbia, some of the owner's war mementoes. Several little Whitman manuscripts formed a permanent display in a back parlor, just behind Miss Beach's desk. An assortment of mostly "flea-market" furniture ringed the fireplace (Joyce appropriated one of the two armchairs—known as good-wife—perhaps associating its blue cushion with *Ulysses*). In the narrow display windows, decorously arranged, rested leather-bound volumes of Shakespeare, Chaucer, Poe, Eliot, and of course Joyce, as well as a prominently displayed edition of *Three Men in a Boat*, a great French favorite and, because it was one of the first books Miss Beach sold, a

Sylvia Beach and James Joyce, rue de l'Odéon, Paris.

permanent window resident and a good-luck charm. Over the entrance, suspended by a "sort of iron finger," hung the shop's ensign, a portrait of Shakespeare, a proper patron saint. Miss Beach marveled that the artist, Charles Winzer, seemed to know instinctively how Shakespeare should look—"rather Chinese, with slanting eyes" and dressed "in black with buttons down the front and a gold chain"; sometimes she even thought Winzer's portrait resembled Joyce, though the artist had never met the author of *Ulysses*.

One senses that during the hectic years when Miss Beach was supervising the publication of *Ulysses* and then serving as Joyce's unofficial secretary and publisher, she must have often looked back nostalgically to that brief period of calm, her apprenticeship days, when learning the job meant being in the midst of it and when the pace at the shop allowed time to savor those bookish rewards so long anticipated. Shakespeare and Company was "like a house with the members of the family growing up in it." Even if she had not met Joyce and published his book, the uses for the shop would have increased, and with them, the tempo of its life. Financially, though, the first three years were almost better forgotten. Some days Miss Beach took in only fifty francs, around four dollars. For 1921 her expenditures (24,858,000 francs) came perilously close to matching her receipts (25,738,550), and if it had not been for the small amounts regularly received from home she no doubt would have had to consider closing the shop. Although financial solvency came slowly and was never a certainty on which she could depend from one year to the next, there was scarcely any delay before the popularity of her shop was a fact. A *Tribune* columnist reported a year before *Ulysses* appeared that "almost all the literary celebrities of the day are Miss Beach's friends" and that hardly "a day passes that some stray poet or novelist does not drop in to browse at her crowded shelves." Among those literary itinerants were the first American exile writers—the vanguard of the vast migration that followed—"pilgrims," Sylvia Beach called them, who in those pre-*Ulysses* days invariably asked to see Gertrude Stein and to whose *pavillon* in the rue de Fleurus she usually consented to conduct them. On Stephen Benet the meeting with Gertrude Stein probably left few traces; but Sherwood Anderson's visit to the rue de Fleurus turned into a banquet of mutual appreciation and admiration that would have long-lasting results for both. In an unpublished notebook Anderson kept at the time he called Gertrude Stein "the very symbol of health and strength" and noted that she smoked and laughed and told stories "with an American shrewdness in getting the tang and the kick into the telling." The generally amiable relations be-tween Miss Stein and Miss Beach quickly worsened, however, when *Ulysses* was published in February 1922. More than anything it was Joyce's fame that bothered Miss Stein, and even Miss Beach had to agree that Joyce's work "had a way of monopolizing the attention of everyone around him," and that it was probably that fact which explained Miss Stein's resentment of Joyce as well as a larger resentment that extended to "the whole writing world" for having been so neglected. Certainly Miss Stein made no secret of her displeasure, something she was almost cer-tainly dramatizing when she notified Miss Beach that she wished to trans-fer her lending library subscription to the American library on the Right Bank.

Of the other early semi- or permanent American residents, Ezra Pound, Robert McAlmon, and Ernest Hemingway were the shop's steadi-est users. Pound, who had just fled England, where, he told Miss Beach, the water was beginning to creep up over the islanders who would prob-ably soon develop webbed feet, found Shakespeare and Company a con-venient and hospitable parliament. McAlmon, besides making the place his permanent mailing address, used it as a club and eventually as a stor-age and distribution center for his Contact Publishing Company. "Pil-grim" Hemingway, who turned up late in 1921 bearing the now-famous letter of introduction from Sherwood Anderson, became Shakespeare and Company's "best customer," for which the main recompense perhaps was unlimited hours of uninterrupted reading in the back room of the shop. Hemingway, boyishly attractive and cosmopolitan, enchanted Miss Beach as well as Miss Monnier, and the two women, their excitement nearly equalling his, often accompanied him to boxing matches and bike races. When he told them he planned to read a story he had just written called "In Our Time" and invited them to attend the reading (for the occasion Hemingway borrowed an apartment from Dorothy and Louis Galantière), they accepted the invitation with honor and later described the event as having the same rapturous sensation as discovering an excellent wine; and Adrienne Monnier remarked that young Hemingway had the "true writer's temperament." Both women added practical support to their praise. In *Le Navire d'Argent* Miss Monnier published "The Undefeated," the author's first French translation. Miss Beach, when asked by Jonathan Cape what American author he should publish, instantly replied: "Hemingway." Cape became Hemingway's first English publisher. In *A Moveable Feast*, his book of rather testy recollections of Paris in the 1920s, Hemingway remembered Sylvia Beach as a "delightful and charming and welcoming" friend. "No one that I ever knew was nicer to me."

II

Joyce, galvanized by the decision to publish *Ulysses*, at once got in touch with Harriet Weaver and recommended that in some way she try to amalgamate her long-planned edition of the book with the Paris publication, a suggestion she rejected in favor of issuing her own edition later on. She did agree, however, to supply Miss Beach with the names of prospective English subscribers, and proposed that, once the Paris book was fully subscribed, sheets be sent to her for an "ordinary" edition which she would sell for 10/6. By the time Joyce conferred again with his new publisher, Miss Beach had had some misgivings that required the reassurance and strength of Miss Monnier to dispel. The enormity of the task ahead had all at once overwhelmed her. After all, she had never before thought of going into publishing, and now, without any clear notion of how to proceed, she had agreed to become the publisher of the one work she most admired. What she realized was that she had picked out "the most difficult book in the world" with which to make her debut. The challenge could hardly have been larger, or the possibilities for failure greater. Although Miss Monnier did not know Joyce, and knew nothing about *Ulysses*, she immediately—and enthusiastically—assured Miss Beach that her decision was sound and that she could depend on her for support and guidance. Together, she recommended, they would visit her printer, Maurice Darantière, who would know exactly how to proceed. They also decided (probably on Miss Monnier's advice) to restrict the first printing of *Ulysses* to a thousand copies, a figure which Joyce later complained was far too high for a limited edition. Miss Beach would be better off printing a dozen or so (on one occasion he reduced the figure to two), and even then, he feared, there might be some left over. Joyce's pessimism failed to deter Miss Beach. Shortly afterward, she announced that her edition of *Ulysses* would be available in three impressions: the smallest, 100 copies, printed on Holland paper and signed by the author, would sell for 350 francs; the next, 150 copies, on Vergé d'Arches paper, for 250 francs; and the largest, 750 copies, on plain linen paper, for 150 francs. (The price in United States currency for the cheapest edition of *Ulysses* at 150 francs was $11.50. During the decade the franc varied from about 13 to 25 for the dollar.) For any who complained that the prices were too high she had an explanation. "Considering the seven years Joyce had spent on the book and the loss of his eyesight, it didn't seem to me as dear as all that."

As expected, Darantière not only listened sympathetically to the account Miss Beach gave him of the misfortunes of *Ulysses* and its creator, but unhesitatingly accepted the assignment of printing Joyce's opus, delighted at having been chosen to do a book by the writer whom Miss Beach described as "our greatest." Perhaps it was his elation that made it easy to accept her rather exacting financial stipulations. Determined not to permit *Ulysses* to plunge her into bankruptcy (she had no reserves and depended on contributions and loans to operate the shop), she had put prospective subscribers on notice that their orders would be filled by registered mail immediately *"on receipt of payment."* They would be notified when the book was available and would be expected to send their remittance before it was posted. Darantière, she requested, must not begin printing *Ulysses* until enough money had either been collected or promised by subscribers to cover the costs of printing. And he must not press her. Further, she asked that he agree to have his bill settled in installments when, or if, "the remittances for the subscriptions came in." That he accepted these terms struck her as "very sporting."

For the job of actually selling subscriptions, she could depend on a small band of loyal and energetic friends: Adrienne Monnier, who said it was "everyone's duty" to subscribe to *Ulysses*, and Léon-Paul Fargue and Valéry Larbaud collected the names of interested Frenchmen; Harriet Weaver, as promised, supplied the list of *Egoist* readers, all long-time Joyceans, as well as the names of others who had inquired about the book; André Gide paid a personal visit to the shop to place his order, not so much to subscribe to *Ulysses*, she thought, as to show "a friendly interest" in her enterprise and to support the "cause of freedom of expression." From the *Little Review* crowd, now settled on the Left Bank after having suffered the "curtailment of so many of their pleasures," the final one being the suppression of *Ulysses*, came numerous orders. Ezra Pound, himself a subscriber, brought in many more from all over the world, and one from his friend W. B. Yeats. Hemingway was down for several copies. No one quite outsold Robert McAlmon, however, who, with his pockets perpetually stuffed with subscription blanks, moved from café to café, waiting for an opportunity to inveigle his drinking companions into signing up for a copy of Joyce's book. On opening the shop Miss Beach would often spy a batch of signed orders ("hasty bunches," McAlmon called them) that McAlmon had deposited under the door sometime during the early morning hours. The most famous non-subscriber was George Bernard Shaw. Though he admitted that *Ulysses* was a truthful book and though he wished it success, Shaw accused Miss Beach of not knowing Joyce's countrymen very well if she believed any of them, particularly the elderly, would spend 150 francs for a "revolting record of a disgusting phase of civilization." Reading only fragments of *Ulysses* had convinced him that Joyce had written an obscene book, and if Miss Beach preferred to regard it as art, then she was probably "a young barbarian beglamoured by the excitement and enthusiasms that art stirs up in passionate material." Miss Beach, while admitting Shaw was right in saying that *Ulysses* had certainly stirred her, and lots of others, more than anything Shaw had ever written, resisted the urge to tell him so, preferring to enjoy his denunciations privately with Joyce. On one point, however, Shaw was wrong. Among the nearly five hundred names that finally filled the subscription list were several "elderly"—and presumably affluent—Irishmen. Approximately one-third of the subscribers lived in Paris, one hundred or so in New York, fifty throughout England, a dozen in both Italy and Ireland, and one or two in such places as Belgium, Sweden, Norway, China, and Borneo.

With the problem of subscriptions settled, Darantière began setting type, and, as agreed, supplied Joyce with as many proofs as he wanted, usually five, the first batch of which reached him in June 1921. For Joyce, reading proof was "a creative act" which Miss Beach, probably more out of naïveté than an inducement to creativity, abetted by permitting him to make unlimited changes directly on the proof sheets. By the time Joyce had finished developing and rewriting *Ulysses* it had swollen to a third again its original size. Darantière, although alarmed, at first remained silent out of deference to the publisher's wishes and respect for Joyce, but as more and more proof sheets arrived at the printery "adorned with Joycean rockets and myriads of stars guiding the printers to words and phrases all around the margins," he decided he must speak. Did Miss Beach understand that resetting type time after time would increase production costs enormously, and perhaps even plunge her into the "financial quagmire" she wanted to avoid? Could not something be done to curtail Joyce's "appetite for proofs"? Nothing could, and as far as Miss Beach was concerned, nothing would. Neither the protestations of the printer, no matter how sincere and correct, nor the heavy burdens she herself had assumed of reading and rereading the proof sheets sent back from the printery, ever had the slightest effect on Joyce's habits. Doggedly Miss Beach insisted that publishing *Ulysses* was her responsibility. Writing it was Joyce's, and therefore it "was to be as Joyce wished, in every respect." The only salving thought she allowed herself contained a characteristically sturdy puritan rectitude: "It seemed natural to me that the efforts and sacrifices on my part should be proportionate to the greatness of the work I was publishing." And sometime later, when asked about her association with Joyce, Miss Beach referred again to the mutual dedication to work on which their collaboration rested: "He [Joyce] was never a slacker. If he was, I would never have helped him. He did great work. He gave himself to his work and expected you to do the same." So the lights in the old vine-covered Dijon printery continued to blaze all night as Darantière's toilworn printers, none of whom spoke or read English, went on with the tedious business of deciphering Joyce's emendations and resetting their type.

Nearly as worrisome as the author's proliferating proofs was the problem of finding reliable typists to copy his manuscripts. Those who offered their services often left after a short time, necessitating renewed searches for replacements, and at least one volunteer typist introduced changes into the text of *Ulysses*. While copying the Penelope section, McAlmon inadvertently misplaced some of Molly's thoughts, and deciding that the order of her ruminations would not matter much, left the mistakes uncorrected and never bothered to mention the matter to Joyce. When *Ulysses* appeared he was pleased to see that his transpositions had been retained, and asked Joyce whether he had noticed. Joyce replied that he had but decided McAlmon was right and let them stand. The difficulties involving the Circe episode, however, on which nine typists had labored and failed to finish, caused Joyce so much distress that, in desperation, he left the unfinished section with Miss Beach, who promised to have it typed, and soon, for Darantière had at that moment sent word that printing had caught up with the supply of text and that the missing section was causing a delay. First to volunteer (for a short time) was the publisher's sister Cyprian, whose French replacement made "wonderful progress" for someone whose language was not English before she, too, departed. Volunteer three, the wife of a British Embassy official, perhaps would have completed the project had not her husband, scandalized by what he one day accidentally found his wife copying, dispatched Joyce's manuscript to the flames. Horrified by the loss, Miss Beach broke the news to Joyce, who made matters no better by revealing that the only copy of the de-

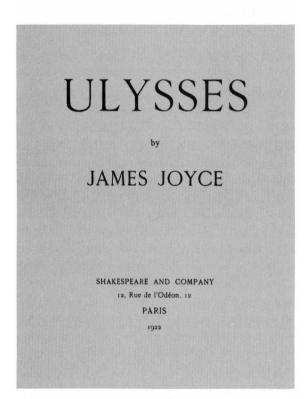

ULYSSES

by

JAMES JOYCE

SHAKESPEARE AND COMPANY
12, Rue de l'Odéon. 12
PARIS
1922

Title page of *Ulysses* by James Joyce (Shakespeare and Company, 1922).
PRINCETON UNIVERSITY LIBRARY

stroyed section had already been sent to John Quinn, in New York. Quinn, who had arranged to purchase the entire manuscript of *Ulysses* and was receiving it from Joyce section by section, stubbornly refused to return the Penelope section to Paris despite the pleadings of both Joyce and Miss Beach. Finally, he consented to allow it to be photographed, and, to everyone's delight, the reproductions came out clearer than the lost manuscript. After only a slight delay a new copy was made (by Cyprian) and rushed to Darantière.

Even the covers for *Ulysses* turned into a problem, one that might have defeated a publisher less determined than Miss Beach. Joyce insisted that they had to be blue, not any shade of blue, but the same as that found in the Greek flag, one of which, "in honor of Odysseus," hung outside Shakespeare and Company during the incubation of Joyce's book. Satisfying Joyce's latest request exhausted and exasperated printer and publisher alike. "Alas!" exclaimed Miss Beach, "merely to look at that flag gave me a headache." First, the color samples Darantière brought to Paris did not match the blue in the flag. Retiring to Dijon, he tried again, and the new samples came no closer. Finally, he traveled to Germany and there tracked down the elusive blue, only to discover at that point that the paper was wrong, a problem he fortunately was able to solve by having the blue lithographed on white cardboard covers, thus producing, perhaps without realizing it, the national colors of Greece—blue and white.

Presumably unaware of the delays his own demands were causing, Joyce began letting it be known, around December 1921, that *Ulysses* would appear about the time of his fortieth birthday on February 2, 1922, just two months away, and despite the announcements Miss Beach had issued to the contrary (the publication date had been changed and reposted again and again) he emphasized in a spate of letters and telegrams to both Miss Beach and Darantière that they must make every effort to meet that date. It was a preposterous demand, considering all that remained to be done, including the blue covers, but knowing how much he looked forward to celebrating the publication of *Ulysses* on his birthday, Miss Beach went to Dijon and held a "conversation" with Darantière, the substance of which was that, although it would be impossible to deliver the complete edition of the book in February, it just might be possible to place "one copy in Joyce's hands" by then. Darantière, however, did even better. On February 1, he notified Miss Beach that he was dispatching two copies of *Ulysses* with a conductor on the Paris-Dijon express, due to arrive in Paris at 7:00 A.M., February 2. On the platform the next morning, her heart going like a locomotive, Miss Beach searched the incoming train for Darantière's emissary. Finally he stood before her, holding a large parcel bearing her name, which, with nearly unbearable excitement, she opened and found did indeed contain two large blue copies of *Ulysses*. Copy Number One was, of course, for Joyce, which she dropped off to him on the way to the shop, where Copy Number Two, her own, went on display in the front window, causing simultaneous excitement and disappointment among those who had waited a good part of the night to claim their copies only to learn that Miss Beach had received only one for herself. Joyce, presumably too delighted with having the book to complain about the numerous typographical errors (in the 732 pages, "complete as written," Miss Beach estimated there averaged one to half-a-dozen per page), wrote to thank his publisher for such a momentous birthday gift. "I cannot let today pass without thanking you for all the trouble and worry you have given yourself about my book during the past year." To commemorate the occasion he had dashed off a few verses containing, along with praise for her Yankee bravery, some clear directives concerning her future responsibilities to him:

> Who is Sylvia, what is she
> That all our scribes commend her.
> Yankee, young and brave is she
> The west this pace did lend her
> That all books might published be.
>
> Is she rich as she is brave
> For wealth oft daring misses?
> Throngs about her rant and rave
> To subscribe for *Ulysses*
> But, having signed, they ponder grave.
>
> Then to Sylvia let us sing
> Her daring lies in selling.
> She can sell each mortal thing
> That's boring beyond telling
> To her let us buyers bring.
>
> J. J.
after
W. S.

As much as Miss Beach would have liked pleasing Joyce, for awhile she had no copies of his book to sell or send subscribers. By this time it had been almost fully subscribed, and after word spread that publication was imminent the demand far exceeded the number of copies she would be able to provide. With Joyce's impatience increasing daily, Darantière labored to correct a flaw in the cover, and a week after publication he had managed to ship only fifty copies to Paris. In mid-March, with deliveries still lagging, Miss Beach and Miss Monnier went to Dijon to confer with the printer, and soon afterward the flow of copies increased. For the next few months Shakespeare and Company was transformed into a wrapping and shipping room. Joyce came in almost daily—more interested, one gathers, in supervising than helping—although occasionally he would glue the labels on the parcels and then tote them to the post office nearby, complaining of their weight (one kilo, 550 grams). Conditioned to view customs men with suspicion, particularly in Ireland, he urged Miss Beach to mail Irish subscribers their copies immediately; he reminded her that "with a new Irish Postmaster General and a vigilance committee in clerical hands" the situation in Ireland could deteriorate at any moment. Joyce was right. By mailing copies to England and Ireland at once, before postal authorities realized what was passing through their hands, all reached their destinations safely. However, finding ways to circumvent American customs officials—who, after passing copies sent to Quinn and a few others, had become more vigilant and were delaying or impounding the book—demanded more ingenuity than either Miss Beach or Miss Monnier possessed. Exasperated, they finally put the problem before Hemingway, and the plan he devised must be one of the most successful booklegging operations on record. A friend of his, a painter named Barnet Braverman, he told Miss Beach, might be persuaded to go to Windsor, Canada, where there was no embargo on *Ulysses* and where copies, therefore, could be safely mailed, and from where, Hemingway explained, Braverman could carry the book to the United States by ferryboat, making as many crossings as needed to transport the forty copies American subscribers were still expecting. Miraculously the scheme worked. Using his artist's equipment as decoys, Braverman began shuttling between Windsor and Detroit, each time carrying at least one copy of *Ulysses*, which he would carefully unwrap on the Canadian side of the border and retie and rewrap on the American. When in early 1923 he had delivered the final copy, he submitted a bill to Miss Beach for $53.34, and asked if she would kindly tell him who in Paris had ever recommended him for such a tiresome job. Young Braverman's accomplishment delighted Joyce, who rewarded him with a signed copy of his book.

If Sylvia Beach wanted to curtail or stop altogether the services she had provided Joyce and even resign from her position as the publisher of *Ulysses*, now that it had been distributed and a second edition was about to appear, she gave no sign that she wished to dissolve their partnership. Despite all the taxing, annoying, and time-consuming demands Joyce had made, she could honestly say she had enjoyed "the Joycean job." Nor did Joyce do anything that would suggest he wanted to close his relationship with his "funny little publisher." In fact, beginning in the months following the publication of *Ulysses*, he practically took over Miss Beach's shop as well as her life. In her words, he became a "perfect octopus." If one did anything for him one did everything. He kept Miss Beach as well as her various helpers (especially Myrsine Moschos, who for several years served as Miss Beach's closest assistant) busy attending to his correspondence and banking; they became "his agents, his errand boys . . . made appointments for him, made friends for him, arranged all the business of the translations of his work published in Germany, Poland, Hungary,

21

Czechoslovakia." Miss Beach herself carefully recorded all his royalties, loans, payments, and expenses in a dozen small memo books. Her own accounts, nearly empty except for a few spare listings of the cost of food and travel, testify to the vast expenditures of time and devotion she willingly granted Joyce. On some days he would appear at the shop around noon, skip lunch, and continue conferring with Miss Beach about the problems of *Ulysses* for the rest of the day. Any unfinished business they completed in the evenings. With his growing fame he had become increasingly dependent on friends to shield him from "strangers, fans, and members of the press," and in Sylvia Beach he had a sentry of steel who guarded his privacy as diligently as she conducted his business. Over the next ten years, catering to Joyce's needs developed into a full time occupation which, with a total lack of self-glorification and in absolute modesty, Miss Beach assumed uncomplainingly, only resisting her "hero" when he threatened to turn Shakespeare and Company into "a Joyce plant"; for although it was true he had given "great lustre to the bookshop"—and from it got his "boost"—she vowed that he should never completely engulf it.

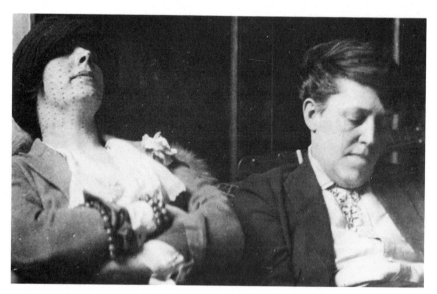

Margaret Anderson and Jane Heap, editors of *The Little Review*, France, 1920s.

As soon as Joyce realized he had underestimated the demand for *Ulysses* and that the thousand copies Miss Beach had printed would not begin to meet it, he suggested to Harriet Weaver that she go ahead with her plans for a second edition. Miss Weaver, who had already published the author's *Dubliners* and *The Portrait of the Artist as a Young Man* and had reluctantly cancelled plans to publish *Ulysses* when the suppression of the *Little Review* made publication of the novel in England inadvisable, had been encouraged first by the appearance and then by the sales of the Paris edition. When she told Joyce she would act immediately, he went to see Miss Beach and, without mentioning his negotiations with Miss Weaver, asked her to allow Miss Weaver to print her edition from plates made from the original type, a request, since it was in Joyce's best interests and not the bookseller's, Miss Beach could hardly refuse. Joyce pressed Miss Weaver to bring the Egoist edition out quickly, first because he needed the funds, second to deter pirates ("My book isn't a bibelot," he said), and third to take advantage of the mounting interest and demand for the book. Miss Weaver asked John Rodker, an experienced printer and publisher of limited edition books, to go to France and oversee the operation. It was agreed that little could be done to correct the errors but Rodker did insert a list of errata and collected more subscriptions. In early October 1922 Darantière finished printing the entire edition of two thousand copies, which was priced at £2.2, not 10/6, as Miss Weaver had originally proposed, and like the first edition it sold out almost at once. While Rodker and the publisher attended to the problems of spiriting copies into England and America (without much success, for in both countries large numbers were either confiscated or destroyed, five hundred of them by New York Postal authorities), Miss Beach suddenly found herself facing a rebellious crowd of Paris booksellers who were among the best customers she had for *Ulysses*. Disturbed by the unexpected appearance of the second edition (Joyce's "precipitated second edition," Miss Beach called it), coming so soon after the first, they accused Miss Beach of having violated the "ethics of a limited edition publication." Not only did the cheaper Egoist book threaten to undercut their sales, but, being almost a duplicate of the first, it had turned hers into a "dishonorable fraud." Moreover, she had not allowed them enough time to dispose of her expensive limited edition. Since it was Joyce who had precipitated the Egoist edition, Miss Beach forwarded the booksellers' complaints on to him and suggested he investigate. Joyce did, and from his son, dispatched to make "oblique enquiries," he learned that in the three leading "English

Inside Shakespeare and Company, *from left to right:* John Rodker,
James Joyce, Sylvia Beach, and Cyrian Beach.

selling shops in Paris"—Brentano, Terquem, and Galignani—only two
copies of both the first and the second editions were in stock, and that
there "was no sign of any angry attitude about edition 2." In a letter to
Harriet Weaver, Joyce defended the publication of the second edition,
noting that it had not only been agreed to "by all parties" but differed "in
size and weight" from the first and, furthermore, was "plainly marked a
second edition in two places for any buyer who can read." In a show of
pique he exclaimed that "no bibliophile has the right to tell me how many
copies of my book are to be inflicted on a tolerant world." Any boycott of
Ulysses that disgruntled booksellers might organize would fail "where
there is a strong demand on the part of buyers."

Fortunately for Joyce—and Miss Beach—the discord over the sec-

24

ond edition, though putting a strain on their relationship, never threatened to dissolve their partnership, and by the time their business association formally ended, in 1939, the year *Ulysses* was vindicated and published in America, Joyce's "funny little publisher" had solicitously watched over the birth of nine more editions of *Ulysses*, totalling at least twenty-eight thousand copies. Subscription and bookshop sales accounted for most of the profits, but tourists would often come to her shop to purchase single copies, for which Miss Beach would prudently provide such suitable jackets as *Shakespeare's Complete Works Complete in One Volume* or *Merry Tales for Little Folks*. Being a banned book, *Ulysses* was of course cut off from "its normal market in English-speaking countries." However, as distasteful as it was for Joyce to have his book relegated to the erotica shelf with *Fanny Hill* and *Raped on the Rail* (he estimated that no more than five percent of *Ulysses* could be called erotic), he was aware that the classification had distinct financial advantages. Warning customers in search of smut that *Ulysses* would be a disappointment seemed pointless to Miss Beach, since its reputation as a "banned book" had been so solidly established. Royalties paid to Joyce remained high—sixty-six percent of the net profits—and often even before those of one edition were gone he would request the royalties for the next, which usually meant that Miss Beach would relinquish her share of the profits even before she had time to clutch them. The practice strengthened her already firm belief that Shakespeare and Company would probably always remain more picturesque than profitable.

III

By 1930, the pirating of *Ulysses*, particularly in the United States, had expanded into a profitable business. For Miss Beach and Joyce, however, it meant shrinking profits. Finding ways to halt the practice concerned them both. Joyce thought that Miss Beach should abandon her bookshop and transplant it to the United States in order "to take up the fight for *Ulysses* in [her] own country," but that was a suggestion she was determined to oppose no matter how dire the circumstances. Her recommendation to Joyce was that he should find an American publisher who would bring out *Ulysses* reasonably quickly. Joyce also suddenly decided to formalize the partnership with Miss Beach, and in a document of his own creation willingly gave the publisher world rights to *Ulysses*, while granting himself the right to authorize the purchase of his work from the publisher, "at a price set by herself," at such time as it was "deemed advisable by the Author and Publisher in the interests of the Author." In May of the same year the last edition of *Ulysses* Miss Beach would publish came off the press; it was the eleventh and the largest (four thousand copies) she had ever ordered, and, since the appearance of the first American edition of *Ulysses* was not far off—unbeknownst to both publisher and author at the time—it was more than adequate to meet her demand for some time. In 1933 Judge John M. Woosley issued his historic decision that freed *Ulysses* for publication in America. *"Ulysses,"* wrote the Judge, "has a rather strong draft, somewhat emetic, but not aphrodisiac." Immediately, Random House announced that it was publishing Joyce's book.

No doubt plans for the American edition had been made with a certain amount of subterfuge on Joyce's part. While negotiations were going on, Miss Beach had only the barest hints of what was happening. At one point when Joyce inquired what she would ask for her rights to *Ulysses* she had facetiously replied "twenty-five thousand dollars." There had also been the unexpected and prolonged visitation of a Joyce emissary, a poet she had long revered, who had spent several days insisting that Joyce's interests had to be understood and advanced and that by remaining his publisher she might be "standing in the way" of his interests and, further, that Joyce's makeshift contract with her was probably worthless. If the object was to convince Miss Beach that any hold she might have thought she had on Joyce was indeed indefinite, if it existed at all, the poet's efforts succeeded. Soon afterward she telephoned Joyce and announced she wanted to be free of the whole situation. He could dispose of *Ulysses* at whatever terms and amount he wanted. The decision, of course, meant she was cutting herself off from the main source of her income. Joyce had not, and would not, pay her anything for the rights she held to his work. The separation, following a decade of the most arduous and rewarding collaboration, could hardly be accepted resignedly, although Miss Beach tried. While confessing she "was not as a rule very grasping," she could not help "feeling the injustice of taking over without any compensation a work . . . [she] had been nursing at least as many years as Joyce had spent writing it." It was a plaint in which an author who had denounced so vehemently those responsible for the wholesale thievery of his property might have found some justification.

Although Shakespeare and Company survived the thirties,* barely, and gallantly remained open even after the Germans occupied Paris and only closed then under threat of confiscation, no period of its history surpassed the remarkable decade that followed the publication of *Ulysses*. Most of Miss Beach's memoir is a reflection of those bountiful years from 1921 to 1932, the years when her shop served as a club, seminar room, lending library, and bookstore for the legions of writers and artists then converging on Paris, and the years when she, in the words of André Chamson, "carried pollen like a bee," cross-fertilizing "her" writers, and doing more "to link England, the United States, Ireland and France than four great ambassadors combined." All the most talented appear in her book. In addition to the prodigious portrait of Joyce and the marvelously illuminating sketches of Hemingway, Adrienne Monnier, Robert McAlmon, and George Antheil, her memoir abounds with incisive cameo-portraits of the many who wandered and worked in the Odéon neighborhood: Bryher, quietly observant, a "shy young English girl in a tailor-made suit"; Janet Flanner, "brilliant," a "great worker" who "always found time to look after people"; Djuna Barnes, "so charming, so Irish, and so gifted"; Thornton Wilder, "rather shy and a little like a young curate"; Mary Butts, "a personality . . . with red cheeks and red hair" whose life turned tragic; Marsden Hartley, "attractive, though perhaps a little melancholy"; F. Scott Fitzgerald, "blue eyes and good looks," a "wild recklessness," and a "fallen-angel fascination"; Mina Loy, a poet more beautiful than her beautiful daughters; André Chamson, "steady, studious, versatile, level-headed"; Jean Prévost, "erratic, temperamental, moody"; Stuart Gilbert, a "delightfully humorous, witty, paradoxical, rather cynical, extremely kind Englishman"; Ada and Archibald MacLeish, talented and considerate; André Gide, "kind-hearted" but impatient with any who "tried to pin him down"; Paul Valéry, "a brilliant talker," kind, "completely unaffected"; Valéry Larbaud, a charming man, with large beautiful eyes, who "was proud of his feet." Dozens more

---

* Besides losing *Ulysses* to Random House, by the middle thirties Miss Beach had started to feel the effects of the Depression which, among other things, had reduced the number of Americans in Europe to a fraction of what it had been a few years before. In 1936 she had reached a low point and let it be known that Shakespeare and Company would probably have to close. Determined that it should not, a group of friends and writers hastily formed Les Amis de Shakespeare and Company and organized monthly readings by Eliot, Gide, Valéry, and Hemingway which brought in enough money to keep the shop operating.

appear fleetingly: Allen Tate, Nancy Cunard, Louis Bromfield, Marc Allégret, Jules Romains, Natalie Clifford Barney, Anaïs Nin, Katherine Anne Porter, Eugene and Maris Jolas, Thomas Wolfe, Berenice Abbott and Man Ray (the unofficial photographers for Shakespeare and Company), Georges Duhamel, Kay Boyle, John Dos Passos, Nathan Asch, Jean Schlumberger, Léon-Paul Fargue, Jo Davidson, Gertrude Stein, Ernest Walsh, Ford Madox Ford, Virgil Thomson, George Moore, Arthur Symons, Ken Sato, Robert Sage, Ethel Moorhead, and Elliot Paul.

Time not spent doing the multitudinous Joycean chores was lavished on her friends and customers. "I wasn't someone," she said, "who received certain days, worried to death if so-and-so wasn't coming, counting great names. My customers were in and out, coming usually on business. Their books were out. . . . They had to meet a transatlantic ship. Readers were prowling in the underbrush. My role was keeping house open for the writing professionals, bringing them in contact with each other and readers, keeping them peaceful if possible, giving them opportunities to appear in magazines or books, translating into French, etc.—someone whose interest in them was that of a mother of a family." With the French, who comprised nearly half her customers, she enjoyed being pedagogical, introducing them to new writers and bringing them "up to date" with a lecture on American literature. As for the Americans, whose attitude was of revolt, not of submission or resignation, and whose influence prevented a precious tone from pervading the atmosphere, there were always introductions to arrange, especially now with Joyce, books to order and recommend, and favors (too many) to grant. Among those favors she generally allowed were requests for small loans or for the return of subscription card deposits, practices which made the shop at times seem more like a "left bank" than a bookshop. Spare minutes she used to catch up on commercial chores—selling, distributing, ordering, and filling orders, and trying to keep accounts with dealers in England and America straight (in New York the Gotham Book Mart, Holliday Book Shop, and Harry Marks; in Chicago the Powers Bookstore and A. Krock; in London the Poetry Bookshop), to and from which flowed an unbroken stream of orders. Besides stocking the publications of major houses in both countries, she carried those of small private presses like Nonesuch, Orioli, Cresset, Fanfrolico, Hogarth, and Egoist as well as the books turned out by little presses in Paris. Accounts—of necessity kept in three currencies (American, French, and English)—always remained the "most puzzling [of] occupations," wasteful of time, and almost as exasperating as trying to fit some customers with books, like the one who returned each year to ask for a copy of Raphael's *Ephemerides*. The always prosperous and popular circulating library that filled three or four large bookcases demanded attention, too. Subscribers, usually averaging around a hundred, many of them Sorbonne students, had to be issued cards (seven francs—fifty cents —per month), and delinquents, like Natalie Clifford Barney and Joyce, had to be notified when they failed to return a book on time. Miss Beach's method of retrieving overdue books was to send delinquent borrowers a card showing a distraught Shakespeare tearing out his hair and weeping oversized tears.

With so many demands competing for her time, what Miss Beach could hardly begin to contemplate was taking on any additional publications. Yet as news of her publishing success spread beyond Paris, even before *Ulysses* had been distributed, writers started plying her with requests to publish their books. A lady author living in Peking, determined to prove to English publishers who had refused her book that she could

F. Scott Fitzgerald and Adrienne Monnier, rue de l'Odéon, Paris.

"live without them," offered to pay all expenses if Miss Beach would publish her study exposing conditions in North India. An English playwright, admitting he had not followed Shaw's advice to send his manuscript to Ezra Pound for submission to Miss Beach, hoped she would consent to print privately, or publish, at least five hundred to a thousand copies of his play. Requests of this sort were easily refused, but others made in person were more difficult, and barely a day passed without another visitor turning up with a manuscript. "I think they let me read [their manuscripts] because I never criticized them," she once said, and modestly added, "They had too much talent for me to pass judgment on anything they wrote." When D. H. Lawrence called on Miss Beach not long before his death to ask if she would consider publishing an edition of his much-pirated *Lady Chatterley's Lover*, difficult as it was to say no, she did, offering explanations she correctly feared would not impress him. Lawrence had his own publishers and he had people to take care of him. Joyce, on the other hand, had no one. In any case, she did not really like Lawrence's work. "It was all preaching, preaching." Just the same it was "hard to refuse such a man," and later she admitted that if he had proposed his poems, which she liked, she probably could "not have resisted him." No explanations, however, softened her refusal to a "blonde lady, aggressively partisan," who one day marched into the shop brandishing a "prospectus announcing the 'forthcoming *Memoirs of Aleister Crowley*' " under the imprint of Shakespeare and Company, as well as the "draft of a contract" stating that Crowley would receive fifty percent of the earnings! More firmness was needed, though, to turn down a tantalizingly immodest proposal made by the major domo of Maxim's, who graciously offered her the first right to his memoirs, the appearance of which, he prophesied— after injecting a reminder that he had "known everybody who was anybody in his time"—would be a literary sensation rivaling and perhaps even surpassing the publication of *Ulysses*. (Miss Beach later commented on the major domo's offer: "I thought it was too small a frame at Shakespeare and Company for such a picture, and that anything so important should be handled by a great firm. I suggested Messrs. Macmillan.") The only book Miss Beach said she might have published probably did not exist at the time it was proposed. Someone representing Tallulah Bankhead offered her the memoirs of the actress, but according to Miss Beach's reckoning, Miss Bankhead "could hardly have been more than a child at the date of that letter."

When she refused *Lady Chatterley's Lover* Miss Beach told Law-

30

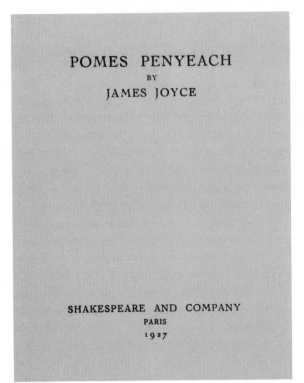

POMES PENYEACH

BY

JAMES JOYCE

SHAKESPEARE AND COMPANY

PARIS

1927

Title page of *Pomes Penyeach* by James Joyce
(Shakespeare and Company, 1927).

rence she "did not want to get the name as a publisher of erotica." Although she stopped short of saying his novel might revive the mistaken impression that many had derived from the publication of *Ulysses*—that she intended to make erotic books a speciality—she certainly implied as much. That misconception, first dramatically publicized in the *London Sporting News* (April 1, 1922) under the sensational title "The Scandal of *Ulysses*," had brought her a cascade of manuscripts "intricate with perversion—love children"—by a flock of writers who, having seen the success of *Ulysses*, assumed Miss Beach would be interested in taking on more books at least as erotic as Joyce's ("a nice career for a minister's daughter"). It seemed at times that all that was unpublished in Anglo-Saxon countries headed for the rue de l'Odéon. "You might have thought," she complained, "I was offering a prize for the lewdest book of the month." Finally, "I got rather sore about this nuisance. I wondered what I had ever done to deserve it." In *Ulysses* the "erotic has its place and certainly part of the importance of the book is due to the way Joyce dealt with the subject. He was the great purifier who rid us of the naughty word and the immoral situation and brought everything out in the good old English language and our poor funny human nature. But Joyce spent seven years on *Ulysses*. He thought it would interest very few readers and he never counted on any financial returns from it. This was the contrary with every one of the authors who turned up with a proposition. They looked on it as an easy way to make money."

Of those who came to Shakespeare and Company ready to read passages from books they believed might titillate Miss Beach and make money, no one quite surpassed the histrionics employed by Frank Harris, who, after ceremoniously drawing up to the shop in a "barouche and pair hired for the occasion," deposited a huge parcel containing a manuscript which, he assured her, "went much further than Joyce." Harris' complaint was that the author of *Ulysses* "was just another of those Thomas Hardys who never get anywhere near a woman." Even in the Penelope episode Joyce had not managed to get "inside a woman." His (Harris') book "showed how it was done." In spite of the spirited reading that doubtless followed that claim (Harris spent the entire afternoon at the shop), Miss Beach remained unenthusiastic. The best she could do was to suggest he try Jack Kahane, a friend and publisher of Obelisk books, who was always looking for "hot books." Harris did not leave without gaining something, however. Miss Beach agreed to sell *My Life and Loves*, but not promote it. Nonetheless, from time to time mysterious people would come by her shop for bundles of Harris' book to sell in England where it had been banned.

What Miss Beach did not tell Lawrence, but what must have been apparent, was that she had made up her mind to be a "one-book publisher." A more accurate description would be a one-author publisher, for in 1927 she had agreed to bring out Joyce's slender volume of poetry *Pomes Penyeach*, and in 1929 had overseen the production of the first apologia of *Finnegans Wake*, which appeared under the inflated title of *Our Exagmination round his Factification for Incamination of Work in Progress*. In the final year of the decade *Ulysses* was going into its tenth edition and still selling steadily, with no likelihood of either an American or British edition appearing soon. It was a sound decision. Having rescued and succored Joyce, one of Shakespeare's company, whom she and a multitude of admirers revered as the "greatest writer" of the time, Miss

Beach had come to occupy the place of a high priestess among Joyce cultists. No book of this century aroused more discussion or more controversy than *Ulysses*, most of which redounded to her credit. That she could ever again publish a book of the same magnitude was neither likely nor desirable. Besides, she once said when asked why she had not published others, "nobody else seemed interesting enough to me."

Ulysses was her trial, her torture, and finally her triumph. It brought Shakespeare and Company a second celebrity, a living bard, who turned the shop into a literary shrine. It burdened our literature with a work of extraordinary versatility. It canonized Sylvia Beach. To those fitfully wondering whether to try and follow in her footsteps she was the object of envious glances and acclaim. What she had accomplished they had only dreamed of doing and, remarkably, she had done it despite a shaky budget and with little knowledge of what the effort would entail. She succeeded partly because she did not know what she could not or should not do. To contend, however, that success was practically guaranteed, given the prepublication publicity *Ulysses* received, is to suggest that the publisher was endowed with a degree of prescience she could not have had prior to February 1922. Even Joyce gloomily predicted dismal sales for his book. Sylvia Beach had what every publisher needs—intuition—and on that quality rested her lasting belief in Joyce and in the greatness of *Ulysses*.

12, RUE DE L'ODÉON

PARIS (VIᵉ)

II

Robert McAlmon's
CONTACT PUBLISHING COMPANY

I

THOSE WHO KNEW Robert McAlmon in Paris in the early twenties began to worry about him in the early thirties. His companion Ezra Pound expressed concern in a letter to a mutual friend: "And what iz gone wrong with McAlmon? The kid just playin' the fool, or watever? Too bad some of his best have been printed, though hardly more than privately printed. I hope he ain't gone plumb to hell." And Sylvia Beach, a longtime friend who had once "quite completely fallen prey" to McAlmon's charms, was saddened by what she described as the slow deterioration of her friend into a "malicious gossip," who by the end of the thirties became "completely soured." Sorrowfully she concluded that McAlmon's opinions, though amusing and even brilliant, were often "influenced by his envy of other people's talents." Even more depressing, since it now seemed undeniable, was the realization that after a tryout of a few years in Paris McAlmon had done little to sustain the belief held by Miss Beach and shared by many others that he would gradually emerge as one of the important young American exile writers in Paris. "No one knew this better than McAlmon himself," she wrote, and it made him "hard and embittered." A sad fate for one whom the irrepressible Ernest Walsh had called in 1927 "the most honest and authentically American of our writers, and the only man writing who can seriously compete with Joseph Conrad and James Joyce." Eventually Joyce, too, found reasons to be concerned and disturbed. For several afternoons in the early months of 1934, McAlmon, at Joyce's invitation, read Joyce portions of his just-completed memoir, mockingly entitled *Being Geniuses Together*. In the

34

presence of his friend, Joyce professed to be amused, but privately he expressed disappointment at finding so much "malice" in the writing, and McAlmon later learned that Joyce had curtly dismissed the memoir as "the office boy's revenge." What McAlmon's memoir revealed about his expatriate years and his friends in Paris remained more or less a secret until 1938 when the book was finally issued, unceremoniously, in England. It was the last of his books he would live to see published.

Undoubtedly, with the passing of the early exciting years in Paris, years when McAlmon regarded writing and publishing as integral parts of a noisy and amusing and ruttish social life rather than activities one practiced faithfully in the quiet after-hours, he began experiencing the first shivers of self-doubt and frustration and of disappointment with himself and with others. Friends like Kay Boyle, aware of his state, discovered that well-intentioned efforts to inspirit him could often release wild, violent outpourings of disgust and even despair. And at least one other friend, the journalist-publisher Bill Bird, with whom McAlmon joined forces in the mid-twenties, mentioned betrayal. He confided to Kay Boyle (in 1929) that he could tell the "exact story" of how their friend McAlmon had been "done in" by nearly every American writer of the twenties, and "some English writers too." Whether real or imagined, betrayal, an unshakable feeling that he had too often been the victim of undeserved rebukes and injuries, blotted a good part of McAlmon's life after 1930. After his death in 1956 (he spent his last years living on a sand dune near Desert Hot Springs, a virtual eremite), McAlmon's sister said that her brother, "even as a little boy, had believed everyone was out 'to get him' and that he had feared betrayal even before he had been so bitterly betrayed." If this be the case, then his propensity for perceiving situations in which deceit, if not outright betrayal, loomed as a possibility must have intensified during the twilight years of his exile, for by then, after nearly a decade devoted to writing and publishing, both admittedly often done in a slipshod manner, he alone among his compatriots, including those whose careers he had assisted by publishing their first books in Paris, remained an unpublished author outside of his own Contact Editions. But if McAlmon passed the last years abroad fending off obscurity and defending himself against detractors and the smooth-talking American editors who invariably ended up rejecting his books, he spent the first cultivating friendships that would stimulate and help shape his art, and in some ways his life as well, not the least important of which was the association he struck up with Sylvia Beach.

Robert McAlmon, 1925.
PRINCETON UNIVERSITY LIBRARY, SYLVIA BEACH COLLECTION

II

Despite the tantalizing manuscripts that began descending on the rue de l'Odéon shop, Miss Beach wisely decided that Shakespeare and Company, whatever claim it had as a publishing house, would have to support that distinction on the basis of a single book, and, as it turned out, *Ulysses* was almost more than she could manage. Her hope, of course, was to see that Shakespeare and Company remained primarily a bookshop and lending library. Nonetheless, the experience of publishing *Ulysses* had convinced her that a publisher for exiled writers in Paris was "very much needed," a conviction shared by McAlmon, who first turned up at Shakespeare and Company in the fall of 1921, and whose charm, fine profile, "Irish sea-blue eyes and nasal drawl" had immediately enchanted its owner. Alone—having come to Paris from London without his new wife, Bryher (Winifred Ellerman)—he, like so many who followed him, made Miss Beach's shop his headquarters, stopping by almost daily between sittings on the nearby café terraces, where he would become as ubiquitous a figure as Harold Stearns, the indisputable champion of all café habitués. In England, earlier that year, he had made the acquaintance of Harriet Weaver, Joyce's generous patroness and publisher, whose Egoist Press had printed, in addition to *The Portrait of the Artist as a Young Man* (1917), T. S. Eliot's *Prufrock* (1917), Ezra Pound's *Dialogues of Fontenelle* (1917) and *Quia Pauper Amavi* (1919), Jean Cocteau's *Cock and Harlequin* (1920), Wyndham Lewis's *Tarr* (1918) and *The Caliph's Design* (1919), and Richard Aldington's *Images* (1919), and would, in 1922, issue Joyce's *Dubliners, Exiles*, and *Ulysses*, and in 1923 (with Elkin Mathews) an edition of *Chamber Music*. The retiring Miss Weaver had liked Bryher and her American husband and had welcomed their proposal to underwrite an edition of Marianne Moore's *Poems* and Hilda Doolittle's *Hymen*. Miss Weaver also agreed to take on, at McAlmon's expense, a volume of his poems called *Explorations*, which appeared in the winter of 1921 in an edition of five hundred copies. The little book, McAlmon's first and the last on the Egoist general list, found an admirer in Emanuel Carnevali, who reviewed it for *Poetry* in June 1922. Granting that it contained the "very spirit of quest and struggle," Carnevali nonetheless warned that McAlmon's impression could be "unpleasant" and perhaps rude, like "a youth, agile and attractive, passing by without taking his hat off to anybody." Predictably, though, except for Carnevali, the book went unnoticed, thus obviating, McAlmon later wryly observed, the need to make apologies for its contents. *Explorations*, however, did contain a poem that was "rather harsh on Eliot," and McAlmon wondered whether it might make calling on the elder American poet a little awkward. But the evening he spent with Eliot passed amiably. "I like your mind," Eliot told him, "and that is all that matters." When McAlmon sent him some poems to read soon after arriving in France, Eliot took the opportunity to reply at length concerning the "right way to take Paris." One must see it as "a place and a tradition, rather than as a congeries of people, who are mostly futile and time-wasting, except when you want to pass an evening agreeably in a café." McAlmon would do well to realize that Paris is a "strong stimulus, and like most stimulants, incites to rushing about and produces a pleasant illusion of great mental activity rather than the solid results of hard work." His own stay in Paris, he told McAlmon, had been rewarding because he had had "only the genuine stimulus of the place, and not the artificial stimulus of the people, as I knew no one whatever, in the literary and artistic world, as a companion —knew them rather as spectacles, listened to, at rare occasions, but never spoken to."

Eliot's admonitory letter convinced McAlmon that the two men would never "agree on what makes literature or life." This retiring, elusive, spectatorial author of *Prufrock*, so dependent (in McAlmon's opinion) on literary and cultural traditions to mitigate his fears of the "interchange of relationships, with their attractions and antagonisms and experiences," stood almost no chance of making an impression upon the man who had declared in the first "manifesto" of *Contact* magazine (a short-lived publication started by McAlmon and William Carlos Williams in 1920) that that "art which attains is indigenous of experience and relations, and the artist works to express perceptions rather than to attain standards of achievement." *Contact*'s credo celebrated "contact with the local conditions"; and good writing provided the "essential contact between words and the locality that breeds them." The animating idea of *Contact* was direct experience with life. It was that, combined with intelligence and talent, rather than the dead traditions of the past, which made writing real and authentic. For McAlmon, Eliot would always be a temporizer, overcautious and snuggly insulated from the living world, as retiring and shy as McAlmon was gregarious and brazen, a man who deliberately shunned the life experiences that gave "validity to tradition."

McAlmon descended upon Paris in 1921 as determined as any springtime tourist to savor its legendary riches, and at the same time as certain as Eliot was uncertain that it would provide the "conditions" needed to nourish his art. In time, however, he would find that the city he envisioned as a Parnassus in reality often resembled a Sodom, where carnality was the least offensive excess, and from which he would regularly flee, seeking in isolated Swiss and Riviera villages the quiet and privacy that would restore his burnt-out energies. Alternately repelled and attracted by the only place he could possibly call home, McAlmon became a "veritable dromomaniac," vanishing whenever he had had too much of Paris, and reappearing after some saunterings, ready to renew the "socializing" that had precipitated his departure in the first place. Society, he told Sylvia Beach, was no boon, "even to those most gregariously sociable, if it's carried beyond the point where one wants it." The rooms and apartments he took in the Quarter, and the cafés through which he ceaselessly glided were always crowded with friends, new and old, as well as strangers and hangers-on and the curious and the predatory, all of whom joined McAlmon on his nocturnal rambles, talking, talking, talking— McAlmon's only real passion—encouraged by his "sympathetic" way of listening to pour out their frustrations. To those like Sylvia Beach who had come to admire his spirit and ambitions, and who looked forward expectantly to the time when he would fulfill his promise, he "was talking away his talent." McAlmon disagreed, of course, contending that all the midnight confabulations would one day appear in print. Nothing would be wasted. It would be some time before he would realize the truth of what Eliot had said about the illusory and often debilitating stimulus of Paris.

Harriet Weaver had given McAlmon a warm introduction to Joyce, and the two men were soon on friendly terms. From this new American in Paris, Joyce was soon receiving a monthly check ($150), and McAlmon would occasionally help with the preparations of *Ulysses*, on which Joyce would often work sixteen hours a day. Despite Joyce's awesome schedule, McAlmon did not hesitate to send him a batch of stories he had written, in just six weeks, soon after coming to France. Joyce thought they sounded, "in a way," like *Dubliners*, "not in treatment or the characters—rather the mental predisposition," and with their slangy language and Americanisms he labeled them "a hasty bunch," a phrase McAlmon at once appropriated for the title. Would he publish his stories through Shakespeare and Company, too, Joyce wondered, or would he do it himself? With the long-awaited publication of *Ulysses* still several months off, there was no chance that Sylvia Beach would take on another book, not even McAlmon's; *A Hasty Bunch* would have to be done on his own. Darantière, though still grappling with *Ulysses*, agreed to print McAlmon's little book, perhaps seizing upon it as a welcome relief from Joyce, and managed to produce an edition of three hundred a month before *Ulysses* appeared.

In February 1922, Ezra Pound reviewed *A Hasty Bunch* for the *Dial*. After reading Pound's comment, Joyce wrote McAlmon: "I think it will serve you." How much it served him, or in what way, can be debated; but Pound, after stating that McAlmon's stories showed "little skill," praised the author's "capacity for presenting the American small town in a hard and just light, no nonsense, no overworking, or overloading. . . . McAlmon has written in the American spoken language. He, or his printer, even goes to the length of using 'had went,' not in the person of a character but in that of author; this is . . . a daring effort to maintain the atmosphere." Williams, excited enough by his friend's book to send it to his literary agent at once, described McAlmon's problem another way: "The thing is that what you have to say is too important, too finely grained—in its adjustments, while it is at the same time too casual and unlettered in surface appearance for anyone but a most unusual person to penetrate it for its real value." The plotless, unfinished, often sketchy stories of *A Hasty Bunch*, honest if somewhat oppressively fatalistic, and as brooding and questioning and rebellious as *Dubliners* (Joyce was right about the matching of a "mental predisposition"), can be taken as the prototype of McAlmon's subsequent Contact books, even though, ironically, it was the only one of his publications that did not bear the Contact imprint, nor did it carry a date or place of publication.

No doubt the nearly simultaneous appearance of *Ulysses* and *A Hasty Bunch*, the services of the masterprinter Darantière in Dijon, and Shakespeare and Company in Paris as a distribution point, helped convince McAlmon that *Contact* might be turned into a publishing enterprise. Moreover, as had been the case in New York a few years before, when, with Williams, McAlmon had started *Contact* magazine in order to get their poems into print, *Contact* would serve as an outlet for the books he was planning to write himself. In America, *Contact* magazine had given McAlmon some status in literary circles, and at least a nominal acquaintance with editors Harriet Monroe (*Poetry*), Scofield Thayer (*Dial*), and Margaret Anderson (*Little Review*), and for a while, in 1922, he even considered reviving the magazine, and, as was to become increasingly his habit, he outlined his plan to Sylvia Beach. "I feel an impulse to get out a *Contact* magazine . . . the idea being this: I'm weary of hearing and reading that America has had no literature; that it is just beginning this generation. Don't believe it." Rereading Cooper, Poe, Twain, Harte, Melville, had apparently been a revelation to McAlmon, for unlike Eliot, Henry James, and especially Pound—all of them in his estimate "too admiring of the thing foreign"—they possessed an American quality; perhaps this quality was the "simplicity and directness" he specifically admired in Cooper, which he equated with "life," the "thing that finally makes or breaks writing." The "raw, pioneering past" of America was indeed a force, and "some of the bigoted, austere, ignorant, roughneck quality of the past" had to be accepted as a "quality" too, and part of the nation's history. The idea for the new *Contact* was a comparison of "American, French, English, and Italian and Spanish literatures, [to] see if the same period of time hasn't produced something in America that lets us stop saying—'We ain't got no culture. Nor no literature.'" An encyclopedia of all America's past, and all her writings, done in an unliterary way, by people not too intently "literary men, pedants, and scholastics, with a 'great love of art,' is what I'm after." Williams, he told Miss Beach, had already written articles on the "voyage of the Mayflower, on Columbus, Sir Walter Raleigh" and had discovered "some journals of explorers, Spanish and otherwise." Could it be that there are "some undiscovered, simple old boys, who had personalities and qualities, and wrote journals, badly perhaps, but that had life?" Convinced there were, he asked Miss Beach to send him whatever she could find, beginning with Cotton Mather, and after that catalogues of names and titles.

McAlmon's plan to revive *Contact* in Europe with an issue celebrating the unacknowledged greatness of early American literature failed to materialize. He did not mention it again to Sylvia Beach, but throughout the year he made a point of keeping her informed on the progress of his own work. "I have more tomes ready than I know what to do with," he wrote in a letter from Rome in the fall of 1922, "but will within a few months have a book of short stories out somehow, somewhere." Not to be published for some time, however, were a long family novel set in the North Dakotas, and eight short stories ranging in length from six to fifteen thousand words. All together, he estimated he had written 150,000 words in the first ten months of the year, an achievement he must have hoped would dispel any lingering doubts Miss Beach might have about his ability and willingness to work, and perhaps offset what she had presumably disapprovingly heard about his "pretty strenuous night life." Of the latter, he admitted that since "I've been fifteen I've gone through long spree periods. My temperament. And I am a social being; not expecting much of very many people. I can't let myself be disturbed by their impositions, as those impositions can only be financial. That I can't bother myself about, and couldn't when I earned six dollars a week only. Of the various figures who drift through Montparnasse I have my judgments, and find a few worth satisfying one's social need through. The others hang on without my being able to tell them to beat it out of my sight."

Proof sufficient to quiet any doubts about McAlmon's right to be included among the "producers of his time" came in 1923. Although by then he had taken to shuttling about Europe and England with the frequency, if never the ease, of a roving ambassador (so like his itinerant minister father, Sylvia Beach remarked), he somehow arranged for the publication of seven books: two of his own; and one each by his wife Bryher, Mina Loy, Marsden Hartley, his former associate and friend William Carlos Williams, and a new acquaintance he had met at Ezra Pound's retreat in Rapallo—Ernest Hemingway. Their order of appearance was never established, nor could it have been, for McAlmon, whose office was wherever he was, conducted his publishing business almost entirely by mail. Manuscripts and proofs addressed to him in care of Shakespeare and Company were forwarded to Rome, Madrid, Amsterdam, Eastbourne, Copenhagen, or wherever his ramblings had taken him; and from wherever he was, often in an amazingly short time (for McAlmon was a notoriously sloppy and impatient editor and proofreader), he would forward the material to Darantière in Dijon.

McAlmon's two books, *A Companion Volume* and *Post-Adolescence*, neither of which carried a date or a place of publication, were the first to bear the Contact Publishing Company imprint, and like *A Hasty Bunch*, were harbingers of what McAlmon hoped his publishing house could achieve. *A Companion Volume*, so named because of affinities it had with *A Hasty Bunch*, was another collection of short stories, set mainly in mid-America, and filled with the sort of raw experience McAlmon insisted was a neglected but important ingredient of the American past. Again the stories seemed close to dramatized autobiography, and even though he had confided to Miss Beach that "small-town stuff" no longer seemed possible, he had nonetheless managed to fill the two volumes with some poignant and disquieting accounts of his youth. *Post-Adolescence*, actually McAlmon's first book, having been written previously to *A Hasty Bunch* in 1920, continued the story, with the scene now shifting to Greenwich Village, where McAlmon had lived briefly in 1920, and where he had met four of the authors he was publishing in 1923—

Williams, Mina Loy, Hartley, and of course Bryher—each of whom, with the exception of Bryher, appeared, thinly disguised, in McAlmon's book. Williams, reviewing *Post-Adolescence* in 1924 for *Transatlantic Review*, called it "a *journal intime*," emphasizing that the book had only one character, "a young man hounded in his own body by the realities of love and sex, which just at the close of adolescence are seen introspectively possessing him."

The stress Williams placed on McAlmon's being possessed by the "realities of love and sex" might have resulted as much from Williams' observations of his friend as from his reading of *Post-Adolescence*, for the two men, after meeting in 1920, had seen each other often for nearly a year before McAlmon left for France in February 1921. It was Williams who introduced McAlmon to Bryher, who had come to New York with Hilda Doolittle, the Imagist poet and Williams' friend of many years. Neither Williams nor McAlmon knew then that the "small, dark English girl with piercing, intense eyes" was the daughter of Sir John Ellerman, "the heaviest taxpayer in England," and apparently neither Bryher nor H. D. deigned to tell them. At least not immediately, and when McAlmon learned who Bryher really was he had not only already married her, but had agreed to her proposal that, once married, they would lead "strictly separate lives," except for obligatory visits they would have to make together to her parents. The "marriage of convenience" held advantages for both. Bryher would at last be freed from parental restrictions and the conventional mode of life certain to be reimposed if she returned home. For McAlmon there would be immediate passage to Europe (he wanted to go to Paris to meet Joyce but lacked the money), and the assurance of a generous allowance as well. Once the pact was made, events moved swiftly, beginning with a civil ceremony on February 14, followed by a bon voyage supper at the Brevoort Hotel with H. D., the Williamses, Marianne Moore, Marsden Hartley, and McAlmon's sister, after which the couple (and H. D.) sailed for Europe on the White Star liner *Celtic,* "on which Sir John had reserved the bridal suite" for his daughter and new son-in-law. Tearfully, Williams saw his friend off, unable to decide whether what moved him was the loss of McAlmon's companionship, or joy for his "good fortune," or the feeling that perhaps McAlmon carried with him a "disastrous story."

McAlmon's fourth publication was Bryher's *Two Selves* which, like his own *Post-Adolescence*, was a continuation of an earlier volume of thinly disguised autobiography called *Development* (1920). Taken as a fictional account of events preceding the author's visit to America with H. D., *Two Selves* provides revealing glimpses of the protagonist's life (here named Nancy) between the ages of fifteen and twenty-four. Nancy possesses two selves: one, an "obedient" girl who answers "Yes, no, yes, no"; the other, "a boy, a brain, that planned adventure and sought wisdom"— two distinct personalities "jammed against each other" and "uneasy for their juxtaposition." Aggravating Nancy's condition are her doting parents, kind and conventional but insensitive to her real longings—poetry, travel, America—from whom escape, in order to develop, is a necessity. In an imaginary conversation with them Nancy expresses her desire to be free, to live alone, and to write. Escape, though desirable and necessary, is not something easily done, however. Marriage, the conventional avenue open to young girls, is denied Nancy: ". . . she hated men. And to cut the knot that way was playing the game wrong. It was to create the same situations over again. And when people married they had children. That was awful." America, new and more tolerant of girls than England, "was something to hold one to," but getting there posed a problem. A friend? "If she had a friend something would burst and she would shoot ahead, be the thing she wanted and disgrace them by her knowledge. Because she would care for no laws, only for happiness." Escape for Nancy, fortunately, does finally materialize in a lady poet she writes an admiring letter to and who possesses all the pulchritude and intelligence she could hope for. After searching out the poet's remote seaside cottage, Nancy tremblingly knocks and waits, prepared "not to be disappointed if an elderly woman in glasses bustled out." But "a tall figure opened the door. Young. A spear flower if a spear could bloom. She looked up into eyes that had the sea in them, the fire and colour and the splendour of it. A voice all wind and gull notes said: 'I was waiting for you to come.' "

III

In the spring of 1923 McAlmon stopped at Rapallo to see Ezra Pound. Pound was away at the time, but Ernest Hemingway and his wife Hadley were there. McAlmon had never heard of Hemingway or of the others with him, Mike Strater and his wife, but he settled down with them for some work and moderate drinking. Hemingway told him the now-familiar story of how Hadley's suitcase, containing originals, typescripts, and carbons of nearly everything he had written for almost a year, had been stolen in Paris, leaving him with only a few poems and stories, including one called "My Old Man," which Edward O'Brien had accepted for his short story anthology of 1923. McAlmon did not stay long at Rapallo, but a short time later he saw Hemingway again in Paris, and with Strater's help they began planning a trip to Spain, a country Hemingway had scarcely seen at that time, and McAlmon not at all. It was understood that McAlmon would pay expenses. In May, they left for Madrid, where they were joined by Bill Bird, the Three Mountains publisher, and then traveled on to Seville, Ronda, and Granada, seeing bullfights at each stop. Despite the hostility that Bird, to his alarm, had observed growing up between his two traveling companions and for which he held Hemingway responsible, McAlmon announced on returning to Paris that he would publish Hemingway's stories (three) and poems (ten), which, since at that moment they comprised the author's entire output, left Bird, who had included Hemingway on the Three Mountains prospectus, with nothing to print.

About the middle of the year, Sir John bestowed upon his son-in-law the generous sum of £14,000, sufficiently bounteous to enable McAlmon to expand his limited publishing activities, and as word of the windfall spread through the Quarter, he was besieged by friends and strangers bearing manuscripts, few of which he could ever have seriously considered for publication. Although many had contended he would publish "almost any writer who came along," a tantalizing rumor to say the least, McAlmon had by mid-1923 pretty much decided whose books would be issued under the Contact imprint, at least for the remainder of the year. Furthermore, the first announcement of the Contact Publishing Company contained some bluntly discouraging news: "It is highly improbable that Mss. submitted to us would be read, or returned. Unfortunately we have not the time to discover new writers in wading through offerings. This slip is no request for material." Elsewhere, however, there were more hospitable words. "We will bring out books by various writers who seem not likely to be published by other publishers, for commercial or legislative reasons." Readers were also assured that both the "popularly commercial" and "esthetically fashionable" standards would be rejected in favor of "personality, conviction, intelligence, and skill," the ingredients indispensable to a book with an "identity of its own." Echoing the anti-establishment credo of *Contact* magazine, and at the same time denying that the fledgling press would espouse a "new consciousness," or a "new art," or even an "uplift intention," McAlmon maintained that "certain works like other organisms have a life, and they are the ones we wish to publish even if they have deformity and many limitations." Listed as Contact's first publications—books it would publish "simply because they are written" and because "we like them well enough to get them out"—were William Carlos Williams' *Spring and All*, a volume of verses by Mina Loy eventually titled *Lunar Baedecker* (misspelling was McAlmon's), *Twenty-Five Poems* by Marsden Hartley, *Short Stories* by Ernest Hemingway (titled *Three Stories* and *Ten Poems* before publishing), and of course McAlmon's two books. For the future, the publisher announced "other things [were] in the air." Wyndham Lewis "intends to have a book that he has been working on for some time ready to publish soon. We will publish it if he lets us. H. D. has also for some time been working upon a **several volumed prose piece** [no doubt this was *Palimpsest*, published by Contact in 1926], which we will bring out should it be necessary to have it published as she writes it."

The distribution of Contact books was to be conducted on as individualistic a basis as the selection. From the three hundred copies of each book printed, a handful would "be sent to what few publications or individuals we care about the opinions of: others will be given away to friends or enemies of the writers." The rest "may be bought at prices from one dollar (four shillings, fifteen francs), to five times these amounts." Contact was also ready "to send copies of any leftover number" to a "few bookshops," the one most important being Shakespeare and Company, whose address at 12 rue de l'Odéon the publisher inserted at the end of the announcement as the location of the Contact Publishing Company. Sylvia Beach gave McAlmon more than just permission to use her shop's address. When the first batches of Contact books began arriving from Darantière, she agreed to look after them, storing some, selling as many as possible, and of course always forwarding a few to McAlmon wherever he happened to be. But handling the distribution of McAlmon's publications went beyond her limits, a fact that must have been on the publisher's mind when he went to see Bill Bird. For about a year Bird had been printing books by hand, a laboriously slow process that nonetheless satisfied the owner's long interest in printing and made even a stack of unsold volumes a matter of small concern. Whereas McAlmon never had more than a hotel room and a mail drop, at most, Bird had outfitted a tiny office and had hired a secretary to handle book orders and correspondence. Bird and McAlmon agreed "to join forces as far as distribution went," and the following year (1924) they issued a prospectus headed "Contact Editions, including books printed at the Three Mountains Press," beneath

46

Marsden Hartley, artist and poet, Paris, 1926.
PRINCETON UNIVERSITY LIBRARY, SYLVIA BEACH COLLECTION

which were listed the publications of both firms. McAlmon's association with Bird continued until 1926 when the latter sold his press to Nancy Cunard.

The remaining Contact books all appeared before the end of the year, and at least in one place they were reviewed together. Edwin Muir, writing in *New Age*, congratulated the new firm on providing a much-needed outlet to writers "whom America . . . finds it hard to tolerate." His only quarrel was that McAlmon had chosen the wrong selections to publish. Williams' *Spring and All* was "a naive betrayal of the triteness flavoured by insecurity upon which the aesthetics of Mr. Williams and his friends are built." Williams' "central dogma"—that "art is not a mere reproduction of nature, but a separate creation, independent of us as Nature is, with its own laws, its own *Wirkung*"—could in itself hardly be questioned. But the point he and his company had missed was "that art must also be organic and complete, like Nature, and, being that, must, like

Nature, be comprehensible, universal, inevitable." No concentration on one aspect of art could possibly constitute a revolutionary position. Not only could the poet's thesis on aesthetics be questioned but Williams' attempts at demonstration struck Muir as totally unsuccessful. The critic's attack was hardly a serious reproach to Williams, who admitted his book was at least partly a "mixture of philosophy nonsense. It made sense to me, at least to my disturbed mind—because it *was* disturbed at that time—but I doubt if it made any sense to anyone else." At one level, he went on, it was a combination of fancy and satire, a travesty of the typographical revolution waged by the dadaists and surrealists; a record of experimentation set down during the creative process; an open-ended celebration of thought, emotion, and imagination; and certainly a reiteration of the Contact principle that only life can invest art with vibrancy and meaning. But what Williams intended to do Muir denied he had done.

In Marsden Hartley's *Twenty-Five Poems*, Muir detected the same tendency to "intellectualise life without ever coming to conclusions about it," which, by implication, meant that the poet might be unable "to face life," or "to face the fact that [he] cannot face it," and was therefore forced "to create another world where other laws operate." Muir's complaint about "cerebralists," aside from their inability or unwillingness to come to grips with life and nature, was that they left "everything as it was before." In the case of Hartley, McAlmon himself had noted how often his friend had asserted that the seriousness of life bored him; and once, in Berlin, heard him renounce art and "grim reality," choosing, when he could afford to, to languish in "divine trivialities," and then, in time, to go back to his painting, more as an antidote for boredom than as a creative necessity. Marsden, the "eagle without a cliff," as someone called him, had made his mark as an expressionist painter at the beginning of the First World War, though his bold, raw canvasses, full of shooting stars and "flaming globes," had generally attracted more attention than sales. It was Hartley who, in Greenwich Village in 1920, had introduced him to Williams. After the war, Hartley had returned to Berlin, where, like so many other impecunious exiles, he found that on very few American dollars the inflated German economy permitted him to live "as he liked to live." McAlmon joined him in Berlin for a while, and the two men immersed themselves in the fervid, squalid night life of the city. Hartley acquiesced to be the center of an adoring circle of girls and boys with whom he was comfortable whether speaking or listening and to whom he would distribute marks. McAlmon, as always, "accompanied by a retinue of various sexes," remained absorbed by the atmosphere of that joyless city until, depressed and restless, he finally moved on. Later, in his book *Distinguished Air*, he would re-create his Berlin sojourn.

To Mina Loy's *Lunar Baedecker* Muir granted compromising approval. The author of "a very unequal, but an arresting book" of poetry, Mrs. Loy, Muir conjectured, was "good" when she was "not cerebral," not at all good when she was. Still, this book by another of McAlmon's Greenwich Village friends was the "surprise of the bunch." By the time she had arrived in New York, before World War I, she had already written "some attractive verse," according to William Carlos Williams, who found her "very English, very skittish, an evasive, long-limbed woman too smart to involve herself, after a first disastrous marriage, with any of us—though she was friendly." She had also known Paris in the same period—"in the days of Apollinaire, Arthur Craven (whom she later married), Picabia, Marinetti," and after the war she had returned there and opened a tiny shop off the Champs-Elysées, where she exhibited and sold her paintings, abstract designs, and curiously decorated lampshades. Mrs. Loy's industry as much as her beauty and wit ("slightly overcerebral") impressed McAlmon and Sylvia Beach, and her poetry, written "whenever she had time," drew admiration from all who read it.

Muir called Hemingway's first publication *Three Stories and Ten Poems* "an able little volume." There was a faint echo of the Contact credo in his comment that the stories attempt "to render artistically things as they are," and while granting that the stories "are told with economy and impartiality," he faulted the author for being "too noncommittal." Gertrude Stein, to whom Hemingway had shown the proofs and who had seconded his proposal that the table of contents ought to be printed on the cover in bold type, sent a short and, for her, a rare review to the Paris *Tribune*. "Three stories and ten poems is very pleasantly said. So far so good, further than that, and as far as that, I may say of Ernest Hemingway that as he sticks to poetry and intelligence it is both poetry and intelligent. Roosevelt is genuinely felt as young as Hemingway and as old as Roosevelt. I should say that Hemingway should stick to poetry and intelligence and eschew the hotter emotions and the more turgid vision. Intelligence and a great deal of it is a good thing to use when you have it, it's all for the best."

From New Jersey, Williams sent over his praise, which McAlmon forwarded to the author, then in Canada working for the *Toronto Star*. In the weeks following publication, Hemingway had naturally expected

American reviewers to note that his book at least existed, and was annoyed when he learned that that was about all Burton Rascoe, then a columnist for the *New York Tribune* (Sunday Edition) had, in fact, done. The supposed slight irritated him enough to write to Edmund Wilson, who had called Rascoe's attention to Hemingway's pieces in the *Little Review*, asking for the names of four or five people who might review his book. Wilson replied that he had read *Three Stories and Ten Poems* and had found the prose superior to the poetry, and offered to include a short comment in the "Briefer Mentions" section of the *Dial*, for which he was then reviewing. Though pleased, Hemingway suggested that he wait until December, when he expected Bird's Three Mountains Press to bring out *in our time*, and then review the two books together, a recommendation presumably acceptable to Wilson, who did review both books in the October 1924 number of the *Dial*.

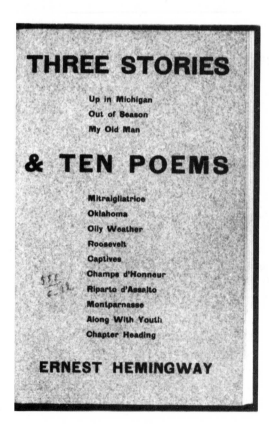

Cover of *Three Stories & Ten Poems* by Ernest Hemingway (Contact Editions, 1923).

IV

Anticipating a reunion with a friend not seen for some time can be more disconcerting than the meeting itself. So when William Carlos Williams and his wife Flossie arrived in Paris in January 1924, on the first stop of what would be a six-month sabbatical leave—urged upon them, incidentally, by Ezra Pound—and looked up their friend McAlmon, they must have been relieved to see he had not only retained his familiar "western manners and counsels" but had even come "to easy terms" with Paris and everyone in it—"the best and the worst." In fact, Williams thought, Paris seemed his "very twin," a place in which McAlmon was at home "as only an American expatriate could be." Ample proof of that observation came in the next few weeks, during which, with McAlmon serving as a self-appointed guide and impresario, the Williamses found themselves being shuttled around the city at an exhilarating and exhausting pace. Besides the essential café-hoppings, dinners, and parties, climaxed by a farewell gathering at the Trianon with James Joyce—a gay, exuberant Joyce, not the staid man-of-letters that McAlmon believed Williams expected to meet—McAlmon introduced his friend to the publisher Bill Bird, who the previous year had printed Williams' *Great American Novel* at his Three Mountains Press; to the young composer George Antheil, of whom the poet had received excited accounts from Pound; to Brancusi, whom Williams would remember as a "mild-mannered" peasant sitting in a clutter of "blocks of stone" and "formless wooden hunks and stumps"; and, of course to McAlmon's special friends, Sylvia Beach and Adrienne Monnier, who at once arranged a dinner for the visitor with Valéry Larbaud, an occasion made memorable by the "tremendous expectancy" Williams and Larbaud shared.

Williams also noted, approvingly, that McAlmon's mind had become "far less youthful" and "more discerning." To Williams he described, "for the first time in full," the "disastrous outcome" of his marriage to Bryher, and "of H. D.'s part in the affair," and it seemed to Williams that his friend's heavy drinking was "a natural consequence." When he expressed interest in meeting a few of the young French writers, especially the dadaists and surrealists, towards whom, unbeknownst to him, McAlmon had developed a coolness if not an outright antagonism, the accommodating guide suddenly became intractable. Where Williams saw profundity and "significant impetus" in the work of the French, McAlmon was certain he had spotted opportunism and contrived iconoclasm. They also found, somewhat ironically, that their opinions of H. L. Mencken differed, with Williams holding that Mencken was among the most important critics of the day, and McAlmon professing astonishment at his friend's respect for a "Babbitt iconoclast exclusively for Babbitts," a man hopelessly incompetent to criticize contemporary writing. McAlmon attributed their opposing views to a "difference of generation," and—in a remark that contained larger implications—to Williams having located in a "suburban town full of residents whose reading fare consists of the *Saturday Evening Post* [and] the *American Mercury.*"

On the potential value of McAlmon's publishing enterprise, however, there was no discord. Williams at once saw that his friend was in a position to direct the course of contemporary writing, direct it, that is, if he wanted to, and if he could. Partly because McAlmon had learned to spend Sir John's money "like a prince," Contact "had really come to life this time as a publishing venture. If it could go on this way, in no time at all it was bound to become the most powerful influence in the publishing field that we have ever known." Along with Bird's Three Mountains Press, Contact had created a "front," Williams believed, that everyone could profit by, providing, of course, the money held out. But he must have known that more than an unexpected financial collapse threatened this promising "front." Others had observed, and Williams did, too, that Mc-

William Carlos Williams,
mid-twenties.
PRINCETON UNIVERSITY LIBRARY,
SYLVIA BEACH COLLECTION

Almon often fought and helped people at the same time. And his friend's "excesses" also worried him. No one, he concluded, "could go on at that pace forever; he knew no limits, physical or for intellectual honesty. Nothing pleased him." Put somewhat dramatically perhaps, the "mark was on Bob's face."

In February, McAlmon accompanied his friends to Villefranche, where they lingered for a month and then temporarily parted company, the Williamses going on to Italy, McAlmon remaining behind before returning to Paris, where, in May, they rejoined for a last and even more enervating round of visits and parties; and then in mid-June the Williamses set sail for America, their "memorable" European "debauch" at last ended. Exhausted, McAlmon made straight for Territat, a remote Swiss village where Bryher and H. D. were living and where McAlmon would often go whenever he needed solitude for his work and relief from the strains of too much socializing. He was soon in touch with Sylvia Beach, complaining that this time it had taken a week to get over Paris, and that "too many personal relationships, too many problems Americanly and Russianly discussed" had reduced his present wants to hiking, swimming, and wandering around. There was a real danger, he told her, that if he tried writing too soon after Paris he "might begin to interpret, or go in for mysticism, or problems, or propaganda," all of which were being done, or overdone, by enough Americans already. About the same time, in another letter to Miss Beach, he mentioned sending his only completed manuscript, *Village*, to Harcourt, Brace and Company, assuring her, in terms by now familiarly pessimistic, that when it was rejected he would send it to Boni and Liveright, and "afterwards, as a course," publish it himself in the fall. Earlier that year he had confided to her that *Village* was his best "by far . . . better rhetoric, cooler thinking"; however by June his feelings had turned ambivalent: "I like it myself at moments, and detest it other times." Nonetheless, at the end of the summer, *Village* turned up on the list of forthcoming Contact publications.

In early summer McAlmon resumed his perambulations, thereby forcing postponement of plans to prepare a few of his stories for translation and to start a jazz opera based on the history of the "world towards machinery." In July, again in Spain, he spent a few weeks fishing, hiking, and watching bullfights with Hemingway, the Birds, Dos Passos, and Donald Stewart. Two months later, on a swing through northern Italy, he stopped to see Emanuel Carnevali, the Italian-American poet and critic who, after the war, had worked briefly as associate editor of *Poetry* in

Chicago, and with whom McAlmon, at that time a rather desultory student at the University of Southern California, had conducted a steady and fervent correspondence, sensing in the young Latin poet a plentitude of life which underlined his own narrow experience. "He was purely Italian," McAlmon said of him in *Geniuses*, "with the Italian lack of cant about 'morals' and 'soul' and 'conscience.' " But the Carnevali McAlmon found languishing in a small town near Bologna, suffering from encephalitis lethargica, then untreatable, had only a short time to live. Still undiminished, however, was his mental vigor, amazingly quick and alert and curious; but the disease had depleted his energy and reduced the time he could spend writing. Nonetheless, for his friend he produced a pile of manuscript containing "fresh" and "interesting" portraits of local characters— "the village barber, the *sage-femme*, the priests, the nuns, the male nurse, the town whores, workers, housewives"—enough material, McAlmon speculated, for the makings of a book. How McAlmon climaxed his visit with Carnevali, undoubtedly done with the same spontaneity that characterized so many of his actions, could hardly have been more restorative to the ailing poet, who excitedly reported what had happened to his friend Kay Boyle. "A great man, Robert McAlmon, came to see me here . . . and when he saw the conditions in which I was living, he paid a year in advance for me in a private sanatorium. Besides this, this unbelievable man whose smile is like a scar from the many wounds he has borne took all my writings with him, and he will perhaps make a book out of them!" The following year, after McAlmon announced that Contact would issue his book, Carnevali wrote again to Miss Boyle, beginning his letter with a reference to "the prince of men"—Robert McAlmon.

By the time *Village: As It Happened Through a Fifteen-Year Period* was about to appear, in late fall, McAlmon discovered he liked it even more. For a while he considered discarding the brown covers he had used on the earlier Contact books for one that would make a "splashy window display"—say, a shiny green, orange, or blue. He assured Sylvia Beach that *Village* would be proofread, presumably in reply to her chiding him on his failure to do so in the past, and then added, self-deprecatingly, "God, it's nice to always have an appreciative audience of oneself." Although *Village* showed that McAlmon had done little to improve the plotlessness and disorganization that had weakened his earlier books—in fact, if anything, it must be considered a retreat—it did evoke, perceptively, if somewhat too solemnly, the stagnant atmosphere and smothering puritan respectability that Lewis and others had condemned as so damaging to life in small midwestern towns. It was also intended to be an indictment of the "whole ideal of American propriety," the obstinate nature of which McAlmon had once tried to describe. "It's the puritan training perhaps, not that it got me, but the 'Have a purpose,' 'Succeed, make people accept you' 'Don't think or feel, just work and earn your living' atmosphere that permeates all America, relives in one at moments in spite of Einstein."

Village brought McAlmon more favorable reaction, public and private, than any other book he ever wrote. Ford Madox Ford, already enchanted by the work of Americans from the Midwest, although decidedly not with McAlmon's writing, printed an episode from the novel in *Transatlantic Review*; and Ethel Moorhead, in her magazine *This Quarter*, wrote admiringly of the "new and good form" of *Village*, and its racy, convincing language, so robust alongside the stilted, tradition-bound English still favored by her countrymen. In America, a *New York Evening Post* critic, Walter Yost, also praised the author's prose ("unliterary and as direct as an invoice") and described portions of *Village* "as beautiful and dramatic as sunlight" creeping "upon one unpretentiously." In London, the *Adelphi* reviewer called McAlmon a "mind" and prose writer of original talent. The Italian critic Carlo Linatie acclaimed *Village* a "masterpiece in miniature" and McAlmon an artist whose style, rude and resilient, the "style of a true chronicler," had endowed the "whole village throng" with a "festive and dramatic" life. Hemingway, away in the Austrian Alps, wrote McAlmon that his book was "absolutely first-rate and damned good reading. We've all read it down here and everybody thinks it a knockout. It is swell." Dorothy Richardson reported that *Village* was like a "woodcut," and added that H. G. Wells had "found it vastly more detached and intelligent as a picture of American life than Anderson or Lewis." Ludvig Nordstrom, a Swedish author and critic McAlmon had met in Italy the previous year, wrote, somewhat fulsomely, that McAlmon had developed a "new melody, a new rhythm, and new vibration," and predicted that *Village* would one day be regarded as "epoch-making" and that "American novel writing" would have to follow the direction it set." Gertrude Stein's response to *Village* combined self-flattery and encouragement. "I find your young people to be as I knew them and as I know them and America as I know it. . . . I like the general resumés which you do of what happened and what did not happen to each of all of them in detail. It is present past and future. Like Trollope you ought to write a lot." Miss Stein enclosed an amusing letter she had received from a farmer who had read *Village*, a portion of which McAlmon dutifully copied into his scrapbook.

> *Village* amused me tremendously. I was especially taken by Daisy the cow. Am quite familiar with cowology and she is the most cowy cow in literature. The fact that she was outraged in her higher cow nature will go a long way to keep her place and her memory green and it will be long before another cow will replace Daisy. It seems to me that she really marks the entry of cows into literature, anyway she far surpasses anything that could have been done. The whole book is interesting, and mainly wonderfully done.

At the end of the year McAlmon settled again in Territat, maintaining what he called a "strict drinking diet" (nothing but beer and mild whiskey punch before bed) and an exacting writing schedule, the writing consisting now of two panoramic novels, *The Politics of Existence* and *The Portrait of a Generation*. Of the latter, intended to be a portrait of Sir John and Lady Ellerman, he wrote enthusiastically to Sylvia Beach. "Have done a hundred photographic pages of my in-laws, and Bryher says she can't stand it. To [*sic*] real. I know it's much the maturest stuff I've done; getting away from the too American stuff." He had evidently concluded that being American was "getting to be too much of a stunt and pose," although turning away from American themes did not mean he wanted to write "good English." But on the other hand he did not want to go in for creating an "American language" either. He regarded the new direction as part of his growth as a writer, and reminded Miss Beach that "plants grow, they don't need forcing."

V

Between the time Gertrude Stein began looking for someone to publish *The Making of Americans* and the date the book finally appeared, her magnum opus (once estimated to be 2,428 typewritten pages) must have logged more mileage, going and coming from agents, publishers, and friends on both sides of the Atlantic, than any book ever sent on a pre-publication safari through the mails. Though it was McAlmon who published it in November 1925, the first one to see a portion of the manuscript fourteen years earlier, in September 1911, was the English publisher Grant Richards, who was also the first to reject it as something not likely to be successful. Undaunted by Richards' rejection, Miss Stein next asked

56

two friends in America to circulate the manuscript; their efforts, though intense, were no more successful than her own, and when the First World War erupted a short time later she decided to place *Americans* in storage. There it remained, quite forgotten, until 1922, when her friend and admirer Carl Van Vechten inquired about the status of the book and encouraged her to try placing it once more in the United States, perhaps beginning with Knopf, his own publisher. Her hopes revived, she lost no time sending Van Vechten the first three volumes early in 1923, which he dutifully deposited with the New York firm. Meanwhile, in Paris, the long-buried manuscript had also begun to create a stir, as Miss Stein later remembered in *The Autobiography of Alice B. Toklas*.

> One day Hemingway came in very excited about Ford Madox Ford and the *Transatlantic* . . . and said that Ford wanted something of Gertrude Stein's for the next number and he, Hemingway, wanted *The Making of Americans* to be run in it as a serial and he had to have the first fifty pages at once. Gertrude Stein was of course quite overcome with her excitement at this idea, but there was no copy of the manuscript except the one that we had had bound. That makes no difference, said Hemingway, I will copy it. And he and I between us did copy it and it was printed in the next number of the *Transatlantic*. . . . Hemingway did it all. He copied the manuscript and corrected the proof.

Hemingway did even more. As subeditor of the *Transatlantic*, he had become well enough acquainted with the editor, Ford Madox Ford, to know that the latter believed Miss Stein received "big prices" for her work, a mistaken notion Hemingway told her he had in no way tried to correct. "Be haughty but not too haughty," he advised, and accept Ford's offer of thirty francs a page, reminding her that it was all John Quinn's money anyway. Whether Hemingway told Ford at the outset that *Americans* consisted of six volumes, an impossibly long manuscript for serialization, is a matter still contested by the partisans of both writers. In barest outline the facts are these: Hemingway, in a letter to Miss Stein dated February 17, 1925, wrote that he had told Ford *Americans* ran to six volumes, but in a letter Ford wrote to Miss Stein six months later, after four installments of the book had appeared, with no end in sight, Ford insisted Hemingway had given him the impression that *Americans* was a "long short story which might run for about three numbers." Had he known what it was, Ford continued, he would have offered her a "lump sum"—serials fetching less than shorter pieces—and delayed publication until his own serial (*Some Do Not*) had ended. As things turned out, John Quinn died suddenly in June, and although Hemingway miraculously found new backers for the magazine—Krebs Friend and his wealthy but penny-pinching wife—it, too, expired by the end of the year, however not before the seventh installment of *Americans* had come out (the last few at reduced rates introduced by the Friends, who hoped to cut costs by inducing writers to contribute their manuscripts free). Although only a small portion of the book had appeared in Ford's magazine, it was enough to rekindle interest in publication, which, rather surprisingly, came this time from Harold Stearns, Horace Liveright's Paris representative, who, in Miss Stein's words, "made me a very good proposition subject to Liveright's approval." Unhappily, Liveright's approval never came; nor did Knopf's, that firm having found a "reader's response sampling" disappointing, and thus Miss Stein was once again back where she started. Except for an unsuccessful attempt made by the determined and loyal Jane Heap to interest T. S. Eliot in printing parts of *Americans* in the *Criterion*, and the promise that she, too, would look into possibilities for publication in the United States, and an inquiry from Jonathan Cape who, having learned of the book from McAlmon, asked about securing the English rights, all prospects that even remotely held out the possibility of publication seemed as moribund as the expiring *Transatlantic*.

McAlmon's first meeting with Gertrude Stein (in the company of Mina Loy) turned out to be an unexpected surprise. Close up she was not as bad as she seemed from a distance. Pontificate, reiterate, and stammer she did, as McAlmon expected she would, but he found she was also human. She even shared his passion for Trollope's novels. As proud and egotistical as she, McAlmon had quite prepared himself not to like this "oracle," and certainly not to allow any of her pronouncements to influence him in the slightest or, if they did, not to admit it, and he had all but ruled out the prospect of there being any friendship between them. At best, they would circle each other, like friendly foes, wary and respectful, so long as neither attacked or made demands upon the other. McAlmon had long admired "Melanctha," the second story in Miss Stein's *Three Lives* (her one "sound book" in his estimation—"a *clarified* Dostoevskian depiction of niggers"), and it was probably with the hope of obtaining something as good that he wrote to the author in August 1924 to announce he intended to publish the following year a collection of new works by "various writers," mostly his Paris-based friends, with a few "names" admitted for their "public value" to help sales, and to ask if she would like to be included. Miss Stein replied that she would, and sent him "Two Women," which was short enough to meet his request for a piece not exceeding five thousand words. In view of what promised to be, if not a close, at least a relationship based upon respect, Miss Stein must have wondered whether this young American publisher might agree to take on the luckless *Americans*, particularly if she were able to guarantee him a sale of, say, fifty copies. When they met again in January 1925, at her invitation, to discuss the subject, she proposed that McAlmon should proceed to publish her book, "in a series of four to six volumes throughout a two-year period." With surprising ease, McAlmon agreed to the plan, promised to honor her request for a contract that would state *Americans* belonged to her (this being necessary, according to the author, in case anything happened to McAlmon's firm), and soon afterward announced that Contact Editions would publish *"The Making of Americans* in four to six volumes, appearing over a period of a year or more." He added that Miss Stein's book "has been awaited with impatience, but which, because of the timorousness of commercial publishers, has thus far appeared only in brief extracts, in the *Transatlantic Review*, now unhappily suspended."

Almost at once, however, McAlmon raised two potentially explosive matters. *The Making of Americans*, he informed Miss Stein, had turned out to be a much longer work than he had supposed, a third longer than even *Ulysses* (he and Bird, after a word count, estimated that *Ulysses* contained 379,000 words; *Americans*, 550,000), and therefore if the book came out in the four or six volumes that she had suggested, the cost would be prohibitive. He had decided, therefore, that it must not exceed one or two volumes. He also reminded her that subscriptions to help defray the expense of printing such a large book would have to be gathered at once. No doubt Miss Stein's acquiescence averted a sudden end to their relations. It was "hard to know how long a thing is until one has tried," she replied, and added that she thought "one volume would be nice." As for subscriptions, he could expect a "fair amount fairly quickly as soon as the subscription blanks are out. . . ."

Tucked in among the reviews and mementos in McAlmon's scrapbook is a catalogue of names bearing the title: Producers in Montparnasse, Paris and France. Spurred by the complaints of a journalist friend annoyed by a spate of articles in American newspapers that had pictured expatriates as dissolute, non-working Bohemians noisily going to seed in Paris, McAlmon and a few friends retired one evening to a café to draft

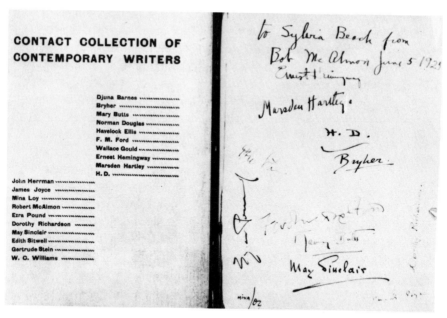

CONTACT COLLECTION OF CONTEMPORARY WRITERS

Djuna Barnes
Bryher
Mary Butts
Norman Douglas
Havelock Ellis
F. M. Ford
Wallace Gould
Ernest Hemingway
Marsden Hartley
H. D.

John Herrman
James Joyce
Mina Loy
Robert McAlmon
Ezra Pound
Dorothy Richardson
May Sinclair
Edith Sitwell
Gertrude Stein
W. C. Williams

to Sylvia Beach from Bob McAlmon June 5 1923
Ernest Hemingway
Marsden Hartley
H. D.
Bryher
May Sinclair

Opening of autographed copy of *Contact Collection of Contemporary Writers* (Contact Editions, 1925).
PRINCETON UNIVERSITY LIBRARY, SYLVIA BEACH COLLECTION

their reply. What they produced was a list of more than a hundred writers and artists, mostly Americans, who, in their opinion, comprised the most talented and promising creators of the age. Besides listing the most prominent names—Hemingway, Stein, Cummings, Joyce, Ford, Pound, Djuna Barnes, Man Ray, and Elliot Paul—the compliers included part-time residents of the Quarter, such as Fitzgerald, Sinclair Lewis, John Dos Passos, and Edna Ferber, presumably because they had absorbed both material and stimulus while living abroad. After each name, along with a note saying how long that person had lived in Europe, was a synopsis of his accomplishments: Fitzgerald wrote *The Great Gatsby* and short stories in Paris or in the south of France, Pound wrote sixteen cantos while living in Montparnasse, Nathan Asch wrote *The Office* in the Quarter.

Although McAlmon's list was never published, and was probably not intended to be, it did refute the easy notion that the exiles were frittering away their time and talent. It may also have assuaged any misgivings the compilers themselves might have had about their own output as well as reenforced the conviction that Paris was still the creative crossroads of the world. Whether it inspired McAlmon to go out and gather samples of unpublished writing by many of these same "producers" for his Contact anthology of "works in progress," he never said, but by the end of 1924 (the list was drawn up in the fall) he had made arrangements for a sizable volume to be called *Contact Collection of Contemporary Writers*. Contributions—all quickly forwarded to Dijon—began arriving early in 1925: Miss Stein's "Two Women," a parcel of poems by Mina Loy, two contrasting views of Greece by H. D. and Norman Douglas. Ready for distribution by summer, the *Contact Collection*, running to 338 pages and imposing in light-gray covers, offered selections by ten of McAlmon's Contact writers—Barnes, Bryher, Butts, Hemingway, Hartley, H. D., Herrmann, Loy, Stein, and Williams; four of Bill Bird's Three Mountains authors—Ford, Hemingway, Pound, and Williams; and seven "unaffiliated" writers—Norman Douglas, Havelock Ellis, Wallace Gould, James Joyce, Dorothy Richardson, May Sinclair, Edith Sitwell, and, of course, McAlmon himself. As eclectic as other samplers of expatriate writing, notably Peter Neagoe's *Americans Abroad*, McAlmon's offerings possessed no recognizable similarities beyond an interest in displaying the "interior life," which at times amounted to exhibitionism. John Collier, reviewing it for the *New Age*, took aim at Mina Loy's contribution (fifty-eight pages), complaining that it was a surfeit of verse by one who "has nothing but faith and pomposity." Whether she deserved more or less space than May Sinclair (fifty-nine pages) or Gertrude Stein—who, Collier wrote, was "not even pompous"—could hardly have mattered to McAlmon, undoubtedly pleased to have all three as contributors. Collier brushed off H. D.'s long prose study, "Hedylus," as so much Greekiness poured out "in a formless, intolerably sweetened flood." In his opinion, the short stories of May Sinclair and Dorothy Richardson far excelled those of Djuna Barnes and Mary Butts, both faulted as strained and artificial, as well as the contributions of Hemingway ("Soldier's Home"), John Herrmann ("Work in Progress"), and McAlmon ("Spring Leaves to Consider")—all of them arid and insignificant. As for Joyce's excerpt from the as-yet-untitled *Finnegans Wake*, its very "fragmentariness" made more than a general comment impossible. Collier awarded the laurels for the best poetry to Pound's "A Canto" and Edith Sitwell's "The Drum" and "An Old Woman Laments in Spring-time."

In a rare comment on his publishing days McAlmon once said that of the twenty-odd authors he published only two ever got "temperamental" and that they were both Gertrudes. He went on to say that both women

61

were also megalomaniacs who had the idea that "to know them was to serve them without question about their demands." As had been the case with Gertrude Stein, serving Gertrude Beasley, a Texan whose early experience as a teacher in Abilene prompted observers to praise her as a "very successful teacher" who "doesn't believe in sparing the rod," began pleasantly. After a brief teaching career and stay at the University of Chicago, Miss Beasley had turned up in Paris, where in the early twenties she began writing her autobiography, rather forcefully titled *My First Thirty Years*. McAlmon liked Miss Beasley's "naturalistic" expression and recommended that she finish her book which he promised to publish.

McAlmon's amiable relations with Gertrude Stein began to deteriorate about the time Darantière started sending her the first proofs of *Americans*. While acknowledging that the proofs looked good, she was unhappy about not having a contract, and the draft of one McAlmon hastily drew up and sent her was a disappointment. It was "too indefinite" about royalties, profits, expenses, and the disposition of sheets, she complained. She also reminded McAlmon that she was saving him money by doing the proofreading herself, and that the revised agreement should clearly state she would receive ten free copies of her book, a matter that had the appearance of being almost an obsession with Miss Stein. McAlmon incorporated her demands in his revision, modifying a few of them somewhat. It granted her royalties of ten percent after 350 copies had been sold, not 250, as Miss Stein had suggested, although even a sale of 300, McAlmon cautioned, would barely cover costs. He ruled out charging a higher price for the book—they had agreed on 150 francs—since that would only encourage collectors to buy it up and sell it at even higher prices to other collectors, with the result that the book would have few readers. As for the proofreading, McAlmon acknowledged that Miss Stein was doing her own, and explained that he had brought the subject up "simply to insure against long inserts and changes in the text," a practice he believed the author eschewed, but with writers inclined to "change more" the contract could serve as a model. Their agreement at last signed, Miss Stein and Miss Toklas left Paris for Bilignin, their country residence south of Paris, where they passed the summer struggling "with the errors of French compositors," sometimes checking and rechecking the proofs as often as four times. In August, Miss Stein reported to Sherwood Anderson that *Americans* had come to 925 pages. Preparing it for publication had been a pleasant but rather "strange" experience, strange because for twenty years she had not read her book and there were places where it seemed to her "foolishly youthful." Nonetheless, she had decided to leave things unchanged: ". . . lots of people will think many strange things in it as to tenses and persons and adjectives and adverbs and divisions are due to the french compositors' errors but they are not it is quite as I worked at it and even when I tried to change it well I didn't really try but I went over it to see if it could go different and I always found myself forced back into its incorrectness so there they stand." More proof sheets from Dijon arrived in Bilignin or Paris regularly throughout the summer and early fall, and after a close scrutiny by both Miss Stein and Miss Toklas were returned to the printer. At the same time, unknown to McAlmon, Miss Stein and Jane Heap were pressing their search for an American publisher to bring out *Americans*, and the near success of their "secret" negotiations with one New York firm, once McAlmon learned precisely what terms had been agreed upon, created a crisis that eventually led to a permanent separation between the author and her publisher as well as to a threat which, if it had been carried out, would have resulted in the destruction of all the copies of Miss Stein's book.

VI

Fortunately, preparations for the publication of Mary Butts' novel proceeded more smoothly. Widely believed to have been based on the author's "distinguished" family history, *Ashe of Rings* presented a plethora of ancestoral shenanigans that included witchcraft, incest, heathen gods, adultery, nepotism, and spiritualism. Published in the spring, in pale-green paper covers and a silver slipcase, it made the author "most effusive." First married to John Rodker, the publisher of Ovid books and Casanova Editions, Mary Butts had fled to the Continent with a "tall Scot who practiced black magic and took drugs" and who died, suddenly, soon after they had arrived in Paris. It was through Mary Butts that Virgil Thomson—and many another—experienced the "opium world," though Thomson discovered that part of her magic also came from religion and great poetry. Anyway at all, he opined, she was "strong medicine," a strong woman, hardened by personal tragedy, possessed with formidable "mental powers" and inflexible habits—a vertitable "storm goddess" who was at "her best surrounded by cataclysm." With McAlmon, whom she would address as "my lamb," she spoke sighingly of the depravity of Europe, of the sinister forces, like dark clouds, threatening to "overwhelm us all," and against which "clean, young, pure" Americans like McAlmon

—naive and inexperienced—were defenseless. Such fermentations made him "squirmy," though he wondered if perhaps she was not right in saying that "healthy, young Americans didn't know anything about the depths of Europe." Yet to become like Mary Butts seemed to him impossible. "Mary, Mary, to be one of you? I ask myself, do I want that?"

McAlmon had had at least a glimpse of Mary Butts' depraved Europe during his Berlin visit with Marsden Hartley, and in *Distinguished Air* (subtitled, sardonically, *Grim Fairy Tales*) he had tried to re-create the ambience of the place. In July (1925), the same month *Ashe of Rings* appeared, Bill Bird finally finished hand-printing *Distinguished Air*. It was the last he would do before selling the Three Mountains Press. Around the same time McAlmon also released Carnevali's *A Hurried Man*, which for the co-editor of *This Quarter*, Ernest Walsh, was an event of unprecedented importance. In *A Hurried Man*, Walsh wrote, "we have a book that is something never before done. The collected writings [the volume contained Carnevali's collected poetry, short stories, and essays] of a young writer still under thirty published while he is still living and edited by his contemporaries [actually only by McAlmon] and published by a publishing house devoted only to the work of a small minority whose work appears to have those qualities that suggest the major performance in art." With Carnevali's book still in mind, Walsh predicted that McAlmon's Contact books would "outlive the hurried reading of one generation and be part of the mental equipment of the generation now on the way to maturity." Walsh's certainty that Carnevali would assume his rightful place among the next generation rested partly on his belief that Carnevali had been mistreated during the eight years he had lived in the United States. Remonstrating that America had had no use for the poet "except to starve him and put him to serving his inferiors as a waiter in a cheap restaurant," Walsh warned that Carnevali would challenge and destroy the usual inheritance passed from one generation to the next and claim the allegiance of America's children, becoming part of their mind and soul, "their Father, and the beginning of the Republic of Youth." Obviously as impressed with Carnevali as McAlmon had been, and not wishing to be outdone in his appreciation, Walsh compared him to Keats, claiming that Carnevali was more important than Keats, because, unlike the English poet, Carnevali lived in a "more important age" and knew a "larger world," and thus had more to say. On a visit to the writer in Italy Walsh had been as profoundly moved as McAlmon by his power "to entertain and buoy" those around him despite the presence of almost continual pain. One never "felt death in him," Walsh declared. "He is a live warm laughing and fighting man; and, beyond that, he is a 'major poet,' the equal of Pound, Sandburg and Williams, whose record of the 'life of the youth of this age' . . . will live beyond this century."

Up to 1925 McAlmon had managed to avoid any run-ins with British and American customs officials, but suddenly in that year his privileged status ended, with disastrous results for several Contact publications. He had of course realized that in both countries books printed in Paris were automatically suspect and often confiscated simply because they were believed to be obscene. Still, he was appalled that American customs men had rejected a shipment of Carnevali's "clean" and "distinguished" book and had also refused a packet containing five copies of *The Making of Americans* as well as a shipment of John Herrmann's "boyish" and "naively innocent" book *What Happens*. In England, Gertrude Beasley's *My First Thirty Years* could not be distributed, and in America three hundred copies of the book "were lost." Miss Beasley, unfortunately for both author and publisher, had angered British immigration officials by failing to register as an alien, and the subsequent outlandish news coverage given the event—all while Miss Beasley was reading the proofs of her book—had dissuaded McAlmon from even trying to circulate her book in England. News of its suppression convinced Elliot Paul that it was "one of the cleanest books" he had ever read. "If it is obscene," he pontificated, "then intellectual honesty itself must be counted as abominable. If it is indecent, then pretending to see straight must be made a crime." As inspiring as Paul's words were they did little to improve the testy exchanges that passed between author and publisher on the matter of how to rescue their beleaguered book. Finally, McAlmon had his own book, *Distinguished Air*, to worry about. If copies reached England and customs officials discovered the frank treatment of homosexuality and the rather hopeless sort of heterosexual love McAlmon had depicted in the third story, there would certainly be repercussions that might produce additional restrictions on Contact publications. From London, he sent specific instructions to Miss Beach: "For various reasons I don't want a copy [of *Distinguished Air*] to get into England unless I know who it goes to, so I don't want to let any copies be sold in Paris, except to people I know." When he heard from her that she had had "callers" at Shakespeare and Company who had asked questions about Contact books, he replied he was certain "somebody is out to get us," and whoever it was had even tipped the porter at his apartment "to give them information" and gone to the expense of subscribing to a "clipping agency for notes." In the midst of all this it would be "quite impossible" to circulate *Distinguished Air.* With four "dead" books now on his hands—Hermann's, Beasley's, Carnevali's, and his own—he sent Miss Beach a rather plaintive message expressing the hope that she was selling a few of the new Contact books in Paris "to finance the dead ones." The check she sent him two weeks later seemed to relieve him somewhat. "We are sliding more easily now, but there's lots of flummery business in the world. Though it ain't as if I didn't dern well know that aforehand. About publishing I mean."

In Paris again in September McAlmon picked up a shipment of sheets of *Americans* and took them to the bindery. He especially wanted to have one copy bound—and signed—for Joyce. He also had important news for Miss Stein. In England he had met a representative of the newly formed firm of Albert and Charles Boni, who, having been alerted to the forthcoming publication of Miss Stein's book by the hard-working Miss Heap, had proposed that McAlmon instruct Darantière to print a thousand instead of five hundred sets of sheets, which the Bonis would bind and distribute in America. Since only fifteen orders for *Americans* had arrived during the several months he had advertised it, McAlmon lost no time outlining the proposal to Miss Stein, who, while naturally appreciative of his efforts, persisted in her demand for ten author's copies of *Americans* and, if the Bonis published the book, for ten additional copies from them. If the Bonis bought the edition and hence took over her contract, McAlmon replied, they would have to furnish the ten books. Still adamant, Miss Stein answered that even if the Bonis purchased the edition McAlmon must supply the ten copies as promised. Then, with the impasse still unsettled, plans for an American edition unexpectedly collapsed. First McAlmon discovered that the instructions he had sent Darantière to double the printing of *Americans* (that is, to a thousand) never reached Dijon. All mail addressed to the printer had been held in England on the grounds that Darantière was publishing obscene books, and by the time McAlmon learned he had never received his message, the printer had already distributed part of the type. Next, McAlmon reported to Miss Stein that the Bonis had "backed down" when he requested part payment at the time of shipment and the balance in thirty days, claiming that their London representative had misunderstood the proposal. The climax, however, came later the same month when Jane Heap notified Miss Stein that she had found someone ready to pay McAlmon a thousand dollars for the five hundred sets of sheets, and urged her to put pressure on him to accept

Djuna Barnes, Paris, 1928.
COURTESY OF MISS BARNES

quickly. Miss Stein did, emphasizing the mutual financial advantages of the offer: "Their proposal is to buy *The Making of Americans* from you that is the 500 copies minus the 40 copies already ordered [evidently additional orders had arrived, or McAlmon and Miss Stein had different counts], for a thousand dollars which really means 1620 dollars or 1000 dollars for the 460 books and 40 ordered at 8 dollars and the five bound in vellum at $60." Despite Miss Stein's figures and her belief that the offer was an "important opportunity" for her, McAlmon rejected it as barely enough to cover even a third of the printing costs. Miss Heap's next maneuver sent McAlmon into a rage. A London book distributor named Stanley Nott, whom Miss Heap had contacted, agreed to take four hundred sets of sheets. McAlmon quickly notified Miss Heap that Nott could have only two hundred sets. But the opportunity of disposing of almost the entire edition must have proven irresistible to Miss Stein, for without telling McAlmon she instructed Darantière to forward the four hundred sets to Paris for shipment to England, assuring the skeptical printer she

67

was merely conveying McAlmon's wishes. Darantière, unsatisfied with Miss Stein's explanation, telegraphed McAlmon for verification. That Miss Stein had arrogantly ignored his orders McAlmon had no doubt, and he angrily dismissed as false her story that she had acted on the instructions of Jane Heap, who, she claimed, had received authorization from McAlmon to ship the four hundred sets to Paris. Curtly he informed her that the printed sheets belonged to him and had been stitched and would be bound. She would receive *her* ten copies, "sufficient for your friendly gifts," review copies would go out to "some special reviewers," if Miss Stein supplied names and addresses, but "further panic and insistence, and " 'helping us' " would not be welcome. Disinclined to admit guilt, Miss Stein nonetheless did concede that his anger was "not without reason." In reporting what had happened to Sylvia Beach, McAlmon admitted he was less surprised by Miss Stein's action than he told her he was. "Somehow we get instincts."

The Making of Americans, the last Contact book of 1925, reached Paris in October and most copies never left. Miss Stein reserved her compliments for Darantière, ignoring McAlmon who had selected "the paper, the print, the binding and designed the jacket and make-up." Nott, stunned by the Beasley affair and the seizure of her book, abandoned plans to import two hundred copies, and although the Bonis did finally purchase one hundred sets of sheets (at a fifty percent discount), *Americans* seemed close to being another "dead" book on the publisher's hands. (A year later the "tome" he hoped might sell "a little" had sold only 103 copies, 74 of them paperbound.) Nevertheless, with *Americans* at last launched, though barely, McAlmon could get back to his own writing. He confided to Sylvia Beach that the "summer's activities, publishing, home office [probably visits to the Ellermans], and G. S. [Gertrude Stein] and her very Hebraic insistence [have] made me want not to look at proof for a year." And while waiting for that mood to pass, he assured her, once more, he was getting much work done.

VII

The year just ended had been a trying one for McAlmon, but at least the new one would begin differently, far from Paris and far from the concerns of book publishing. Travel had always calmed McAlmon and often set him writing again, and in January he reported to Miss Beach that traveling with Bryher and Lady Ellerman—in the Middle East, Egypt, and then Greece—was having a salubrious effect on him. "I feel a change coming on. . . . Much reading, working, and travel makes that." He was actually writing more since he no longer held drink well, and from Athens he reported that, though still working, Bryher "finds me very froggy [*sic*] as a writer." In April, alone, he stopped over in Cagnes-sur-Mer, staying with people who were "actually working," one of whom was the American artist Hilaire Hiler, whose painting McAlmon considered "about the best America is producing." Hiler had already finished a number of woodcuts that the publisher would later use in his last Contact publication, *North America, Continent of Conjecture*. Two new Contact books were already in production for 1926: H. D.'s *Palimpsest*, mentioned in the 1923 Contact announcement as a possible future publication, and John Herrmann's novel *What Happens*, as lucid as *Palimpsest* was complicated, and one which McAlmon had agreed to sponsor "for its plain, easily read, direct and honest writing." Both were scheduled for release in the summer, to be followed in the early fall by Robert Coates' *The Eater of Darkness*, after which, at the end of the year, would come McAlmon's book of poetry, *The Portrait of a Generation*. It was certainly a lighter publishing schedule than the one just closed and, hopefully, one that could be more agreeably managed.

One problem, however, carried over into the new year: Gertrude Stein. In April, still rankling over her high-handed intrusion into his publishing affairs and cool toward her efforts at reconciliation, McAlmon sent the author an ultimatum:

> Contrary to your verbal statements that you would help rid us of your volume, you have done nothing. The Dial review I got for you. The Irish Statesman review came from a book sent them at my instructions. Books were sent to people you asked to have them sent to. Ten books were GIVEN you. You *asked* me to take on the book. You knew it was a philanthropic enterprise as the Ms. had been some twenty years on your hands. There is no evidence of any order having come in through your offices except from your immediate family . . . the family, one judges, mentioned in the book. . . .
>
> If you wish to purchase the rest of the books you may do so. . . . As the Three Mts. Press is now non-existent, and any pub-

lishing I do will be as a private person, using the name Contact, and as Mr. Bird is out of it, I do not choose to bother storing a book of that size, when its author so warily fears we might get back a portion of the amount paid for it.

. . . If you wish the books retained, you may bid for them. Otherwise, by Sept.—one year after publication—I shall simply rid myself of them en-masse, by the pulping proposition.

In addition to the *Dial* review McAlmon mentioned, which Marianne Moore wrote, Edmund Wilson in the *New Republic* and William Rose Benét in the *Saturday Review of Literature* both reviewed Miss Stein's book, but neither critic did so with any discernible enthusiasm, Wilson even going so far as to say he had not read it through, and Benét, who presumably had, expressing amazement over what he called an exhibit of "the most complete befuddlement of the human mind." Although McAlmon himself later wrote that *Americans* "got few and mainly unfair reviews," the one he submitted to *The Outlook* and which appeared the same month he sent the ultimatum to Miss Stein contained surprisingly few recommendations. With barely veiled asperity he granted that Miss Stein was a "writer of quality in that she uses words in a new way," that is, "repetitiously, darkly, sluggishly understood, slowly utilized, in vast quantities, like mud, and plenty of mud." He also granted that *Americans*, like *Three Lives*, was a "good stolid, solid, recordation of slow, undistinguished life among slow people." It lacked, however, almost all of the quality of American life McAlmon had tried to render in his own work. Except for some cursory attention to the "American background," *Americans* was "eminently Jewish," a picture of the "thick, ingrown, murky life of a bourgeois Jewish family through three generations in America"—a life monotonously slow, devoid of ideas, and responsive only to threats to its middle-class virtues and property. It followed that the book could only be the work of a "low-tensioned being," one "whose pulse throbs with utter lethargy," and who is satisfied with the simple process of putting words—often the same words—together over and over, rather like a baby playing with clay who asks her nurse repeatedly: "Shall I make a man? Shall I make a man?" The trouble was "none of Miss Stein's characters [had] even the distinguishing characteristics the baby's clay man would have." The really regrettable thing about *Americans*, McAlmon concluded, was that it did not "frankly admit more of the primitive child, the naif discovering incident." Her few efforts "to be instructively and analytically intelligent" could have been "her error."

If McAlmon, out of pique over what she had done to him, intended to damage Miss Stein's reputation as a leader of modern literature, a position he suspected she was already having trouble maintaining, he may have succeeded. He stopped short, however, of pulping the leftover copies of *Americans*, perhaps as many as two hundred, and Miss Stein never hinted she would consider buying them. Of those distributed to bookstores in America, England, and on the Continent, not more than two hundred, according to the publisher, were ever paid for. What happened to the rest neither McAlmon nor Bird could recall.

For *Palimpsest* and *What Happens*, both ready in June, McAlmon wrote introductions, or in the case of *Palimpsest*, a "Forewarned." *What Happens* was John Herrmann's first book. Herrmann, a native of Michigan, had studied art history in Munich before arriving in Paris, where he met and married the novelist Josephine Herbst and settled down to become a serious writer. *What Happens* satisfied McAlmon's Contact criteria admirably. It was an example of "good, plain, simple, direct, and honest writing," which gave a "very fair picture of adolescence in America," direct and authentic, and was totally unaware of the "glamor and romance and great love interest needed in a book which is to sell." What a *New York Times* reviewer called "a saga of the jazz age" rendered exactly what McAlmon believed happened to young men growing up in America. Its very ordinariness—"the gangly, awkward, fumbling-bewilderment of its youthful quality"—while anathema to a commercial publisher, was what gave Herrmann's book its individuality. Although hardly a book that promised to return his investment, McAlmon was unprepared for its being banned both in England and America (it had been designated primarily for the American market), and when Herrmann's attempt to have the restriction revoked by circulating a protest signed by notable writers failed, McAlmon wrote it off as another loss, remarking later that the "venture was not a cheering affair."

Fortunately, H. D.'s *Palimpsest* was. Not only were there no problems with customs officials, but McAlmon actually sold seven hundred sets of sheets to Houghton Mifflin (the Boston firm released the book before the end of the year), an unprecedented event for a Contact book, although given the author's considerable reputation as a poet it was perhaps not entirely unexpected. *Palimpsest* was the author's first book of prose, a fact McAlmon believed required an explanation, not so much because her shifting to prose demanded it, but because he thought her prose style did. "Forewarned as regards H. D.'s Prose," the title of his introductory essay, appeared neither in the Contact nor in the American edition of *Palimpsest*, although it was set up in type and printed, perhaps for promotional purposes. A pity it did not appear, for McAlmon's analysis of the author's intentions and what he regarded as her achievements was one of the best pieces he ever wrote. Perhaps with *Ulysses* in mind, McAlmon granted that *Palimpsest* had the "capacity to start sensation," despite its obvious inherent difficulties and demands and despite the " 'intellect' of the author—so insistent upon intellect, not here an escape, but a necessity, an inevitable assertion." *Palimpsest* was an unavoidable and necessary break with the past—H. D.'s past—a fact revealing how disconnected the author had become with the acclaim awarded her and how determined she was to go on "knowing life, and going on with it." Rejecting any "haven of security," she had forged her own style, studiously avoiding both English and American traditions, and writing "as an individual with an individual's rights," without the slightest deference to any of the fashions in vogue among her contemporaries. Her writing, McAlmon contended, was based on "direct perception; direct origination; direct rejection of the parasitical fungi of 'taste' as understood because either Britain or America need pattern-minded types to 'carry on the tradition.' " Like *What Happens*, although its opposite in style and substance, *Palimpsest* was an "outsider," a book that defied established standards and popular tastes and asserted its own aestheticism.

The always gracious and accommodating book editor of *The Outlook*, Louise Morgan, was among the first to review *Palimpsest*, and echoed McAlmon's appreciation in language nearly as poetic as the author's. Of H. D.'s three interrelated stories (now is the time to say that a palimpsest is a parchment or tablet containing sometimes two, sometimes three, texts, all of which are visible at the same time), Miss Morgan selected the second, "Murex," as the author's best, being not only an "aesthetically fine, moral revaluation of life" but a picture of the "brutality and the ecstacy of war London." The first and third stories, the former set in first century B.C. Rome, the latter in Egypt soon after the First World War, were remarkable achievements for an "expatriate American," convincing evidence that the author, unlike many of her compatriots, could write about subjects entirely divorced from her own origins or her own nation or even West Philadelphia, where H. D. had lived while a student at Bryn Mawr. In Miss Morgan's opinion, H. D. was obviously "interested in writing not as a method of national self-glorification, or as a social pose, or as a paying profession, or as a means to any end whatso-ever outside itself. It is writers like H. D., who are above the vulgarities of affection or the stupidities of propaganda, writers whose immediacy of thought and feeling burn to ashes all intervening falseness, that have always been the hope of life as well as of literature."

McAlmon and Bryher spent the summer of 1926 in London, and except for a brief visit to Dublin, where he met Joyce's father, McAlmon was increasingly unhappy. Part of the malaise, no doubt, was caused by the familiar uncomfortableness that usually overcame him on visits to England. "I'm hating London so intensely that there's no use trying to work much at the moment," he complained to Miss Beach. "Mould and decay and dirt and ingrown Britishness without the one time stability and dependability of it. Paris is my town, and I think after this year I'll not take on a long stretch of London again." Even the "season" had conspired to annoy him. "London having done the Sitwell season—with Gertrude Stein a presiding mass—and the Sitwells' three rabbits made in wood to conceal their rabbit frights—London will now have the Ballet Russe." After much perturbation, Miss Stein had accepted invitations to lecture at Cambridge and Oxford, her text on both occasions being *Composition as Explanation*, which, before going back to Paris, she managed to place with Leonard Woolf for publication in the fall at his Hogarth Press. (A year or so after publication Woolf reported to Miss Stein that her book had sold "quite fairly." Of the thousand printed, nearly five hundred had been sold.) In spite of the grim London sojourn, McAlmon was looking forward to publishing a new book of short stories by Claude McKay and a strange collection of tales by Ken Sato tentatively called *Yellow Jap Dogs*. Also, he told Miss Beach, besides having "lots of work to re-work a little" [probably *Portrait of a Generation*, still scheduled for the fall], he was getting out a novel, already being delicately nibbled at by two publishers, but probably a "bit continental for the American" firm, and "too Ameri-can for the English, and too 'really, you cant [sic] use these words' for both." Despite his misgivings, however, he had decided to send a copy of the novel (the never-to-be-published *Family Panorama*) to America, not by mail, but "with somebody," for from Bird he had learned that Scotland Yard was still vigilantly watching the mails for Contact books and had recently photographed a London bookseller's order for the forthcoming *Portrait of a Generation*, contending that the book was "obscene."

VIII

When Robert Coates' *Eater of Darkness* came up from Dijon, the author was in Paris to receive it. McAlmon, however, was heading for California by way of the Panama Canal, loaded with manuscripts. Coates had written the first part of his book in New York while replenishing his finances after a year's stay in Paris; he finished it in Giverny, the scenic town south of Paris popularized by Claude Monet. By his own admission, he never "expected to see it published," and presumably would not have gone out of his way to show it to a publisher had Gertrude Stein not urged him to. He later described his attitude at the time as "a confused, variable and thoroughly jejune mixture of Francois Villon (the medieval influence and also general rascality, though a more law-abiding rascal than I was in those days could hardly be imagined); Sir Philip Sidney (the great six-teenth-century English poet, representing the aristocratic impulse) and Dada, or devil-may-careness." While Villon and Dada certainly influenced what Coates put into his book, it was Sidney's example that determined what he would do with it. If Sidney, instead of stooping "to seek out a publisher for his writing," had just had a "fair copy" of them made for circulation among his friends, why should he not do the same? The care-fully bound transcript Coates passed along to friends eventually reached Gertrude Stein, who "read it, liked it, and immediately set about getting it published." Ordinarily Miss Stein's endorsement and support would be welcomed as an important step toward publication, but for the author who subscribed to the dadaists' credo forbidding "anything so vulgar as wide circulations and financial profits," it created at least a philosophical prob-lem. What if *Eater of Darkness* turned out to be a success? How could such a "failure" be explained? Before him loomed the example of Louis Aragon, who had dramatized his contempt for literary commercialism by sending a warning to all the Paris book editors that he would "horsewhip them if they so much as mentioned his new book." In an introduction written for a reissue of his book, Coates admitted that at the time his resistance to the prospect of publication must have been limited to a delicate yawn. In fact, he "was pretty darned pleased at the way things were turning out." Objecting to the mingling of "art and commerce . . . was basically simply hedging: I wasn't at all sure that anybody was going to want to publish the thing in the first place."

McAlmon remembered that the script Coates delivered was "a beau-tiful affair: a work of art in itself with the cover and inside pages designed by himself"—really a "modern illuminated manuscript." McAlmon was certain, however, that Darantière's printers would never be able to unravel its "mystery," and since he did not want to go to the expense of having the binding and pages photographed and reproduced in color, he asked the author to retype his manuscript. At the same time Coates drew up a "dadaist" dedication of eighteen names: alongside Paris friends like Kathleen Cannell, Harold Loeb, Gertrude Stein, and, of course, McAlmon, he included the *New York Times*, which had helped finance his book by buying some of his "color stories" for its Sunday magazine section; Nick Carter; "Snapper"; and Fantomas, their French counterpart, on whose thrillers Coates had modeled *Eater of Darkness*; and Gerald Chapman, "a bank robber and gunman very much in the news at the time." Arthur Moss, at McAlmon's request, contributed a two-page preface, "A Soft Note of Introduction," in which Moss gracefully endowed Coates with familiar Contact credentials: no obeisance to tradition, a "lonewolf" character, a "young Mahomet blazing his own new religion."

If Coates had any real qualms about the consequences of success and how it might affect his status as a member of the "non-commercial" group of writers, events must have eased his mind. While *Eater of Darkness* "wasn't an actual flop," it had, in Coates' words, "a gratifying lack of success in the proper quarters, and a pleasantly comforting *succès d'estime* elsewhere." In his estimate, McAlmon took note of the author's intention to write a surrealistic novel which at the same time would be a satire of surrealism, and hence of itself; however the experiment had not quite come off, perhaps because Coates had "pondered too long a book which should have been written with gay and malicious joy." Instead, he had produced a "book for authors." In Paris Coates' work caused a momentary stir, dramatically mirrored in two strongly opposing reviews printed in the *Tribune*, one by Elliot Paul, the other by Alex Small. Paul focused on the author's skill as a parodist. Only Gertrude Stein, who, Paul surmised, was probably "too difficult to approach, either reverently or irreverently," was spared; but there for those acquainted with contemporary writing to enjoy were delicious stylistic parodies of James Joyce, Waldo Frank, E. E. Cummings, Sherwood Anderson, Jean Toomer, Max Bodenheim, Frank Harris, and even Ben Hecht. Furthermore, for anyone who found Van Vechten, Donald Ogden Stewart, Walt Mason, Christopher Morley, Aldous Huxley, Irvin Cobb, Heywood Broun, H. L. Mencken, or Franklin P. Adams "stupid ought to like Mr. Coates." To Alex Small, noted for his vitriolic attacks on Left Bank writers, Coates' book was "worthless," beneath even the limited value of a nursery tale. Small took the opportunity to lambast both Gertrude Stein and James Joyce, two of his favorite targets, to whom Coates, he believed, was mistakenly trying to ally himself. Were they, Small wondered, bringing forth a "new and great revelation," or was it all the "raving of madmen, just as significant and just as important as the hallucinations of any maniac"? There was no doubt in Small's mind. A halt should be called at once! How much longer, he wailed, would "intelligent people in the Quarter . . . be bullied by the sort of stuff and nonsense which Mr. Coates has the infernal cheek to put into print?" A friend of Small's, a onetime associate editor of *transition* named Robert Sage, conjectured that a book that perfectly reflected its environment was usually the first to die. *Eater of Darkness*, unfortunately, was such a book, but it was also "one of the lonely handful of recent novels . . . that an adult mentality can honestly recognize as being funny." Happily, *Eater of Darkness* possessed more lifeblood than Sage seemed willing to allow. In 1929, two years after his review, it was published in New York, and thirty years later reprinted in an American paperback edition.

The final Contact book of the year, *The Portrait of a Generation, Including the Revolving Mirror* contained nearly all of McAlmon's poetry, some of which had already appeared in the *Little Review* and *Poetry*. Throughout the year he had worked hard on *Revolving Mirror*, a nine-hundred-line poem intended to complement the "portrait of the age" contained in the short lyrics which filled the rest of the volume. Unsurprisingly, it turned out to be a realistic, sardonic, occasionally cynical interpretation of the author's life on two continents, in which he had tried to trace the breakdown of traditional values and the search for fundamentals much as Eliot and Hemingway had attempted to do in *The Waste Land* and *The Sun Also Rises*. In the end he had come closer to embracing Hemingway's stoicism than Eliot's resurrection of the past. The poem offered more than a comment on the destiny of a generation, however. The passages containing cameo portraits of the author's friends and in-laws, along with the lyrical sections, are the best parts of the poem, and the former were all that Ethel Moorhead could find to praise. Neither she nor her co-editor Ernest Walsh had ever thought much of McAlmon's verse, and Walsh had once sharply criticized it. Referring to the *Portrait*, Miss Moorhead accused the author of "disguising under a cloak of cynicism his better self." In place of Robert McAlmon we have "mostly the clever, cynical observer," flaunting his observations with a jeer, but betraying at the same time an ineptitude and a lack of self-assurance. Mc-Almon had been "daring about others, but not sufficiently courageous about himself." Only the "highest moments have a fleeting and shame-faced tenderness." The acerbic William Rose Benét, reviewing it in the *Saturday Review of Literature*, found even less than that to praise; in fact, after maliciously noting that McAlmon's last effort had been a "fairy story" (*Distinguished Air*)—foolishly recommended by Walsh as an example of a new prose style—Benét proceeded to demolish *Portrait*, first as an exercise in incoherence that succeeded, and next as a depiction of an age that did not exist. Dismissing *Portrait* was tantamount to rejecting the whole "lost generation":

> So "the generation" sits in its café in Paris, and its eyelids have grown more than a little weary. There is no health in us. The world revolves in the revolving mirror. The mind is a mere kaleidoscope of preposterous patterns, ever shifting and reforming. The news of the day, the babble of small-talk, amorous memories. Language is a mere box of anagram letters spilt all over a cracked marble table. Sex is a persistent thorn in suppurating flesh. Existence is drab, sad, and hopeless. Everything is stale and outworn. Remains the sneer. Remains the weary pastime of disconnected sentences. That is nepenthe. That is art. At least, all the art we have. The world is still shell-shocked.

Having seen on his trip to America the "hell and corruption at the customs in New York" and still alarmed over the confiscation of the Beasley and Herrmann books, McAlmon requested Miss Beach to look over his new book very carefully and advise him whether it ought not to be in too much evidence at her shop. He especially cautioned her about letting Arthur Moss get hold of a copy, as he did not want him "columnizing too much about that poem" in the Paris *Times*. "I'll give it away to some people," he told her, "and carefully sell the others. I won't get rich on it . . . [but] it is better than to be made target for gossip chatter." His instructions given, he left Paris for Monte Carlo, where during the quiet and uncrowded off-season, and without the usual bevy of friends around, he looked forward to rest and writing and an opportunity to review the year just ended. In due time a report reached Miss Beach. His writing was progressing well, spurred by ideas he had picked up in America. He was putting them down as fast as he could, which was "too fast for things to be finished products." He had decided against sending out a completed novel called *The Family Panorama*, which contained valuable historical material but "too many characters, and varieties of scenes." Maybe he would let it lie for "several years," for after all, he had watched too many "great" books come out "to be in a frenzy now about being 'discovered.' " Another book, a third of which he had finished, entitled *The Politics of Modesty*, would also have to wait, at least until he had shaken himself loose from the "psychoanalytic laboratory of phobes, manias, blackmailing distrusts, and [his] own anti-England phobe." Also at rest ("for a long time") was a voluminous work on a "financial genius and its family," 120,000 words of which had already been written. But he did have ready another collection of short stories, which he thought a London publisher might take. Lastly, he reported that he and Bryher were separating. It was a decision neither entirely unexpected nor unwelcomed by their friends. McAlmon, deciding that their marriage was not a "go," had been the one to suggest the separation, and there was obvious relief to have it over in his report to Miss Beach. "I'm glad to be out of the thing, and able to be free of the need of false addresses, and of being within 'getting back to Paris or London within 36 hours distance' all the time." From now on, he assured her, he would be less "impulsive." But she should know that Bryher and he did not "treat each other badly, except in going into that damn fool, 'intelligent' arrangement." Finally, the marriage had represented to him "more things that [he] did *NOT* want in life than . . . [he] could cope with." While he was still in the United States on his second trip home their divorce became final. Sir John solemnized the event by bestowing on his former son-in-law a settlement of such generous proportions that wags in the Quarter began calling him "Robert McAlimony." The same year, 1927, Bryher remarried, and with her new husband, Kenneth Macpherson, a Scottish novelist and amateur film-maker, launched a cinema magazine called *Close Up* (the "first periodical to approach films from any angle but the commonplace") as well as a new publishing house they named Pool, whose first offering was Macpherson's *Poolreflection* (highly recommended by H. D.), followed by *Gaunt Island*, also by Macpherson, and *Civilians* by Bryher.

IX

Going back to the United States the second time must have been less a homecoming for McAlmon than a kind of grand tour in reverse. Before leaving Europe he had said he was returning to take another look at the land some Europeans acquainted with his writing insisted he perfectly represented, an observation McAlmon always found slightly baffling. He began his odyssey in Los Angeles, then moved on to Taos, and eventually reached New York, thus retracing the route he had followed ten years before. The country had probably not changed much, or at least not enough to make him want to prolong his visit or to settle down permanently. He must have marveled again at the splendid American scenery and detested, again, those flaws he found so obnoxious a part of the American character. Both subjects had figured importantly in a short story called "Deracinated Encounters," which Walsh printed in *This Quarter* while McAlmon was still away. Like many Americans in Paris who rejected their country and then found they had rejected the only heritage they had, McAlmon could be ambiguous when he tried to define how he felt about his homeland. In his story, a young Turkish friend asks Alaric, the protagonist, whether he will not soon leave for America. The answer in a word is no, but Alaric feels obliged to explain to the Turk, who is himself eager to see America, why he prefers other lands to his own.

> I feel no wish to be there. There are stretches of sea-coast that are marvelously lovely there; mountain regions, forest and lake districts; the desert, and many scenically wonderful things in America. But—I can't explain easily to you. Our backgrounds are so different—there is a weariness in me about the country. I can see a foreigner loving it, as a spectacle, for its vibration, and for the beauty of the people too. They are beautiful en masse, and individually, just as bodies, as healthy animals. Can I make you understand? They pry, and permit little privacy to anybody. Mainly they are neither simple or cultured but they are aggressive and pretentiously ambitious. Advertising there goes in for impertinences about peoples' personal habits as though the whole population were still unwashed, badly bred school children to be taught how to take care of themselves. They are too eager to be cultured, but it isn't generally so much a wish for culture as a sensitive thing, as it is a commercial impulse to increase one's social market-value. Can you understand that, having been born to class and caste, and the traditions and responsibilities of that system? You might be most unhappy in America, except that there is a kindness, in a manner, apart from the custom there of judging so much by money standards.

When McAlmon returned to Paris in the spring of 1928, he found a few new faces in the Quarter, among whom were the two young Canadians John Glassco and Graeme Taylor, who, like many others, had come

79

to Paris to write and play. For the next several months they formed an inseparable trio. McAlmon was certain that the new arrivals were two of the most promising people he had met in some time, and Glassco and Taylor, enchanted to be adopted by one they regarded as "a minor legend," were alternately intrigued by McAlmon's "charm, loneliness and bitterness . . . touched by his vanity and refreshed by his rudeness." They were also flattered by the interest he took in their writing—Glassco worked desultorily on his autobiography inspired by George Moore's *The Confessions of a Young Man*, Taylor on short stories—and by the efforts he intended to make to get it published. Glassco's autobiography, the first chapter of which McAlmon read, seemed "god-damn arch" but he was sure it was a "genuine . . . human document." There was a chance, he told him, that, if Glassco could maintain the same quality to the end, he would publish it himself. Meanwhile he persuaded Ethel Moorhead to print the chapter as well as two excerpts from Taylor's "work in progress" in *This Quarter*, and since it was to be the final number of the magazine she would edit, she also agreed to include extracts from McAlmon's *The Politics of Existence* and *North America, Continent of Conjecture* (his current projects), jesting that they would probably be like all the rest of his work. McAlmon never had a chance to publish Glassco's autobiography. The next year he suspended Contact, and Glassco, seriously ill with tuberculosis, returned to Canada and a long period of hospitalization and convalescence. Nearly four years passed before he could finish his memoir (winter of 1932–33), and by then he had turned away from his youth and did not look at the manuscript again for over thirty years, when, without revision, he published it under the title *Memoirs of Montparnasse*.

Glassco and Taylor were not the only young writers McAlmon met in 1928. There was Edwin Lanham (the two men met on the beach at Le Canadel), a Texan, who, after having been in Eastern prep schools and Williams College, had gone to sea for a year. McAlmon liked Lanham's sea yarns and suggested he put them down, and if they read as well as they sounded he would publish them in a book. Lanham spent the summer re-creating his life as a sailor. Kay Boyle was another McAlmon began seeing more often in 1928. She had been one of the first to answer Ernest Walsh's request for contributions to the maiden number of *This Quarter*, and Walsh had printed her poem "Summer" and a prose piece "Passeres' Paris." Soon afterward, living near the editors of the magazine, she assisted Walsh with the editing and correspondence and discussed with him the value of McAlmon's contributions to contemporary letters. Although

Walsh had never met McAlmon and Miss Boyle had seen him only once, they agreed he deserved to be called "a great white god." When Walsh died in October 1926, Eugene Jolas informed Miss Boyle that he intended to continue the work Walsh had not been able to finish in a magazine he was founding called *transition*, and invited her to submit stories and poems for the first number. When Miss Boyle went to live in Paris in 1928, she began seeing a lot of McAlmon and even more of Jolas, whom she assisted with *transition*; but maintaining a balance between two men with such contrasting views on writing was not easy, and although helping Jolas was almost as exhilarating as working for Walsh had been, McAlmon's opinion of the former and his magazine was, to say the least, disconcerting. Sometimes, after joking about the editor and the contents of the latest *transition*, McAlmon would tweak Miss Boyle by asking how she could possibly spend hours with the *transition* editors talking about the " 'reevaluation of the spirit in its intercontinental relations,' and the 'destruction of mechanical positivism' " (Jolas' phraseology). Once when he volunteered to tell her that his grudge against Jolas was not ideological, that it was based on Jolas' having printed a prose piece in the issue of *transition* devoted to the surrealists "just to show how bad . . . [his] writing was," Miss Boyle mischievously dared him to submit some poems to Jolas under a nom de plume (Guy Urquhart). Miss Boyle herself gave McAlmon's poems to Jolas, one of which appeared in the next *transition*. When Jolas learned of the ruse, Miss Boyle was told there was to be no more of "that kind of subterfuge."

The same year Miss Boyle met Harry and Caresse Crosby, the fledgling proprietors of the Black Sun Press, to whom she enthusiastically recommended McAlmon's poetry, particularly the poems in *North America*, which she considered completely original and perhaps even prototypes that would stand for years to come. Crosby, however, barely responded to her entreaties, and when she mentioned to McAlmon what she had done —the occasion was a New Year's Eve party at Crosby's mill house outside Paris—and added that, if Crosby did ever decide to print his poetry, the first poem ought to be the one she had often spoken aloud, McAlmon replied in a manner shockingly different from her expectations. What had been clearly done to inject some much needed hope into a man whose writing career had become increasingly desperate and which was in danger of collapsing altogether with the cessation of his publishing company, and whose bitterness and animosity and cynicism threatened to destroy his own well-being as well as his relations with his friends, produced instead a torrent of self-vituperation that left no doubt how deep the inroads of self-defeat had penetrated. " 'The God-damned, fucking, quivering pieces of me! Good enough to be flushed like you know what down the drain! Stinking enough to be tacked on the barn door in warning to the young!' he shouted. 'Fouled up enough for—what? You finish it! I'm fed up with whatever it is I'm carrying around inside this skin, rattling around inside these bones!' He struck his chest violently with his fist, and his face was as hard as stone. 'For Christ's sake, don't care about me! Stop it, will you? Let the God-damned pieces fall apart!' "

Still, as Edwin Lanham and others noted, McAlmon remained a compulsive worker; he wrote constantly, incessantly, necessarily sustained more by the prospect than the fact of publication, except when he printed his own books; and he protected himself from too much hurt by a defense of cold-eyed objectivity. The depressing nocturnal admissions Kay Boyle listened to that New Year's Eve belie the optimistic reports he gave Miss Beach in the early months of the new year. In May he described a short novel entitled *My Susceptible Friend, Adrian*. It is the "best thing I've ever done, but it is shocking in what it says and knows, though by no means a fairy story." It was rather the "life of any one of several of the boys about Paris," a "composite, with other characterizations and episodes therein." He had no doubt the book would sell but he had to find "some new way of distributing" his books in England and America. For a reprint of *Distinguished Air* (presumably he intended to publish it himself later in the year), he had written three new stories. He had also finished the third volume of *Politics of Existence*, and would soon have the first volume ready for the printer, which, he thought, Williams would have done either in France or America. But if not—for there were "some bits that might not get by," although things seemed "to be opening up there [America] considerably"—he would bring it out himself in the spring (1930). And as for *Family Panorama*, on which he had worked intermittently since 1924, would Sylvia Beach please give him her opinion of the manuscript she had read? This unfinished autobiographical work, in which McAlmon recounted his origins, beginning with family scenes set in the 1880s, was not one he wanted to bring out himself. It should appear first in the United States, but, "if it has stuff," there was no reason why it had to be done "right away." That "has to be my attitude towards my work anyway, as it was and is naturally, mercifully, as I get rejected," but he hastened to add, "I must be arriving." Edward O'Brien had chosen his story, "Potato Picking" for *The Best Short Stories of 1929*, and the editors of *The New American Caravan* (Alfred Kreymborg, Lewis Mumford, and Paul Rosenfeld, all of them "messes" as editors, McAlmon thought) had deigned, "after ninety years," to take one of his stories ("An Illiterate but Interesting Woman"). *Transition* No. 15, due in February, had printed "Potato Picking" and "The Jack Rabbit Drive, as well as "Mr. Joyce Directs an Irish Prose Ballet," which Miss Beach had just reprinted under a slightly altered title in her first publication since *Ulysses—An Examination of James Joyce*. Lastly, he asked Miss Beach to send Edward Titus the "American script" of *When Blood Flows Young* (the original title of *Village*), and advised her that *North America*, with woodcuts by Hiler, had gone to the *transition* printer, André Brulliard of Saint-Dizier. This, the last Contact book, was the first not printed by Darantière.

Even though McAlmon mentioned in his miscellany of news that he might one day print more of his own books, it never happened. *North America* was the last, and since it had been done by the *transition* printer, McAlmon had evidently ended his association with Darantière. The last two books Darantière printed—Lanham's *Sailors Don't Care* and Ken Sato's *Quaint Stories of Samurais*—both appeared in the spring, and the former at least had a modest success. In March, McAlmon ordered one hundred copies of Lanham's book sent to Shakespeare and Company (the edition consisted of 501, with numbered copies from 1 to 10), saying he thought it would sell well "once it gets known of and the summer tourists start coming in." *Sailors* recounted the author's experiences, at sixteen, while working his way around the world on a freighter. Long before he met McAlmon, he had set out to be an artist, and after studying at the National Academy of Design had worked at his painting for several years in Paris. Having his sea adventures published just may have given Lanham a new career. McAlmon liked his "punch" and Lanham's book was "simple and direct . . . a narrative yarn of the sea . . . rather strong, but authentic to sea life." Like one or two other Contact authors, Lanham paid a share of the print bill, and on the day of publication had the unforgettable experience of seeing his book "under the arm of a customer at the Dome," who turned out to be a visiting celebrity—Maxwell Bodenheim, then in a "prosperous period of his life." Though, as Lanham put it, *Sailors Don't Care* was "innocuous enough even for that time," American customs men disagreed, and "after due notice" at least one shipment was burned. The incident may have brought a compensating benefit to the author, however, for soon afterward the publisher Harrison Smith cabled

Lanham that he was interested in publishing *Sailors* and asked for a week's option, at the end of which he accepted it with the proviso that the author "expurgate several passages and also . . . put it in the first person (because Joan Lowell's 'Cradle of the Deep' was a current sensation not yet exposed as a hoax)." With "neither harm nor help to anyone," Lanham carried out Smith's requests. In addition to being published in America, the book came close to being translated into French, and at one point McAlmon indicated that neither he nor the author would mind if Miss Beach took on the job, but after its American appearance no further plans were made for a translation.

What McAlmon had intended to be a double volume of Ken Sato's work—Sato's translation of *The Quaint Tales of Samurais* by Saikaku Ibara and Sato's own stories—turned out to be a drastically shortened book consisting mainly of the translations. "About half of the stories," McAlmon reported to Sylvia Beach, "got lost in the mails," but there were still enough (111 printed pages), he reckoned, to provide amusement "without the matter getting wearisome." He had read the Sato manuscript on his trip to America and had found a pleasing naiveté in the stories as well as "situations so completely horrifying to Anglo-Saxondom" that he vowed "they'd better be done." To Miss Beach went four of the ten deluxe copies printed on special China paper and bound in vellum, "rather arty," McAlmon admitted, but still "good to look at too," and he asked her to try and sell them for 500 francs instead of the 250 announced in the folder ("if she did not think that was too high"), since disposing of all ten at that price would "pay most of the print bill."

Despite the promise of heroic pederasty among conscience-unstricken samurai in feudal Japan—a promise Sato advanced in the Translator's Note along with the suggestion that there might be similarities between the "pretty" lads the samurai took as lovers and "certain young men of [the] present day in Europe and America"—McAlmon rightly feared that Sato's book probably had "too limited" an appeal. "Those that want it," he conjectured, "want sentimentality, mainly." Still, he took pleasure in the way Sato "used the language, particularly in the primitive 'No don't kill you; let me kill me or I kill the third man' sort of quality." The subject matter was unimportant except that it made the language funnier. The publisher remained Sato's lonely admirer. Even Ethel Moorhead, usually effusive about anything McAlmon wrote or published, called the book a "bore." One "wearies of their nobility," of their tragic nature, of their "nursing a nostalgia that must always elude." Tragic though they may be to themselves, she concluded, to others they were merely "comic," at best.

X

In mid-1929 McAlmon finally decided to close Contact and leave France. Besides the restlessness that made vagabondage a necessity and variety an essential ingredient of his life, there were certain practical reasons why he was closing his publishing company and leaving Europe. First, he had always insisted that publishing was not a profit-making business. From the start Contact operated to publish the books commercial firms would not take a chance on. As he put it, they were printed "to help create new literature, not to supply public demand," and not to make money. But even though he was determinedly, almost aggressively, noncommercial—and fortunately could usually afford to be—he could not completely ignore the problems that concerned all publishers: distribution, publicity, and, alas, even for McAlmon, payment from bookstores. In Paris, distribution was limited to placing Contact books at Shakespeare and Company and at a few other shops like Titus' Black Manikin. The large bookstores on the Right Bank, Brentano's and Galignani's, "had not shown much interest in limited editions," and from bookshops abroad that stocked Contact publications—for example, William Jackson in London and the Holliday Bookshop in New York—he seldom collected sums due him. Had he done so, Contact might have more than paid its expenses. Serious losses, of course, had started occurring in the mid-twenties when customs in England and America confiscated shipments of Contact books at the docks, and even when the publisher was notified of such actions, which was not often, he had usually not been able to prevent their destruction. Aside from financial woes, he had had the demoralizing experience of being scorned by critics like William Rose Benét, who either ignored or condemned Contact books—McAlmon's as well as those by other Contact authors—simply because they were "Paris or expatriate productions," while at the same time praising works vastly inferior. It was almost as bad as having books arbitrarily censored and confiscated for the same reason. Although these problems had become more acute as the years passed and seemed insoluble at the end of the decade, they probably could have been remedied, though never eliminated, if McAlmon had been more efficient.

85

But neither his background nor his convictions about publishing would permit that. As Miss Beach remarked, McAlmon "knew nothing about business. [He] only saw the literary side of publishing," never kept accounts, or at best very sketchy ones, and generally left most matters in the hands of Contact's "foster-mother"—Miss Beach herself. When McAlmon summoned a London bookdealer named Jake Schwartz to gather up the leftover Contact books, he was surprised to find he still had "four *Villages*, and several *Hasty Bunches* and *Companion Volumes* left." Of the latter he intended to keep about a dozen, but the rest—"books that never would sell"—Schwartz removed and undoubtedly sold, as booksellers were beginning to do in America, for ten to twenty times their original price. Schwartz, an American who once had a prosperous dental practice in Brighton, opened the Ulysses Bookshop in London in the late twenties, from which, besides publishing an occasional book under the Ulysses imprint, he conducted a successful rare-book business for several years, purchasing considerable memorabilia as well as large book collections from, among others, Samuel Beckett, James Joyce, and Nancy Cunard.

In *North America, Continent of Conjecture*, the final Contact, finished just before the author left for America in October, McAlmon had tried again to write a "little epic," something he had set out to do in *The Portrait of a Generation* and to which *North America* was a natural corollary. Small, only forty-three pages, but attractively illustrated with Hiler's woodcuts and a decorative initial, it tried to define the psyche of a nation ("North America,/ a continent but limitedly apprehended," the poem begins), a nation which, like his poem, was unfinished, still in the process of becoming. The ambitiousness of the undertaking had apparently exhausted both his will and patience, though he always professed to be satisfied by it; but the critical reception, what there was, could hardly have increased his pleasure. One of the few positive reactions came from Harriet Monroe, who found the poem vigorous "in many separate statements" and impressively realistic "in several episodes," but badly marred by "indiscriminate selection, careless understanding, and a reach too wide and too eagerly attempted to insure mastery."

Edwin Lanham once described McAlmon as the "most tragically lonely person" he had ever known, but also "one of the most stimulating to those who were not put off by his elaborate defenses," and, he continued, "it can be said that the publication of books in Paris in the 1920s

86

was in part one of those defenses. It was the act itself that counted for him—that, the act of getting something into print he wanted to see published . . . and it can be argued that he had this drive to 'get it into print' because he had published so much of his own work himself, because he was ignored by publishers in England and the United States, and because so many of the writers he published, from Ernest Hemingway on down the list, went on to find publishers and a public outside the little presses." Lanham's last point may help to explain not only McAlmon's reasons for going to America but what he did after his arrival. He was, after all, the author of seven published books and as many unpublished ones, as well as the publisher of Hemingway, Butts, H. D., Stein, Coates, and Lanham, all of whose Contact books had been or would be published in America. McAlmon must have believed he could not be forever ignored in his own homeland. And the belief that in America he might do for himself what he had helped others accomplish received considerable support soon after he arrived home, first, in Albuquerque (near Norman MacLeod) and, then, in New York. "I have done a great deal of new work," he reported to Miss Beach, "so that the agent has four new books in her hands to place, two of them very quickly done, the others done more leisurely." He asked for a list of the Contacts she still had on hand in Paris, and to send him— probably with the intention of using them as promotional material in his meetings with publishers—the deluxe copies of *North America*, ten copies of the Sato stories, all the remaining copies of *Village* (there were only two), and "two copies each of all the others." Reports Miss Beach received in January 1930 remained hopeful. The country, he wrote, was "crazy" and there were times when he did not know how to adjust to its "social patterns and attitudes," but staying on had already "cleared some things out of" him and he had decided to remain for the year, "for whatever impress it will make." Scribner's was still holding *Village* ("Probably waiting till I get out of town to reject it."), and some new stories had been taken by *Pagany* and *The Hound and the Horn*.

A visit to Mexico City was a disappointment ("second-hand and vin ordinaire"), but Guadalajara and Sonora, towns similar to his favorite Riviera retreats, were pleasant surprises and ideal for work. For eight months he lived in one or the other, seeing nobody, living quietly, and going on with his writing. Gradually, however, the rejection slips accumulated, always courteously worded, but reconfirming his conviction that publishing in America was a "racket." It was insulting, even arrogant, to be told he had a "deadly smooth way of telling about the kinds of things people do, that shouldn't be told of in literature, when at the same time everyone talked about him with hearty laughter." There was little hope that a Chicago publisher would "dare" bring out a revised edition of *Distinguished Air*, with illustrations by Charles Demuth ("a fine painter"). The only good news was that a Texas magazine had accepted a few poems and praised his "distinguished mind," and that Norman MacLeod had taken "New York Harbour," which had appeared in *A Hasty Bunch*, for his new periodical, *Morada*. "Mercifully for the Scotch in me," he wrote Miss Beach, "I like my own work and when people begin throwing too many rocks at me I gain pep. . . ." He stayed on in Mexico until June, working hard to finish everything to turn over to his agent before he returned to Europe "to begin on a new line." How new it would be, however, must have been on McAlmon's mind when he wrote "Mexican Interval," a short account of his visit, finished just before departing, which ended with a disarming truth: "Suddenly I realize that my stay here has been a vacation of variation only; it has not been release, and I don't want to escape from the world I knew before."

While in New York McAlmon met two booksellers, David Moss and Martin Kamin. Moss, who had once been the manager of the Gotham Book Mart, the New York counterpart of Sylvia Beach's Shakespeare and Company, had just opened (with Kamin) a new bookshop in the Barbizon-Plaza Hotel. McAlmon was amazed to discover that Moss and Kamin had on hand a large stock of Contact and Three Mountains books which they were selling at prices well above the original. How they had managed to import so many without running afoul of the customs officials and, indeed, where they had found such a rich trove, remain mysteries. It is possible, however, that Jake Schwartz was the supplier. Obviously impressed with McAlmon's work as a publisher, the booksellers suggested that he consider serving as the editor of a new series of Contact books which they would underwrite and sell at their shop. Although it was a tempting offer, for besides the editorship he would have an American distribution center for Contact books, his interest waned and he refused. Without McAlmon, but with the editorial assistance of Dashiell Hammett and John Sanford and the blessings of William Carlos Williams, Moss and Kamin got out one Contact book, Nathanael West's pastiche of fantasies, *The Dream Life of Balso Snell*. It was their first and last publication, and one from which McAlmon hastened to disassociate himself, calling it "an adolescently smart and naughty novel" by an author who had obviously read "too much of Anatole France at his most senile-mischievous and tried to convince himself and his readers that he was still concerned about soul and Christ and the insularities of religion." The booksellers also tried to interest McAlmon in reviving and editing *Contact* magazine, which they also agreed to support and distribute. To this proposal, however, Mc-Almon was even cooler. A "purely literary periodical was passé," he thought, and neither Moss nor Kamin showed any interest in his counter-plan to edit a magazine that would incorporate economic and political writing. Moreover, McAlmon had concluded, somewhat tentatively, that little magazines "did not help the working artist to arrive," and that they could "create antagonism on the part of publishers and in the minds of certain people who insist upon seeing all their contributors as a school, and therefore, precious boys and girls." Again, without McAlmon, the booksellers proceeded with plans to resurrect *Contact*. Williams, whose belief in small magazines had never faltered, responded to their call for an editor, a "calling" he joked about in a letter to Ezra Pound. "I'm editor of a new quarterly, CONTACT! up again and soon to be at 'em. . . . All I does is to pick out what goes into the mag—if it ain't too dirty or lood, whatever that means." He did not mention that, with McAlmon out of the picture, he had invited West to serve as associate editor. For West, joining Williams in the latest *Contact* venture was an opportunity to align himself with an illustrious group of magazines and their editors—the *Little Review* and Margaret Anderson and Jane Heap, *transition* and Eugene Jolas —both of which, though defunct, had printed work by most of the important writers of the previous two decades, and whose responsibilities *Contact* would now naturally assume. The two editors agreed that *Contact* should again emphasize what Williams called "American super-realism," and what both editors announced would "attempt to cut a trail through the American jungle without the use of a European compass."

The first number of *Contact*, now subtitled "An American Quarterly Review," contained Williams' "The Colored Girls of Passenack" and McAlmon's short story, "It's All Very Complicated," which, he was disappointed to find, Williams had used in an old rather than a revised edition, a matter that could have been avoided had Williams mentioned he intended to include the story. Presumably *Contact* I impressed McAlmon enough to give him reason to reconsider the Moss and Kamin offer. He wrote Miss Beach from Majorca (February 1932) to say he was thinking about returning to New York in the fall to "take on the publishing of the magazine very earnestly," adding he wanted "writers who aren't too precious or too mannered under the name of being 'modern.' The kind of thing that was 'modern' five or ten years ago isn't so now, and I'm not interested in people's work which becomes what they imagine surrealist or Joycean, then years too late, and five million years off understanding." The second number of the magazine, containing his "Mexican Interval" and a long excerpt from West's *Miss Lonelyhearts* (one part had already appeared in *Contact* I), pleased McAlmon even more than the first, and although some things in it he would not "want responsibility for even as co-editor," he urged Miss Beach to send him or Williams any work by promising authors who might turn up in Paris. Moss also got in touch with Miss Beach (at McAlmon's suggestion), asking if she would agree to handle *Contact* and Contact publications, the first of which (*Balso Snell*) he was sending her. So long as Moss and Kamin continued to support *Contact* McAlmon thought that it would be good, and he expressed interest in "getting some generally bright articles, not alone on literature and making the magazine a real review, with fewer of the arty movements, precious 'novelities' and stunts, and wider in its scope." The third and final *Contact* (October 1932)—irreconcilable differences between editors and sponsors made continuation impossible—was the best of all, despite Kamin's insistence that it should be a communist number. Besides Williams and West, contributors included Caldwell, Farrell, Perelman, Herrmann, Hiler, and Yvor Winters.

XI

Again in Europe, a changed and changing Europe, emptied· now of all but a few self-supporting American expatriates, McAlmon resumed his familiar routine, reconciled to a way of living he had grown accustomed to, and convinced that Europe at least for a while sheltered "fewer morons and bigotries" than the United States. As before, he wandered, pausing occasionally to report to Miss Beach. In a letter from Munich (late in 1931), he spoke cautiously about placing a novel and two volumes of short stories with the British firm of Longmans Green, and about a "long book" he was doing which a friend in London (almost certainly Otto Theis, an editor at Secker and Warburg) had told him would be a "sensation." It was also giving him some second thoughts, however, even "tremors," and, he confided, if it were "too sensational" he might have to go to "darkest Africa." When Longmans Green rejected the short stories, he complained, but mildly, noting that his novels were being "nibbled at"—sometimes by as many as four publishers at once—his stories were being published, two in *Pagany* in 1931 and another the following year; one in Samuel Putnam's *New Review* in 1932, besides the *Contact* pieces. In 1932 Louis Zukofsky printed two of his poems in *An Objectivists' Anthology*, which, with Williams' help, was printed in France; and Peter Neagoe included the poem "Leavetaking" in the anthology of exile writing, *Americans Abroad*. The same year, after a long delay, Caresse Crosby published a collection of his stories in the newly created Crosby Continental Editions. Entitled *The Indefinite Huntress and Other Stories*, it contained nine stories, chosen by everybody but McAlmon, "after Caresse Crosby had consulted everybody and thing but any possible inclination she herself might have." While disappointed that the book was not of his own making, he conceded that "maybe some of it [was] all right, an estimate Ezra Pound supported in a review of the book he wrote for the *New English Weekly*. Pound invited readers to show him "an author in whose pages I or any other European can learn more about the nature of contemporary Americans, and I will endeavor to do him justice." Pound's acquaintance with "current American prose" allowed that only McAlmon had "covered such an extent." More exciting, though, than the appearance of these stories and poems was his "sensational" book. He mentioned to Miss Beach that he was still "scary" about releasing it but was sure it would be published. For the time being it would have to keep.

The book McAlmon had been alluding to for over a year was a memoir he was calling by the extravagant title, *Being Geniuses Together*, in which he had poured out the "truth" of what he had observed during the years of his exile from America. Any forebodings he had about his book received a first testing when Joyce asked to hear it, and for several afternoons sat listening to McAlmon read, saying little until he had finished, and then confiding to Miss Weaver that McAlmon's book had made him feel "actionable." To McAlmon, however, he laughingly recommended that it be entitled "Advocatus Diaboli," a jest that evoked a sharp retort from the author: "What in hell do you think the title means, that I take genius without salt?" Whatever prompted Joyce's comment, whether McAlmon's description of the author of *Ulysses* as a hard-drinking Bohemian or the generous use of "salt" in treating the "geniuses" of Montparnasse—he had plainly disliked his friend's book. Over the next few months McAlmon let several others read it, including Katherine Anne Porter, who had a copy of the uncorrected first writing, before the author had "blue-pencilled it and had it retyped." It was the same copy McAlmon asked Miss Beach to borrow and show to Jack Kahane, the Obelisk publisher, in case he might be interested in adding it to his list. Kahane was not, nor was Miss Beach who, like Joyce, took displeasure in a book "totally lacking in sensitivity," one that reminded her of "some shadows on a stone wall." When *Geniuses* was published three years later in 1938 by the London firm of Secker and Warburg (probably with considerable assistance from Otto Theis), it caused no stir, certainly nothing remotely like the sensationalism McAlmon had once anticipated and feared, and except for occasional appearances in excerpted form, was not heard of again until 1968, when Kay Boyle, using the author's original manuscript, edited and reissued the book under its original title, with autobiographical interchapters describing her own early experiences in France and Montparnasse. *Geniuses* was only the second of McAlmon's books ever to be published in America. The first, a volume of poetry wistfully entitled *Not Alone Lost*, was published in 1937 by New Directions at the behest of William Carlos Williams.

In 1934, the year he finished his memoirs, McAlmon was thirty-eight. Contemplating turning forty, a milestone that can shake even the most lymphatic, produced some predictable remarks: "Life begins, they say, at forty. . . . It ought to be interesting when it really gets under way." More self-disparagement? Probably. For he must have suspected that the greatest adventures of his life lay behind him, and that what remained—revising manuscripts, resubmitting his stories and poems, receiving more rejections, travel, and drink—could only be anticlimactic. Still in Europe in 1939 and already ill with tuberculosis, he traveled through occupied France to Lisbon and from there sailed to America, where he settled in El Paso and worked, as long as his health permitted, in the family business. Then as the disease worsened, he moved to warmer climates, first to Mexico and then to Desert Hot Springs, where he lived, alone, until his death in 1956. He was fifty-nine.

Of those closest to McAlmon—Sylvia Beach, Bill Bird, William Carlos Williams, Ezra Pound, Ernest Walsh, and Kay Boyle—all had unstinted admiration for his accomplishments as a publisher. And for his writing they had almost as much praise. "It was McAlmon," Kay Boyle wrote, "who, in liberating himself from genteel language and genteel thought, spoke for his generation in a voice that echoes, unacknowledged, in the prose of Hemingway and that of other writers of his time." Ezra Pound, while noting the perfection of Hemingway's work, still regarded McAlmon as one who had "opened up a whole new vein of writing. Tough realism." Others, Pound believed, "could go on from where he started." For the man who was their friend, however, they had opinions that were often equivocal and defensive, and generally at odds with McAlmon's own views of himself. In his autobiography, he recalled how Williams had once said he had a "genius for life." If by that his friend meant that he had a capacity for indifference, despair, "long and heavy spells of ennui which takes bottles of strong drink to cure, and a gregarious but not altogether loving nature," he might be right. Everyone concurred with Sylvia Beach that McAlmon, "potentially a greatly talented writer," had not fulfilled his high promise. His own protestations to the contrary, McAlmon failed because he was too impatient to commit himself completely to his writing. He "refused absolutely to revise," exclaimed Pound. Though doubtlessly aware of his friends' criticism and their disappointment, he nonetheless saw himself as one of the producers of the time, perhaps the only one with enough integrity and courage to go his own way, resisting at any cost all restraints that threatened to standardize literature. McAlmon wanted to be heard, he wanted to be a force, he wanted to direct things—friendships, parties, journeys, careers, and literature—and he often did them well, very well. But he was impatient with pretension, and any signs of cheating drew his ire. Williams wrote he had a "fierce tongue when he saw others among the writers about him, liars in one form or another, who were lying to make their reputations." And Sylvia Beach recalled that the "ruthless honesty which drew people to him demanded that those he faced with his icy stare look closely at themselves and their pretenses. It was a demand that made the presumptuous turn the other way." Was he a Diogenes of Montparnasse, sniffing out sham, or was McAlmon a misdirected writer recklessly squandering his talent and health in pursuit of the experience of living? Or was he a man, as Bird believed, who "had been exploited, betrayed, neglected, deceived, and imitated beyond recognition . . . preyed on by the vultures of the writing world"? He mentioned two: "Stein driving out to the printer's in a taxi and absconding with what amounted to the better part of the whole edition of *Americans*, and Hem making Bob the goat of that trip we took to Spain." His having a fortune at his disposal meant he could be as independent as any tramp. He could afford to be prodigal, wasteful of his money, of his talents, and of himself. He could afford to publish his own books after they had been rejected by commercial publishers. He could do it without changing a word. Perhaps, as Sylvia Beach suggested, the very luxury of being rich, of having that affluence which gave McAlmon the freedom to accomplish so much and to defer doing so much more, literally brought about his downfall.

CONTACT EDITIONS

29, QUAI D'ANJOU, ILE ST.-LOUIS, PARIS

III

Bill Bird

AND THE THREE MOUNTAINS

IN THE SPRING of 1922, William Bird, the European manager of the fledgling Consolidated Press Association, of Washington, D.C., dispatched himself to Italy to cover the Genoa Economic Conference. Also attending was reporter Ernest Hemingway, who must have been surprised to learn that Bird, a tall, angular, academic-looking man, had recently set up a small printery in Paris and was looking around for publishable manuscripts. Hemingway mentioned that Ezra Pound might be willing to let the new press have portions of a long poem on which he was busily working, and suggested that Bird look in on Pound when he got back to Paris. He did, and Pound, "after a couple of days of reflection," recommended that Bird start his press off with a series of six books, the first to be one of his own. Bird agreed and appointed Pound editor.

That same year Hemingway introduced Bird to Robert McAlmon who, by then aware that his Contact company might actually turn a small profit if it could somehow be run according to established business practices, proposed that they join forces, at least for the purpose of improving the distribution of books. Bird agreed, and McAlmon, at least figuratively, installed himself in his new partner's already cramped quarters on the Ile Saint-Louis, from which, at irregular intervals, for the next several years, flowed publications that often bore the joint imprint of Bird's Three Mountains Press and McAlmon's Contact Editions. A short time later, into this burgeoning publishing nucleus moved Ford Madox Ford, one of the five authors Pound had selected for his series. Ford, who had just agreed to be the editor of a new English-language magazine that would bear the ecumenical name of *Transatlantic Review*, found himself in the

Robert McAlmon and William Bird, Spain, 1923.
PRINCETON UNIVERSITY LIBRARY, SYLVIA BEACH COLLECTION

rather desperate position of not being able to locate a home in which to oversee its birth. Bird offered Ford space in his shop, and the advent of the *Transatlantic Review*, in the form of the first number (January 1924), occurred there—"rather shabbily," Joyce thought. For the next year, operating from his perch in a gallery resembling a "bird-cage," which spanned the rear of Bird's shop, Ford presided over the business of the new magazine, descending when summoned to help Bird pull the immense levers of his great old seventeenth-century press, and, without coaxing, writing fraternal reviews praising the little books printed by his American neighbors. Joining Ford for a time as assistant editor was Ernest Hemingway, who, much to the editor's eventual exasperation, added Gertrude Stein to the list of *Transatlantic* contributors, which by 1924, besides Hemingway and Ford, included Pound, McAlmon, and the composer George Antheil, whose talents and theories Pound would later celebrate in the magazine and in his Three Mountains book, *Antheil and the Theory of Harmony*. Thus, sheltered in quarters so inadequate that only collaboration or penury could explain the unnatural neighborliness that prevailed, labored the functionaries of the two foremost avant-garde presses then in Paris, and the avuncular editor of the only magazine devoted to Anglo-

96

American writing; and linked to them both, by a bond of mutual dependence and interest, were the principal creators of the time.

Florence Gilliam once remarked that no one would ever connect the reserved, self-effacing Bird with the publication of avant-garde editions. The occurrences that brought about this apparent anomaly were as fortuitous as they were absorbing. Being one of the founders of the Consolidated Press Association (his partner was David Lawrence) and, after 1920, its European manager, Bird could hardly have foreseen that he would find in Paris both the time (though in perpetual shortage) and the materials to turn a long-standing interest in hand-printing into an inexpensive and remarkably influential hobby. Strolling on the Ile Saint-Louis one day soon after arriving abroad, he came upon a small printery operated by a French journalist named Roger Dévigne who, to his delight, was printing books by hand on an old press. Apprenticing himself to Dévigne—at the same time supplying him with a full series of Caslon type and a few short manuscripts, including one of his own (*A Practical Guide to French Wines*)—Bird absorbed the rudiments of typesetting and printing with rare ease, and in a short time had gained enough skill and confidence to consider seriously the prospect of starting his own shop at the first opportunity, which, as it turned out, came unexpectedly soon when the place next-door fell vacant. Bird promptly moved in, installing an ancient Mathieu press as the centerpiece, and announced the formation of the Three Mountains Press. That imprint (he found the reference to three mountains in Psalm 121 reproduced as a type specimen in a book on printing) not only emblemized the three mountains of Paris—St. Genevieve, Montparnasse, and Montmartre—but to his delight could also be conveniently shaped into a colophon forming his initials, the three peaks making the W and the framework the B.

In all likelihood Bird would have gone on indefinitely printing small books of no special value had he not met Hemingway who put him on to Pound. For it was Pound who impressed upon Bird that no more reprints of the classics—books similar to the well printed but otherwise undistinguished Mosher type—were needed. Do the moderns, he urged. Print what authors are writing now. His recommendation that Bird begin with the series of six books rather than wait for whatever happened to come along contained as much commercial as literary merit. Once subscribers knew that each volume would be part of a single series devoted to the investigation of the same subject, Pound reasoned, they would be encouraged to purchase the lot, thus all but guaranteeing the publisher a

Ezra Pound, Paris, 1926.
PRINCETON UNIVERSITY LIBRARY,
SYLVIA BEACH COLLECTION

sizable number of buyers in advance. The topic Pound chose for the series was announced as a "manifest of the present state of English prose," later modified and reduced to "an inquest" into the state of English writing. As for the important matter of who would conduct the "inquest," Pound nominated at least seven candidates besides himself—T. S. Eliot, Wyndham Lewis, William Carlos Williams, Ford Madox Ford, Ernest Hemingway, and two others with formidable names but rather dusky credentials and backgrounds: B. C. Windeler and B. M. G. Adams. Bird hastily printed a notice announcing that the series was under the aegis of Ezra Pound and that each volume, besides being a contribution to the "inquest," would also be an "experiment in hand-printing." Editions would be numbered and limited to three hundred copies ("in certain cases fewer"), and since there would be no second editions, their value as "rarities for collectors" would be assured.

By mid-summer (1922) Pound was in high gear and obviously enjoying his assignment despite the protestation he made to Williams that it was "hell the way [he] always [seemed] to get sucked into editing something or other." In the same letter, in which he invited Williams to join him and the others in the series, Pound advised his friend that since Bird would pay contributors one hundred dollars ("50 dollars down to author,

98

and another 50 later") and would retain no copyright privileges, Williams was being offered a "means of getting in 100 dollars extra before one goes to publisher." He reminded Williams that the same practice had netted Yeats "a good deal," and he recalled that his own Cuala Press book (*Certain Noble Plays of Japan*, 1916) had brought in nearly as much as the "big" Macmillan edition of *Noh*. Further, he suggested that private limited editions encouraged one to be "more intimate," and, if more intimate, perhaps "really interesting"—the essential, in his opinion, which would determine the "general success or point of the thing." Instead of writing for the public, Pound advised Williams, write as though talking to one's friends—friends among whom, he hoped, would be former *Contact* subscribers likely to want Williams' "stuff" and who, along with friends of the other authors included in the series, might comprise the bulk of Bird's buyers.

The first Three Mountains book, *Indiscretions or, Une Revue de Deux Mondes*, Pound's fragment of autobiography up to his sixteenth year, did not quite satisfy what Bird described as an "amateur's fondness for typographical experiment." Although this first experiment had fallen "considerably short of his ideal," he consoled himself by vowing that "next time" he would approach it more closely, and that, anyway, selling books was of secondary importance. As for the literary value of *Indiscretions*, Pound defended it as an example of early experimentation that one did and then stopped doing when something else more important came along. Actually, he had composed it three years before in Venice, while still writing art and music criticism for A. R. Orage's *New Age*, at whose request, Pound confided in the dedication to Orage, the "fragment" had first been "hitched together," after having appeared, piecemeal, in *New Age*. He explained that *Indiscretions* was intended to serve as "a sort of foreword" to the series, now definitely set at six books, Eliot and Lewis having dropped out, in which each author would endeavor to write a "work in accord or in discord with" his own criteria, books which the editor stated, with homey assurance, "We ourselves have read without being bored, and which we believe to have some durable value as literature, or at any rate to have, as a series, the value of a landmark as had Des Imagistes volume in 1912, the Vorticist manifestos in 1913, or, in 1917, the grouping of writers in the *Little Review*." Finally, in a statement obviously intended to elevate Bird and other small publishers above their commercial counterparts, Pound explained that, although the books in the series averaged only fifty pages, the aim of the press was "to free prose writers from the necessity of presenting their work in the stock-size volume of commerce"; after all, he added, a book can be a "unity without filling 250 pages," or some other arbitrarily established figure.

Indiscretions appeared in March 1923, and the following month Bird finished printing the second book in the series, Ford Madox Ford's *Women and Men*, a collection of reminiscences that demonstrated in seasoned colloquial language the author's prodigious anecdotal and storytelling powers. In his exploration of the relations between women and men, Ford reached the egalitarian conclusion that not only could all those legendary attributes generally associated with men be found in women— and vice versa—but that the only important difference between the sexes (that is, what one has been commonly taught to regard as a difference) was the "difference between employments"—the "functions we perform in society." Ford's assault against the hoary beliefs that had divided the sexes for generations ended in a complete victory for the cause of equality: so far as immorality was concerned, the "number of immoral women must be exactly the same as the number of immoral men," and as for the behavior between sexes, Ford confessed he had noticed that each behaved abominably toward the other—tactfulness as well as coarseness were remarkably evenly distributed between both.

While Pound faithfully performed the duties of editing, he carefully avoided becoming entangled in the business operation of the Press and, of course, left the printing to Bird, who soon discovered the incompatibility of being a practicing journalist by day and a novice printer by night (as well as on weekends). Hopes of maintaining a reasonably strict publishing schedule when the books being produced had to be set by hand, a slow process even for the experienced printer, faded as the spring wore on, and, finally, when progress on the Williams book slowed, Bird called for help. The man who came to his assistance was a tall, white-haired, elegant, courteous Britisher named Herbert Clarke, who seemed even more out of place in a printing shop than Bird. For some time, however, Clarke had had his own printery in Paris, conveniently located in an old courtyard off the rue Saint-Honoré, where, practicing the protocol suggestive of the English country gentleman he resembled, he presided in a large front office, personally greeting all clients by name. Behind him, at the end of a long corridor, was the actual printing plant, off-limits to all but a few, where Clarke's master printer, M. Servant, "a very genius in his line," solved "with infinite ease any problem of composition or page make-up brought before him."

The Great American Novel, which bore the note "Finished printing in May 1923, by H. Clarke and William Bird at Paris and in St. Louis Island," was the second of Williams' two pieces of experimental writing published in Paris, the other being *Spring and All*, which McAlmon brought out about the same time, and, like *Spring and All*, it was an arresting and rather bewildering salmagundi of irony, satire, and parody, loosely conceived and even more loosely expressed. Soon after it appeared, Williams conceded to Kenneth Burke that his experiment may have misfired slightly, particularly insofar as there seemed to be no beginning to the book. But he went on to defend the omission by declaring that that was what he "must have wanted to say. And that's how you get me, one of the ones with *that* in him that I am after." Without trying to justify the formlessness of the book or its raw animation, he advised Burke that *The Great American Novel* had "to be said to be read. I *am* trying to speak, to tell *it* in the only way possible—but I do not want to *say* what there is. It is not for me merely to arrange things prettily. Oh, purple anemones! You get what I mean? . . ." Whether Burke understood the message is less important than the fact that Williams said it, and had

Ford Madox Ford, New York, 1927. Portrait by Georg T. Hartmann.
COURTESY OF
GEORG T. HARTMANN

The Great
American Novel

CHAPTER I.

THE FOG.

 F THERE is progress then there is a novel. Without progress there is nothing. Everything exists from the beginning. I existed in the beginning. I was a slobbering infant. Today I saw nameless grasses—I tapped the earth with my knuckle. It sounded hollow. It was dry as rubber. Eons of drought. No rain for fifteen days. No rain. It has never rained. It will never rain. Heat and no wind all day long better say hot September. The year has progressed. Up one street down another. It is still September. Down one street, up another. Still September. Yesterday was the twenty second. Today is the twenty first. Impossible. Not if it was last year. But then it wouldn't be yesterday. A year is not as yesterday in his eyes. Besides last year it rained in the early part of the month. That makes a difference. It rained on the white goldenrod. Today being misplaced as against last year makes it seem better to have white—Such is progress. Yet if there is to be a novel one must begin somewhere.

Words are not permanent unless the graphite be scraped up and put in a tube or the ink lifted. Words progress into the ground. One must begin with words if one is to write. But what then of smell? What then of the hair on the trees or the

[9]

Page from *The Great American Novel* by William Carlos Williams (Three Mountains Press, 1923).
PRINCETON UNIVERSITY LIBRARY

ELIMUS

D RIVING RAIN beat on the deserted quay, clearing black scum from the man-messed waters of the basin—
Derelict bottles jostled against the hard stone sides, and the vulture cranes kept sentinel, wrapped in their own warm steam.
Elimus leaned on the bulwarks.
He did not like it.
He had imagined other lands sunny; the family had never spoken of rain—that was wrong of them—perhaps they didn't know — he must tell them.
There was shouting from a tug; he could not hear what they were saying:—
JOHN PARKER
COLLINGWOOD
Collingwood was an admiral—
Sweat drops squeezed from octopus hawsers, clutching their prey—a coir rack wringing staccato cries from engine room bells, stilling slow pulse throbs.
The cranes turned on their iron heels nosing fresh carcase to be disembowled; little bunches of

Opening page of *Elimus* by B. C. Windeler, illustrated by Dorothy Shakespear (Three Mountains Press, 1923).
PRINCETON UNIVERSITY LIBRARY

attempted to particularize it in his book. What he concluded later he had done was to write a travesty of what he considered "conventional American writing," including the burdensome challenge that summoned every American author to deliver the "great American novel." He exhibited his talent for comedy by making the central characters a pair of lovers, a "little Ford car . . . very passionate—a hot little baby" who "falls more or less in love with a Mack truck," prototypal lovers, needless to say, who have spawned a sizable latter-day progeny.

Determinedly iconoclastic (*The Great American Novel* espoused the new credo: "To hell with art. To hell with literature"), Williams found in Bird and McAlmon cooperative companions who were as eager as he to print the "unprintable" (e.g., *The Great American Novel* and *Spring and All*) and to flout the debilitating standards imposed upon writers by commercial publishers. Our salvation, he reminded Burke, is the print shop. It must be "forwarded" and we must "print and distribute here and there until we all land in a (patriot's) jail. . . . That or Paris for us all—but *never* silence." What staved off silence for Williams at a time when experimentation outbalanced the concerns of popularity and salability, he admitted years later, was Bird and McAlmon—"They saved me."

Both *Elimus* and *England*, the former also completed in May, introduced relatively unknown names into the series, although two of the four stories printed in *England* had appeared earlier in *The Criterion* and *Dial*, the author of which, B. M. G. Adams, was an upper-class English woman Pound had met in London around 1910. Bored with the restrictions class imposed upon her, she sought diversion and relief in the company of poets and artists, two of whom were Yeats and Pound. The poet's relation with her, certainly already close while he resided in England, apparently lost none of its intensity after he moved to the Continent. In the early twenties they were together in Verona (Pound mentioned the occasion in "Canto 29"), and in Paris he introduced her to the sculptor Brancusi. The same year Bird printed *England*, Mrs. Scratton (she published *England* under her maiden name, B. M. G. Adams) returned to England and was divorced by her husband "who named Pound as co-respondent." Following the publication of her book, and for many years thereafter, Pound continued to correspond with Mrs. Scratton and to encourage her with her writing.

Elimus was the work of B. Cyril Windeler, a British wood merchant and another of Pound's acquaintances, who wrote his story of a "young emigrant's disappointments in Canada" while serving as a colonel in the

British Air Force in India. Although insignificant contributions to the ongoing enquiry into the state of contemporary prose—Adams' writing is Edwardian, dry, and impersonal; Windeler's, more colorful but larded with inflated metaphorical language—the two books did demonstrate how far Bird's typographical experiments had advanced since *Indiscretions*. *Elimus*, a more subdued book than *England*, contained a number of woodcuts by Dorothy Shakespear, Pound's wife, and a frontispiece, also a woodcut, by Robert Dill, which blended harmoniously with the printed text. *England*, too, exhibited the successful fitting together of text and typography, most strikingly in the cover designs Bird had devised, large floral and bird patterns, tinted rose and blue, and faintly suggestive of Morris—the whole being a charming evocation of the setting of Miss Adams' stories.

In the first announcements of the Three Mountains series, Bird had listed each book by title with the exception of Hemingway's, the sixth and final volume. In place of a title, Bird had simply inserted the word "Blank" next to Hemingway's name, which, in view of McAlmon's rather sudden decision that summer to publish *Three Stories and Ten Poems*, turned out to be doubly necessary. For the moment, at least, McAlmon had taken all the writing Hemingway had ready for publication. Nothing remained for Bird. The solution to the problem of how to fill the blank Bird himself provided. He recalled that in the spring number of the *Little Review* six of Hemingway's miniatures had appeared under the title "In Our Time." If he could compose, say, a dozen or so more, there would probably be enough material for a book. It was a good idea, and Hemingway set to work, spending the summer revising five of the six miniatures that had appeared in the *Little Review* and writing twelve new ones. Charles Fenton rightly observed that these miniatures, or vignettes, "were a blueprint of what Hemingway was attempting stylistically and a definition of the attitudes he was forming about his experiences." And those experiences up to mid-1923, when he delivered the completed manuscript to Bird, were concentrated into three areas, to each of which he accorded exactly the same number of vignettes: six were devoted to newspaper experiences, six to war, and six to bullfighting. As mechanisms of self-instruction they had the utmost value, as he would declare in 1932 when, with his Three Mountains book in mind, he discussed his apprenticeship years. "I was trying to write then, and I found the greatest difficulty, aside from knowing truly what you felt, rather than what you were supposed to feel, and had been taught to feel, was to put down what really happened in action;

what the actual things were which produced the emotion that you experienced."

Hemingway finished his work for Bird in early August and sailed at once for Canada, where he and Hadley had decided their first child should be born. He had also decided to try writing interviews and special features for the *Toronto Star* at the impressive salary of $125 a week. No doubt Bird had every intention of finishing his friend's book by the end of the year, its publication date having been announced as 1923; but as the fall wore on, progress slowed, and any expectations he had of completing it by December eventually faded. Bird's experiments with different typographical designs and illustrations were probably one reason for the slackened pace. In September, he wrote Pound from Venice, suggesting that the pages of Hemingway's book be framed with a border of newsprint, a nice decorative addition, which he thought would be just as appropriate as the title he and Hemingway had chosen. Pound forwarded Bird's idea to Hemingway, with the following postscript:

> For yr
> Ap----or
> disap-----proval
> R. S. V. P.
> romptly.

The title they had agreed on was really the same one Hemingway had used in the *Little Review*, but Bird decided that it should be set in lowercase type, a typographical liberty which prompted Hemingway to remark to Edmund Wilson that if that was "all the fun [Bird] was getting out of" printing the book, he "could go ahead and be a damn fool in his own way if it pleased him, so long as he didn't fool with the text." As the months passed, Hemingway became more impatient. Why was Bird taking so long when McAlmon had got *Three Stories and Ten Poems* out in such short order? Sometime later, he told Louis H. Cohn that the fact that the book was being printed by hand and that Bird had had "plenty of other things to do" accounted for the irritatingly long delay. Finally, in November, Bird managed to ship fifty copies of the thirty-two-page *in our time* to Hemingway in Toronto, all of them "spoiled," he regretted to say, by the ineptitude of a printer who had used watermarked paper in reproducing the woodcut portrait of the author that appeared as a frontispiece. Nonetheless, he hoped there would be 170 perfect copies eventually, and meanwhile the fifty, despite the flaw, ought to be useful as gifts and review copies. Of the latter, one of the first went to Edmund Wilson, whom Hemingway had asked to write a joint review of his two books as soon as Bird's became available.

Bird officially released the book in March 1924. It was dedicated to him and to McAlmon and to a professional British soldier named Captain Eric Dorman Smith. Although the pages were unadorned (Bird had apparently discarded the idea of decorating them with newsprint), the covers resembled, in the words of Kate Buss, the "disordered parterre of a news clipping bureau—five dollars per hundred clippings." Ford printed reviews of both books in the April number of the *Transatlantic Review*, as well as Hemingway's story "Indian Camp," including it, without a title, in a Literary Supplement devoted to "work in progress." Marjorie Reid, Ford's secretary, evidently enthralled by Hemingway's succinct style and ability to capture and project those moments when "life is condensed and clean-cut and significant," filled her review of *in our time* with a bounteous selection of excerpts in an effort to make the point that each tale was "much longer than the measure of its lines." To review *Three Stories and Ten Poems*, Ford got a twenty-year-old American named Kennon Jewell, whose literary mentors included Dostoyevsky, Laforgue, and Flaubert; Jewell wrote appreciatively of the author's sensitive feeling for the emotional content of a situation and, with obvious relief, of his refusal to overstate his meaning by indulging in the "shallow hardness of photography."

A notice on the last page of *in our time* read: "Here ends the inquest into the state of contemporary English prose, as edited by Ezra Pound and printed at the Three Mountains Press." Ford naturally honored the occasion by discussing the series in one of the "Literary Causeries" he was then writing for the Paris *Tribune*. After noting that the six books had been selected by his "friend Ezra Pound as marking the high-water mark of English literary psychology and execution of the present-day" and that the authors had all been "profoundly influenced by the curious, indefinable, unmistakable spirit of workmanliness that breathes in the Paris air," he explained why four of them could not be discussed at all. As for the three English writers—Adams, Windeler, and of course Ford himself—he admitted, sardonically, there was no need for comment, for any "English critic—I mean Reviewer—will tell you he had never heard of one of them." Discussing Pound's *Indiscretions* was inadvisable, "for reasons of sensitivity toward the people mentioned" in it. That left Williams' *The Great American Novel* and Hemingway's *in our time*, both of them, in

Ford's estimate, examples of "almost unsurpassed" care of handling. Reading Williams was "to be overwhelmed by the bewildering remembrances that . . . are all that remains to us of life today," while reading Hemingway was "to be presented with a series of—often enough very cruel—experiences of your own that will in turn be dissolved into your own filmy remembrances." Together they represented what Ford called the two main literary trends of the time: the pre-digested pablum of life (Williams) and the raw material (Hemingway).

Since Bird had agreed to retain no copyright privileges—the same was true for McAlmon—Hemingway was at liberty to try and place one or both of his Paris books with American publishers. He did not wait long. At the urging of his friends John Dos Passos and Donald Stewart, he gathered up the prose contents of *Three Stories and Ten Poems* and the vignettes of *in our time*, to which he added several new stories, and sent the collection to Stewart in New York. The next month (October 1924) Wilson's review of both books came out in the *Dial*. Wilson concluded that *in our time* contained "more artistic dignity than anything else about the period of the war that has as yet been written by an American." Delighted, Hemingway thanked the critic and alerted him to the manuscript he had sent Stewart. Around Christmas, Stewart wrote that Doran and Company had refused the manuscript but went on to say that he intended to take it next to H. L. Mencken, in hopes that Mencken would pass it on to Knopf, and should Knopf reject it, then there remained Horace Liveright, Harold Loeb's publisher, with whom Loeb had already agreed to speak on Hemingway's behalf. The long-awaited message arrived in February (1925), in duplicate—two cables, one from the resourceful Stewart, the other from Loeb—both announcing that Liveright would publish *in our time*. The news that Liveright would be his American publisher may have brought Hemingway more displeasure than joy. He wrote to Loeb that "he felt as if he had been punched in the cojones." To Liveright, however, he wrote he was happy to be accepted by his firm and hoped he would become one of the company's regular authors. Before proceeding with production, Liveright asked the author to make two changes: one, the deletion of a passage in the story, "Mr. and Mrs. Elliott," which the publisher feared might be considered obscene; the other, the substitution of another story for "Up in Michigan," which he was certain was too outspoken for the American public. Hemingway complied and sent a new story called "The Battler," which he had written after having heard from Liveright, and warned him that nothing—not even a word—should be changed without his permission. Perhaps in obedience to the rule that volumes of short stories, especially by unknown authors, seldom paid their way, Liveright wreathed the jacket of *In Our Time* (Bird's lower case letters were lost in the transatlantic crossing) with testimonials by Gilbert Seldes, John Dos Passos, Edward O'Brien, Waldo Frank, and Sherwood Anderson, who also wrote the catalogue description and to whom Hemingway belatedly acknowledged his debt for Anderson's part in persuading Liveright to take on his book. The publisher also took the added precaution of limiting the edition to the rather safe number of thirteen hundred copies, just in case the bouquet of tributes miscarried.

Even before Bird had started to print *in our time* Pound was announcing plans for the book that would follow it, which, unsurprisingly, since he had once said he intended to use the facilities of the Three Mountains Press for his "annual outburst," turned out to be one of his own. What he had in mind was an elegant edition of sixteen of his cantos, a volume that would aspire to the level of the medieval manuscript, he explained to Kate Buss, "one of the real bits of printing" that would combine large, clear type on outsized pages and, as an added touch of finery, "specially made capitals" and illustrations in color by Mike Strater. Bird agreed to print an imposing prospectus for the book, which he completed the following April (1924), using the opening of "Canto Four" as a specimen. In November a selection of specimen pages went on exhibit at Shakespeare and Company. Bird also recommended that together they go over the entire text, so as "to get it as near as possible letter perfect" before the poet left for Italy. Bird evidently planned to include "detailed glosses in smaller print beside the main text," but they did not appear in the finished book. This "dee looks edtn . . . of UNRIVALLED magnificence," as Pound called it, would be limited to ninety copies, of varying quality and price, the highest being five leather-bound copies printed on Imperial Japan paper that would sell for "100 bones." Fifteen copies, modestly bound in vellum and printed on Whatman paper, would go for fifty dollars, and the other seventy, the regular edition, printed on Roma paper, would be available for twenty-five dollars. It would take Bird over a year and a half to produce Pound's opus (it appeared in January 1925), much of the delay attributable, however, not to Bird, but to Pound, who became dissatisfied with Strater's work.

The same month Pound excitedly outlined the canto project to Kate Buss, his old friends Margaret Anderson and Jane Heap—the joint editors

Ernest Hemingway, Paris, early twenties.
PRINCETON UNIVERSITY LIBRARY, SYLVIA BEACH COLLECTION

of the *Little Review*—introduced him to the composer George Antheil, who had just arrived in Paris, and whom they had befriended several years before at the start of what was to be a meteoric career which would quickly reach its peak in the uninhibited performances of the *Ballet Mécanique*. The friendship between Pound and Antheil, based at least partly on what each saw could be gained from the other, was instantaneous. Antheil, exuding admiration for Pound's vast musical knowledge, announced in an article published in the Paris *Tribune* that he had seldom read a "statement of the theory of harmony" that was as clear and simple as the one Pound had written for the *Transatlantic Review* the previous month. "With one stroke," effused Antheil, "it brushes away a world of imbecilities carefully cultivated and cherished by impotents since the time of Bach." His concluding observation, he had reason to know, had plenty of extra-literary support: Ezra Pound was a "poet who wanted all of his life to become a musician." Pound had, in fact, been music critic for

George Antheil, Bernardsville, New Jersey, 1920.
COURTESY OF ALLEN TANNER

Orage's *New Age* magazine in London from 1917 to 1920, writing under the pseudonym of William Atheling, and as Antheil also knew, he had labored to compose music of his own, his current effort being an opera entitled *Le Testament*, based on Villon's work of the same name. And for this Antheil reserved additional superlatives. *Le Testament* "is a work of colossal talent; a genial work; a work gaunt and bare, but with a new richness, and an approach that is as new as new planets." What he did not mention was that at Pound's invitation he had joined him as a collaborator, working out the orchestration of the opera while Pound "sang the score and tapped on his desk." Nor did he say that Pound had made arrangements with Bird to publish a little book called *Antheil and the Theory of Harmony*. Issued the following month in an unusually large edition of six hundred copies, it consisted of a sheaf of Pound's *New Age* reviews ("with marginalia emitted by George Antheil"), the treatise on harmony, most of which had appeared in the *Transatlantic Review*, and a short, laudatory article on Antheil in which the composer was classified as "possibly the first American or American-born musician to be taken seriously." Bird's edition, even though priced at only ten francs, sold slowly; however, by 1931, Pound told a friend that Bird had sold all the copies and that the book had actually "made expenses at 10 francs a copy." Four years before, however, Pound had arranged for an American publication of the book by Pascal Covici, who also printed three numbers of Pound's short-lived magazine, *Exile*.

That "flamboyant book," as Antheil later called Pound's appreciation of him, predictably did little to enhance the composer's reputation in Parisian or American music circles, and among critics it provoked more guffaws than respectful admiration. In his autobiography, *Bad Boy of Music*, Antheil wrote scornfully of having permitted such self-serving effusions of praise to be printed, and blamed his poor judgment on an overriding desire to blast his way into the "tight-as-a-drum salons" with Ezra's book as the ammunition. The expected detonation had fizzled. Instead of clearing the way for concerts, the book produced an "active distaste for the very mention of the name 'Antheil.'" Even as late as 1945 he still believed it had been partly responsible for the decline of his career.

A query from the critic R. P. Blackmur, asking Pound why he was issuing the *XVI Cantos* as a limited edition and charging twenty-five dollars for the cheapest copy, received a teasingly mocking reply. "Why the 100 readers? There were only five men hanged with Villon, or rather without him. Nobody can pay 25 dollars for a book. I know that. I didn't make the present economic system. The book, of course, can't be made for 25 bucks. Not if Strater and Bird and I were to be paid. That is not the point." The point Pound wanted to make was that he was being forced to publish his work in expensive limited editions outside America. It was not his fault that America was "so mentally and spiritually rotten as to permit filth like Article 211 of the U. S. Penal Code to lie around empesting the atmosphere." Unlike Joyce and McAlmon, however, Pound had yet to experience the baleful ways of American or British postal authorities. (When in 1929 United States authorities confiscated a copy of *XVI Cantos* and tried to prosecute the buyer, a New York bookseller, Pound declared that all his notions about the entrenchment of American puritanism had been reaffirmed.) Moreover, he admitted to Blackmur, American and English publishers no longer entered into his "calculations." Henceforth it would be necessary to support, though he himself would not devote much energy to it, presses like the Three Mountains and Contact, which, he hoped, might "lead to some more general system of printing" abroad. Meanwhile, he would "never again take any steps whatever to arrange publication of any of [his] work in either England or America." However, trying to sell Paris publications in both countries was another matter, and one which Pound, as Bird would soon discover, had learned to do with an impressive shrewdness. Working with Strater on *XVI Cantos* had been a distressing experience. At one point Strater had outraged him by "bitching" his original idea for the initials and illustrations by trying to get "sophisticated" (i.e., losing all quality) and straying all "over the page." He professed to be satisfied with the finished book, however, which Bird sent to him in Italy in January 1925. Even Strater's "effex" which had worried him earlier now seemed satisfactory; and as for Bird's labor, he proclaimed it "Vurry noble work. . . . A bhloody ghood job. After awl yr. night sweats." As for marketing the book, all Bird had to do to sell the ninety copies was to announce that Ezra Pound's *Sixteen Cantos* is "part of a long poem" (the full title was *A Draft of Sixteen Cantos for a Poem of Some Length*) and that at an "auction recently a copy of Mr. Pound's *A Lume Spento* published in 1908 at $1.00 (One dollar) was sold for $52.50." The collectors and bibliophiles, to whom the statement was clearly directed, "will prefer this half-time report on the poem to a pretended complete edition." Bird faithfully reproduced Pound's words in an ad which Ford printed in the June number of the *Transatlantic Review*.

Like most other little-press publishers, Bird placed far more value on the books he printed than on any profits he might make for himself or for the author. In an article on the ills of commercial publishing, he called for the repeal of copyright laws as the first step toward transforming the publishing industry. If the laws no longer existed, thus opening the way for wholesale piracy, publishers would stop seeking or "creating" the highly profitable bestseller and would instead seek the book of worth, the really "first-rate" book that would reflect credit on the publisher. In the same article, he advised the author to sell his manuscript to the highest bidder, thereby getting his money all at once rather than on a "contingent basis." Although Bird had managed to incorporate these innovations into the operation of the Three Mountains Press, as a publisher he still had an obligation to sell whatever he printed however long it might take, which, practically speaking, often necessitated making the most of the cumulative value of a limited-edition publication, such as Pound's *XVI Cantos*, in hopes of attracting buyers among collectors and booksellers interested in obtaining it primarily as an investment. The fact that both Bird and Mc-Almon scorned the practice of buying up limited editions with the intention of disposing of them later at greatly inflated prices did little to halt or impede it, and in fact it might be said that in the case of Pound's book Bird tried to capitalize on the very practice he abhorred. The bookseller who traded in small-press books with the primary intention of eventually reaping a sizable profit, though generally despised, nonetheless played an indispensible part in disposing of the publisher's stock. When Blackmur implied that both the high price and the small edition of *XVI Cantos* worked against the author's best interests, Pound's rejoinder that the United States Penal Code and economic system were to blame probably comprised only a part of the truth. Seemingly as important, given Pound's experience, might have been the tantalizing certainty of being able to dispose of ninety volumes at a profit.

With Pound's opus launched in January (1925), Bird turned to *Distinguished Air*, McAlmon's three stories of the homosexual milieu in Berlin, which would be the last Three Mountains book Bird himself would print before selling his press to Nancy Cunard. The book that had caused McAlmon so much worry was considered by many his best. Pound and Joyce much admired the second story, "Miss Knight," a portrait of a male homosexual who "manages to be simultaneously funny, pathetic, and repulsive," and at Joyce's suggestion it was translated into French. The other two stories, "Distinguished Air" and "The Lodging House," contrast debauchery and neuroticism and sexual aberration with the more ordered but equally "joyless' vagaries of heterosexual relationships." Ernest Walsh, in the second number of *This Quarter*, praised McAlmon's successful presentation of people often considered "disgusting by the average reader," but who, in McAlmon's hands, appeared as the comic figures they are in real life. McAlmon, in Walsh's opinion, was Whitmanesque, but without the bard's propensity for arguing with his readers; like Whitman, though, he concentrated on the "humanity" that was in the lives of his twisted characters, rendering them without explanation, without apology, in the manner of a "great white father watching the brood." Realistic and disinterested, *Distinguished Air* showed what "a really distinguished mind" could "do with difficult material."

In December (1925), with no new books scheduled for publication, Bird drew up an inventory of all the books he had sent to Miss Beach's shop, the major local outlet for Three Mountains books. Her year-end check for 3360 francs had just arrived, a welcome remuneration Bird claimed had saved him from "bankruptcy, lawsuit and other calamities." By return letter he assured her that the bookseller's discount of thirty-three percent she requested would be allowed on all Three Mountains books, except *XVI Cantos*, which had to be exempted because of the royalty arrangement with Pound. Hoping to balance his figures with hers, he supplied two lists, one showing the number of books he had sent to Shakespeare and Company, the other the number of books she reported as sold. Both lists underscore the modest turnover for printer and bookseller alike, and provide an amusing comment on the preferences of some of Miss Beach's customers. Of the thirteen books Bird listed, his own account of French wines had far outsold, at sixty-eight copies, all other Three Mountains publications, with the cheap edition of Pound's *Antheil*, at thirty-nine copies sold, a distant second.

	Supplied	Sold
Indiscretions	12	9
Women and Men	10	3
Elimus	13	None
Great American Novel	25	19
England	10	2
in our time	30	25
Distinguished Air	17	10
French Wines (1st ed.)	97	60

French Wines (2nd ed.)	25	8
Antheil (Ordinary ed.)	54	38
Antheil (De Luxe ed.)	5	1
XVI Cantos (Roma ed.)	2	None
XVI Cantos (Whatman ed.)	1	None

The last book to bear the Three Mountains imprint, though unofficially, was a small collection of poems by Krebs Friend, the shattered, death-haunted war veteran whom Hemingway had inveigled into backing the ailing *Transatlantic Review* after the death of its first patron, John Quinn, in June 1924. Married to a wealthy woman more than forty years his senior, who lived "to make a functioning human being out of him," Friend seemed a godsend to everyone except Ford, who feared, rightly, that these new patrons—Mrs. Friend especially, since she had the money—would eventually try to wrest control of the magazine from him. In August, Ford, hard-pressed for money, was forced to sell the Friends additional shares in the Transatlantic Company, which gave them a controlling interest. Friend was made president of the company, Ford was relieved of all financial responsibilities, and Mrs. Friend launched a series of ill-fated austerity measures designed to put the company on a sound financial footing. By the end of the year both Ford and Hemingway were disenchanted with their benefactors and their policies, and since no new sources of financial support seemed likely, the *Transatlantic Review* was allowed to expire.

Friend dedicated his poems—the collection bore the title *The Herdboy*—to his wife Henrietta, who almost certainly subsidized the private printing of sixty copies (forty on Madagascar paper, numbered 1–40, and twenty on Rives paper, numbered I-XX). Typographically, the volume is impressive. The frontispiece, a woodcut by Marcel Poucin, showing an intense, raven-haired shepherd standing before his flock, a staff in his hand, a dog at his side, blends nicely with the Caslon Old Face type used for Friend's poems. A note at the end stated that the book had been hand-printed by Maurice Lévy at the Three Mountains Press, December 1926.

In 1928, apparently not having done any printing since *Distinguished Air*, Bird decided to sell the ancient press on which he had printed nearly all his books, a tray or two of Caslon Old Face type, and even some wooden furnishings. The buyer, an even more inexperienced novice than

Bird had been a few years earlier but possessed with the same intense desire to print books by hand, was an ebullient, glittering British aristocrat named Nancy Cunard. The move to her house in the country, some fifty miles north of Paris, a colossal effort requiring the dismantling and reassembling of the press, Bird himself supervised. And to instruct Miss Cunard in the intricacies of operating a press over a hundred years old, Bird procured the services of Maurice Lévy, the printer who had so artfully designed and printed Krebs Friend's book of poetry.

IV

Edward Titus
AT THE SIGN OF THE BLACK MANIKIN

I

I T IS HARD to imagine how such an industrious, indomitable, imperious person as Helena Rubinstein could have been even remotely connected with the Left Bank literary life. Yet money from her burgeoning cosmetics fortune subsidized a bookshop, an avant-garde press, and one of the best little magazines of the era—all ventures organized and directed by her *littérateur* husband Edward Titus. None of them, however, really interested Madame Rubinstein, but from her Right Bank apartment she maintained a devoted interest in Edward Titus, who, in the opinion of Madame's biographer, "remained to the end of his days, and hers, the only passion she was to experience as a woman." If Edward Titus was a "waster," and she thought he was, he was a beloved one. Supporting his costly literary hobbies was a foolish extravagance, but she went on doing it, and, in return, received his advice on investments and purchases of the paintings, antiques, and books which formed the centerpieces of her impressive collection.

Before Madame Rubinstein and Edward Titus lived in separate quarters—she in a luxuriously renovated eighteenth-century house on the Ile Saint-Louis, he in a small but elegant apartment at 4 rue Delambre, around the corner from the Dôme—they lived together on two continents. Both Polish—Madame had fled Poland for Australia as a young girl and Titus had settled in New Orleans as a small boy—they had met and married in England, where at the turn of the century Madame opened the first of many successful salons. In 1908 she extended her business to Paris, and in 1913 the Titus family (two sons had been born in England)

Edward Titus in his bookshop, rue Delambre, Paris, 1930s.
COURTESY OF MRS. WILLIAM FRIEDMAN

followed her there. The outbreak of war the next year forced another move, this one to America, a country Madame rejoiced to find was populated with women with whitish faces and "oddly grayish" lips, all in obvious need of lipsticks and powders. While Madame concentrated on building a cosmetics empire in the New World, Titus and his sons languished in a country house in Greenwich, Connecticut, through which passed a covey of "nice women" hired by Madame to watch over the children, and with one of whom, in 1916, Titus incautiously disappeared to Chicago. That indiscretion produced such an upheaval in Madame that she demanded and got a legal separation.

What had happened, according to her biographer, was that Madame had succumbed to Titus' charms, perhaps even been enslaved by them, had then grown increasingly jealous of his attentions to other women, and after his flight with the family nursemaid, had been humiliated by him. Yet Titus "was always to have a hypnotic power" over her, and she would continue "to see him, love him, and occasionally live with him." Their separation, whether caused by peccadillos or, as one of Madame's maids contended, by money, or both, was frequently interrupted by reconciliations. He remained one of the three men "who really mattered in the strange tapestry of her family life" (the others being her sons). When he "tortured her . . . she repaid the compliment by frequently refusing him funds." But before she stopped the flow of funds once and for all, Madame found that she had cast herself, quite against her will, in the role of benefactress for a coterie of talented artists and writers, of whose work she could hardly have had less knowledge or appreciation. "How was I to know all those writers were worth a sou," she remonstrated after Titus, with Madame's money, had published books by Lawrence and Lewisohn and a naughty memoir, for which Hemingway had written an introduction, by the Quarter's most famous model-mistress, Kiki. "I never had a moment to read their books. To me, they were meshugga . . . and I always had to pay for their meals!" Even the most celebrated did not escape Madame's scorn. Joyce "smelled bad . . . couldn't see . . . ate like a bird"; Hemingway was "a loud-mouth and a show-off. Women liked him, but I didn't"; Lawrence, whose novel *Lady Chatterley's Lover* Titus published in 1929, was "a nice little man . . . shy," who would sit for hours staring into space "while his pushy wife held the stage." Nothing Titus did promised any return, she complained, and, furthermore, he had too many expenses and spent far too much of her money on trivia. Convinced as she must have been that her husband, like others, had fallen in with a com-

pany of Left Bank "wasters" whose nonsense she was foolishly supporting, Madame must also have recognized that Titus' literary ventures were
far from frivolous enterprises and that the high quality of the magazine he
edited and the books he published was acknowledged both in and well
beyond Montparnasse.

Nothing prepared Edward Titus for life with Madame. Nothing
could. Dismayed by the inexhaustible and thundering energies she lavished on the thriving family business and increasingly short-tempered because of her domineering, bullying efforts to control him (one of Madame's
maids of many years said that her employer "treated all men—relatives
included—as employees. . . . She eats them alive . . . even her own
sons!"), he understandably sought relief and refuge in the quieter and
more rarefied world of art and books. It was a world he finally created for
himself in Paris in 1924, inside the crowded confines of a bookshop
enigmatically named At the Sign of the Black Manikin. Unlike the one
Miss Beach operated several blocks away, Titus' shop was what in France
is called a *librarie*, a sort of rare book room and gallery combined, within
which, a reporter from the Paris *Tribune* one day discovered, Titus had
amassed a collection of priceless literary treasures. "In one afternoon of
browsing one is confused not only by the rich array of very good books,
but by the special rarities which he shows with the pride and pleasure of
the intelligent collector. There is first of all his collection of books on
constitutional law, for he aims to have a reference library on this subject
which serious students may consult. He is an amateur of Americana, and
has picked up many a curious thing on this side of the Atlantic, such as a
letter by . . . George Washington, in which the first President commissions
a dentist to repair his false teeth. There is also a manuscript account of an
exploit in the life of John Paul Jones, with notes in the handwriting of the
great admiral. He has a first edition of *Leaves of Grass*, and an account in
the writing of the poet of Camden of his own life, written for a newspaper
on his sixty-fifth birthday." Titus' library of European books and manuscripts was even more impressive. He has "what is undoubtedly the best
collection of first editions of Verlaine, together with two postcards which
the poet wrote to a friend, in a most curious English. He has Mallarmé's
translation of *The Raven*, signed by the great symbolist himself, and
illustrated by Manet. . . . And there is a richly bound first edition of that
manifesto of the Pleiade, dating from 1549, the *Défense et Illustration de
la Langue Francoyse*. And there is a copy of Eyckliffe's *Apology* dating

from 1550, and a 1633 Elzevir, and one of the very rare copies of the Cromwellian Bible of 1651, with its astounding errors."

Obviously, the visitor from the *Tribune*, Alex Small, whose testy comments on expatriate life in Paris had long rankled the members of the American colony, had found in Montparnasse what he least expected to find: someone with erudition and an encyclopedic knowledge and an acquaintance "with the personal history, writings, and manuscripts, not only of the acknowledged great, but with many an obscure but interesting and eccentric figure." Just talking with Titus, rhapsodized Small, was to make a "voyage to the kingdom of the mind, that place open only to those who believe that the intellect alone is important, and the rest of life so much annoying and trivial nonsense." Though only one side of Titus' nature, the intellectualism and high seriousness that Small lauded was the side that most people saw, and sometimes to their discomfort. Not infrequently visitors to the Black Manikin would find that they were being closely scrutinized for the slightest hint of bad taste or unrefinement. Those who betrayed either might be conducted out of the shop, silently and firmly. Nor did Titus restrict such close critical examinations to his own purlieu. Once, spotting a friend carrying a copy of the *Reader's Digest*, fully and shamelessly exposed, he initiated a tongue-lashing that extended over a week. Another time an unwary acquaintance with an abridged book in his hand was the surprised victim of an unexpected burst of vituperation. Lordly within and without his baliwick, impatient with all who failed to meet his standards, irascible, and often disagreeable, Titus was hardly one to ingratiate himself with the throngs at the cafés around the corner from his shop. Titus never tried to move with the crowd. His acquaintances, always few, and his friends, even fewer, were mainly the writers whose books he published at the Black Manikin Press—Ralph Cheever Dunning, Ludwig Lewisohn, William Van Wyck, Morley Callaghan, and D. H. Lawrence—and a few others such as the Pierre Lovings, Polia Chentoff, Lily Wolfe, and the irrepressible Kiki.

For those with enough courage and intellectual and aesthetic fortitude to face Titus, in or out of the Black Manikin, there would be rich rewards. Ostensibly, Titus had started his bookstore not to make money but to create a focus in Paris for bibliophiles (*cum* Titus) and lovers of art. It was the same sort of formalizing of a hobby Bill Bird had achieved when he founded the Three Mountains Press. Never the crossroads, or hangout, that Miss Beach's Shakespeare and Company was, and not even her rival commercially, the Black Manikin resembled a cloister, the private artistic sanctuary of one who aspired to play the role of Maecenas to those who shared his tastes and, in Alex Small's words, to those "who write books" and "who do reading not as a recreation, but as the serious business of life." So long, however, as Titus merely remained the obscure proprietor, or curator, of the Black Manikin, the opportunities of enjoying the literary esteem that came to the supporter of Vergil and Horace, no matter how modest, seemed decidedly limited. Some more direct way to share his bounty and extend his influence among his creative friends had to be found, and in mid-1926 Titus found what he was looking for, the first sign of which Sisley Huddleston detected on one of his many visits to Titus' shop. There were fewer new releases, Huddleston noticed, and more "significant books" and others of "a special esthetic character." The place had really ceased being a bookstore and its owner a booksalesman, changes that foreshadowed the transformation of the former into a publishing house, the latter into a publisher. To his friends, Titus announced he was ready to publish their poems, stories, and even novels, and in the case of artists, their cover designs and illustrations. He would call the new press the Black Manikin, and the printing, he was pleased to discover, could be done by the Crète printery, at 24 rue Delambre, a few doors away.

II

Titus never liked large things, Howard Simon said of the man who backed his first exhibit (at the Black Manikin) and who then commissioned him to make three woodcut illustrations for the first Black Manikin publication. Certainly Simon's observation aptly describes Titus' maiden book, a slender volume of poetry, twenty-two pages, by Ralph Cheever Dunning, whom Ernest Walsh, with typical hyperbolic flaccidity, accused of having "the soul of Dowson and Swinburne and Keats and Shelley as well as their petty agonies and florid importance of expression." Entitled *Rococo*, it provoked nearly as much controversy as the news the previous year that Dunning had won *Poetry*'s verse contest. That announcement had also drawn some caustic comments from Walsh, most of them aimed at Ezra Pound, who, Walsh contended, had only surveyed Dunning's poetry and hence had mistakenly praised what he had not read. What Pound had said was that "anyone who cannot feel the beauty of [Dunning's] melody had better confine his criticism to prose and leave the discussion of verse to those who know something about it." Walsh's death soon afterward ended their bickering over Dunning, but the poet remained the whetstone on which others sharpened their critical powers, whether as defenders or detractors, none of whose comments probably made the least impression on the silent, elusive man Ford Madox Ford called "the living Buddha of Montparnasse."

Wambly Bald, whose position on the Paris *Tribune* elevated him to the enviable rank of Boswell of the Lost Generation, once accompanied Dunning to his "shelter" in rue Notre Dame des Champs and found it to be "virtually a wooden box," its furniture a stove, a cot, a bookcase, and a single chair. Outside in a tiny garden, seated at the foot of a huge chestnut tree, he composed his verses. At the time Bald visited the poet's sanctuary Dunning had lived in Montparnasse for more than twenty years and, according to old acquaintances, had scarcely spoken more than a few sentences the whole time. Never a recluse, he frequented the noisiest and most crowded cafés, sitting still as a skeleton, impassive and unbothered by the scrambling activity going on around him, one hand gripping a glass of hot milk, the other a book—an "apparition," in Samuel Putnam's words, "weirdly out of place there." Putnam, later Titus' assistant on *This Quarter*, defined Dunning's nature as Oriental, by which he probably meant more than the poet's addiction to opium, but the habit may have intensified his obsession with terror and death, an obsession which so concerned his friend Ezra Pound that, on leaving Paris, he gave Hemingway a can of the drug with orders to deliver it to Dunning in the event of an emergency. When the emergency came, Hemingway, carefully following Pound's instructions, delivered the drug to the distressed and dying poet, only to have Dunning dismiss him with an epithet and a barrage of flying milk bottles. To those who had broken through his communion of silence, Dunning seemed to be a man in love with death, perhaps one who had been most of his life. Bald concluded death was the final experience Dunning had spent forty years of contemplation preparing for, and which he would accomplish by simply refusing to eat. Putnam, in a tribute to the poet printed in *This Quarter* at the time of his death, declared that Dunning "had willed to die, as the one last great adventure that was left to him in life," an adventure completed without "bawdy accessories" or "showmanship," totally without vulgarity. His was a "poet's death" which Putnam claimed had restored his own "unspoiled Idea of Death."

While many in Montparnasse undoubtedly urged Dunning to publish his poems, it was Titus who had the means to see that it was accom-

Elliot Paul, writer and Paris *Tribune*
book critic, Paris, 1930s.
PRINCETON UNIVERSITY LIBRARY,
SYLVIA BEACH COLLECTION

plished. What critics Elliot Paul and Pierre Loving, both Titus' friends, had to say about the small gathering of poems, the fruits of slow, silent labor performed in the privacy of his room or garden, probably never reached the poet. To modernish Paul, Dunning's work was hopelessly antiquated, *terza rima* being a meter, in his opinion, that was "never useful in English and of doubtful value in Italian." It was simply another fault in a list that already included "mawkish and distorted lines and metaphors" (glancing at Dunning's pages gave Paul the sensation of "walking between long isles of badly stuffed birds"), a laughable philosophy of love, and a narrative on which the poet had only the most juvenile opinions. Titus the bookseller had "fulfilled his functions creditably," but Titus the publisher, if *Rococo* was a harbinger of future publications, had started with something "manifestly unfit to go on the shelves of his own bookstore," one that brought to mind the dismal American books that "impelled so many writers and readers to seek refuge" in Paris. Loving's reply to Paul in the Paris *Times* defended Dunning's choice of an "outworn and rather conventional language" as enhancing the "beauty of the achievement." Paul, unfortunately, had failed to comprehend that a "poet's ideology of love has very little to do with the quality of his poetry." *Rococo* was, of course, neither as bad as Paul charged nor as good as Loving claimed. Paul, however, had the last word, and he reserved his parting salvo for Titus. Noticing the publisher's announcement that the type used in printing *Rococo* had been distributed, Paul gibed: "By no chance should it ever be assembled again." It never was, but shortly before Dunning's death in 1930, Titus published the poet's second book of poems entitled *Windfalls* (with a portrait by Polia Chentoff that accented the poet's cadaverous appearance). The volume inspired Pound to proclaim Dunning "one of the four or five poets of our time." From Paul there was no reply.

When Titus' second Black Manikin book appeared in the winter of 1926, even Paul had to concede the publisher had "in a measure" redeemed himself. *The Case of Mr. Crump*, a long naturalistic novel recounting the collapse of the author's ill-considered marriage to a woman many years his senior, was the work of Ludwig Lewisohn, a middle-aged, German-born ex-journalist and teacher who had turned up in Paris in flight from a wife who, judging by her fictional correspondent, must have been the equal of Xantippe herself. Finding that he had little in common with the expatriates, except on the "ground of mere human friendliness," Lewisohn set out to document the history of his marital strife, and was soon turning out (with impressive Germanic precision) a thousand words a day, "without pause or hesitation." Four and a half months later he pronounced it finished and shipped the 150,000-word "case" to his American publisher, Horace Liveright, who refused the new manuscript, wary of accepting something so clearly libelous. Disappointed, Lewisohn at first considered printing the book himself (or, at his mother-in-law's expense, if she agreed), but then changed his mind and showed it to Titus. The publisher read the manuscript immediately and offered to print an edition of five hundred copies, an offer the author described as "a very great service" that occurred when "I would have felt with the utmost keenness the failure of my manuscript to reach the finality of a permanent record."

The hasty printing of *Crump* nearly exceeded the speed at which the author had written it. By the early winter Lewisohn rushed first copies to a few carefully selected and influential friends—in America, Carl Van Doren, William Ellery Leonard, Joseph Wood Krutch, H. L. Mencken and Sinclair Lewis—and, in Paris, to Sisley Huddleston—all of whom responded "with the utmost generosity." Orders flowed in, and Titus, anticipating a large American sale, confidently stamped the edition "For America." Lewisohn was jubilant. With *Crump* now "not only on paper but in the consciousness of a few wise and gifted contemporaries," he proclaimed his "moral satisfaction . . . quite complete." After all, he confessed, if a man did not have to worry about earning a living he could hardly ask for more "in the case of any book." Well that he was contented, for it soon appeared that he might have to settle for "moral satisfaction" and the approval of the "few wise and gifted contemporaries." Rumors, first from St. Louis and then from Baltimore, that copies of *Crump* were being delayed arrived just ahead of the jolting news that the United States Post Office had classified *Crump* "unmailable," on the grounds that it violated Section 211 of the Federal Criminal Code, the same regulation which had been cited in denying *Ulysses* entry into America and against which Ezra Pound had never ceased fulminating. Having a "blacklisted" book on his hands, although for Lewisohn an outrageous situation, hardly deterred Titus from spreading the news. An ad in *transition* made the claim that "Nothing could have stopped *The Case of Mr. Crump* from being numerically the Best Seller except the numerical fact that it appears in an edition deluxe limited strictly to Five Hundred copies." *Crump* became the first of Titus' books—and one of three—to go out of print, and it was the only one he ever reissued.

Lewisohn dedicated the book he called a work of the "severest moral idealism" to the memory of his parents and to Thelma Spear, a singer who had replaced the discarded Xantippe and who would herself be exchanged, following a sixteen-year alliance with the author, for a young journalist named Edna Manley. The conjugal serenity Lewisohn apparently pursued most of his life never had a chance to flower in the marriage of Herbert and Anne Crump. Long after it might have made a difference, Herbert, a naive and weak-willed musician, discovers he has married a crafty, dishonest, vulgar woman, who knows that in any proceeding Herbert might initiate to dissolve their marriage she can gain, through stealth and perversion of the truth, the support of the American legal system to guarantee her "innocence" and uphold her claims. In Anne Bronson Farrel Crump (the first Mrs. Lewisohn was Mary Arnold Crocker Childs, an English dramatist and poet, who wrote under the pseudonym "Bosworth Crocker"), Lewisohn created an almost draconic figure, whom he invested with the acquisitive and destructive and creative forces in American life that had tamed an aboriginal civilization and then imposed an only slightly more hospitable rule. Against such elemental power, Herbert, a representative of the cultured and refined and somewhat reactionary aspects of America, struggles ineffectually. Finally, only the fact that Anne will deny him the divorce he so desperately wants (her compromise is a separation and a sizable alimony) and the certainty that she will publicize slanderous stories about his life-saving attachment to a young musician, as peerless as Anne is deficient, if he does not publicly deny the liaison and assure the world he loves only her, forces Herbert to act. Like Clyde Griffiths, Dreiser's trapped hero, Crump mechanically destroys the object that threatens his life, and thereby ruins his own. Despite their different origins and "essentially distinct points of view," Dreiser and Lewisohn, concluded William Smyser, reviewer for the Paris *Tribune*, had arrived at the same result: egalitarian America not only allowed a union of two irreconcilable personalities but regarded any attempt to dissolve it as a threat to national morality. Likewise, Thomas Mann, in the preface he wrote for the 1931 reissue of *Crump* (advertised as "This Great Banned Novel"), blamed American conditions for turning Crump's marriage into an "inferno." Only the "protection of cruel social hypocrisy and of a cruel social fear for the abstract institution" prevented its immediate dissolution. To Europeans inclined to be indifferent to the problems raised by Lewisohn's book, perhaps out of a mistaken belief that their social morality was a trifle more mature, Mann cautioned that the "world has become small and intimate and there has arisen a common responsibility which only a malignant reactionary dare repudiate." Recognizing a "common responsibility" meant joining Lewisohn, Mencken, Sinclair Lewis, Judge Lindsay, and the contributors to the *American Mercury* and *Nation* in the labor of transforming the "handsome, energetic children of American civilization into beings of a ripe and adult culture." Hopefully, Mann concluded, *The Case of Mr. Crump* will "extend its influence back across the ocean and contribute to that Europeanization of America that should be the counterpart of our much-discussed Americanization and which is indeed the aim of the best Americans of our time."

Notwithstanding the excitement created by the publication of *Crump*, Titus managed to bring out a third book before the end of the year. Titled *The Frog* (a play in five scenes), it was the work of a red-bearded American poet named Virgil Geddes, gently described by two Paris *Tribune* associates (Geddes served as the paper's financial editor from 1924 to 1928) as a wanderer in the "realm of fancy," poignantly sensitive to the "tremors of emotional experience," a man without mission, ethics, or stereotyped philosophy, one amused by human antics and troubled by human loneliness. Geddes, who shared Dunning's Oriental detachment from things and people but not his opium habit or his death wish, had somehow attached himself to the gregarious *littérateur* Elliot Paul, who wrote benedictory introductions for his play and for a collection of poems Geddes was issuing privately about the same time called *40 Poems*. Paul detected a vital harmony linking Geddes' work and his life, the first reflecting a "logical and constant growth and expansion," and the second "a constant process of simplification." But it was the poet's powers of observation that most impressed him. While hardly all-absorbing, Geddes instinctively selected the "essential problems reflected in his own experience and that of others immediately around him," and endowed his verses with his "natural gifts" of gentleness, finality, irony, and music. In the summer of 1926, Paul found quarters for his friend in the quirky hotel and bistro in the rue de la Huchette, paradoxically named l'Hotel du Caveau de la Terreur (later memorialized in Paul's *The Last Time I Saw Paris*), where, perhaps inspired by the tranquil atmosphere, Geddes speedily composed *The Frog*, and where, one afternoon, Paul introduced him to a new acquaintance, Katharine Huntington, who happened to be a vacationing director of the Boston Stage Society. On the watch for new works, Miss Huntington agreed to take the play home with her, and the next year, to everyone's delight and surprise, *The Frog* was performed by the Boston Society—most successfully, according to the Paris *Tribune* notices.

III

With the exception of Manuel Komroff's novelette *The Voice of Fire*, the books Titus issued the next year, 1927, were a rather undistinguished lot, although they bolstered Titus' standing as a publisher willing to print first writings by unknown authors. Of the three volumes of verse, *First Fruits* by Thelma Spear (with an introduction by Lewisohn) was marked "Not for Sale, for Private Circulation Only"; the second, a collection of Dunning-like lyrics purportedly by a nineteen-year-old poet named Agatha Itchwyrth and entitled *The Cheese Girl at New Bench*, quickly went out of print, as did the third, Kenneth McNeil Wells' *Absit Omen*. The same year Titus also published an English version of Arthur Schnitzler's reputedly "naughty" drama *Der Reigen* (Couples), which he had translated with the assistance of Lily Wolfe, one of two attractive young women he had hired to work at the press. The other was Polia Chentoff, a Polish artist and sculptor of remarkable beauty and limited talent, whom he commissioned to illustrate Schnitzler's ten "gallant episodes." At least on one occasion, Miss Chentoff's association with Titus threatened to undo his tenuous relationship with Madame. Manuel Komroff reported the episode. "Once I happened to be in the Closerie des Lilas at the end of Montparnasse . . . about a quarter mile from Titus' store. It was evening and soon after I came in I noticed that Titus was at the other side of the café with the handsome young woman, Polia Chentoff. I was alone. They waved to me and I waved back. But then their waving did not stop. He kept pointing at his table indicating that I should join them. I resisted until it got to a desperate state and then I picked up my drink and its saucer and went over. He whispered in my ear. The reason he wanted me was because Mrs. Moneybags (Helena Rubinstein) had just come into the café with a woman friend and he did not want her to see him alone with a handsome dame." Titus himself unwittingly described the contretemps more succinctly in the blurb he wrote for *Der Reigen* in which he credited Miss Chentoff's drawings with possessing humor vying with "consummate artistry."

There were no traces of humor in the woodcuts Miss Chentoff made for Komroff's *The Voice of Fire*. Like Ludwig Lewisohn, Manuel Komroff was that anomaly in Paris: a published author (a collection of his short stories, *The Grace of Lambs*, had appeared in 1925, a year before the author arrived in Paris). One of the first people Komroff met abroad was his friend Whitold Gordon, an artist who, in addition to making several covers for the then newly founded *New Yorker*, had just finished designing the Black Manikin colophon for Titus—a lithe female figure, black except for a festoon of white stars, balancing on a wriggling black serpent (subdued by a sword) and gazing serenely at an open book held gracefully in one hand. With Gordon's help Komroff found in Paris what he had come seeking: the time to write and a quiet place in which to do it. Friends recall seeing him going regularly to a café near the Dôme—a slender, red-haired man, with a straggling red moustache, a long head, and a face often masked in an inscrutable Oriental expression—where, unperturbed by other patrons, he would methodically turn out a fresh batch of manuscript—every day. Gordon, of course, introduced his industrious friend to Titus, and on one of the evenings when they met at the Select, Komroff told the publisher he was at work on a novelette which, for various reasons, he did not intend to publish in the United States. "It was fantasy," he explained, and "was against the Church, and was not suitable for American publication." (Komroff had worked as an editor at Boni and Liveright.) He was writing it to free his mind for a long historical novel he intended doing when he got back to New York (the novel turned out to be *Coronet*, by far the author's most widely read book). Besides, the idea of the novelette plagued him and he had to get it out of his system. What Komroff said was enough to convince Titus that here might be a book worth publishing, appealingly iconoclastic, and a natural companion to *Crump* and *Der Reigen*, both of which he had begun advertising as publications "available only in Paris." Indeed, as soon as he had finished, Titus told Komroff, he wanted to see his work and, as expected, Titus liked what he saw, and Komroff liked what he heard: Black Manikin would publish *The Voice of Fire*. "I had no contract with Titus; never asked for one." Nor was there an advance. "Never asked for one. And no money; never expected any. The subject never came up. This may seem strange but this is the fact." Still, even without the promise of payment, the book was at least being published, and handsomely, too, as it turned out.

Komroff unequivocally enunciates both the cause and the effect of man's desperate situation: "Man does not know where to go. He is blind. He is surrounded by a world that he knows is filled with tricks. There are tricks of two kinds: those that can be explained, like the tricks of business, and those that come from the unknown, like illness, sorrow, and death. Man is content to fight the tricks of the fellowman, but against the dark tricks of nature he is helpless and blind. In this business you (the clergy) have become the middleman so that you may profit and thrive on the illicit traffic between man and the unknown." The middlemen, of course, are exposed and destroyed, tragically in that they fall victims to the ecclesiastical pride that lay behind the construction of a mighty cathedral ("the greatest and most imposing that money can buy"), one intended, ironically, to rebuke and "abase the pride of Paris." The weapon that unmasks such patent clerical despotism and effectively destroys it is laughter, a strange, mocking laughter that emanates capriciously from the cathedral organ (the largest in the world), and which among the clergy produces paroxysms of agonizing embarrassment. The laughter has no extraterrestrial source, but rather is the result of an accident involving a cathedral worker who, while welding the pipes of the organ, discovers that the flame from his blowtorch makes a strange music—"the voice of fire" —and who, after developing a theory of pressures, builds a set of pipes labeled "Hell Fire." He alone knows that the laughter is produced by acoustics, and it is a secret that neither the wrath nor the solicitations of the clergy can pry from him. In the end, the cathedral that was erected to humble the proud Parisians is allowed to go down in laughter.

The slyly malicious anti-clericalism found in Komroff's book assumed solemn and pontifical force in the first Black Manikin publication of 1928, William Van Wyck's *Some Gentlemen of the Renaissance,* a collection of four free-verse portraits of Giotto, Michelangelo, Galileo, and Richelieu which, the publisher speculated, might "give rise to the hope that perhaps we are now arrived at the threshold of a new Restoration," an event long overdue, judging by the gathering of witless ecclesiastics Van Wyck rounded up as targets for his rebellious Renaissance heroes. Thus, Michelangelo, brushing in the final strokes on the Sistine Chapel ceiling, knows that the reward for his labor—knowledge—is far more lofty, intellectually and morally, than what an impatient Pope expectantly looks forward to—a new toy which will picture God for his aggrandizement. And just as certain of his rightness is Galileo, who, charging that "purblind atrophy" has led his oppressor cardinals into senile ways, denies that their glimpse of God is "entirely" and that science can "obscure the face of God." A dying Richelieu hurls the mightiest challenge when he orders a "good varlet priest" to tell his hierophants that "he has gone to play match-wits with God," and that in the event Peter should try to bar him from the gates of heaven, he will take the portals with his naked hands and "show God how his kingdom can be run!" To print the book that Titus believed might usher in a "new Restoration," he commissioned the masterprinter of Dijon, Darantière, whose combination of a large 12-point type and an outsized format assured the publication at least an imposing material majesty.

The same year Darantière also printed a small chapbook entitled *Ladies Almanack* (to use a much abbreviated title), profusely illustrated by the author and bearing her sobriquet, "By a Lady of Fashion," the unpuzzling pseudonym chosen by Djuna Barnes, whom Janet Flanner named "the most important woman writer we had in Paris." A very great beauty, an indefatigable worker, and a remarkable conversationalist, Miss Barnes had already published *Nightwood* (also written in Paris), her novel of sexual aberration and tormented love, and had gathered around her a large and devoted following, none of whom had any trouble identifying Miss Barnes as the author of *Ladies Almanack.* But more than a casual familiarity with the members of the American colony was needed to identify the real-life figures that resided beneath the protective guises Miss Barnes had created to hide—and perhaps to protect—her lady characters. The exception was Evangeline Musset, "who, in the early eighties, had discarded her family Tandem, in which her Mother and Father found Pleasure enough, for the distorted Amusement of riding all smack-of-astride." She could be no one else but the poet, translator, and celebrated hostess of the Left Bank, Natalie Clifford Barney. Janet Flanner found herself cast as one of a pair of journalists bearing the sprightly names of Nip and Tuck. Once Miss Barnes decided to print her book (it was originally written for fun and not for publication), she apparently consulted with Titus. An early announcement of the book, a facsimile of the title page, bears the imprint of the Black Manikin. Plans to issue it under his auspices ended, though, when the publisher, after agreeing to defray all costs in return for permission to retain a few copies which he would put on sale at his shop, provoked Miss Barnes by asking for money and then demanding wholesale and retail rights over the book with no assurance of distribution. The impasse was resolved, at least partly, by Robert Mc-Almon, who paid for the printing as a gift to the author. Miss Barnes paid for the drawings (in fifty copies she and two helpers hand-colored the illustrations), and sold all the books herself: ten dollars for the uncolored copies; twenty-five dollars for the hand-colored; fifty dollars for the ten hand-colored and signed copies.

The manuscript bearing the title *Imaginary Letters* that Mary Butts turned over to Titus in 1928 bore the date "Autumn 1924, Hotel Foyot, Paris." It might have carried the subtitle "notes on the personality of a naughty boy, on poverty, change, and the sexual life of our time." The addressee of Miss Butts' eight letters was indeed an imaginary person, the mother of the author's would-be lover Boris, an exile living far from her son, in Yalta, and destined to see neither the letters nor their composer. Just as well perhaps, for what they reveal about Boris no mother would want to hear. Of a nature unbelievably paradoxical, he is at once cruel, devoted, capricious, selfish, jealous, bold, insensitive, chaste, double-willed, and honorable; but, most pronouncedly, he is a monster of vanity and pride, a parasite feeding on the woman he abuses and scorns and who attempts, vainly, "to create through him. To create him. In his own image." For despite all that is ignoble in Boris, she finds that "his qualities are twisted on a string of poetry." It is perversion that lies at the center of his "badness." Boris is a "fanatical pederast," a deviation countenanced and perpetuated by the "insane" Parisian society in which they both live, and one which Boris recognizes as a "medium for advancing one's career." Following a sequence of tortuous suffering and aversion, of violent separations and short-lived reunions, their relationship mercifully ends, dissolved by the writer who understands that what was once a pleasure has now become a duty and hence must stop. She reports to the "living

LADIES ALMANACK

showing their Signs and their tides;
their Moons and their Changes;
the Seasons as it is with them;
their Eclipses and Equinoxes; as
well as a full Record of diurnal
and nocturnal Distempers

WRITTEN & ILLUSTRATED

BY A LADY OF FASHION

P A R I S

PRINTED FOR THE AUTHOR, AND SOLD BY

~~Unreadable~~

1928

Title page (*right*) and
frontispiece (*below*) of
Ladies Almanack, written
and illustrated by a Lady
of Fashion [Djuna Barnes].
PRINCETON UNIVERSITY
LIBRARY

133

ghost" in Yalta that Boris and she "are walking backwards away from each other, a little chorus of short barks from our friends accompanying us." Though the loss is nearly all Boris', the writer ponders what he might have received if he had come to her "with heart and spirit full"; she dares only half imagine: perhaps a chance for creation, perhaps a "lot of information gained." With the final letter comes a mysterious happiness—not quite pure, not quite cynical. What the letters have done, she assures that other, distant mother, "is to fix a little in this flying world your fleshly and my ghostly son, the black and green boy, who comes less and less often to see me now. The ray, the shadow, the memory, the mirror in which I have looked, seen and understood, imperfectly, many things."

It is remuneration that hardly seems to compensate for the energies expended and the hurt borne, but for the writer it may have been enough. The epigraph from Whitehead that Miss Butts chose for *Imaginary Letters* warned that "we must not expect all the virtues. We should even be satisfied if there is something odd enough to be interesting." Boris, whatever else he is, is interesting, and, finally, of course, exasperating. In a revealing entry Miss Butts wrote in her journal a few months before *Imaginary Letters* appeared, she confided that she had always had "an incomparable pleasure in finding someone psychically sick, and learning about it, and seeing if there is a way out. This feeling very much mixed up with sex—bed not necessary, but it makes things work better. That is, any power I have seems to work better in that relation. I've always wanted to make my lovers well, sense powers liberated in them. . . ." Unfortunately, as the letters make clear, Boris remains stubbornly indifferent to the "link of bodies" and the "living intimacy that resolved all differences," and frustrates her greatest efforts to liberate his powers and to heal his psychic disorder. The differences separating the central figures were strongly stated in a series of line-drawings the author's close friend Jean Cocteau made for the book, the first time, according to Titus, the poet had consented to illustrate a book he had not written. In one, a contorted Boris, bruised and bewildered, writhes next to his neglected and Grecian-clad mistress—serene and benevolent and formidable.

IV

The year Wall Street tottered and then collapsed and precipitated the first homeward-bound exodus of American expatriates from the Quarter, their Parisian sojourn unexpectedly ended by the cutting off of funds from home, Titus announced that he would soon erect an apartment building on Boulevard Raspail, which, besides tenants, would house a "little American theatre" (three hundred seats), decorated in the "most modern style." He would be the sole director and manager, he told reporters, and explained that it was "an experiment," and that he intended to produce plays that had not been "played elsewhere before," by which he meant plays considered "avant garde." Even O'Neill, two of whose one-act plays had been chosen for the first program of the American theatre group in Paris, would be passed over in favor of the "most modern dramatic pieces." Also, he added, there was a possibility that "some of the more modern cinematic productions would be shown," a matter on which he would consult with Man Ray. At the same time Titus outlined his theatrical plans, he announced that he also intended to publish a literary quarterly which would be "devoted to encouraging the modern young American and English writers in Paris." That it would in no way condescend to compete with Jolas' *transition* he made clear in a statement worded to tweak the "revolutionists of the Word": "I wish to emphasize that the English in this magazine will be understood. There will be no attempt to re-create the English language."

That magazine was not the *Titus Quarterly*, as a newsman mistakenly reported, but the bumptious and unpredictable *This Quarter*, the creation of Ethel Moorhead and Ernest Walsh which had burst on the Paris literary scene in 1925 vowing to serve the artist by printing his work with "no greater delay than the editing and printing" demanded and without subjecting it to the customary "literary politics" that infested so much commercial criticism. Its spirit of adventure and outspoken iconoclasm was unique even in the unusually animated world of the little magazines. The editors scornfully rejected "valuations that tried to relate an artist to a "time, motive, or movement," and warned all "critics, labellers, baptisers, slanderers, experts, reviewers and such to be slow in giving us a number or letter or any documentary classification lest they be confounded." Their anarchistic credo outraged reactionaries and academicians: "We are fickle, wayward, uncommitted to respect of respect of the respectable established armies strong because many. *This Quarter* is our search and reason." Hoping to dramatize their brave words, they dedicated the first number to the one indisputable enemy of the "respectable established armies," Ezra Pound, who "by his creative work, his editorship of several magazines, his helpful friendship for young and unknown artists, his many and untiring efforts to win better appreciation of what is first-rate in art comes first to our mind as meriting the gratitude of this generation." Through three issues, each printed in a different place—Paris, Milan, and Monte Carlo—they flaunted their independence and determination "to publish the artist's work while it is still fresh." As well received as the first issue was—especially impressive was a fifty-page supplement devoted to Constantin Brancusi—it was the second that convinced skeptics that *This Quarter* might indeed invigorate contemporary writing. Its appearance was "a literary event of the highest importance," Elliot Paul assured readers of the Paris *Tribune*, and "familiarity with its pages will be necessary to those who wish to keep pace with modern artistic achievement." Besides a "Musical Supplement" consisting of extracts from the compositions of George Antheil, a service that Paul contended would "enable musicians to break through the utter drivel which newspapers have published about his work and examine it for themselves," there were stories by Hemingway ("The Undefeated"), Kay Boyle ("Flight"), Djuna Barnes ("The Little Girl Continues"), and Morley Callaghan ("A Girl with Ambition"), the latter's first appearance in print; and poetry by Pound, Emanuel Carnevali, Kenneth Fearing, Eugene Jolas, Carl Sandburg, and, of course, Walsh.

Shortly before the third number appeared Walsh died, the victim of the consumption that had plagued him for years. Miss Moorhead immediately revised plans for the number so as to accommodate the material on which Walsh had been working at the time of his death and as many tributes to him as she could gather in a fairly short time. Among those quick to respond were Kay Boyle, Eugene Jolas, Archibald Craig, and Emanuel Carnevali, but missing was Ezra Pound, an inexcusable slight, in Miss Moorhead's opinion, in view of Walsh's devotion to the older poet and her own request to Pound for a tribute. His reply that a "tribute 'elsewhere' would do more good"—though hardly what she wanted or expected—nevertheless was interpreted as a sign that Pound would write something about Walsh in the first number of his own magazine, *Exile*. But the maiden issue of *Exile*, which finally appeared in early 1927, carried nothing remotely resembling a tribute to Walsh. Miss Moorhead, bitterly disappointed, retaliated by writing a scathing denunciation of Pound in which she revealed that, among other indulgences granted him, had been his request for £40 as payment for a canto she had planned to print in the second number of *This Quarter*, at a time when all other contributors, including Joyce, were receiving only thirty francs a page. Despite such dispensations, Miss Moorhead added, Pound had never responded to Walsh's request for a critical assessment of the poems he had sent to the poet at Rapallo during the last summer of his life. Pound's unconscionable behavior demanded that the original dedication be retracted, a feat Miss Moorhead accomplished with a few sweeping sentences. "I herewith take back that dedication. I have said before that Ernest Walsh was disillusioned about Ezra Pound before he died. We [presumably it was Walsh's wish too] take back our too-generous dedication."

In the same number Miss Moorhead assured readers that the magazine would continue under her guidance, although she admitted that finding another editor who would be as inventive and adventurous as Walsh would not be easy, and, as it turned out, a replacement for him was never to be found. In the spring of 1929, after a lapse of two years, she rallied and published the final number (No. 4) of *This Quarter* under her editorship. Nearly hidden in the Editor's Notes was the announcement that her "editorship and ownership" of the magazine had come to an end. "But I am glad to announce that *This Quarter* has been taken over, and will be carried on, by Mr. Edward W. Titus, the well-known Paris publisher. Nothing is nearer to my wishes than that *This Quarter* shall last out, and that young writers of worth shall still find here a place for their work." With Robert McAlmon's help, Miss Moorhead set out to make the farewell number an example of what *This Quarter* had always officially stood for: a place where young writers, inhabiting the "right quarter, the only one of importance to a literary magazine," could find a receptive response and, more often than not, acceptance of their first writings. Among the fifteen contributors, nearly half of them being published for the first time, were Edward Dahlberg, Graeme Taylor, John Glassco, and Paul Bowles; and others like McAlmon, Carnevali, Bravig Imbs, and Archibald Craig, old friends of the magazine and its editors, could hardly claim to have a prominence extending far beyond the little magazines.

As the new owner of *This Quarter*, Titus, above all, wanted to assure readers he had no intention of tampering seriously with the policies of the former editors. In reply to questions of why he had taken over the quarterly instead of starting "one from the egg up," whether any "goodwill" had accompanied the transaction, and whether or not he intended to follow in the footsteps of Miss Moorhead and Walsh, Titus could hardly have been more reassuring. "To tell the truth, although we have been watching *This Quarter* from its inception under the courageous editorship of our predecessors, we were never quite sure whither its footsteps led.

Not that it is essential to the quality of a publication of this character that it lead anywhere in particular. Its charm is so much greater if it proceed to unknown destinations and wander aimlessly over unsurveyed territories or drift heedlessly over plumbed and unplumbed seas. If it were Cookled, bent on cut and dried voyages and excursions, time-tabled, measured off correctly down to fractions of kilometers, we would have none of it." That that non-policy of his predecessors had succeeded in enriching the "domain of letters with such a gem as Ernest Hemingway's "The Undefeated," McAlmon's "The Mystical Forest," the haunting rhythms of Pound, and lines from the verse of Ernest Walsh was sufficient reason for providing a "modicum of perpetuation which we are so feebly able to allot to it." As for goodwill, Titus denied that this had played an important part in his acquisition of the magazine. "So far from any goodwill, it was rather, if the coinage be permitted, a sort of unmalicious and to all appearance straightforwardly righteous illwill, in which there was no participation on our part, that became intermixed with the transaction." It was

Ernest Walsh, editor of
This Quarter, Paris, 1925.
PRINCETON UNIVERSITY LIBRARY,
SYLVIA BEACH COLLECTION

Ethel Moorhead's retraction of the dedication to Pound that—however obliquely—had entered into the business of buying *This Quarter*. Disclaiming any interest in Miss Moorhead's motivations, but admitting that, if anything, the dedication understated rather than overstated Pound's qualities, Titus professed to admire the "passion, the *frenesie mystique*, the courage, the moral fervor, the gesture, the utterly rectitudinous illwill and the unprecedented irregularity" embodied in the quarrel, an unparalleled dispute, he concluded, in which a generation's Arbiter Poetarum was "thrown headlong from his eminence by the frail hand of brave little Ethel Moorhead."

Despite such plaudits for the achievements and artistry of his predecessors and the assurances that *This Quarter* would go on being as aimless and directionless and as receptive to new writers as before, the selections in the first number under Titus' editorship intimated that the new director had a marked preference for established professionals over untried novices. A contingent of familiar Anglo-Irish authors, including Herbert Read, D. H. Lawrence, T. F. Powys, Richard Aldington, and Liam O'Flaherty, and several of the Black Manikin authors and artists, notably Lewisohn, outnumbered the few writers like Graeme Taylor, Walter Lowenfels, and Genevieve Taggard who could conceivably be classified as young apprentices. Music was rather cursorily represented by Marc Blitzstein's essay, "Four American Composers," and the five illustrations, with the possible exception of E. E. Cummings' "Bal Negre" and Polia Chentoff's portrait of Dunning, were not much above the ordinary. But the commentaries on modern French literature by Harold J. Salemson and Victor Llona and the assessments of Baudelaire's knowledge of English by W. T. Bandy and "Gobineau and France" by Oscar Levy were informative if somewhat tedious contributions that foreshadowed later issues of *This Quarter* devoted to the art and literature of different European nations.

V

If Titus' first number lacked the originality and sense of surprise and verve that had been the hallmarks of *This Quarter*, it nonetheless offered a solid and respectable collection of fiction, criticism, and poetry, annoyingly academic and uncreative only to the critical few; for most readers, it reflected credit on its editor-publisher who, after noting with regret that both the *Little Review* and the *Dial* had expired the same year, gallantly announced that he intended "to go on marking time," a curious bit of understatement that masked the successful negotiations he had just completed with D. H. Lawrence for a Paris edition of *Lady Chatterley's Lover*, as well as for Lawrence's article "Pornography and Obscenity" for *This Quarter*. Even before he had finished writing the last of three versions, Lawrence had anticipated having trouble with *Lady Chatterley*. Publishers in England and America would not accept something so explicitly sexual; and if they did, it was bound to run into trouble with the censors eventually. Printing the book himself seemed the only alternative. With the help of the irrepressible Florentine bookseller Guiseppe Orioli, the intimate friend of Norman Douglas and the publisher of several of his books, Lawrence watched, alternately amused and appalled, as non-English-speaking compositors slowly brought into being what would henceforth be known as the first Florence edition of *Lady Chatterley's Lover*. A printing of a thousand copies, priced at two guineas each, sold out quickly by December 1928, netting the author a tidy profit. But with the demand still greater than the supply—one unexpected result of the book's publication—pirated editions began appearing on both sides of the Atlantic. Shocked as much by the thievery itself as by the shoddy quality of the facsimile editions—one American product, a "filthy-looking book bound in a dull orange cloth, with green label, smearily produced by photography," particularly bothered him—Lawrence decided to counter-attack by issuing a second edition of two hundred copies, far too few to stem the flood of pirated volumes. Although already seriously ill, but still determined to deprive the enemy of any further royalty-free profits at his expense, he set out to print another—and larger—edition in hopes it would satisfy the demand and thus deny the pirates at least part of the market they had commandeered for themselves. But in Paris, where he had gone looking for a publisher, his search seemed unpromising; even Sylvia Beach, who later remarked she had seldom met a more charming writer than Lawrence, showed no interest in taking on *Lady Chatterley*. She admitted privately that Lawrence's work did not interest her at all and that *Lady Chatterley*, a "kind of a sermon-on-the-Mount—of Venus," bored her more than most of his other preachy novels. She suggested, however, that Lawrence go to see another Paris publisher—Edward Titus —who might be willing to bring it out.

The agreement Lawrence worked out with Titus assured substantial profits for both. Titus would print three thousand copies, the cost price of each not to exceed twelve francs, the profits from which (the retail price was set at sixty francs a copy, with one-third off for the trade) would be divided between them—eight francs for Lawrence and seven for Titus. The cost of production they would share equally. Probably at Titus' insistence, they also agreed that the new edition should be more an inexpensive reprint, "photographed down from the original," that it should, in fact, contain some "new matter." Lawrence provided a twelve-page introduction called "My Skirmish with a Jolly Roger," which Titus promptly sold to Random House, with the understanding that the profits would be divided between them. Titus later told Frieda Lawrence he had violated his policy never to publish reprints only in the case of *Lady Chatterley*, and only then because Lawrence had agreed to supply the "new matter." The introduction gave Lawrence an opportunity to recount his novel's troubled history and to defend what he called the "real point" of the book: that "men and women" must "be able to think sex, fully, completely, honestly and cleanly . . . that the mind has to catch up, in sex: indeed, in all the physical acts. Mentally, we lag behind in our sexual thought, in a dimness, a lurking, grovelling fear which belongs to our raw, somewhat bestial ancestors. In this one respect, sexual and physical, we have left the mind unevolved. Now we have to catch up, and make a balance between the consciousness of the body's sensations and experiences, and these sensations and experiences themselves. Balance up the consciousness of the act, and the act itself. Get the two in harmony. It means having a proper reverence for sex, and a proper awe of the body's strange experience."

To assure the anticipated large sales of *Lady Chatterley*, Titus hired a "traveller," a salesman working for ten percent commission, who collected orders from booksellers outside the country. By late July Titus reported to Lawrence that "about 1000 copies" had been sold, and in August another four hundred. The same month Lawrence informed Aldous Huxley that Titus had sold the first three thousand copies and would be printing again. No doubt spurred by the success of these efforts, Titus approached Lawrence with two requests. "I am looking forward to the day when I shall be able frankly and without apprehension to put my imprint on *Lady Chatterley*, and not only on *Lady Chatterley*, but also on other books by you."* One Titus probably had in mind was *Pansies*, a

---

* Neither the title page nor the spine carried the Black Manikin imprint. The title page contained the following information: The Author's unabridged Popular Edition. *Lady Chatterley's Lover* Including "My Skirmish with a Jolly Roger," written Especially and Exclusively as an Introduction to this Popular Edition by D. H. Lawrence. Privately Printed 1929.

small collection of satiric poems Lawrence had sent his English publisher, Martin Secker, in January 1929, and which the publisher, on the recommendation of the home secretary, Sir William Loynson-Hicks ("Jix"), an outspoken enemy of Lawrence's, had brought out in an eviscerated version. Lawrence had countered by authorizing his friend Charles Lahr (the proprietor of a socialist bookshop in Red Lion Square who, in 1926, had printed Lawrence's story "Sun"), to issue an unexpurgated edition of *Pansies* (five hundred copies, plus fifty on Japanese vellum), plainly marked: "This limited edition is printed complete, following the original manuscript, according to my wish." Signed by D. H. Lawrence, and dated June 1929, the Lahr edition of *Pansies* was sold to subscribers (only) for thirty shillings; Lawrence eventually received £500, £1 for each copy sold. Titus' hope of publishing another edition of *Pansies*, already somewhat dampened by the appearance of the Lahr book, collapsed completely, however, when a second unexpurgated version (bound in plain red covers) appeared in Paris, presumably the work of the "Jolly Rogers."

Throughout the fall and winter Titus continued to petition Lawrence for a short piece he could publish under the Black Manikin imprint. In the same letter in which he announced that the second printing of *Lady Chatterley* had gone forward (September 9, 1929), he wondered if the novelist could send him a story of between 15 and 20,000 words for three or four plaquettes he planned to issue in editions of about 300 to 500 copies. His only request was that the story "would have to pass the censor." For this Titus was ready to pay 75 guineas. In January 1930, just after Titus had traveled to Lawrence's Riviera home at Bandol to turn over to him a payment of 7,672 francs (the author's earnings as of December 31, 1929 had reached the substantial sum of 41,352 francs, of which Titus had paid him nearly 38,000), Titus again proposed that Lawrence send him something. This time he increased the amount he was ready to pay for a long short story to 100 guineas, and reminded Lawrence of their understanding that he would be paid at the rate of "20 guineas each" for contributions to *This Quarter*. After Lawrence's death on March 2, 1930 (Titus attended his funeral), Titus' efforts to obtain an unpublished manuscript from the author's widow, Frieda, were no more successful than his earlier exertions. He was miffed when Frieda rejected his "Noble offer" of £500 for "Apocalypse" and instead gave Orioli permission to print the story, saying that she had promised him an "edition of 800," and that, besides, "Apocalypse" belonged to her, it being a gift from her husband. Even more frustrating was Frieda's rejection of an offer Titus said he was authorized to make on behalf of a London firm. In exchange for rights to publish "Apocalypse," the publisher would pay an advance of £5000, with royalties starting at fifteen percent and going up to twenty-five percent. Orioli had also gone ahead with a printing of *The Virgin and the Gypsy*, which, according to Frieda, Lawrence had approved sometime before his death; and in England, Titus noted, the Nonesuch Press had issued an edition of *Love Among the Haystacks* (with a Reminiscence by David Garnett). "Everybody in London," he complained, "has had new Lawrence stuff published but myself." And in Paris the Crosbys, who had brought out "Sun" in 1928, had printed a second Lawrence story, "The Escaped Cock," six months before his death. When news reached Titus that Orioli's publications had sold out, he redoubled his efforts to extract something from Frieda, this time insisting that he had taken on the publication of *Lady Chatterley* only because he had counted on publishing other Lawrence works, that the author had in fact promised him other things, and that Frieda herself had renewed Lawrence's promise after his death. As for the promise she had made to Orioli, why, he wondered, should that have "greater sanctity than promises made to" him? When Frieda did finally send an essay on Hardy, he was disappointed and replied: "I should not care to publish it because it does not at all fit into the frame of what I propose to do within the near future." With her permission, though, he would like to use two or three chapters in *This Quarter*. The chapters, however, never appeared. Despite his disappointment, Titus never permitted relations with Frieda to deteriorate to the point where *Lady Chatterley* might be in jeopardy. The same date on which he sent her a statement (December 1, 1930) which showed that Lawrence's share of the earnings on the first two printings of *Lady Chatterley* had reached 89,151 francs, he requested and got her approval to proceed with a third printing which, set at five thousand, would be only one thousand short of the total of the two earlier printings.

Whatever losses the two slim Black Manikin publications of 1929 incurred were many times compensated for by the large profits earned by Lawrence's book. The first, called *Windfalls*, was Dunning's second and, as it turned out, his last collection of verse (Dunning, after refusing to eat for weeks, died on July 3, 1930). Serving as a frontispiece was the Chentoff portrait of the poet that had earlier appeared in *This Quarter*. Ready with praise for his old protégé was Ezra Pound. Besides the intensity and vigor and "almost violence of visual imagination" that distinguished Dunning's latest work, Pound vouchsafed the observation that his friend's verse had passed through "thought and reentered the domain of instinct, where certain things are sure and do not need to be argued." Titus did well by his friend, too, ordering up an edition of 500 copies, of which 25 were printed on Imperial Japan paper which, with the author's signature, were offered for 100 francs a copy. The second Black Manikin book was another expensive affair (250 francs). Printed on heavy Monval Gris Rose hand-molded paper, in an edition of only 250 copies "for subscribers" and "friends of the translator and publisher," it bore the title *The Legend of Ermengarde* and was purportedly the work of the troubadour Uc Saine (Hugh Saxon). Titus announced it had been translated "into modern verse from the early fourteenth-century Provençal" by one Homer Rignaut, a pseudonym, Titus divulged, of a "well-known poet in his own right." The "amusing legend" of Ermengarde, as it was described in the announcement, combined weak verse and strong ribaldry.

VI

At the same time Titus was rejoicing over the publication of his "privately printed" *Lady Chatterley's Lover*, a book he claimed to have inspired two years earlier suddenly burst upon Paris, creating a "hubbub" in the press and columns of commentary in journals from the "extreme right" to the "extreme left." The object of all this attention was a loose-jointed memoir by a refugee Burgundian named Alice Prin, known throughout the Quarter as Kiki. Kiki, of course, was the mascot of Montparnasse, a buxom, sensuous, uninhibited café regular, orphaned at fifteen by an outraged mother who caught her posing nude for an old sculptor, and subsequently adopted by a string of artists who, if one judges by their portraits of her, were enraptured as much by her childlike innocence as by her exotic physical traits: slanting, feline, green eyes; bobbed hair, black bangs, and spit curls; and an outrageously painted face. The first to embrace Kiki as model and mistress was the "fierce-looking" Chaim Soutine, who obligingly burned up his furniture to keep her warm. After Soutine, in random order, came Modigliani ("All he did was growl; he used to make me shiver from head to foot."); Kisling ("A great little playmate."); Utrillo, who drew a "little country house" once while she posed for him; Foujita ("He was charming. I was simply crazy about him."); Per Krogh, whose recreation, pinching her in the rump, left her cold; and Man Ray ("He has an accent that I like and a kind of mysterious way with him."), in whose quiet quarters she sojourned longest. Montparnassians occasionally amused themselves by attending well-publicized exhibits of Kiki's work, consisting of one-dimensional studies of nudes, à la Matisse; animated scenes of schoolchildren, sailors, nurses, and circus performers, colorful and naive; and a few inspired portraits of loyal admirers such as Foujita and Henri Broca.

For over two years Titus had urged the laggardly Kiki "to buckle down to the job" of writing her memoirs. "Generous enough with promises, she always stopped short of performance, until a better man made his appearance at court,—the enterprising, persuasive Henri Broca, who understood how to make Kiki alive to the gravity of promises and take pen in hand." And then, responding to Broca's prodding and direction, at twenty-eight, she finally set down the slight but, as Titus admiringly called them, "rough and ready" chapters, which Broca published as *Les Souvenirs de Kiki de Montparnasse*, with an introduction by her friend Foujita. Broca's success with Kiki may have been due to the fact that he and Kiki had quickly become, in the words of Wambly Bald, "excellent friends." Like her, an underdisciplined child, he had shed paternal bonds early, and after an adolescence marred by the most excruciating adventures had landed in Montparnasse, penniless and desperate. The writer André Dahl found work for him first as a cabaret handyman and then as an illustrator for *D'Artagnan, Le Soir*, and *Le Petit Journal*. In 1926 Broca turned publisher, issued a sketchbook of familiar Montparnasse characters, and two years later, in an effort to record the "official life" of the Quarter, founded a monthly called *Paris-Montparnasse*, staffed only by the photographer Man Ray and himself. Functioning ambidextrously as publisher, reporter, copyreader, artist, and editor, he tirelessly doted on the achievements of his favorites: Foujita, Kisling, André Salmon, and Kiki. Being Kiki's publisher brought Broca some acclaim but, by 1931, being the companion of the "Queen of Montparnasse" was beginning to take a toll, and while Kiki, who had "less imagination" but "more vitality" than Broca, was still the "life of the party," Broca had collapsed and retreated to a sanatorium, "obliged to rest."

Couched in his customary donnish idiom, Titus explained that he "could not without affectation show" himself "indifferent to the success which the *Memoirs* had met with." And without mentioning what arrangements he had made with Broca and Kiki, if any, he announced that the "issue of the English version [had] devolved on" him, and that Kiki, no doubt responding to his request, had "amplified" her book "by the addition of about twenty pages of manuscript . . . absent from the French

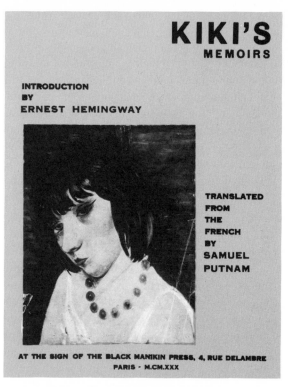

KIKI'S MEMOIRS

INTRODUCTION
BY
ERNEST HEMINGWAY

TRANSLATED
FROM
THE
FRENCH
BY
SAMUEL
PUTNAM

AT THE SIGN OF THE BLACK MANIKIN PRESS, 4, RUE DELAMBRE
PARIS · M.CM.XXX

Title page and portrait of Kiki from *Kiki's Memoirs*
(Black Manikin Press, 1930).
PRINCETON UNIVERSITY LIBRARY

edition." To translate Kiki into English Titus turned to Sam Putnam, a midwesterner and former art and literary critic for the *Chicago Evening Post*, who, after an exhausting study and research junket through nine countries, made possible by a stipend provided by the Chicago publisher Pascal Covici in exchange for translating services Putnam had promised him, had finally settled down in Paris with his wife and child. Like so many others living in the Quarter, Putnam was under the "constant necessity" of earning whatever he could, and so, towards the end of 1929, when Titus asked him to help with *This Quarter*, he accepted and was appointed associate editor. For one who had already devoted years to translating Rabelais, the memoirs of the "Queen of Montparnasse" would hardly seem to be a challenge. Yet, according to Putnam's note on the translation, two problems emerged at once, one so formidable that he professed it was enough "to frighten off a hardier hand than mine." That problem, it turned out, had nothing to do with the text itself. Rather, it arose from the

146

Preface which Titus had inveigled Ernest Hemingway to write, and which he had, for good reasons, not shown to Putnam until after he had started his translation. Hemingway, who had read the original French version of Kiki's book, concluded in his Preface that not only would it be a crime to translate Kiki but that the effort, regardless of whoever undertook to do it, could only end in being a "bad job." He advised prospective readers of Kiki to learn French so that they could read it in the original. No less intimidating was Kiki herself or, as Putnam put it, the problem was "not to translate Kiki's text, but to translate Kiki"; and to do that, he continued, "'one must have the feel of Kiki, the feel of the Café du Dôme at five o'clock on a rainy, bleary, alcoholic morning." And yet even that hardly sufficed. It would not be fair to Kiki. What was needed, he speculated, was the "feel of a St. Theresa who should suddenly materialize in the Café du Dôme at the hour mentioned," for it was St. Theresa that Kiki, as unlikely as it seemed, most resembled, according to Putnam, and it was this inspiring similarity that made him proud to be her St. Jerome, the patron saint of all translators. Rendering the "divine Kiki" into English, however, imposed demands that even St. Jerome might have found strenuous. "Do not be deceived by her naivetés," Putnam warned, or even her gaucheries; her prose is the most subtle that I know. At rare moments, you think of a remote sort of Anita Loos flapper; but the next moment, you banish the thought as sacrilege. I know, absolutely, of no other prose with which to compare this; I know of none so hiddenly delicate, so deceptively nuanced —not even Fanny Hill. . . . In fact, Kiki's prose is as fine an example as any I know of that quality on which French classicists so pride themselves: *clarté*. And *clarté*, the French themselves will be the first to tell you, is a highly deceptive entity." Despite the trials he envisioned at the start of his task, Putnam assured readers that he had approached it "reverently, never once doubting the plenary inspiration" of the text before him, but that, unfortunately, its completion had not completely silenced his nagging doubts about whether Kiki was really translatable. For whatever mistakes he had committed—including that of undertaking the translation in the first place—he asked forgiveness, first of God, then of Kiki, and if granted by both, then of Hemingway himself.

In his Preface, Hemingway showed as much appreciation for Kiki's appearance as for her literary style. "It was very pleasant, after working, to see Kiki. She was very wonderful to look at. Having a fine face to start with, she had made of it a work of art. She had a wonderfully beautiful body and a fine voice, talking voice, not singing voice." As for her book, it was among the best he had read since Cummings' *The Enormous Room*, and he assured readers tired of reading books by "present-day lady writers of all sexes" that it was the work of a "woman who was never a lady"; in fact, a part of it reminded him of Moll Flanders. And by way of suggesting the stature Kiki had achieved in Montparnasse Hemingway evoked the name of another, grander lady, Queen Victoria, declaring that Kiki had dominated the Montparnasse era of the 1920s even more completely than Victoria had possessed the age that bore her name. But like Victoria, Kiki's age had passed too; Montparnasse had "become rich, prosperous, brightly lighted, dancing-ed, shredded-wheated, grape-nuts-ed or grapenutted." Caviar was even being sold at the Dôme. An era, Kiki's, had ended, he proclaimed. It was a period bounded by his arrival in Paris in 1921 and the publication of Kiki's *Memoirs*, a time for which he had already expressed contempt and which, now that it had ended, and even Kiki had begun to look "like a monument to herself," he could again assail in stronger language: "Montparnasse for this purpose means the cafés and the restaurants where people are seen in public. It does not mean the apartments, studios and hotel rooms where they work in private. In the old days the difference between the workers and those that didn't work was that the bums could be seen at the cafés in the forenoon. This of course was not entirely true as the greatest bums, using the word in the American rather than in the English connotation, did not rise until about five o'clock when, on entering the cafés, they would drink in friendly competition with the workers who had just knocked off work for the day. The worker goes to the café with the lonesomeness that a writer or painter has after he has worked all day and does not want to think about it until the next day but instead see people and talk about anything that is not serious and drink a little before supper. And maybe during and after supper, too, depending on the individual. . . . The Era is over. It passed along with the kidneys of the workers who drank too long with the bums. The bums were fine people and proved to have the stronger kidneys finally. But then they rested during the day. Still that Era is over."

The Hemingway and Putnam contributions, despite their contrariness, delighted Titus. The former's Preface, written with "Great gusto," possessed "to perfection, in English, the very idiom which Kiki wields so matchlessly in French." Putnam's translation was a "capital job." As for their being at "loggerheads over the English translation," both men, he concluded, had simply been "decanting poppycock." St. Jerome himself would have liked Kiki's *Memoirs*, particularly the "homespun colloquialism of Putnam's English version," and furthermore would have said so, protected by time and space "against a possible menace of Ernest Hemingway's gladiatorial bulk and sinewy arm." Printed by Darantière in large format, on heavy, glossy paper, with illustrations by Kiki (over twenty-five paintings and sketches), photographs of the author by Man Ray and portraits by Kisling, Foujita, Hermine David, Mayo, and Tono Salazar, the *Memoirs* comprised a sumptuous package, indeed, a fitting valedictory for an era which, Hemingway's notices of interment to the contrary, still showed a few life signs. Wambly Bald, concerned that Kiki had come perilously close to "spreading into a legend," of becoming "unreal," credited Putnam with having rescued her from that fate by revealing that life in her world was as simple as breathing, and, in return, Bald reported, a grateful Kiki had offered to learn English in order to translate anything Putnam ever wrote.

By coincidence rather than design another book Titus published in 1930 assailed the same weaknesses for which Hemingway had berated his fellow Quarterites. William Van Wyck, in his second Black Manikin book, a free verse poem titled *On the Terrasse*, brings together an improbable pair: George F. Babbitt and a Montparnassian named Scott. Babbitt, unsurprisingly, professes to be shocked by everything he sees and hears around the Quarter, and in language that echoes Hemingway's, he complains: "I've seen more bums around this damned café/ In just ten days, than I have seen before/ In twenty years of work in Winnemac." That reputed anathema among Quarterites, work, is what bothers him most. "Where would they be without their monthly checks?" The answer: "Back in the old hometown, and working hard/ For three square eats a day."— like Babbitt. Almost as upsetting, because hypocritical, is the discovery that for the "guzzling" artists clustered at the Dôme, America is the "hope of European art," the bourgeois marketplace supported by industrious "hicks' like Babbitt which all intend to invade. And yet, Babbitt snickers, "These poor bums swill booze and patronize/ The men who do things in America." The sight of so many "boys and girls" slumming out their lives among fairies and lesbians, swilling booze and spilling bunk and experimenting with dope, is an affront to his accomplishments and to the country that made them possible: "Call me a hick or bourgeois if you like,/ But call me a good fellow too, for I/ Have helped my land to prosper and to grow,/ You've got to say that Babbitt is a man."

Scott, in a riposte surprisingly brief and benign, avoids Babbitt's accusations and advances the rather adolescent adage that one "must taste life to get experience," presumably best done in the Quarter. Missing from Babbitt's discourse was any mention of beauty, an important omission, according to Scott, for it not only reveals that Babbitt's aesthetic sense has not gone beyond material comforts and wealth but that Scott and his companions possess, in abundance, what poor Babbitt cannot even contemplate: beauty of soul. "Our eyes see beauty, and our hearts are filled/ With longings to create." Finally, Scott chides Babbitt on a subject he suspects has become as much of a routine as the rest of his life: "We know more of love in one night than you do in twenty years."

On the Terrasse, a late and limp entry in the debate Paris journalists had conducted for years on the vices and virtues of life in Montparnasse, did little to advance either side. Notwithstanding Van Wyck's arguments in favor of the Quarter that he himself inhabited—the dedication to Richard Aldington carefully noted that Aldington "adorns the Dôme terrasse occasionally and letters permanently"—the gusto with which Babbitt defines and delivers his denunciations carries at least the suggestion that the author might have found the detractor more fascinating than the defender. However, two sketches of the Dôme terrasse by the author's daughter, Margery Nahl, showing figures strangely somnolent and serene, and a generous format designed by Darantière, and covers in marbled swirls of red, yellow and green, raised the volume, at least typographically, to an aesthetic level that vindicated some of Scott's claims.

VII

If in the early 1930s Titus thought he had not quite yet received his acclaim as a "man of letters," he must have believed that the time had come to enforce that delayed recognition. Of the little publishers in the Quarter, he had outlasted McAlmon, Bird, and Sylvia Beach (the final edition of *Ulysses* over which she presided as publisher had come out), and of their successors only Nancy Cunard's Hours Press, then itself about to expire, had published the work of unknown writers. Black Sun and Harrison had turned to issuing reprints and the classics. Although one of the two projects Titus announced in 1929 had failed—the theatre never got beyond the planning stage—*This Quarter* had thrived. Contributors to the second number included Natalie Clifford Barney, Claude McKay, André Maurois, Sholem Asch, Countee Cullen, Morley Callaghan, Bob McAlmon, and Rhys Davies. In the same number Titus announced the creation of the "Richard Aldington Poetry Prize" of twenty-five francs "to

Waverley Lewis Root, Paris
Tribune book critic,
New York, 1939.
COURTESY OF RALPH
JULES FRANTZ

be awarded to the ablest young American poet whose work has appeared in *This Quarter*." Three months later Titus matched Aldington's award by offering a prize to the "ablest young English poet whose work has appeared in *This Quarter*," to be known as the "Edward W. Titus English Poetry Prize." And then, in a rush of beneficence that combined "a spirit of sportsmanship with a great love for poetry." William Van Wyck upped the bounty by offering an additional prize of twenty-five hundred francs to the "abler" of the winners of the English and American poetry prizes, the latter, "thanks to Mr. Aldington's personal efforts to enlist public-spirited support" for the contests, now increased to ten thousand francs.

   With Putnam's help (he joined Titus in time to prepare the third number of *This Quarter*, dated January/February/March 1930), Titus produced the first of what would be several issues devoted to the writing of various European nations, the first appropriately being France, represented by Paul Valéry, André Spire, Pierre Minet, Leon Lemonnier, Roger Vitrac, and Arthur Rimbaud, whose half dozen poems Titus translated himself. For the fourth number, Putnam, an aficionado of modern

Italian writing, collected examples of contemporary Italian literature translated by Gabriele d'Annunzio, Luigi Pirandello, Arturo Loria, and a dozen others. Titus announced that the next issue would be devoted to Russian writing and subsequent numbers to German, Spanish, and Polish, an innovation he called "both useful and interesting." More self-serving interpretations turned up in a resumé called "The First Twelvemonth," where, with obvious pride, Titus wrote that after editing *This Quarter* for a year he was pleased to say that he had thrust no manifestos upon the world, had not tried to be "modern beyond the day or reason" (a pointed reference to *transition*), had compiled no platform or programs, had eschewed literary politics despite the difficulties of doing so in the "seething cauldron" of Paris, and had "kept clear of unbalanced isms in literature." Henceforward, *This Quarter* would remain unattached but would open its pages to an even larger number of writers "of all schools." Of his past achievements, foremost was the assemblage of contributors *This Quarter* had presented in its first four numbers. "We venture to say that no periodical published in the English language, certainly none published in that language in a foreign country, has within the covers of four issues brought together such a constellation of contributors as it has been our pleasure and privilege to put before our readers this past year. Side by side with contributions by writers of prominence we have published material in prose and verse by writers as yet unknown or unestablished." Readers were invited to scan the index of the first year's offerings to see for themselves whether the editor had cause to describe the results as "very creditable, discriminating and well-balanced." Kudos, fortunately, came from outside the rue Delambre office, too. A critic for the Paris *Tribune* judged the fourth number of *This Quarter* the "best," and complimented the editor on his spirited criticism of the *Imagist Anthology* edited by Ford Madox Ford and Glenn Hughes. The only disappointment another writer for the same newspaper found important enough to mention was that no English or American poet had yet been awarded either of the poetry prizes. Titus replied, complaining that the "dearth of poetic material" was "astounding," and that the "total amount of good work" upon which he had been able to draw had been "so small as to afford, in reality, no basis for a decision that would mean anything." Still hoping for an improvement, however, the three donors had decided to extend the time limit for an additional year. Can it be, Titus speculated, that "poets no longer need money?" Perhaps, rejoined the journalist: "Evidently all of the creatures we see about the Quarter who look "like what poets are believed to look like are merely posing poverty. Perhaps they have plenty of cash in the bank."

Proof that *This Quarter* was working as a conduit for new writers (Titus repeatedly asked Quarterites, including Sylvia Beach, to send him "young meritorious writers who find it difficult to get their work published") came in an announcement, issued in 1931, that Black Manikin would publish "a series of original novelettes by prominent writers of fiction," in signed and numbered editions of five hundred, available for 150 francs (six dollars). Selected to begin the series were Ludwig Lewisohn, Morley Callaghan, and Kathleen Coyle, all of whom had appeared in *This Quarter*. Titus also disclosed that Black Manikin would print a new edition of *The Case of Mr. Crump*, with a preface by Thomas Mann, as well as a collection of regional verse by Laura Sherry, a midwesterner, who, in addition to being the founder of the first experimental theatre in America—the Wisconsin Players of Milwaukee—had become something of a folklore specialist on the French settlers who had populated a remote region of Wisconsin in the late 1600s. In her Introduction to *Old Prairie Du Chien*—Mrs. Sherry's title was the name of one of the settlements—Zona Gale praised the author's ability to capture the elusive, "the particular of a region, a culture; and the general intimation of us all." Alfred Kreymborg, swelling the chorus of praise, remarked on Mrs. Sherry's "unique evocation of the soil and the spirit of an old corner of Wisconsin," and Carl Sandburg tersely labeled one of her character sketches "an achievement." Titus added that Mrs. Sherry had "done in poetry for Wisconsin what Hamlin Garland and Glenway Wescott had done in prose."

Titus was not the first to publish the work of a young Canadian lawyer-turned-writer named Morley Callaghan. That distinction belongs to McAlmon, or, more accurately, to Ethel Moorhead and Ernest Walsh who, at McAlmon's urging, printed Callaghan's story "A Girl with Ambition" in the second number of *This Quarter*. His appearance in *This Quarter* preceded by only a few months the publication of a second story, "Last Spring They Came Over," in *transition* magazine, with whose editor, Eugene Jolas, McAlmon was also on friendly terms; and a reappearance in the third number of *This Quarter* with the story "A Wedding Dress." Still another short story had been selected by the editors of the yearbook *The American Caravan* (1927), and this one had the good fortune to be read by Maxwell Perkins, the Scribner's editor and friend of

Hemingway and Fitzgerald. When Perkins mentioned to the latter that he had liked Callaghan's work, Fitzgerald showed him one of the stories that had been printed in Paris, and Perkins, his enthusiasm quickened, asked Callaghan to send him another, and meanwhile obtained one of the two stories Callaghan had earlier submitted to Ezra Pound's magazine, *Exile*. By the time Callaghan met Perkins in New York, having sent ahead, in addition to the requested story, a novel called *Strange Fugitive*, Pound had written directly to Perkins, giving him permission to use the Callaghan story but excoriating the editor for having wasted years "publishing worthless junk," despite the fact that Perkins had taken on Hemingway and was now interested in Callaghan. To a "puzzled and aggrieved" Perkins, Callaghan suggested that maybe Pound had just taken the opportunity to vent his rage against all publishers who had failed "to recognize authentic writers," and that Scribner's certainly had "proven they were aware of authentic work." Regardless of whether the explanation satisfied Perkins (he had made it clear to Callaghan that he "had an abusive champion whose temperament was past his understanding"), Pound's tirade did not lessen his interest in Callaghan, for at the end of their visit he remarked, quite casually, that Scribner's would bring out *Strange Fugitive* and, at a later date, his collection of stories.

If Callaghan called McAlmon his "first patron," it was Ernest Hemingway who, ever since the two men had met in the library of the *Toronto Star* in the fall of 1923, had been his "only reader and booster," and who, on returning to Paris at the end of that year, had handed his stories over to McAlmon. Callaghan had kept up a correspondence with both men, desultory with Hemingway, steadier and more intense with McAlmon, who, in one of his letters, complained about a "hardening process" in Hemingway's writing which, McAlmon was happy to report, was not present in Callaghan's. What the Canadian writer learned when he finally arrived in Paris in the summer of 1929 was that his two American supporters were barely on speaking terms, and that McAlmon, apparently piqued by Hemingway's success and convinced Hemingway had forgotten him, missed few opportunities to run down his old friend. Being indebted to both put Callaghan in an awkward position, in no way relieved by the fact that, despite McAlmon's "destructive malice," he still liked the nervous, arrogant publisher with the "contemptuous tilt to his head." For one thing, it was evident that if a "man of talent" needed help, McAlmon would "help him if he could." Though Callaghan's account of his sojourn

in Paris (*That Summer in Paris*) is devoted mainly to the relations between him and Hemingway and Fitzgerald, McAlmon, for once, emerges
from the deep literary shadows to which most memorialists of the period
usually relegate him. Often in McAlmon's company, and even for a time
occupying the same hotel with him, Callaghan saw as much of his "patron" as the summer advanced as he did of Hemingway and Fitzgerald.
And of McAlmon's many café acquaintances two came to have a special
importance for the author. Like Callaghan, John Glassco, and Graeme
Taylor—the "bright boys from Montreal," as McAlmon called them—
had benefited from the interest McAlmon had taken in their work. It was
McAlmon who had persuaded Ethel Moorhead to print their first writings
in her final number of *This Quarter*, and as McAlmon's companions they
had met the Quarter's "celebrities" and were beginning to attract a certain
amount of attention themselves, as Callaghan realized at their first meeting. "Two slender boys in their early twenties, they were inseparable
companions, very understanding of each other, soft-spoken with a mocking opinion about everybody. They were writers. One of them had some
money of his own, but not much. Within a few hours of meeting them we
seemed to know ten or twelve other people at the café."

The boys McAlmon also called, affectionately, the "clever little
devils" were the inspiration of the two pieces of writing—a short story
and a novella—that Callaghan somehow managed to write during his busy
summer in Paris. Both were published in Paris, not by McAlmon, but by
Edward Titus, whom Callaghan and his wife got into the habit of meeting
at the Select, sometimes in the company of Madame Rubinstein, then
"growing stout, but still dark, handsome and full of energy." One evening,
in a reversal of the usual process, Callaghan introduced McAlmon to a
man he had never met, Edward Titus, and while the group sat listening to
McAlmon tell how Zelda Fitzgerald "had cast a lustful eye at him" (a not
unusual assumption, according to Callaghan, when McAlmon "had had a
drink or two"), "along the street came those two willowy graceful young
men from Montreal," Glassco and Taylor. Entering the café "with their
bland and distinguished air," they bowed to the group, and were acknowledged by Callaghan's "lighthearted wave of the hand," a gesture that drew
from McAlmon the remark that Callaghan did not "understand those two
at all." What McAlmon thought of "those two" and what Callaghan knew
McAlmon did not know about them—that their "snickering wit" could be
turned on him in his absence—amused Callaghan, and for every claim

McAlmon made Callaghan returned a contrasting view. Titus, enlivened by their "jibing and jeering at each other" and "brightening and becoming an alert editor," suggested that both men should confide their thoughts to stories which he would publish, "side by side," in *This Quarter*. Though both agreed, only Callaghan set down his impressions in a story called "Now That April's Here," which Titus, true to his word, printed shortly after the author had returned to Canada, after having turned down Titus' offer to be editor of *This Quarter*.

Though the settings of Callaghan's two pieces are different—the story occurring mainly in Paris, the novella in the Canadian northland—the milieu that inspired them is instantly recognizable as the surcharged, frenzied Montparnasse the author saw in 1929. Just as easily identified are portraits of Glassco, Taylor, and McAlmon who, as Stan Mason, describes Charles Milford (Taylor) and Johnny Hill (Glassco) as the "brightest youngsters who had come to the Quarter in years," that is, until the night he overhears them laughing and snickering at him. Masking their conceit behind a wide-eyed innocence the inseparable twosome roam the Quarter, being amused and amusing others, and occasionally interrupting their rounds long enough to write—Johnny, on his memoirs inspired by George Moore's *Confessions of a Young Man*; Charles, on his short stories. In time, however, the fun stops, ironically in April, the month they prophesied would be the gayest of all, but which turns out to be as cruel as Eliot's. Separation, at first only temporary and then permanent, divide Charles and Johnny, their covenant broken by a "fat-faced girl with a boy's body and short hair dyed red," who is ready to live with anyone and gradually allows Johnny to annex her. Charles, "very much in love with Johnny" and appalled at the thought of losing him to the "fat-faced girl," implores his friend not to let "a little tart" smash things. Shocked by the epithet, Johnny strikes his friend across the face, which leaves them both crying and helplessly shaking until they are found by Mason who takes Charles home with him. Later, when he tells Charles that Johnny is returning to America with the "fat-faced girl," he shakes his head and sighs: "How could he hit me, how could he hit me, and he knew I loved him so much."

Although it has been pointed out that the two women in *No Man's Meat* (the title of the novella), Jean and Teresa, are the "counterparts" of Johnny and Charles and that the respective works in which they appear are studies of homosexual love, it is also worth noting that while the male homosexuals are finally separated the lesbian attachment between Jean and Teresa has at least the appearance of permanency, and it is affirmed despite the presence—or perhaps because of the presence—of Teresa's husband Bert, who, unaware of Jean's homosexuality, has shamefacedly made love to her after she had lost a wager in which she staked "her virtue" against his fifty dollars. That experience, traumatic for both, is partly repaired by Teresa who, after she comforts Jean, tells Bert that Jean had left her husband, not for another man, but for a young woman with whom she had fallen in love, and that now "she can hardly stand to be touched by a man." The full import of Lucretias's maxim ("One man's meat is another man's poison.") along with Callaghan's twist descends on Bert the morning after. Having spent the night with Jean, Teresa obligingly drives her to the station, but not, it appears, with the intention of saying goodbye to a friend. At noon, a stranger, a "townman," delivers a note from Teresa informing Bert that she had never known how much she had loved Jean herself and that she could not return to him for a long time.

According to a Paris reviewer, "Morley Callaghan's story had to be printed in Paris, or nowhere. It is strong meat." Nothing of the sort could ever be said, however, about the other two novellas, Kathleen Coyle's *There Is a Door* and Lewisohn's *The Romantic*. Miss Coyle's story is a parable: Johnny, the hero, at times reminiscent of Synge's bumptious hero of *The Playboy of the Western World*, flees the "mainland" believing he is guilty of murdering his father. Taking refuge on an island inhabited by a mysterious figure known only as Her and her beautiful young companion named Andrea, he learns he is innocent of the crime that brought him there. Her tells him: "There was no murder in your heart. Anger is the same substance. It is a slayer." To his protest that he wanted to be "free," Her replies: "You are free now." He is also granted forgiveness, and with Andrea, who longs to exchange the peace of her Edenic bower for the trials of the mainland, he departs, chastised and aware he has been a great fool.

Lewisohn labeled *The Romantic* "a contemporary legend." The exiled Baron of Tamaczvar passes long days pining for his Carpathian homeland and silently ignoring his wife, whose "vapid contentedness" mocks the spontaneity of the young woman his social climbing father once forbid him to marry, and who also forced him to forsake his religious heritage, Judaism, for the national faith, Roman Catholicism. A virtual

stranger at home, even before being forced into exile by a political coup
that put a reactionary dictator in power, the Baron hopes to end his sense
of homelessness when he accepts an invitation to return to Carpathia to
work for the country's restoration. Once inside the borders of his homeland, however, he is arrested and charged with "spiritual treason" and
"opposing the national will," against which his patriotism ("love of the
patria") proves to be a totally inadequate defense. Found guilty of being
an enemy of the state, church, king and Christ, the Baron, now "disgusted
with a homeless world," with himself, with mankind, awaits death convinced that his real crime is being a Jew, one of the "alien benefactors"
the Carpathians secretly long to destroy. If he must die as a Jew, he
decides he will die as the martyrs of his people had. True to his vow, the
Baron gives the command to fire at his own execution, after which an
impressed captain says, "They die game, these Jews."

VIII

Seven years after he had published the first Black Manikin book and
four years after taking over *This Quarter*, Titus decided to end his joint
career as publisher and editor. In the spring of 1932 the last book to bear
the imprint "Published at the Sign of the Black Manikin" appeared, and it
was followed at the end of the year by the final number of *This Quarter*.
He allowed neither to expire ingloriously. The last Black Manikin selection, *D. H. Lawrence, An Unprofessional Study*, by Anais Nin, became one
of the most sought-after books the press ever issued. As she confirmed in the
first volume of her protracted *Diary*, Anais Nin in the early thirties inhabited a "beautiful prison," in the village of Louveciennes, tantalizingly
close to Paris but where visits were discouraged by a disapproving and
watchful mother. In protest against the dull, uninteresting "ordinary life"
of the village ("I mend socks, prune trees, can fruits, polish furniture. But
while I am doing this I feel I am not living."), Miss Nin, like Walter
Pater, pursued "only the high moments" of existence, what the surrealists
were calling the "Marvelous." Her writing, which for a time she thought
would provide the "only escape" from imprisonment, would extol those
exalted moments when life was at its "highest level," when it consisted of
"infinite space, infinite meaning, infinite dimension." The inspiring force
behind her effort was D. H. Lawrence. It was he, she confided, who
awakened me, and for whom, "out of gratitude," she had decided to write
her first book.

Although she later doubted whether being a writer would accelerate her "escape from Louveciennes," it is a fact that it took her just sixteen days to write her appreciation of Lawrence and that she herself delivered it to Titus in Paris. The publisher, presumably unimpressed with the velocity with which the work had come into being and then into his hands, and feeling no obligation to rush it into print, handed it over to an assistant to revise, an action which, understandably, brought from Miss Nin the familiar protest that a book should be published when it is "hot out of the oven, when it is alive within one's self."* To help her draw up a contract with Titus, Miss Nin called on Richard Osborn, an American friend, who, in her words, was "trying to be both a Bohemian and a lawyer for a big firm," and whose fate, she predicted, would be to "fall somewhere between his lawyer's office (on the Right Bank) and Montparnasse." In the meantime, Osborn had developed "two recurrent monologues"—plagiarism and Henry Miller—and of the first, he complained to Miss Nin, he was the defenseless victim, having lost the manuscript of a novel someone else had just published. Of the other, however, he was pleased to tell her, he was a grateful benefactor. Miller, after wandering around Paris for months, cadging meals and drinks and sleeping in a different place every night, had accepted Osborn's offer to share his hotel room and salary. Every morning Osborn would leave ten francs on the table near Miller's bed, and on his return in the evening he would find a batch of writing in place of the money. One day Osborn showed Miss Nin a review Miller had written of Luis Buñuel's film *L'Age d'Or*. It struck her with the potency of a bomb. The "primitive, savage quality" of the writing was like "hearing wild drums in the midst of the Tuileries gardens," or in her own imprisoning garden at Louveciennes, which increasingly resembled a form of hibernation. Predictably, with Osborn serving as emissary, it was Miller who effected her release. When Osborn showed Miller her Lawrence manuscript, the novelist remarked that he had "never read such strong truths told with such delicacy." That encomium, added to Osborn's insistence that she should meet his friend, brought an invitation to visit Louveciennes, a visit Miss Nin anticipated would bring together "delicacy and

---

* Miss Nin later lodged other complaints against Titus. In the third volume of her *Diary* she wrote: "The book was but partially distributed, half lost, not sent to reviewers [Waverley Root, however, reviewed it in the Paris *Tribune*], and no royalties and not even copies for myself." She does add, though, that the book caused Titus to go bankrupt.

159

violence" to "challenge each other." That first encounter verified some of her premonitions.

Henry Miller, she perceived, was capable of showing two sides of himself simultaneously: "acceptance and passivity in life, rebellion and anger at whatever happened to him. He endured, and then must avenge himself, probably in his writing." But it was his newness, toughness, his Dostoyevskian character, his worldliness, his vast experience and intelligence that both delighted and intimidated her. How could he, who seemed to have lived so completely, be interested in her, an innocent, sheltered and conventional in so many ways? The question, today, seems redundant, for almost immediately Miss Nin was completely absorbed by Henry Miller and, one gathers, he by her. His needs—whether a typewriter, a set of Proust, a meal, or "a home, an income, security," were what she lived to provide.

What Anais Nin came to admire in Henry Miller she had already picked out as the key to Lawrence's philosophy: his was a philosophy that demanded a "transcending of ordinary values," values that would be "vivified and fecundated by instincts and intuitions." To experience Lawrence one must realize philosophy as a "passionate blood-experience." His system was a "system of mobility," a constant shifting of values which discarded "stability" as an "obstacle to creative livingness." Since the liberating forces she discovered in Lawrence had precipitated her own sudden awakening, which had led to the end of imprisonment in the "beautiful garden," it is scarcely surprising to find her extolling Lawrence as a savior. "He hit the center, the vulnerable center of our bodies with his physical language, his physical vision. He hit us vitally." Not only had he thought and felt everything, "he greatly cared . . . and his voice had strange, potent accents." Alone, "he went . . . through hell. And the more experiences he went through, the more he understood." All that he had finally understood, she felt, had gone into *Lady Chatterley's Lover*, paradoxically his "fleshliest" and "most mystical work," and artistically his "best novel because one idea is sustained to its conclusion with intensity and clarity." Lawrence's celebration of the "ecstasy of the flesh which transfigures" must have approximated, even if only vicariously, those experiences of high emotion for which Miss Nin ostensibly lived. The ecstasy, however, as she came to appreciate, was not intellectual; certainly love could not be "mentally directed love." It was instinctual, a correspondence of blood. In *Lady Chatterley's Lover*, Lawrence gave "an honest picture of all the aspects and moods of physical love," awakening

Outside Hilaire Hiler's Jockey Club, Montparnasse, 1930s. *From left to right, seated*: Tristan Tzara, Jean Cocteau; *standing*: Man Ray, Hilaire Hiler, unknown, Ezra Pound, unknown, unknown, Curtis Moffit.

those who wanted to be awakened, and doing it by deliberately using "naked words" to revive the primitive feelings and responses that evasive language—and living—had atrophied. As a mentor, Lawrence had clearly guided his pupil away from the sheltered life of Louveciennes; and what she called Lawrence's "chief preoccupation"—a "choice between life and death, or rather, between complete life and death"—became, in time, her own.

Putnam's association with *This Quarter* was predictably brief. In the first place, he had joined Titus out of necessity rather than out of any interest in or regard for the editor or his magazine, and the two men often disagreed over the contents. Titus' conservative tastes, the result largely of the literary precepts he had absorbed while living in England, collided with Putnam's more progressive views. Since only "name" writers, according to Putnam, would lead Titus "to violate his personal preferences," his list tended to run to Ludwig Lewisohn and Michael Arlen. Inevitably, they quarreled over James Farrell who, besides lacking a "name," had struck Titus as a man who could not write. For weeks during the spring of 1930 Farrell had inundated Putnam with bundles of short stories so impressive that Putnam was determined to get them published, if not in *This Quarter*, then in a magazine of his own devising, if necessary. Titus' reaction, however, exceeded Putnam's worst expectations. "This is rot!" he exclaimed. "For God's sake, tell that chap out in Chicago to stop sending us this tripe!" In the end, determination proved stronger than invective. The last number of *This Quarter* with which Putnam was associated (July–September 1930) contained Farrell's story "Stud," his first to be published abroad. It was the "only thing I accomplished" as associate editor of *This Quarter*, Putnam later admitted. The expected showdown with Titus—probably hastened by the Farrell quarrel—came in the fall of 1930; and, as the account Putnam later sent to his friend Bob Brown suggests, it was both noisy and dramatic. "Some weeks ago, I gave Mr. Titus a verbal kick in the belly, walked out. . . . I don't think he's recovered from it yet. He had gone through life without anyone's ever having told him a few grains of truth about himself, and the shock proved almost too much, but I felt that I simply wouldn't go to heaven when I died, if he didn't hear it from somebody. He heard it!"

The rupture with Titus freed Putnam to do what he had decided to do if he could not find a mgazine willing to publish Farrell: start his own magazine. Called the *New Review*, it appeared for the first time in mid-December—the same month the next number of *This Quarter* came out—and to the immense surprise of the editor it lasted for four more issues. Competition between the two magazines barely existed—the dissimilarity between the policies of the two editors all but ruled it out—but neither editor could resist taking opportunities to tweak the other. When Titus went about the Quarter gloating over an arrangement he had made with Edward J. O'Brien, editor of the short story annual,* to publish some of O'Brien's selections in *This Quarter*, Putnam inserted an ad for the *New Review* in a Paris daily which read: "Special Attention! No O'Brien Short

---

* O'Brien's short-story annuals should not be confused with *Story*, a bimonthly in English edited from Vienna beginning in mid-1931 by Whit Burnett and Martha Foley. *Story*, described as "the only magazine devoted solely to the short story," lasted until 1941.

Stories!" The cafés reportedly exploded with guffaws, and Putnam and Eugene Jolas, who shared Putnam's aversion to *This Quarter*, "laughed over the discomfiture of the common enemy." Putnam, however, got his comeuppance when Titus, writing in one of his omnibus editorials, lambasted his former associate for turning out a slovenly translation of George Rheims' *An Elegant Peccadillo*, then just published in America, and for calling (in the introduction) Kiki's *Memoirs* a "much over-rated book" that played up "saleable nothings." Putnam even wrote that Rheims' book was the one that "Kiki or her 'ghost' would like to have written, had they been able to write, and had they not been deliberately holding out." Titus replied by reprinting excerpts from Putnam's "Note" in the *Memoir* in which he had lavished praise on Kiki, her book, and her style.

Titus' alleged fondness for "names" might have influenced his choice of the winner of the Aldington Poetry Prize, finally announced in mid-1931, and intensified his disappointment over Aldington's nominee. The single, indisputable winner for Titus was E. E. Cummings; but for Aldington, who had ignored the contest ruling stating the final decision would reside with *This Quarter*, the recipient was Walter Lowenfels. Aldington argued that Lowenfels, unlike Cummings, who, after all, was read on both sides of the Atlantic and had been honored with the *Dial* award, needed and deserved the recognition the prize would bring him. Aware that he was not putting his money on the "favourite," he nevertheless defended his choice by citing Lowenfels' "genuinely subtle mind and sense of humour," as well as his poetry which, like Wallace Stevens', nearly always excluded emotion and presented "an imaginative treatment of entirely intellectual material." What this "unknown" would do when he had "thoroughly absorbed his material" was a tantalizing thing to look forward to, Aldington suggested; "I want to see if these bones can live, and therefore my award goes to Walter Lowenfels." Titus, obviously piqued, rebuked Aldington for violating the regulations and added that "under duress" he had agreed to a division of the prize. It was a worrisome matter, however, and Titus could not resist trying to convince Aldington that he may have misunderstood his nominee's intentions. As proof, he flourished a note he had received from Lowenfels about the time the award was made. "I'm getting into shape a prose book that might be, but will not be, called *No More Poems*." It was being done, Lowenfels explained, because there is a "poetry crisis." The "poetry crisis is the empty world. The empty world is the empty word. And the empty word is the empty *heart*." If Lowenfels' slogan was "No heart, no poetry," and if he was serious about forswearing poetry for ten years "because of a vacuity of heart," as he had written elsewhere in the note, then, Titus reasoned, he had clearly disowned "Daddy Aldington," who had placed him among those "guided entirely by their mental equipment." Lowenfels was really "a Romantic of 1931 vintage," Titus concluded, only Aldington had been "too busy with *The Colonel's Daughter* to notice it." The second award, the English Poetry Prize sponsored by the publisher, went to John Collier, who also received, without contest this time, the Preferential Prize offered by William Van Wyck to the "abler" of the winners.

Until March 1932, when Jolas suddenly revived *transition, This Quarter* was the only little magazine appearing regularly in Paris, a fact that may account for the high quality of the contents of the final five issues, each of which the Paris journalists—some of them, such as Waverley Root, Titus' friend—greeted warmly and often with assurances that the copy before them outdid the last. An anonymous *Tribune* reviewer (but probably Root) complimented Titus on the "uniformly good" contents of the December 1931 number, citing for comment "two excellent articles on esthetics," one by Joseph Wood Krutch, the other by Otto Rank; Lewisohn's essay on Henry James, another chapter from his forthcoming work on American literature; "outstanding" poems by E. E. Cummings and Selden Rodman; and a "particularly strong" collection of short stories, including Hemingway's "The Sea Change." How Titus had obtained the Hemingway story led the reviewer to make two assumptions: one, "that Hemingway has never turned his back on the humbler publications in which he once often appeared simply because he can now command the higher prices of the big magazines (and that without altering the quality of his work in the slightest); the other, that the theme of his story would cause more editors to think twice, or possibly oftener, before running it, despite the essentially chaste character of Hemingway's writing." Remarkably similar to Callaghan's *No Man's Meat*, Hemingway's story describes the separation of a man and woman, the latter leaving the man, not for another man, but another woman. Practically unnoticed, at least by reviewers, were Titus' lengthy and often tedious editorials and commentaries, typical of which were a laborious dissection of the then popular psychoanalytical method of art criticism, which wallowed and floundered in its own prolixity, and an indictment of censorship which, although convincingly done, belabored the point that obscenity resided in the reader's mind not in the author's words. More successful because more amusing were the salvos Titus lobbed at leading literary figures. Eliot was accused of misapprehending the nature of poetry; Pound's book, *How to Read* was adjudged unreadable; Joyce's prose was described as "strange words" having all the "glamour of the lady of fashion dressed up for the ball." Titus joyfully likened the resurrection of *transition* to the revival of an "obese pythoness," the 325 pages of its revivified number, in his opinion, consisting of more "mediumistic experiments" designed to expand Jolas' "mantic laboratory of orphic creation."

In a gesture that must have sent a ripple of surprise through the Quarter, Titus turned the penultimate number of *This Quarter* over to the surrealists, ostensibly to satisfy a longing for some sort of distraction. The change, he announced, would also help allay the "fear of growing blasé with encomiums on the quality of the material *This Quarter* [had] printed consistently during the three years" of his "incumbency, and—*unconsciously* perhaps—to countervail the risk of imperilling editorial judgement by a long wearying, vacationless pursuit of an undiminishing standard, even if this standard has been of that worth which generous readers have again and again attributed to it, we were casting about for a passing distraction." The surrealists appointed André Breton the editor and insisted that Titus respect their demand that the issue be devoted entirely to their work, a request to which Titus agreed, asking only that they eschew politics and "such other topics as might not be in honeyed accord with Anglo-American censorship urges," a request that Breton honored with just a trace of displeasure. Although Titus' efforts to come up with a workable definition of surrealism did not get very far, reading the surrealist poetry spurred him to issue a prophecy: "If, by the evocation of the unconscious or subliminal self, poems are produced such as some of those printed in this issue, the day may come when the need for reexamination of every known definition of art—certainly of the art of poetry at least—will force itself upon us." Besides Breton, the poets Titus commended were Paul Eluard, Benjamin Peret, Tristan Tzara, and Salvador Dali, who also contributed prose pieces and, with Luis Buñuel, the scenario of the enigmatic film, *The Andalusian Dog*; Marcel Duchamp submitted excerpts from a long, unpublished collection of notes, tentatively called "The Bride Stripped Bare by Her Own Bachelors," which was intended to accompany his painting of the same title; Breton, René Crevel, Eluard, Dali, and Max Ernst all tried, in essays of varying lengths and complexity, to illuminate the subtleties of surrealism; and Giorgio di Chirico, Ernst, Eluard, Breton, Tzara, Valentine Hugo, Man Ray, and Yves Tanguy combined to provide a sampler of surrealist art. To translate the mass of material into English, Titus hired Richard Thoma and Samuel Beckett, the latter earning Titus' "special acknowledgement," particularly for his rendering of the Eluard and Breton poems, "characterizable only in superlatives."

Josephine Herbst, Samuel Beckett, Neville Brand, and even James Farrell had stories in the valedictory number of *This Quarter*. Allen Tate and Oscar Levy supplied essays; Charles Williams and A. L. Rowse, poetry; and E. E. Cummings, another line drawing. Appropriately, the common theme of Titus' two editorials was disintegration—intolerable in the case of the crumbling League of Nations, the victim, in the editor's opinion, of corrupt governments intent on not advancing mankind but precipitating it into "a vale of tears," and unavoidable but sad when the victim was a once-proud member of the transatlantic fleet of ships, like the *Roussillon*, which Titus remembered seeing lying half dismantled in the quiet bay at Hendaye, a melancholy sight that overshadowed the inspiring experience of watching the "launching of a great vessel like the *Normandie*." Though the new addition to the transatlantic fleet was the "world's biggest ship" and bore such a "splendid" name, it was still regrettably true that "ships are mortal," and like little magazines, "they shall lie down alike in the dust, and the worms shall cover them."

Titus' exodus from Montparnasse was eerily complete. He retired to an old house he had renovated at Cagnes-sur-Mer, where with a new wife he lived comfortably surrounded by a large collection of paintings and books. When Titus ceased to be Maecenas, he simply vanished, and as his friend Waverley Root observed, "he did not even leave an empty space." The modest literary esteem he got from playing Maecenas to writers and artists who met his criteria, while sustaining at the time, could hardly survive his disappearance from the Quarter. And yet Titus had unquestionably accomplished a good deal more than many who came to Montparnasse in its heyday with intentions of leaving their mark on the place. *This Quarter*, though often as dull and cantankerous as its editor, still had the appearance of a professional journal, and the selections, despite a shortage of truly experimental writing, maintained an enviably high quality. Almost as much can be said for the books Titus published. Attractively printed, illustrated and bound, they reflect the collector's taste for the pleasing and well-made book. As a publisher Titus may have been too easily diverted by manuscripts containing erotic material, and a few of the writers he published for the first time might better have been denied until they had become more certain of their craft. But as the one responsible for *The Case of Mr. Crump, Imaginary Letters, Kiki's Memoirs,* the novelettes of Morley Callaghan, Kathleen Coyle, and Ludwig Lewisohn, the first book by Anais Nin, and the Paris edition of *Lady Chatterley's Lover,* Titus is assured of a place at least as constant as Maecenas' in the history of Montparnasse.

EDWARD W. TITUS

at the sign of the black Manikin

4, Rue Delambre, Montparnasse

V

Harry and Caresse Crosby
AND THE BLACK SUN

HARRY CROSBY, the Harvard-educated nephew of banker J. P. Morgan, had lived in Europe three years with his wife Mary Jacob Crosby (known as "Polly" to her oldest friends) before they began publishing their own books, although in 1924 Harry had made an almost unnoticed appearance as the editor of a poetry anthology (with a preface by his friend Ellery Sedgwick), which the Dijon printer Maurice Darantière turned out in a small, attractive limited edition marked Not for Sale. Despite the protection of a quiet birth and a noncommercial status, Harry soon heard rumors that Rudyard Kipling had somehow learned that the book existed and planned to sue him for including two of his poems without permission. No action was ever taken, however. The Crosbys' joint appearance in print, albeit in separate books, occurred the following year and was even less conspicuous. Settled in a spacious apartment, located just behind the Gare d'Orsay, accessible to everything and sufficiently "orderly" for Polly, they spaced their days into "riotous hours of entertainment and secluded hours of work," a fair number of the latter spent composing poetry. "Being thrown into ecstasies about each other's work," according to Stuart Gilbert, formed the "mainspring of their zest for living." It was Polly's poetic output, a collection of verses entitled *Crosses of Gold*, that was ready first, its publication held up only slightly by the puzzling problem of how her name—or rather which name—would appear on the title page. Should *Crosses of Gold* be by "Polly Crosby," which to the author sounded "unpoetic," or by "Mary Crosby," which sounded "blue-stocking"? Harry ruled that she must have a new name, preferably one beginning with a "c" to go with Crosby. A ransack of the dictionary for "feminine c's yielded only the rather strident-sounding Cara." It ought to be "more like a caress," Harry proposed. And why not Caresse, with the final "e"? Both pronounced it the perfect choice, although one admittedly likely to scandalize the Boston Crosbys. (They were right. It was like "undressing in public," remarked one unidentified relative.) Family feelings and pride notwithstanding, the sobriquet Caresse was affixed to the title page, and to Harry's great joy, with the "r's" joined, their names formed an acrostic. Called the "Crosby Cross," it would later be used as a colophon.

In January 1925 a local printer named Leon Pinchon delivered over one hundred copies of *Crosses of Gold* to Caresse, all marked Not for Sale; in October appeared Harry's reply, a small book called *Sonnets for Caresse*, hand-printed for him by the English typographer Herbert Clarke, in an edition of seventeen copies, also marked Not for Sale. (A larger edition of the *Sonnets*, priced at five dollars, came out the next year, the printing being done this time by Rimbaud's first publisher, a coincidence that delighted Crosby.) Seeing their poetry in print for the first time inspired the young poets to repeat the magical transformation from manuscript to printed page again as soon as possible. And for a time "experiment in rhyme" became something like a domestic game, each using effusive praise to coax verses from the other. Sending their "experiments" to a publisher would only delay publication, and, after all, they had already discovered that the easiest and quickest way to get their poems into a book was to print the book. With plenty of poems on hand as well as several well-printed books that could serve as models—an edition of *Héloïse and Abélard, Boussole des Amants*, and the Bodley Head edition of Donne's poem—they set out to find their own printer.

The owner of a tiny printery a short distance from the Crosbys' apartment must have often wondered what benevolent force guided two such elegant Americans to his inconspicuous shop "at the bend of the rue Cardinale." His curiosity must have soared when he came upon them one morning peering in his fly-infested shop window and learned they wanted neither a marriage nor a christening announcement, his customary work. What then? That they had come to ask whether he, Roger Lescaret, *Imprimeur*, could print a "whole book" momentarily threatened to deflate his ego. "A whole book is a lot of work," he remonstrated. The Crosbys agreed, but could he not copy the layout and the typography of a deluxe edition like the one Harry had spread out before him? Yes, his confidence

Above: Printery of Roger Lescaret, 2 rue Cardinale, Paris, 1928.
SOUTHERN ILLINOIS UNIVERSITY LIBRARY

Below: Harry and Caresse Crosby, France, 1925.
SOUTHERN ILLINOIS UNIVERSITY LIBRARY

now returning, it would be possible to duplicate "what he saw," but the paper and special type (*Astrée italic*) would be *très cher*. Costs were inconsequential, Crosby assured him, but his next query was not: "It will be hand-set?" Certainly, and the proofs might even be ready within a week. Lescaret did better. Two days later the obviously surprised and delighted printer called on the Crosbys, proudly waving a set of proof sheets that exceeded all their expectations; the poems (*Sonnets for Caresse*) they had left with him had a Shakespearean look and were as handsomely printed as the model. In Lescaret, the Crosbys had had the immense good fortune to find a craftsman with the skills of a master printer, a man with a deep pride in his craft, and one whose simplicity and honesty and *joie de vivre* were as attractive as his work. For the tyro publishers, dropping into Lescaret's little shop, "just for the fun of seeing the pages emerge crisp and fair from the hand-worked press, and [to] smell the good strong ink that permeated the place," became an exquisite and irresistible new pleasure.

Henceforward, interested onlookers they could no longer be. With their own printer they could now publish whenever and whatever they wanted. Caresse set to work designing a colophon for the imprint they adopted—Editions Narcisse—a pool-gazing Narcissus, named after their whippet, "Narcisse Noir." They agreed that together they would select the paper and the binding, that Caresse would plan the pages and format, and that Harry would decide what the new firm would publish. On his first list, issued in 1927, were four more lavish books of their own poems: *Painted Shores* and *The Stranger* by Caresse; *Red Skeletons* and another edition of *Sonnets for Caresse* by Harry. Aside from demonstrating once again the demanding nature of the sonnet form (a fact more than once violated by both authors), the poems in the four volumes provide some intriguing glimpses into the Crosbys' not-so-private lives. In *The Stranger*, a mercifully short (only twelve pages) reply to Harry's *Sonnets* to her, Caresse guilessly claimed to be Harry's "moulder," recollecting that under her guidance he had started writing sonnets years before. Their union, permanent and exalted, is apotheosized in a Yeatsian image, in which Caresse and Harry appear as birds of gold and silver, both "harnessed" to her (Caresse's) "chariot of Hope," thrusting upward toward a distant sun.

The poems in *Painted Shores* and *Red Skeletons*, both longer, attractively illustrated collections, were considerably more arresting than their private love messages. In *Painted Shores* Caresse combines newsy revelations of their social life with some disquieting reflections on its conse-

171

quences. In "Journey's End," for example, she urged suppression of prohibitions against continuing the "riotous hours of entertainment":

> For you remember that the voyage was made
> To be a holiday of flight and thought.
> Since we have loved and learnt, and wept and played
> Have we not realized everything we sought?
> > Though you and I, my heart, are sealed with pain
> > Would we not turn and seek it all again?

Despite poems bearing such titles as "Necrophile," "Lit de Mort," and "Uncoffined" and the faintly Beardslean illustrations created by

CRUCIFIXTION

WAR was romantic in the days of old,
The knight rode forth to battle unafraid,
Wearing the favour of some royal maid
Who loved him for his courage lionbold.
And thus he sought adventures manifold
In joust and tourney, heard fanfaronade
Of trumpets, or else fought in red crusade
With infidels, his honour to uphold.

But modern war is not at all the same,
There are no plumes to catch my lady's eye
In dugouts damp or trenches lashed by rain,
Where poison gas creeps in to suffocate,
Where bullets slap against the parapet,
And barbèd wire crucifies the slain.

Harry's Hungarian artist friend Alastair for others like "Our Lady of Pain," "Salammbô," and the "Massacre of the Innocents," *Red Skeletons* was far more than an adolescent exercise in the macabre. Though two years later Harry himself would call it a "rotten book," *Red Skeletons* was actually a litmus paper of his life, past and present. Mainly, however, as the title suggests, Crosby wanted to exhibit and perhaps exercise a living past, a past in which the incubus of war seems both infernal and consoling. From the ideas of T. S. Eliot and Edwin Muir, he may have derived

Poem (*opposite page*) and frontispiece (*below*) from *Red Skeletons* by Harry Crosby, illustrated by Alastair (Black Sun Press, 1927).
PRINCETON UNIVERSITY LIBRARY

the direction and the support for his concentration. "Contemplation of the horrid or sordid or disgusting by an artist," wrote Eliot, "is the necessary and negative impulse toward the pursuit of beauty." Muir hypothesized that what distinguished the sincere artist from the rest was his concern "with the things that make him suffer, the things, in other words, which stand between him and freedom." Both dicta (Crosby copied them on the flyleaf of his copy of *Red Skeletons*) as well as his devoted reading of Poe, Mallarmé, Rimbaud, and Huysmans probably inspired some of the effusions of loneliness and Baudelairian hymns of despair (in a sonnet dedicated to Baudelaire Crosby wrote: "Within my soul you've set your blackest flag"); but the passion that filled the war poems scattered throughout the same volume came directly from his own past, and though often trite and sentimental, they express the deep anxiety that engulfed him whenever he contemplated the conflict he had once described as "God-ordained" and destined to bring forth "a finer, cleaner, and squarer place." It was that sort of war-inspired idealism, so pronounced in the letters he wrote to his family during the sixteen months he served with an ambulance corps in France, that had dissipated entirely by the time he returned home in March 1919. Harry, however, had solemnized his arrival abroad by declaring that the war was "all for bettering men and women," although he foresaw that the cost would be tremendous. Just how great it would be he learned not long afterwards while driving an ambulance full of wounded men to a field hospital. Forced suddenly to stop when a truck ahead stalled, he spent several long and agonizing minutes exposed to a heavy German bombardment. When the road was cleared, Harry was still alive, but others, among them his friends, were not. For the rest of his life he honored the day (November 17, 1918) of his narrow escape; the day the "hills and the charred skeletons of trees and the river Meuse" stood silhouetted against a "red sun" and the "black shells" sent up columns of dirt along the road. On the same day he wrote "Shadow Shapes" (February 1, 1925), a grim study of a guilt-ridden soldier included in *Red Skeletons*, he entered in his diary the following brief reminder: "We who have known war must never forget war. And that is why I have the picture of a soldier's corpse nailed to the door of my library."

Harry's vow never to forget what had happened to him and to his dead friends permanently altered his life, perhaps to an extent far greater than even he realized when, on the occasion of the tenth anniversary of the November bombardment, he wrote in his diary that "the ride through red explosions [had been] the violent metamorphose from boy into man." The change was not only "from boy into man," however; it was a change from a vibrant boyhood into an empty manhood, in which youthful aspirations succumbed to wild diversion and excitement, in which a once-secure future crumbled into desperation and despair. Malcolm Cowley has suggested that the change effected by the war was from life into death. It was a death which expressed itself in estrangement from family and country, in an obsessive guilt at having survived the war which destroyed his friends, and in a morbid preoccupation with suicide. Until he died the incubus of war haunted Crosby, partly because he nurtured it, more fervently, it seemed, as the conflict receded into the past. In November 1929, a month before he died, Harry wrote in a diary entry that one of his lost comrades had been dead eleven years. The only counterweight and antidote he found to impose against the "deadness" inside him was the mystical belief in sun-worship which, he explained in "Uncoffined" (perhaps the best poem in *Red Skeletons*), released the torment caused by the "ill-considered strife" and the "misconceits" of "my past life." Eventually, however, what seemed to be a sustaining, even restorative, force in his life could not arrest the drive toward annihilation; in fact, since it was the sun that lay at the center of Crosby's sun-worshiping system, and since at the center there was emptiness and death, and since the ultimate experience toward which he moved was union with the "Red-Gold (night) of the Sun," the system itself only served to propel him faster toward self-destruction.

It was with Edward Weeks (an ambulance driver with Crosby, Weeks had witnessed his friend's ordeal) that Harry first discussed plans to publish a deluxe edition of *The Fall of the House of Usher*. He warned his friend that the volume would be expensive, probably around two hundred francs, but would be attractively bound and printed on heavy Van Gelder paper; it would also have five original drawings by Alastair. Two months before the Poe book was scheduled to appear, in November 1927, Harry had sent Arthur Symons copies of *Red Skeletons* and *Sonnets for Caresse* and had asked him to write an introduction for *Usher*. Symons agreed, delighted with Harry's offer of £20 and intrigued by Alastair's *fin de siècle* drawings ("He has genius, his coloured designs are wonderful"). With a volume combining Poe, Alastair, and Symons (in Harry's estimate a "perfect mating"), and with Weeks, now the firm's American representative, standing by ready to dispose of the entire edition of three hundred, safe passage into the world of commercial publishing, if only at the level of limited editions, seemed assured. When Weeks sent word that *Usher* had been accorded a warm critical reception and was selling well, the Paris publishers interpreted the news as a signal to expand their business; at the same time they rechristened it the Black Sun, because, as Caresse noted, "black was Harry's favorite color and he worshiped the sun."

Usher was one of two books the Crosbys published in January 1928. The other one, whose commercial potential was as poor as the Poe volume was promising, was a small collection of verses by Gerald Lymington (later the Earl of Portsmouth), whom the Crosbys had met in New York and who had become their devoted companion and friend, solicitous of their welfare and genuinely interested in their publishing firm. Accompanying the Crosbys in their "maddest hours," Lymington quickly shed his British reserve, and on one memorable occasion, the annual "Quatre Arts" bacchanalia, was seen dancing "savagely, lance in hand," the length of the Champs-Elysées, before a swaying elephant bearing Caresse, naked to the waist. Even his epicurean and gastronomic excesses seemed to match theirs, as Harry once noted: "When we got to Paris we discovered Lord L. waiting for us and we all drank gin fizzes and took cold baths and put rouge on our toenails and then we went to Git-le-Coeur where the Sorceress cast her spells over my heart and C. and I and Lord L dined at Le Doyen on sherry cobbler two sherry cobblers three sherry cobblers. . . ." Moreover, Lymington's fondness for poetry was as well developed as the Crosbys' and in time he, too, had an accretion of verses, a portion of which he deposited with his friends towards the end of 1927. One gathers that the title poem "Git le Coeur" must have possessed somewhat stronger amatory connotations for Harry than for others who read Lymington's book. His first sight of the street of that name occurred in the spring of 1924 when, entering it, he saw "a minuscule apartment perched like a nest on the roof of the house (stork's nest) looking out over Notre Dame and the Seine, ideal for lover and mistress," a purpose for which the place must eventually have been put, if one may conclude that an inhabitant bearing the name of "Sorceress" might conceivably be a mistress. Lymington's poetic recollections of the "stork's nest" seem to remove all doubt.

II

It could almost be said that a meeting between D. H. Lawrence and Harry Crosby was foreordained. Of Lawrence, a fellow sun-worshiper, Harry must at least have been aware in November 1927, when he recorded in his diary that it was probably Lawrence who said "that a man

176

can only be happy following his own inmost need, and my inmost need is the Sun." That inmost need Harry came close to satisfying two months later while on a trip through Egypt, though less by the sight of Heliopolis and the golden artifacts of Tutankhamen's tomb than by the hot Egyptian sun, always a constant, and, for Harry, a welcome companion, and by his sudden impulse to have a sun-image tattooed on his back, but, above all, by his impassioned reading of Lawrence's novel *The Plumed Serpent*. The discovery of so absorbing and enthralling an embodiment of his own version of sun-worship was an electrifying experience, which, in a letter immediately dispatched to Lawrence, Harry enthusiastically recorded along with a fulsome description of the Egyptian sun and confirmation of his own belief in the "Sun God." He also asked Lawrence to send him "any sun story" that he might publish in a limited edition, adding that he was ready to pay the munificent sum of one hundred dollars in "twenty-dollar gold pieces, the eagle and the sun."

Lawrence apparently thought Crosby wanted to buy a "sun" manuscript, for he replied that he had never sold one and hated to sell anything; he added, however, that in this instance he would make an exception and send Crosby a manuscript as soon as he could determine what he had not lost or burned, and for which he would be glad to accept "as much gold as Crosby" could "easily spare." At the same time he asked Curtis Brown, his British publisher, if by any chance the manuscript of his story *Sun* was still in London, mentioning that he had been offered a one-hundred-dollar "windfall" for it. In mid-April, by which time *Sun* had turned up, Harry sent Lawrence some poems from his forthcoming book *Chariot of the Sun*, and asked him to write an introduction. Lawrence agreed to supply about "2000 words" as soon as he had received the "complete book of poems." But by the end of April Harry had not sent it, so Lawrence, anxious to finish the assignment, proceeded to write the introduction and was on the point of posting it, along with *Sun*, when the rest of Harry's poems arrived. The latecomers, Lawrence feared, were "not very sensitive," and they were too "long" and "unwieldly" and should not be included in *Chariot*, which must be left "as it stands."

The same day *Sun* reached the rue Cardinale printery Lescaret began setting type while Caresse and Harry poured over the Holland Van Gelder paper samples, looking for just the right texture. The book would have to meet the most exact and tasteful requirements, and, meanwhile, Lawrence would have to be paid. Harry had not forgotten his promise to reward him in gold, but an interminable wait for the delivery of the gold pieces from America nearly ruined the plan. Finally, the tardy courier, a young Bostonian named Bill Sykes, showed up at the rue de Lille apartment, carrying the bullion in his shoes, a hiding place, he proudly announced, that had eluded the customs officers. Harry, anxious to dispatch the money immediately, nevertheless took time to swathe the coins in cotton before placing them in a "small square Cartier box"; then, after a mad dash to the Gare de l'Est, where he arrived minutes before the departure of the Rome Express, he hurried along the quay searching for an "honest man" with whom to entrust the box with its precious cargo. And it was not until the final moment that he found his man, a "distinguished Englishman," calmly leaning out of a compartment window. Would he mail the box in Florence? "It's gold for a poet." He would, indeed, reaching down and taking the package and waving as the train jerked forward and vanished in the smoke and mist.

The gift of gold made Lawrence "feel almost wicked." Knowing nothing of Crosby's resources, he confided that if by chance Harry were not a rich man he would "feel really bad about it." Accompanying his thanks, however, came the hope that someday he would be able "to square it" with him. Meanwhile he suggested that Harry should check his version of *Sun* with another one in the possession of Allanah Harper and make any substitutions he wanted. He also promised to write to the British and American firms that had published the story for permission to reprint it, explaining that, if Crosby wrote, they would probably "want to fleece" him. Early in August Lawrence forwarded a small gift to the rue Cardinale office: a watercolor painting of the sun that he had made from a Maya design. "Keep it if you like it," he told Crosby. Harry used it for the frontispiece of the Black Sun edition of *Sun*.

In the fall Harry had his own unexpected embarrassment of riches when his cousin, Walter Van Rensselaer Berry, a longtime resident of Paris and a man Caresse called the "epitome of elegance in the Jamesian manner," died and bequeathed him his large library. According to the terms of Berry's will Harry was to receive the entire library, "except such items as my good friend, Edith Wharton, may care to choose." When Mrs. Wharton interpreted Berry's wishes too liberally for Harry and attempted to annex practically the "entire library," he resisted "tooth and nail" and eventually reduced Mrs. Wharton's share to about five hundred books, leaving him with a veritable treasure of close to eight thousand volumes, including such rarities as a leaf from the Gutenberg Bible, the first edition of De Quincey's *Opium Eater*, sets of Casanova, Bacon,

Henry James, Maupassant, volumes of private-press books, and in Crosby's words, "Italian Books, French Books, English Books, Spanish Books, Books in Latin Books in Greek every kind of Book imaginable from the oldest Incunabula down to the most recent number of transition"—all of which, as directed, were delivered to the Crosby apartment by "solid men" who spent close to a day constructing a pyramid of books in Harry's library and filling Caresse's atelier to the ceiling. The overflow blocked the staircase, the guest room, and the front hallway. As Berry's legatee, Harry also inherited a voluminous correspondence which, among other treasures, contained letters to Berry from an admiring Marcel Proust, who, Harry was surprised to learn, had dedicated *Pastiches et Mélanges* to him in gratitude for what Proust construed to be Berry's successful efforts in bringing the United States into the First World War. Both Harry and Caresse foresaw that if the Proust letters were published they would most certainly secure "Cousin Walter's immortality"; they would also add an impressive name to the Black Sun list.

Although four books were already on the fall schedule, with others in the planning stage, the Crosbys made room for one more, seductively described on a miniature announcement card as a "rare and interesting edition minutely reproduced for Harry and Caresse Crosby from an ancient erotic illuminated manuscript recently found in Damascus representing in twenty-two colored miniatures the various positions of love." Even the edition would be diminutive (only twenty numbered copies), a limitation that seemingly would confine the amatory secrets of the ancient Persians to the discriminating and affluent few. In the meantime Harry was preparing two other projects, one being the French and English editions of Oscar Wilde's *The Birthday of the Infanta*, for which he had written a prefatory note lauding the spiritual content of Alastair's illustrations, and his ability to transmogrify evil into something beautiful, and concluding that the "collaboration" between the artist and Wilde had been fated. The other project was the first volume of his diary, *Shadows of the Sun*, restricted to forty-four copies, none of which were for sale. It would also be the first book to bear the Black Sun imprint, and although the shortest of the three volumes of the diary (the second and third appeared in 1929 and 1930), it would encompass the longest period of time, from January 1, 1922 to December 28, 1926.

The Crosbys had come to cherish coincidences as much for their sheer delight as for the happy consequences they so frequently had for the press. Wandering into the rue Cardinale and finding Lescaret's shop had been the first of them; then had come the exciting revelation that Lescaret was a talented printer; after that there had been "Cousin Walter's" bequest and the discovery of the Proust letters. The scene for the next was the Lilliputian office Harry and Caresse had fixed up above the printery, and into which one morning, unexpected and unannounced, came a New York bookseller named Harry Marks, nearly prostrate after picking his way through the thicket of streets leading to the shop. The Crosbys and Alastair had just finished going over the illustrations for Wilde's *Infanta*, and listened, awed, as Marks regaled them with some of the loftiest praise they had ever heard, inspired, it seems, by a single Black Sun book he had spied in a Right Bank bookshop. What awaited him at the end of his junket Marks of course had no way of knowing. Were these two strangers who looked so radiant and exuded such an unmistakable "Shelley-like quality," and who sat surrounded by a "glorious disarray of proofs, manuscripts, pictures, and bindings," wondered Marks, beating their "luminous wings in the void in vain," and, if so, what could be done about it? Though Marks had come prepared to do business, it was not business in the usual sense he was able to do. When, after asking to buy the entire edition of the *Infanta*, he offered to handle all the Black Sun books at his New York store, the Crosbys refused to discuss money or contracts, preferring, at least for the moment, Marks remembered, an agreement "above the usual routine of mere business." The sudden appearance of Marks in the rue Cardinale, coming just as the Crosbys had made final preparations for the publication of Wilde's book, would have important consequences for the Black Sun. Harry wondered, however, if it was any more of a coincidence than the occurrence just before luncheon, when he went up to the library to get his copy of *Chariot of the Sun* and found "the long gold finger of the Sun touching the very center of the Sun engraved in the book."

Though coincidences are fortuitous, whims are not, and the Crosbys, both impulsive and often impatient, seldom waited long before gratifying their whims, large and small, and suddenly it was the French countryside they longed for, the "real countryside where one could bask and muse." A weekend spent at the Comte Armand de la Rochefoucauld's chateau in Ermenonville, a few miles from Paris, confirmed and at once satisfied their latest caprice. Strolling about the vast property with the Comte, who had inherited it the previous year on reaching his majority, the Crosbys suddenly spotted an old mill, derelict and half-crumbling, but enchantingly located. Immediately certain it would make the perfect country retreat, they announced to their speechless host they must have it, and at once; and before the Comte had had time to protest, Harry, anxious to close the matter and quite unruffled by the sudden discovery that he had left his checkbook behind, ripped off one of Caresse's white cuffs and on it wrote out a check for the down payment. Christened the Moulin de Soleil, it burgeoned through renovation into a cross between "an Adirondack camp and an Arizona ranch," complete with swimming pool, and, for Harry, a tower for sun-bathing, and (for the crowds of guests who descended on the place weekends) suites of rooms (ten small bedrooms in the tower, each a different color).

One often invited to the mill was Kay Boyle, then still an unpublished young writer and friend and assistant to Eugene Jolas at *transition*, where Harry's poetry would soon be published. From the start Harry had always respected Miss Boyle's literary judgment (Jolas brought them together at the Bal Negre in 1928) and, along with Hart Crane, E. E. Cummings, and Archibald MacLeish, regarded her as one of the few great writers their generation was likely to produce. Perhaps because Harry respected her so much he accepted her rather trenchant criticism of some poems that would appear in his forthcoming book *Transit of Venus* (issued, *hors commerce*, in an edition of only forty-four copies), a title he had decided on after noting that Venus, the "youngest Princess of the Sun," at her "inferior conjunction," occasionally passed directly across the disk of the sun and that the phenomenon was known as a "transit." Miss Boyle's precisely worded assessment reached Harry the same month *Transit* appeared (September 1928): while his poems seemed "far better than any she had recently seen in print," Miss Boyle ventured that only the "testament of the sun [had] the conviction and despair of originality." Something "stronger and harder" from him would be necessary; that is, in Harry's own "view of those two qualities." She admitted the poems had a "center and a warm glory," but she hinted that better things would come if he wrote out what was churning inside him. That would be "something else again." Harry, as always, reverently distilled her advice in his diary, along with mention of a hashish party and his horse "Mad Queen," on whom he had just lost a thousand francs.

That same autumn the Crosbys experienced yet another windfall. For weeks they had been "weeding out and rearranging" Berry's library, uncomplainingly clearing dust from their throats and dirt from their hands, and on one of their last forages they had come upon an old pasteboard box containing a packet of sixteen letters to Berry from Henry James—affectionate, beautifully composed testaments showing James' admiration for his elegant countryman, and every bit as impressive as the Proust letters to Berry; in fact, the Crosbys were so taken by their find (they had also uncovered letters from Emerson, Ruskin, Valéry, and Foch) that they decided to edit the letters at once and issue them in October along with *Sun* and the erotic Damascus manuscript. The three October publications, diverse in subject and typography, would mark the first time the firm had issued more than one book in a single month. The combined editions of the three books reached 301 copies, also a record, and for the first time all were for sale, both *Sun* and the *Letters of Henry James to Walter Berry* bearing the notation: "to be sold at Marks'." Since the twenty copies of *Moon Letter* (the original title of the Damascus manuscript by Dehzad Nezaki was *Mah-Name*) would undoubtedly have run afoul of customs officials in America and England, despite the fact that it was smaller than one's palm, Harry arranged to dispose of them in France, discreetly, and for the substantial sum of a thousand francs (forty dollars). Hopefully he found twenty connoisseurs with prodigious eyesight—and imagination— or, lacking both, at least with access to a strong magnifying glass, for the illustrations in this miniscule book, while purporting to show the twenty-two positions of love, carried minuteness to the brink of invisibility. The performers, a distinctly Persian couple, half clad and wearing scarves and beads and using two pillows for a bed, assume the various poses with a perpetual look of boredom, which, when added to the bewildering inex-actness of the tiny drawings, must have done as much to frustrate one's expectations of enlightenment or pleasure as the untranslated text and the reverse pagination—page one, according to the Persian custom, being the last, and the last being the first.

Ever since May the Crosbys had dutifully kept Lawrence informed of the progress of *Sun*, and, in return, he had from time to time surprised them by supplying illustrations for the volume—a headpiece and tailpiece for the first part, and a drawing of a phoenix ("quite small nest and flames might be red and bird black") for the cover. At one point he even suggested that *Sun* ought to sell for "at least ten dollars." (In September, Caresse offered Marks 150 copies for four dollars a copy, and eight dollars for signed copies printed on Japan paper. By October, however, the price had escalated to twenty dollars.) Having found the Crosbys so amenable to his recommendations and delighted with his drawings, Law-rence reciprocated by promptly returning the proofs and signed sheets, and at the same time warmly complimenting Caresse's design and even insisting that she subtract her expenses before sharing any profits with him. After Harry, in a lavish display of gratitude, had dispatched two copies of *Sun* to Lawrence in "golden boxes," Lawrence replied that he liked the book immensely and found the "print and the paper very elegant and aristocratic and lovely." By coincidence, *Chariot of the Sun*, Harry's second collection of poems issued in 1928 and for which Lawrence had written an introduction the previous spring, became the ideal companion volume to *Sun*. Both authors expressed their common belief in the rejuvenating and transforming powers of the sun. Though Juliet, the "nervous New York woman" in *Sun* finally releases herself to the sun and experiences a "cosmic influence" that confers insight into her real self buried "in the dark flow of the sun within her deep body," she nonetheless remains tragically bound "to the vast, fixed wheel of circumstance" as well as to her "clean-shaven, grey-faced, very quiet and really shy" husband, Maurice, who is "utterly sunless" alongside Juliet's admirer and would-be lover, a passionate Italian peasant, so "like the sun to her." What he dramatized in his story Lawrence tried to elucidate in his introduction. In Crosby's inchoate descriptions of the sun and in his "glimpse of chaos not reduced to order . . . a glimpse of the living, untamed chaos," Lawrence claimed to have found a "new Naïveté" that was destined to be the "New spirit of poetry and the new spirit of life"; it would also be a liberating force leading "back to the pool of renewal, where we dip ourselves in life again, and let the old case-hardened self-conceit wash off us, and let the body unfurl in all its sensitiveness and naïveté again, like a magnolia, to the suns." Since *Chariot* embodied a new faith and awareness in the sun, it was, despite the "defects and nonsense," a "book of poetry"—a book of poetry with a distinctly Lawrencian message.

Besides Lawrence, one other persona inhabited *Chariot of the Sun*: Polia Chentoff, the diminutive Russian artist the Crosbys had "discovered" that year at the Salon d'Automne and whose prize-winning painting, *First Communion*, they had purchased for their rue de Lille apartment. It was Miss Chentoff's portrait of him ("strange and portentous," according to Caresse) that Harry had used as the frontispiece for *Chariot*, and although the book was dedicated to Caresse ("Queen of the Sun"), the portrait, in addition to a poem bearing the artist's name, gave Miss Chentoff a rather noticeable prominence. Caresse observed that, like so many of their mutual enthusiasms, Miss Chentoff "soon became entirely Harry's," and the situation was not helped by a portrait she made of Caresse, which St. J. Perse found a subtle and skilful portrayal of one woman's distaste for another. Eventually, it was Harry's portrait, however, which served as an object of revenge. On returning to Paris from New York following Harry's death, Caresse burned the painting, declaring that she found it "metaphysically disturbing." Caresse had her own *hors commerce* edition of poems ready in 1928. Entitled *Impossible Melodies*, it contained a frontispiece portrait by Angelès Ortiz, showing the author seated imperiously on a divan, swathed in a Roman toga. Her verses, still personal, provocative, and gossipy, contained this bit of teasing: "All all of the day's delight/ And half of the moon's mad rise/ I fling at the feet of 'I saw you once/ With deception in your eyes.' "

III

Surrounded by friends, Harry spent New Year's Eve, 1928, at the mill, crouched in front of the "red-gold of the fire," smoking his pipe, drinking red wine, and watching the last minutes of the year vanish on his stopwatch. At midnight, when the "Oneness (mid) for Eternity (merged) into the Red-Gold (night) of the Sun," he rose up and pronounced the departed year the "Year Magnificent." Among the multitude of things Harry probably had in mind when he uttered that benediction must have been the record of the Black Sun. Good as it had been—twelve books in as many months—the year just ending would eventually be seen as far less deserving of Harry's accolade than the one that had just begun. In January, Harry sold stocks worth four thousand dollars, most of which he earmarked for two new Black Sun publications—*A Sentimental Journey Through France and Italy* by Laurence Sterne, with illustrations by Polia Chentoff, scheduled for June; and an unusually large edition (1,020 copies) of Ernest Dowson's translation of Choderlos de Laclos' *Les Liaisons Dangereuses*, for which Alastair would do the illustrations. By mid-month he was correcting proof sheets of *Mad Queen*, the book of tirades he had begun after returning from Egypt and while still in a "spirit of tirade," Caresse remembered, and still under the influence of *The Plumed Serpent*. About the same time he became affiliated with *transition*, and came directly under the influence of the review's editor, the energumen and spokesman of avant-garde expression, Eugene Jolas, who introduced Harry to an American poet whose personal and creative agonies the Crosbys would share, and sometimes assuage, almost continuously for the next twelve months.

Hart Crane arrived in Paris on January 7, 1929, relieved to leave behind "wonderful but sad, heavy" London, and excited about the "incredibly free and animated" life of Paris. Within hours he had looked up Jolas, who introduced him to a number of carefully chosen people, including Crosby. The first meeting with Crane left Harry enraptured. "I've met the most wonderful poet," he exclaimed to Caresse. Crane's reaction to Crosby was nearly as enthusiastic. A few days later they met again and, with Jolas, went off to Prunier for oysters and Anjou. That night Harry read the "White Buildings" section of *The Bridge* and immediately asked Jolas whether Crane had made arrangements to publish his poem. The other sections of *The Bridge* that Harry read with mounting enthusiasm over the next several days were enough to convince him that it was a very important work, and that if Crane consented to its publication he would publish it at the Black Sun as soon as possible. At the first opportunity the Crosbys arranged to meet the poet for lunch and listened reverently as he discussed his poem, read a few excerpts for them, and then, without the least resistance, agreed to let them publish it in a limited edition.

Crane—dilatory, quarrelsome, self-indulgent, despondent over the

Hart Crane, Le Moulin,
Ermenonville, France,
1929.
SOUTHERN ILLINOIS
UNIVERSITY LIBRARY

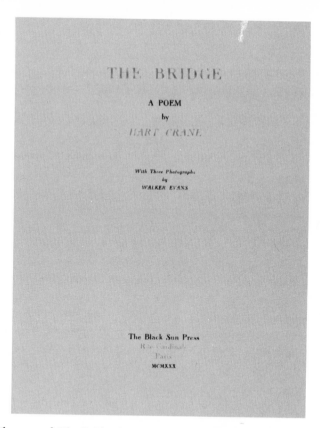

THE BRIDGE

A POEM
by
HART CRANE

With Three Photographs
by
WALKER EVANS

The Black Sun Press
Rue Cardinale
Paris
MCMXXX

Title page of *The Bridge* by Hart Crane (Black Sun Press, 1930).
PRINCETON UNIVERSITY LIBRARY

slow progress of his work—could hardly have placed himself in better hands. Harry proved to be a paragon of understanding and tolerance and generosity. When Crane, for example, pressed him to use a full-color reproduction of Joseph Stella's *Brooklyn Bridge* for the frontispiece of *The Bridge* (Crosby had never seen Stella's painting), he agreed at once, enthusiastically. And he was similarly receptive to Crane's entreaty on behalf of Malcolm Cowley, whose collection of poems, *Blue Juniata*, he hoped Harry would publish at the Black Sun. Though neither project ever materialized, through no fault of Harry's, the publisher's efforts to provide at least the surroundings that might inspire the poet to finish his work had sudden and dramatic results. The first weekend in February Crane joined a crowd of Crosby's friends at the mill where, as Harry noted in his diary, he was far from being overlooked. "Hart Crane here and much drinking of red wine and he reads aloud from *Tamburlaine* and he is at work on his

186

long poem *The Bridge*." The following day, however, Crane's performance changed: "Mob for luncheon—poets and painters and pederasts
and lesbians and divorcees and Christ knows who and there was a great
signing of names on the wall at the foot of the stairs and a firing off of the
cannon and bottle after bottle of red wine and Kay Boyle made fun of
Hart Crane and he was angry and flung the *American Caravan* into the
fire because it contained a story of Kay Boyle's (he forgot it had a poem
of his in it) and there was a tempest of drinking and polo harra burra on
the donkeys and an uproar and confusion so that it was difficult to do my
work on the Bible."

When the weekend of what Crane called "new atrocities" had finally
ended, there seemed little doubt that Crosby would withdraw the invitation he had made to him to return to the mill "at any time for any period
to finish *The Bridge*." But Crane had underestimated his host's liberality.
Completely unperturbed by what had happened, Crosby assured him the
place would be his whenever he wanted it. He decided he wanted it at
once. In a letter to Waldo Frank he admitted that though Paris was the
"most interesting madhouse in the world," it was a test for an American
that he was far from feeling "equal to." Moreover, he told Frank, he had
not written "anything longer than scratch notes" for over a year, and that
the time had finally arrived "to get into myself again, and into my work."
Waiting for him at Ermenonville were Harry's vacant sun tower and the
"service the millionaires are used to having." Above all, however, there
would be solitude. On February 10, Crane moved into the Moulin de
Soleil, the sole guest, and for the next three weeks, except during weekends
when Harry and his friends came out from Paris, he lived alone, alternately intimidated by the opulence of his surroundings (using, among
other articles, Caresse's silken chaise-longue, Crane transformed Harry's
spartanly furnished tower into a regal abode) and stimulated by the
"solitude and study" of the place. At first he worked slowly and sporadi-
cally; then more concentratedly. First to be delivered to Harry was a
nearly finished draft of the "Hatteras" section, which Harry praised as
fulsomely as he had the "O Carib Isle" part Crane had sent him earlier,
and out of gratitude for which Crane had given him a manuscript copy of
the "Grand Canyon" draft. Crosby's reply was ecstatic:

> Hart what thunder and fire for breakfast! "Such thunder in their
> strain!" by Christ when you read something like that all the dust
> and artificiality and bric a brac are swept magnificently aside and

187

one becomes clean like those "clean enamel frames of death" you talk about. I am so damn glad to have this poem in MSS—someday when we are all dead they will be screaming and cutting each other's throats for the privilege of having it. . . . I am no critic but I know gold when I see it. You write from impulse and imagination not by rules—everyone should of course but they simply don't—the result is you have a clean virginity of language, a male strength. . . . It is thoroughbred poetry and that too is a rare quality.

Though happy to be receiving bits and pieces, both Harry and Caresse rightly feared that as soon as Crane left the mill he would again stop writing. What they did not foresee was that he would also gradually disappear after returning to Paris. Except for an occasional visit to the mill, they saw little of him, and when Caresse learned he was leaving for a trip to the south of France, presumably before supplying any more parts of the poem, she proposed that *The Bridge* be published as it stood. "I wanted to say about *The Bridge* that when I saw it, it seemed already to be one poem. Why do you think it must be added to? It is eternal and it is alive and it is beautiful—why don't you let us print it as it is? Afterwards if you add more you can have a second edition. If it seems too fragmentary to you it is because you already know the pieces that should fit in—but I feel that if you published it now, it would give you a fresh impetus for the rest. Think it over." Crane did and agreed to let the Crosbys go ahead with their edition in September, even if he were unable to supply additions by then.

By 1929, the aura of hero worship surrounding James Joyce, whose genius Sylvia Beach so passionately proclaimed and protected and Jolas so successfully perpetuated in the pages of *transition*, had reached colossal proportions. Even for the most intrepid among the Montparnasse literati catching a glimpse of the "great man" demanded careful timing and considerable perseverance; and an actual meeting with Joyce was almost as difficult to obtain as an invitation to Gertrude Stein's salon, and nearly impossible without the intercession of someone who belonged to Joyce's "inner circle." Fortunately for the Crosbys, Eugene and Maria Jolas belonged, and one afternoon they conducted Harry and Caresse to the "tidy and unimaginative" apartment Joyce occupied with his family near the Gare Montparnasse. Bored and uncommunicative, Joyce remained silent behind his "thick mysterious lenses until something was said about Sullivan's concert the evening before." The mention of the Irish tenor John

Sullivan, whose career Joyce had tirelessly worked to advance, brought him to life, and, sensing his sudden enthusiasm, the Crosbys joined the other guests in "enthusing" with him as he expounded on the singer's greatness. Perhaps it was their appreciation of Sullivan that prompted Joyce to invite them back for a concert the next week. Several weeks passed by however before they returned, during which time they slowly worked up enough courage to ask him if they might print a segment of *Work in Progress* at the Black Sun. It is unclear whether they finally went directly to Joyce with their proposal or negotiated with him through his friends, but they at least participated in the drawing-up of the preliminary publishing arrangements. Caresse recalled that Joyce seemed relieved to learn he would not have to supply many pages and that he could make unlimited corrections on the proof sheets, a concession the Crosbys later regretted giving as much as Sylvia Beach. Joyce must have been pleased, too, when Stuart Gilbert told him that Crosby would pay in advance whatever sum he believed "right for a single limited edition."

The day after their meeting with Joyce, Gilbert appeared at Lescaret's shop with three fragments from *Work in Progress* bearing the fanciful names "The Mookse and the Gripes," "The Muddest Thick that Ever was Dumped," and "The Ondt and the Gracehoper." It was agreed that they would be published under the title *Tales Told of Shem and Shaun*. In reply to Harry's suggestion that someone of Joyce's choice should write an introduction, Gilbert reported that Joyce had recommended either Julian Huxley or John Sullivan. Both, however, declined, and Joyce next suggested the mathematician and inventor of Basic English, C. K. Ogden, who accepted and "was enthusiastically signed up." The Crosbys had also suggested that a portrait of the author would make a suitable frontispiece, and, if Joyce agreed, favored Picasso to do it. The idea excited Joyce, who kept asking Harry if he really believed Picasso could be persuaded. By the end of the month that possibility seemed remote when Caresse, who had not yet approached the artist, learned from a close friend that Picasso was "going through a 'crise morale' and would not even see his best friends."

Meanwhile the Crosbys began a series of "working visits" with Joyce, full accounts of which Harry entered in his diary. On March 27 Joyce showed them the "corrections and additions" he had made in *Work in Progress* since it had appeared in *transition*. He "seemed very blind," Harry noted, "and he knocked into the tea table trying to show us the painting of his father by an Irishman named Thohey who has also painted

Joyce and his son. . . . Joyce then asked me to read aloud one of the passages we are going to edit 'Can you not do her, numb? asks Dolph, suspecting the answer Know. I cont, ken you, ninny? asks Kev, expecting the answer guess' whereupon Joyce explains this passage and I realize how ignorant I am from the scholastic point of view and how sane a writer is Joyce. . . . I liked the flash of triumph when Caresse asked him how much he enjoyed doing this new work, the same flash of triumph as when one is sleeping with a woman one loves, the same flash of triumph when one bets high on a horse and sees him gallop past the winning-post a winner. . . ."

On April 3, Joyce and the Crosbys met in a lawyer's office on the Place Vendôme and drew up a contract which all signed three days later. "How I despise lawyers," Harry complained. "They waste so damn much time and their bird-brains are spotted with technicalities." The technicalities that Harry found so irksome gave Joyce an extremely favorable contract, which he acknowledged in a letter to the publishers the following day:

I hereby acknowledge the receipt from you of the sum of ONE THOUSAND ($1,000.—) DOLLARS, being the one-half payment of the sum agreed upon for the publication of the three fragments from my "WORK IN PROGRESS"; I also wish to say that I am in perfect accord with the terms of your letter as follows:-

"We, Harry and Caresse Crosby, hereby confirm
"our verbal arrangements in connection with
"the editing of three fragments of your 'WORK
"IN PROGRESS'.

"These fragments which have already appeared in
"the magazine 'Transition', to wit:-

   " 'The Ondt & Gracehoper',
   " 'Mookse & Gripes',
   " 'The Triangle',

"are to be edited by the Black Sun Press, of No.
"2, rue Cardinal, in one volume, this volume to
"contain also a preface. The edition will be
"limited to SIX HUNDRED (600) copies, of which
"ONE HUNDRED (100) will be signed, and, in addition
"thereto, you are to receive TWENTY-FIVE (25)
"Author's copies, and there shall be TWENTY-FIVE
"(25) press copies for critics, and SIX (6) library
"copies. The corrected proofs of these fragments

"will be our property. We agree and bind ourselves
"to see that the plates are broken up and the type
"distributed as soon as the above copies are
"printed.

"We furthermore understand that the copyright to
"these fragments is in your name, and that you are
"at perfect liberty to immediately apply for
"additional copyrights in America on any matter
"not heretofore covered by your American copyright.

"We herewith recognize in every way your right
"of American copyright and your copyright in France
"and other countries.

"Moreover, we agree that upon the first page of the
"above edition, at the bottom thereof, there shall
"appear the words: 'All rights of publication,
" 'reproduction, and translation are reserved for all
" 'countries—Copyrighted by James Joyce—1929.'

"This book is to be the next publication of the
"Black Sun press after the receipt of the Manuscript
"from you, and it is agreed that no other edition,
" 'de luxe', or otherwise, of these fragments,
"whether alone or included in other works, is to be
"made until EIGHTEEN (18) MONTHS after the day of
"publication of this book, that is to say, the day
"the printer delivers the first copy and the book is
"off the press. It is furthermore understood that the
"payment to you of the second half, to-wit, ONE
"THOUSAND ($1,000.—) DOLLARS, is to be made on the
"day of publication, as heretofore mentioned.

"Will you kindly acknowledge the receipt of the first
"half payment, to-wit, ONE THOUSAND ($1,000.—) DOLLARS,
"which we have already made to you, and also of your
"accord to this arrangement.

"Very truly yours.

Joyce began going over proof sheets in mid-April, usually working at
the Crosbys' apartment, although only after he had received Caresse's
assurance that their whippet would remain tied up and muzzled while he
was there. Then seated in the largest chair in the library, near which stood
a lamp with an "enormous light bulb," he would patiently explain each
revision. Caresse recorded his first visit:

"Now, Mr. and Mrs. Crosby," Joyce said, "I wonder if you understand why I made that change?" All this in a blarney-Irish key.

"No, why?" we chorused, and there ensued one of the most intricate and erudite twenty minutes of explanation that it has ever been my luck to hear, but unfortunately I hardly understood a word, his references were far too esoteric. Harry fared better, but afterward we both regretted that we did not have a dictaphone behind the lamp so that later we could have studied all that had escaped us. Joyce stayed three hours, he did not want a drink, and by eight he hadn't got through with a page and a half. It was illuminating.

Joyce was still making corrections in May and the Crosbys had still not managed to see Picasso. With the publication of *Tales* scheduled for the following month, each departed one morning on separate missions—Caresse to Picasso, Harry to Joyce—from which they vowed not to return without having made substantial progress toward bringing the book closer to completion. At Picasso's Caresse heard the upsetting news that he "never did portraits any more, and never *sur commande*," and that, anyway, he "wouldn't do a portrait of Joyce," although he hinted that he might make a drawing for the Black Sun some time. It was a decision he would live to regret, Caresse told him. Harry found Joyce "feeling very poorly," partly because he had been "working terribly hard on the three fragments," which had begun to look like "a multitude of corrections," one of which Harry was amazed to learn had taken three days to write— "a difficult mathematical sentence," Joyce explained, "with the clue at the end (the word Finish to show that the words in the sentence are of Finnish derivation)." With a mixture of awe and exasperation, Harry commented: "This has even Flaubert beaten."

Though disappointing, Picasso's refusal did not deter Caresse, for she had already decided on her next choice: Brancusi. To her delight he accepted at once and quickly made several sketches of Joyce, all close likenesses, one of which the Crosbys selected and then rejected, deciding that it detracted from Ogden's preface and the text and was "not enough in advance." Joyce concurred and helped to dispel their reluctance to return to the artist to ask for an "abstract conception" of Joyce, a request he agreed to honor provided he were given "absolute freedom." Composed of three vertical lines of varying length and an elongated curlicue, Brancusi's quintessential portrait was sufficiently *au courant* to delight the

192

Crosbys, amuse Joyce, and annoy Sylvia Beach, who dismissed it as a "bit too basic." Some years later the artist told Richard Ellmann the portrait was "intended . . . to express the *'sens du pousser'* which he found in Joyce—the sense of enigmatic involution." Brancusi's hasty completion of the portrait revived the hope that *Tales* would appear on schedule after all, a prospect that Joyce himself enhanced when, a week after Harry's visit, he delivered the final corrected proof sheets of the "Ondt and the Gracehoper," and then returned again to make additional corrections. It was a visit that enlarged Harry's estimate of him:

> Joyce here to correct final proof sheets on the Triangle. He loves to talk about his work and if ever the conversation goes off at a tangent he always coaxes it back to the Work in Progress. He is very shy almost like a schoolboy at times blushes squirms about in his chair is eager for praise laughs a lot. Never pedantic so that even when the subject matter is way over our heads it still remains interesting. And he says amusing things. For instance he compares the Gripes to an octopus and a plate of tripes à la mode de Caen. Himself he compares to a trapezist who has accomplished a difficult acrobatic feat and then is called upon to perform this feat again and again and again. I liked the way after he had signed the bon à tirer for the Mookse and Gripes how he thought of another word and rushed over to the Black Sun Press in a taxicab to change it. Still another proof of his seriousness.

Delayed for only a few final additions that Joyce insisted on inserting after mid-May, including the title, his corrected proof sheets at last went to Lescaret, and the Crosbys began to relax. Not for long, however. One more crisis, oddly enough created by their usually meticulous printer, suddenly demanded an immediate solution. Due to a miscalculation, an embarrassed Lescaret explained, he had committed an offensive typographical blunder. After setting the type for the Joyce book, he found that the last page contained only two lines, which left a large square of blank space that would somehow have to be reduced. Would Mrs. Crosby do him the favor of asking Joyce for, perhaps, an additional eight lines? Annoyed by what seemed a preposterous request, Caresse refused, but when she returned to the printery the next day Lescaret's customary ebullience had been restored. Beaming, he handed her the final page, to which eight lines had been added. "Where did you get these?" she wanted to know. "Madame, I hope you will forgive me," the printer replied. "I went to see Mr. Joyce personally to tell him our troubles. He was very nice—he gave me the text right away—he told me he had been wanting to add more, but was too frightened of you, Madame, to do so."

In a spring that had already been devoted mostly to the affairs of Crane and Joyce, the Crosbys still managed to publish two books and complete negotiations for two others. In March the first Black Sun publication of the year appeared, *Short Stories* by Kay Boyle, which also happened to be the author's first book. Dedicated to Laurence Vail, the American artist and future husband of the author, the volume contains seven short stories, all but one of which had appeared previously in various little magazines, four in *transition*. Harry's estimate of Miss Boyle's work remained faithfully laudatory: "Again I say that Kay Boyle is the greatest woman writer since Jane Austen." And corroborating Crosby's assessment in his unmistakable hypermetaphorical idiom, Eugene Jolas declared that Miss Boyle's "organic impulses" accounted for the "savage beauty" of the narratives. In prose that was "hard, yet flexible enough to present the 'limit-states' of her consciousness," she had captured a "universe of anguish, confusion and a desperate search for liberation." *Short Stories*, he concluded, marked a "turning point in the evolution of American literature." Robert McAlmon, however, disagreed. They "were by no means as good" as some she did later, although he admitted they had helped the author "get recognition from more commercial publishers," one of whom, Jonathan Cape and Harrison Smith, published Miss Boyle's first trade book, *Wedding Day and Other Stories*, the following year.

That April Harry issued a second volume of his diary, *Shadows of the Sun*, as sumptuous as the first and again limited to just forty-four copies for private circulation. Besides a dedication to Caresse, "Queen of the Sun," it bore an ominously provocative inscription: *"si madame mourroit je mourrois avec elle."* Harry was also preparing a new edition of *Transit of Venus*, much praised by Archibald MacLeish. "I should rather have a sincere word from him," Harry wrote, "than a thousand and one laudatory effusions from the average critic." After living abroad for a number of years, the MacLeishes had just gone home to Glencoe, Illinois. Through Joyce they had met the Crosbys and had often been weekend guests at the mill. The correspondence that flowed between Crosby and MacLeish that spring dealt principally with *Einstein*, a long poem which American critics, with the lone exception of Conrad Aiken, had proclaimed a failure. As a prospect for the Black Sun, however, both Mac-

Leish and Harry believed it had obvious attractions, and the poet assured his friend that he could publish it on his own conditions. In March they reached an agreement; McLeish would receive two hundred dollars—"a fine lot of money," he wrote Harry. For the frontispiece MacLeish suggested the drawing that Paul Emile-Bécat (brother-in-law of Adrienne Monnier) had made of him in 1927, still available, he correctly remembered, in Sylvia Beach's bookshop.

In the meantime the Crosbys had a letter from Lawrence acknowledging payment for *Sun* ("4000 francs . . . seems to me quite a large sum"), and asking if they could recommend "some decent bookseller or publisher" who might be entrusted with the publication of a Paris edition of *Lady Chatterley's Lover*, which the author himself would underwrite. He would like it to be "a stock edition at about 100 francs," he told them, "something like Joyce's *Ulysses* or *The Well of Loneliness*." A letter to Sylvia Beach proposing that she look after the book if he paid for publication had not yet brought a reply. Nor had he heard from the Pegasus Press, where he had sent a similar inquiry. Already ill and loath to exchange the warm climes of Bandol for the usually chilly spring of Paris, Lawrence next asked Richard Aldington and Aldous Huxley to intercede for him with the unresponsive Miss Beach. But when their calls at Shakespeare and Company ended unsuccessfully, it appeared that a trip to Paris would be necessary after all. In March, Lawrence and his wife Frieda arrived in Paris, and at the end of the month they accepted an invitation to pass a few days at Crosby's mill.

Meeting the author of *The Plumed Serpent* was an enlightening experience for Harry. From a distance he had come to revere this fellow sun-worshiper, viewing him as perhaps the only one to whom the mysteries of the sun were comprehensible, even inspirational, and one whose thoughts and opinions seemed to coincide almost exactly with his own. Proximity, however, produced bewilderment, and then disappointment, for instead of the kindred spirit Harry expected, Lawrence seemed more like an autocrat, and to his surprise, also something of a prig. Just before coming to stay at the mill, Lawrence joined Crosby for lunch in Paris. The occasion, in Harry's words, contained bodeful meanings for the future: "D. H. Lawrence for luncheon and we disagreed on everything. I am a visionary I like to soar he is all engrossed in the body and in the mushroom quality of the earth and the body and in the complexities of psychology. He is indirect. I am direct. He admits defeat. I do not . . . Lawrence stayed until

Left: D. H. Lawrence, Le Moulin, Ermenonville, France, 1929.
SOUTHERN ILLINOIS UNIVERSITY LIBRARY

Below: First page of *The Escaped Cock* by D. H. Lawrence; decorations in color by the author (Black Sun Press, 1929).
PRINCETON UNIVERSITY LIBRARY

THERE was a peasant near Jerusalem who acquired a young gamecock which looked a shabby little thing, but which put on brave feathers as spring advanced, and was resplendent with arched and orange neck by the time the fig-trees were letting out leaves from their end-tips.

This peasant was poor, he lived in a cottage of mud-brick and had only a dirty little inner courtyard with a tough fig-tree for all his territory. He worked hard among the vines and olives and wheat of his master, then came home to sleep in the mud-brick cottage by the path. But he was proud of his young rooster. In the shut-in yard were three shabby hens which laid small eggs, shed the few feathers they had, and made a disproportionate amount of dirt. There was also, in a

1

four attacking my visionary attitude but my fort withstood the bombardment and I marshalled my troops and sallied out to counter-attack all of which took time. . . ."

The day Lawrence and his wife arrived at the mill Harry insisted on playing a gramaphone recording of James Joyce reading from *Ulysses*. Afterward Lawrence growled: "Yes I thought so a preacher a Jesuit preacher who believes in the cross upsidedown." Worse yet, Lawrence hated the "Empty Bed Blues," one of Harry's favorites, and was shocked when Harry gave a "dissertation in favor of *la morsure* in love-making." The rest of the visit was spent taking long walks in the woods, riding in the donkey carts Harry had hired for his guests, and listening to Lawrence's leisurely descriptions of New Mexico, Australia, and Florence— the vacated haunts of his perpetual odyssey. On Easter Sunday ("at supper time around the fire") Lawrence read a story about the "wanderings of Jesus after his resurrection and of how he met a priestess of Isis in a little temple on the coast of Phoenicia and how they lived together and how this is the missing link in the history of the Christ." Lawrence called it *The Escaped Cock*, and although one section had already appeared in the *Forum*, the Crosbys learned that the complete version had never been published. Obviously the chance to print another Lawrence story could not be allowed to slip by, and a few days later when he came back to the mill to be sculpted by Caresse, Lawrence brought along a typescript for the Crosbys to look over. Despite a brief reappearance of that divisive topic—James Joyce—Lawrence's second visit with the Crosbys passed quietly. "Caresse and I," Harry noted in his diary, "pro-Joyce, Lawrence and Huxley [Aldous Huxley accompanied Lawrence to the mill] anti-Joyce and I proclaim the Word itself the Word is a talent of gold but it is a friendly discussion this time (no need to call out my shock troops) and there was tea and glasses of sherry." Before leaving, Lawrence agreed to let the Crosbys publish his story, advising them, however, to secure a copyright to protect him and themselves from the plundering pirates.

Harry Marks turned up in Paris in June for the publication of *Tales of Shem and Shaun*, and joined Harry and Caresse "for luncheon and cocktails and champagne and a great talk about the Black Sun Press." Except for the fifty *hors commerce* copies of *Tales* the Crosbys retained, Marks took the entire stock of Joyce's book: one hundred copies on Japanese Vellum, signed by the author; and five hundred copies on Holland Van Gelder Zonen. He also arranged to take the second June publication, an apple-green-covered edition of Sterne's *A Sentimental Journey*

Through France and Italy, numbering over two hundred pages and illustrated, rather skimpily, by Polia Chentoff, who with this book ended her commercial relationship with the Crosbys. Only two books appeared on the summer schedule, both Harry's: the second edition of *Transit of Venus*, and a miniature book he called *The Sun*. In late June, however, he added a third, Bob Brown's collection of calligrams, *1450–1950*, which the author consented to subsidize.

When Hart Crane returned to Paris in early July, only two months remained before his agreement with the Crosbys came due, and since he had not brought *The Bridge* much closer to completion during his travels, he speculated that perhaps he would do better if he returned to America. In the meantime he told Caresse he was "through playing around" and would spend the rest of his stay preparing the manuscript of *The Bridge* "for your hands." His promises to reform notwithstanding, Crane found that Paris was still an irresistible "madhouse." One night at the Café Select an argument over a bill suddenly degenerated into a swinging battle between Crane, several waiters, and, unfortunately, a gendarme. Overpowered finally by a swarm of policemen, he was beaten into insensibility and dragged off to jail. The incident mobilized the American colony. Crane's painter friend, Eugene MacCown, set up a defense fund and gathered statements condemning the police action from André Gide and Jean Cocteau; Kay Boyle tried unsuccessfully to reach Harry, who was traveling, and Whit Burnett (then a reporter on the Paris *Herald*), E. E. Cummings, and other friends descended on the office of the chief prefect of police protesting the injustice of their friend's arrest and succeeded in so outraging the prefect that he refused to release Crane without a trial. By then Harry had heard what had happened and had begun coordinating efforts to secure Crane's release, which finally came on July 10, a day Harry described in unusual detail:

> To the Black Sun Press. . . . Then to take a taxi to see McGown [MacCown] about Hart Crane. I arrived in front of the Deux Maggots and hailed a taxi. Just then McGowan stepped out of the café with Vitrac and a girl called Kitty Cannell. We drove off to the Palais de Justice. It was quarter to one. I had a date with Marks at the Ritz Bar so I rushed off and got him (we drank two cocktails) and brought him back with me to the trial. Hart was magnificent. When the Judge announced that it had taken ten gendarmes to hold him (the dirty bastards, they dragged him three blocks by the feet) all the court burst into laughter. After ten

minutes of questioning he was fined 800 francs and 8 days in prison
should he ever be arrested again. A letter from the Nouvelle Revue
Francaise had a good deal to do with his liberation. They wouldn't
let him out right away so I went with Marks to Le Doyen to eat
and to drink sherry cobblers in the sun. We got tight and he went
off to see Eugene O'Neill and I went to the bank. On my way back
I started off towards the race-ticker bar on the Rue Cambon to see
if Tornado had won, but on the way I saw a pretty American girl,
so I talked to her and we went to the Ritz for a sherry cobbler (her
name was Sheelah—I like it) but I had to rush off to the Conciergerie
where I found Vitrac and Whit Burnett and I drove over there (we
saw a truck run over a cat) and here we had to wait from six until
long after eight (we spent the time drinking beer and playing
checkers and talking to the gendarmes). At last the prisoners began
to come out, Hart the last one, unshaved hungry wild. So we stood
and drank in the Bar de la Bonne Santé right opposite the prison
gate and then drove to the Herald office where Burnett got out to
write up the story for the newspaper, Hart and I going on to the
Chicago Inn for cornbread and poached eggs on toast . . . and Hart
said that the dirty skunks in the Santé wouldn't give him any paper
to write poems on. The bastards.

The next day Harry bought Crane a second-class ticket to New York
on the *Homeric*, and in the time that remained before sailing Crane dutifully showed the Crosbys revisions of *The Bridge*, or discussed its format,
and tried however he could to convince his friends he was indeed making
progress. When Crane finally left for America, accompanied by Harry's
bon-voyage gift of a bottle of Cutty Sark, the Crosbys wondered how
much more of *The Bridge*, if any, they would receive before the deadline.
Their worries diminished somewhat when the poet—in a letter post-
marked July 23 and written from the *Homeric*—reported that he was
working, and offered the Crosbys some suggestions for the typography of
the Black Sun publication. "Here are some stars. . . . I think that 'A' is the
best—if made smaller—for the end of the book. And I'm not at all sure
now that I want one at all on the title page. If so, it ought to be very small.
But I leave it to your taste entirely." In the same letter he listed the poems
in the first edition of Harry's *Transit of Venus* that he had liked—"Even-
tuate," "Fire-Eaters," "Were It Not Better," and "Beyond" (in the last he
found a Rimbaudian vigor)—all of which, along with ten new poems,
Harry reprinted in the second edition distributed that summer. Also ready
about the same time was Harry's miniature book, *The Sun*. Measuring 2.5
by 1.75 centimeters, with a red leather cover on which blazed a gold-

embossed flaming sun, and encased a tiny felt-lined green-flowered box, in which lodged a magnifying apparatus, it looked like an exquisite jewel. Each poem was framed by a black-rule border and had been set in Roman Corps 3 type, type so minute that reading the words was nearly impossible without the magnifying glass. Like pendants, Caresse's drawings nicely complemented the poems.

In August Harry delivered one hundred and fifty copies of *1450–1950* to Brown, who quickly sent most of them on to publishers and friends, sixty of whom he had listed opposite the title page under the heading "Free Copies." In return, Brown hoped for a few kind words that might be useful in reviving a writing career that had been quiescent for close to fifteen years. *1450–1950* is an amusing mixture of ideography and calligraphy, examples of which Brown had been amassing—with obvious pleasure—for many years. "I like looking back/ at the/ Illuminated manuscripts of/ 1450/ And forward/ to the/ more Illuminations/ Movie Scripts of/ 1950 I like to see/ Fly Specks/ on yellowed pages/ I like too/ Leaving my own on/ New ones/ My Fly Speck." In his dedication to "all monks, all early oriental artists—Omar—Gutenberg, Caton—, Jimmy-the-Ink, Boccaccio, Rabelais, Shakespeare, Defoe, Goya, Blake, Sterne, Whitman, Crane, Stein, Joyce, Pagliacci, and Myself," Brown playfully attempted to locate his work in the history of innovative printing and himself among those authors celebrated as much for their matter as for their manner of expression. By early fall, he had gathered a garland of testimonials from, among others, Gertrude Stein, H. L. Mencken, and William Carlos Williams.

IV

Five months before he took his life Harry cabled his family to sell stock worth ten thousand dollars; he also informed them that Caresse and he had decided to "lead a mad and extravagant life." To their protestations, not long in coming, he replied in a way that could only have exacerbated their fears. Part of his reply, along with additional comments, Harry recorded in his diary:

> . . . . perhaps it was the "we intend to lead a mad and extravagant life" that upset you. This should not be taken seriously in the common sense of the words but it should be taken seriously in the true significance of the words. The abysms and swamps of red skeletons have been swept clean by the diamond winds of Velocity

and Madness. Stagnation is the past. Whirlwinds and Hurricanes are the present and future. Mamma says she fears disaster 'what is your life leading you to' I can say that it is arrowing me into the Finality of Fire of Sun by means of Catapults and Explosions Gold and Sorceresses and Tornados I believe in giving to my life new and violent associations and I agree with Jolas there is only one action I can believe in and that is the action that leads me to eternity. If we appear to you unwise because we like looping the loop and other aerial acrobatics (never forgetting however the directness of an Atlantic Flight) it may be true and there might come a crash but there is no crime in an explosion whereas there is I think a crime in ending life the way so many people do with a whimper. And when we think of the comets and meteors and the moon and the stars and the planets and the Sun all whirling whirling far above us in the great harmony of the spheres how trivial and ephemeral became dinner parties auction bridge horse-races the editions of books or the investing and selling of stock. For the poet there is love and there is death and infinity and for other things to assume such vital importance is out of the question and that is why I refuse to take the question of money seriously.

Prophecies of death abound in Harry's diary: on August 1, he wrote: "today I read in the 'White Devil' what must be for me prophetic—'Of all deaths the violent death is best/ For from ourselves it steals ourselves so fast/ The pain once apprehended is quite past.'" An entry made on August 8, perhaps occasioned by a rendezvous with the "Sorceress," fore-shadows the circumstances of his death: "In the evening gin fizzes color of green and silver and the Sorceress girlish like young actress feline as a puma she is even more feline and amorous by night and now we are together would that we might vanish together into sleep and. . . ." A few days later Harry destroyed the "pages of statistics" he had faithfully re-corded, as though ridding himself of some noisome relic of the past that he had just discovered was superfluous: ". . . who in hell wants to keep track of the number of drinks he has drunk (it ruins drinking) or the number of cigarettes smoked or the number of cold baths taken or the number of sun-baths or the number of orchids sent or the number of times I have made love. . . ." The same month he marveled at the speed at which the year was elapsing: "the fastest I can remember like a flash of lightning not one vibration of a clock since a year ago and perhaps now I can destroy time as I have destroyed statistics. But this will be harder much more difficult. . . ." Two days after he had watched a "mad aviator" do "slide-slips tail spins loops and flying upside down" over the beach at

Deauville (aerial acrobatics he configured as a miraculous poem), Harry enrolled as a student pilot at a small flying field at Villecomblay. He was pleased to find that with his instructor he shared "the war, girl friends, love of adventure, detachment, drinking, misunderstandings with our families, attitude towards money, restlessness. . . ." A week later Harry took his first flight.

The accelerated intensity that Crosby's life had assumed inevitably affected his writing. "I wake up dreaming of aeroplanes and orchids whirling in circles around two figures the Sorceress and the Fire-Princess [sobriquets for current loves]," he wrote in September, the same month he began *Aphrodite in Flight*, short prose observations on the "aerodynamics of love." Around the same time he finished three experimental pieces for *transition*, and had "kindled the fire" to another book, a book of dreams, soon to be christened *Sleeping Together*; and, at irregular intervals, he went on translating more of the "damn Proust letters," which by this time he admitted he would not think of doing had they not been to "Cousin Walter."

The Escaped Cock appeared in September on time, despite the crowded schedule, and from Bandol Lawrence sent congratulations. As he had done with *Sun*, Lawrence supplied the Crosbys with drawings for the new book—a headpiece and tailpiece (brightly colored gamecocks) for Part I as well as a frontispiece, and for the back cover a black phoenix enveloped in bright red flames. Probably because he was fond of his story (it was one of his "thin-skinned ones"), and perhaps more so now that it was being published in complete form for the first time, he made some forthright recommendations to Caresse regarding sale and distribution of the book. One of his concerns was Harry Marks. Why, he asked her, should Marks be sent the whole edition? "Why don't you print 750 and let Marks have 500, and keep 250 to dispose of this side? I don't see why Marks should have the monopoly. And do please tell me what price he is going to charge—it should be at least $10., and what terms does he make with you? He ought, of course, to pay you $6.65 for each $10. copy—and no bookseller would take more than 40%—which means he would give you $6. on a $10 copy. What are his terms? Have you already fixed them? This is a book that will soon be snapped up—why give it away to Harry Marks?" Finally, he wondered whether Caresse was planning to "halve profits" with him. "Write me a business letter with all details, we may as well have it all square. What I don't see is why all copies should go to New York. Why should not some be sold in Europe?" Reassuring Lawrence would not be easy, but Caresse reported that the price she planned to ask Marks would be considerably higher than the one she had recommended earlier; she also reminded him that, since Marks had to "give one-third off to bookshops and pay 25% duties and tax de luxe as well," the book would have to retail "for over twice" what she asked him for it. At any rate Lawrence's figure of ten dollars for the regular copies would be the minimum price he could ask.

A matter nearly as worrisome for Lawrence was the safe arrival of his book in America. Having received no news from Caresse a month after publication, he asked if she had heard "anything of copies sent to New York. I do wonder how they will fare. . . . If they are stopped, we must make a plan for getting them to England." Lawrence, in fact, had already arranged with Martin Secker (London) for the publication of an ordinary unlimited edition to be released six months after the Black Sun book. In November he was still anxious about the fate of *The Escaped Cock*, and enquired again whether it had "passed or not," and this time learned that the Black Sun shipment had reached New York and gone through customs without incident. Almost at once, however, Lawrence reopened the row with Marks, expanded now to include all "exploiting booksellers," and exacerbated (no doubt quite unwittingly) by Caresse's report that she had sold the entire edition of *The Escaped Cock* to Marks for a price Lawrence ridiculed as absurd. After barely acknowledging her check for his story, forwarded the following February (1930), Lawrence queried: "But did you really sell that whole edition for $2,250.00? It seems absurd, for Marks was retailing it at $25.00 a copy, as I know from two sources. He may have had to come down in price, later. But did you sell the whole edition, *including the vellums*, for $2,250.00? If you did, you are not the good business woman I should expect you to be: and I resent bitterly these little few booksellers making all that money out of us."

The problems that bothered Lawrence were not ones likely to haze the horizon of Gerald Lymington. In early October Harry issued his friend's second Black Sun book, a poem in three parts entitled *Spring Song of Iscariot*, which Lymington had dedicated to one who understood his first book, *Git le Coeur*. In his prologue the author confided that the new poem rendered a man's "attainment for the spirit," not in the "hard prose of philosophy" but in philosophy burned to poetry. Attesting that the form his poem had assumed lay beyond his conscious choice ("it grew of itself"), and that its rhythm aped "no modernity," Lymington hoped he had imbued his ruminations with urgent and spiritual meanings, the inspiration of which he attributed to the nameless person of the dedication: "Because of you I have tried to tell of the bitter desert men must cross between the booths of common mating and that attainment—wherein enough loving light and enough each other, they became light internal, which is God."

Spring Song of Iscariot confirmed that, along with Harry and Caresse, Lymington had enlisted in Eugene Jolas' campaign to purge the language of "monotonous syntax," a campaign the Crosbys announced they supported by signing the manifesto "Revolution of the Word," which Jolas printed (with the signatories) in the June 1929 number of *transition*. A few of Harry's short pieces had appeared in the February issue of the review, and others, including his spirited reply to Max Eastman's attack on Joyce which had come out in the April number of *Harper's*, would be printed in later numbers. By mid-year Crosby, along with Elliot Paul, Robert Sage, Matthew Josephson, and Stuart Gilbert, was listed as one of *transition*'s advisory editors, a suitable anchorage for one whose writing had begun to show unmistakably Joycean characteristics, and who had discovered that the "deformation and reformation of old words" could be as exciting as a horse race. Already strongly under the sway of Jolas (he had long before subscribed to one tenet of Jolas' "Proclamation," that "time is a tyranny to be abolished"), Harry aggressively supported the offensive against the "hegemony of the banal word, static psychology, descriptive naturalism," against all the classic and reactionary literary forms, against the barriers that protected a world and a literature long dead in his opinion. It was, after all, part of the campaign he had always waged against the stifling restrictions of his own past and which he had only recently notified his family he intended to intensify.

The book on which Harry worked steadily through October and November was the book of dreams called *Sleeping Together*, which probably owed part of its inspiration to Jolas, who taught that dreams were capable of producing the "fabulous, the romantic, the magical," what he had named "kinetic romanticism," which, in addition to dreams, included the study of the primitive, and of such "mythic states of mind as approach the fairy tale, the legend, and the ballad." Jolas' own version of this new mythology, as Kay Boyle once called it, was the next Black Sun publication, *Secession in Astropolis*, a seminal book illustrating the twelve points set forth in the "Proclamation." As expected, the illustrations could be as baffling as the pronouncements. Two scenarios—"Flight into Geography" and "Elysian Invention"—delineate the wanderings and troubles of a nameless, lonely youth, as does the last section called "Document," and both may be read as hyperbolized descriptions of Jolas' early years in America and France.

> My mother is an old woman with snow in her hair. She bore me under Gemini shadowed by skyscrapers. I grew into the day amid the spawn of strangers and listened to the first rumblings of the industrial revolution. On the cliffs of the Indian river, my parents dreamed anarchic dreams, and crossed the ocean again in search of the ancient loam. My childhood blossomed in the shadow of a cathedral. Hunger for the absolute gnawed me, when blackbirds brought marvellous words of dusk, folk-songs sank out of star-dew, a gothic wind blew over aryan strings.

Childhood fantasy ended, the demands of life began: "Machines carried me along. I had no longer time to dream. I was hemmed in. It swirled around me, mass, darkening my joys, shrilled into the sonata of a fairy tale. The demi-urge! Speed! Forward! One. Two. Three." Satisfied by liberty, presumably found abroad, perhaps in Paris, he exalts for awhile, then returns to the "new world" escarped in his own mind: "Alone I brew my magic. New world, miraculous humanity of my mind, I kneel before you, dusty refugee in my century's shambles!"

Archibald MacLeish's poem *Einstein* emerged next from Lescaret's shop, its large format impressive and the sixteen-point Caslon type bold and inviting. MacLeish had placed a poem ("Tourist Death") in the February number of *transition*, but he was far from being one of Jolas' "transitionalists," and of course he had not signed the "Revolution of the Word." *Einstein* plainly shows the divergent course the poet pursued, at least stylistically. Reacting with a humanist's skepticism to the claims and speculations of modern science, MacLeish makes Einstein a symbol of science impaired by its own incomplete constructs, best exemplified by the practice of reducing all things through reason to atoms. Thus handicapped by a self-imposed myopia, the scientist occupies a small and deceptively secure world, rather like inhabiting a "garden in a close." Yet this solitary figure does control the universe, or that universe he can shape into comprehensible abstractions, destroying as he does the individual quality of things by submerging "all differences in the indifferent flux."

Harry spent November putting the final touches on *Mad Queen*, the book of tirades he dedicated to "T. N. T." ("never so mad a ladye") and to which Caresse contributed a drawing of the Mad Queen. The author's most devastating salvos ("tirades") were aimed at Boston and America. The former, the subject of "Target for Disgust," is cursed for its sins of hypocrisy, flatulence, and uncleanliness; it is a place where the beverage is the "water of the Dead-Sea," the food "Salt Peter and the Juices of Cod," where libraries "clogged with Pamphlets and Tracts" have no Joyces, Gertrude Steins, or Maldorors, and where churches "crowded with Sabbatarians" have no prophets, fanatics, or Sun-Gods. In "Enquête" Harry found America guilty of the same sins. Only exile provided relief from the burdensome reminders of his childhood as well as an opportunity, since he is already an "enemy of society," to hunt with other "enemies of society." In "Heliograph," another attack on America and the most self-revelatory document outside the diaries, Crosby recounted how he had tried to pursue his own "amenable soul":

Omens and Astrology.
A desert flat and undisturbed, stupid and
forlorn. Sunless. A caravan of failures. Pons
Asinorum and the Feast of the Ass and revolt
against standardized American childhood.

War and Violence.
Catapults and Torches and the first stray thrusts of
Sun into the Soul. Bombardments and Bordels.
Heraldry and High Walls. Too rigid to crumple
but not too strong to fracture.

Post-War Depression.
Extensive swamps formed by alcohol stagnating
in the brain. Away from the gregariousness of
the elephant towards the singleness of the hawk.

Omens and Astrology.
From Fog to Sun. Leaves and Inflorescence. Four
columns of red marble. The scorification method.
Love-Madness. Torchbearer and the complete
entrance of Sun into Soul. Sunfire.

Boa-Constrictor
through the thick grass. Red Skeletons. Silver Scar
by Silver Image and Cicatrix. Reculer pour mieux
avancer. The beaten forces were at last withdrawn
safely into the Island.

The Primitive Method
of strengthening the soul by dropping red-hot

206

sunstones into it. Rimbaud and Van Gogh. Counter-
Attack. Turbulence. Chariot of the Sun.

The Mad Queen.
The violent state of fusion. Her Sun tattoed on my
back. The bold progressive march to the Sun.
Multiplication of Madness. Anarchism. I lay Siege
to the Sun.

Shortly before *Mad Queen* was released (winter 1929), Harry finished and immediately printed his book of dreams *Sleeping Together*.
Made up of sixty-four short prose lyrics, it had so obsessed him that the
actual composition had taken only "three or four days"; behind him,
however, he noted in his diary, lay "three or four years of hard work."
Reviewing the manuscript before sending it to Lescaret, he found what
he had written "funny and fantastic and absolutely individual." *Sleeping
Together*, published on November 14, bore the inscription: "These dreams
for Caresse." It also included a verse from *Ecclesiastes*: "If two lie together then they have heat but how can one be warm alone." Caresse
entitled her frontispiece "Dormir Ensemble."

Harry devoted his last days in France to flying, resolved to solo
before departing for America on November 16. His diary entries for the
period reveal an extraordinary determination and concentration. "I fly in
the afternoon I refuse to go to America until I have flown alone" (November 4). "I am nervous. I wish they would let me fly alone" (November 6). "More flying more wanting to fly alone" (November 7). "I fly
three times but I am not let loose. If I don't fly alone soon I shall go mad"
(November 9). "I fly four times with Detri [Crosby's instructor] twice in
the morning twice in the afternoon and now I hope I shall be let loose"
(November 10). Let loose he was, the following day, November 11, the
day Crosby had unfailingly hallowed in deference to his dead comrades.
His terse diary entry for Armistice Day 1929, however, simply reads: "I
fly alone for the first time at 11 o'clock this morning." A victor by four
days in his race to solo before going home.

Among the items the Crosbys packed for their trip were presentation
copies of *Sleeping Together* for friends and family in America, including a
blank one, elegantly bound by Gruel of Paris, in which Harry would make
a holograph of the poem during the voyage (a feat he accomplished
without a slip despite a "terrific storm"). For Caresse the journey turned
out to be a nervous one, due partly at least to a fellow passenger she
identified, using Harry's "sun-name" for her rival, as "Constance of the

Golden Horse." After landing in New York (the city of "Arabian Nights") on November 22, the day before the Harvard-Yale football game they had hurried home to see, they at once left for Boston. Harry spent the next morning with Josephine, with whom he would be found dead two weeks later in New York.

After Harry died, many, including Caresse, recalled that death, a subject never distant from his mind, had had an almost preternatural fascination for him during the time he was in America. In the longest diary entry he wrote after his arrival (most are terse one- and two-line capsulations) he described what he liked about the room he and Caresse had taken at the Savoy Plaza. "I like living in one room more concentrated more for the poet and high up 27 stories and the round disc of the Sun miraculous place for the sun-death room of the rising sun." The morning of the day before he died, a morning filled with dazzling sun, Harry suddenly proposed to Caresse that they together achieve their "sun-death" at once. "Give me your hand, Caresse," he said. "Our window is open wide. Let's meet the sun-death together." Frightened and protesting, she insisted that they had too much to live for. But Harry's anguished reply revealed that that lay at the very basis of his decision: "There is too much. I cannot endure it all." The moment of paralyzing terror passed. But Caresse demanded that they depart "very soon," and Harry agreed and promised to book return passage to Paris on December 13, adding, however, that they might just "keep on round the world. I don't want to stop." Caresse memorialized that portentous morning in her poem "Invited to Die":

> Our eyes were opened to a blaze of Sun
> New York beyond the sill flashed from
> That wed white structure to our dawn
> And found us storied high, in wool and lawn,
> Above New York
> Our eyes strung level with the Fuller's shine
> (Ritz Tower windows flashed
>   your smile to mine!)
> 'My hand in yours Caresse, unblind?'
> That morning knew
> The sudden wave-length of my longing too,
> 'But we so strong so one so true,' I said
> 'To seek the sunvast splendor through negation'
> Fled the future

Flew the star-filled pennant of my hopes
   across our skies
Over the sun-hung cauldron of your eyes. . . .

Clean sunbuilt dawn the day we owned New York
Rose into noon, the day returned to dark,
Your goddess flown
('To tempt us less' you said).

I did not guess.
I did not guess.

That madder beauty waited unawares
To take your hand upon the evening stairs.

It is difficult to believe that Crosby could have possibly accomplished any writing during this period. Yet Caresse remembered that "he wrote daily and worked feverishly on the last volume of *Shadows of the Sun*," although his diary entries included no mention of any such work. Rather they reveal that his involvement with "J" (Josephine) was consuming most of his time. There were also friends to see and parties to attend, one of which Hart Crane threw on December 7 to celebrate the long-delayed completion of *The Bridge*. After returning to New York, Crane had settled down and managed to expand and revise his poem; progress reports sent to the Crosbys, beginning in September, were often accompanied by revisions, with instructions to substitute them for the sections left behind in Paris. But in October, again despondent, Crane had stopped working once more, and the Crosbys, alarmed by the sudden interruption, wired him that he would have to decide either to publish *The Bridge* at once or wait until February. Deferring publication, he explained, would allow him "to see at least the bulk of the poem in proofs"; besides, he added, "Haven't been well lately, but hope to improve as soon as I can get the 5-year load of *The Bridge* off my shoulders. You can't imagine how insufferably ponderous it has seemed, yes, more than once!" Then, slowly and with the help of friends, Crane had finally lifted the ponderous burden; to celebrate the occasion he had invited all who had helped him to a party at his apartment in Greenwich Village, among them Malcolm Cowley, William Carlos Williams, E. E. Cummings, and Walker Evans, whose photographs had been chosen to illustrate the poem, and, of course, the Crosbys. Midway through the party, Harry and Margaret Robson walked together to Pineapple Street to replenish their host's gin supply, and along the way

Mrs. Robson listened to Harry's confused talk about the "complicated splendors of love and death, and of a great love that somehow should be fulfilled in his own death."

The following day, at a party given by Harry Marks, Crane accepted an invitation to join Caresse and Harry, Harry's mother, and Margaret Robson for dinner and the theater on December 10. That evening when Harry failed to appear (he was not given to lateness) Caresse knew that "something was very wrong indeed." A call to Stanley Mortimer, a close friend of Harry's, produced no information, but he promised to check his studio, which Harry sometimes used, and call her back if he had any news. Just as the group prepared to go on to the theatre, Mortimer telephoned to say he had been to his studio and found the door locked from the inside. He would call again as soon as he had been able to get in. At ten o'clock Hart Crane took Mortimer's message at the theatre, dreading what he would say. Inside the studio Mortimer had found Harry dead. In his arms lay the body of Josephine, in his hand a pistol. Each had died from a bullet in the temple. Harry's death haunted Crane for months. To Allen Tate he wrote: "I've been all broken up about Harry. I had just had a party or so for them—and all our friends immediately fell in love with them both. I was with Caresse and Harry's mother the evening of [the] so-called suicide, and had to break the news to them. I haven't been worth much since." On December 13, as planned, Caresse sailed for France, carrying Harry's ashes with her, and accompanied by Harry's mother. Crane told her before she left that he would send the final version of *The Bridge* by New Year's Day, but he finished the day after Christmas and posted it at once.

V

In Paris, Eugene Jolas hastily organized a memorial section—a tribute to Harry—which would appear in the next issue of *transition*. Caresse ordered Lescaret to stop work on *Sleeping Together*, which the editors of the *American Caravan* had decided to print in the spring. To Bob Brown she confided that Harry thought *Sleeping Together* was the "best thing he had written" and that it was "good to know that he wrote it for [her] . . . just before he died." She had arrived in Paris in time to supervise the final Black Sun publication of the year: a sumptuous, two-volume (French and English) edition of Choderlos de Laclos' *Les Liaisons Dangereuses*. But the most pressing matter of course was *The Bridge*, and Caresse lost no time putting it into production. The previous July Crane had signed a statement giving the Crosbys permission to publish his poem, or "such parts of a poem of mine, called *The Bridge* as I have left in their hands on the date of the heading of this statement" (July 11, 1929); the only proviso was that he be allowed to supervise the correction of at least one set of proofs before publication. In the same statement Crane explained that his contract with Horace Liveright made it impossible to offer the Crosbys any copyright privileges. It was understood the Black Sun edition of *The Bridge* would be a "special, advance and deluxe edition." The review copies Caresse sent to Crane for distribution in February met all the criteria they had agreed upon. Earlier, Crane had gone over the proof sheets and asked Caresse to lower the explanatory passage at the end of "Harbor Dawn" and print another passage at the top of "The Dance" section in red; and, besides the page layout and typographical alterations, he had made a few other textual changes. The two hundred and fifty copies, two hundred of which were printed on Holland paper (price: ten dollars) and fifty on Japanese vellum (price: twenty dollars), had been hand-set (Dorique type) and bound in cream paper covers. Caresse had selected red ink for the title as well as the section titles and marginal explanations, and black for the text. The three Walker Evans' photographs of the Brooklyn Bridge Crane had chosen were spaced throughout the book in locations also selected by him. Opposite the first poem, "To Brooklyn Bridge," was a picture showing the underside of the bridge: the photo of barges and a tug Crane instructed Caresse to place between the "Cutty Sark" and the "Hatteras" sections, since that was the " 'center' of the book, both physically and symbolically." The star Crane had drawn in July on the *Homeric* and sent to Harry with the suggestion that it appear at the end of the book and which Caresse had placed at the conclusion was missing from the published version, presumably the casualty of a last minute change of mind.

The heretofore amiable relations between the publisher and poet suffered a setback in the early months of the new year when Crane informed Caresse, who had become increasingly alarmed by the delays in the distribution of the twenty-five review copies she had posted to him, that reviews of *The Bridge* would be postponed until after the Liveright edition appeared at the end of March. She rejected such dilatoriness as inexcusable and she reminded Crane that she had worked hard to have review copies ready six weeks ahead of the Liveright book, which, although published too close to the Black Sun edition, she had not objected

Kay Boyle and Harry Crosby, Le Moulin, Ermenonville, France, 1928.

to; her single demand was that the Black Sun book should be reviewed first. Crane's friends, she recalled, had promised to write reviews if she supplied the copies. That the Black Sun edition was being shelved until the Liveright book came out so that it would, at best, be reviewed along with the commercial edition was "one of the most unkind and disloyal things" she had ever experienced. Crane, hurt and apologetic, reminded her that acquiring important coverage for an edition as small as hers was more than either of them had a right to expect. It was possible, he went on, that she had misunderstood him. What he intended to do, "wherever possible [was] to have the two editions reviewed together, with [hers] listed first, and with as much description of the [Black Sun] edition as [he] could properly influence the reviewers to attempt within the restrictions of the periodicals they were writing for." This he had done. Gradually tensions between them eased. The Liveright edition appeared and the critical reception, though extensive, was mixed, with reviewers often confining their praise to certain sections of the poem and making some disapproving comments about the structure. This was not the reception Crane had wanted, of course, and yet he found nothing in the commentaries to shake his belief in the poem's greatness.

Fortunately no hitches developed with the publications that followed *The Bridge*. The French and English editions of Proust's letters to Walter Berry, now titled *Forty-seven Unpublished Letters from Marcel Proust to Walter Berry*, were turned out in white paper covers, with heavy gold-colored slipcases. The Crosbys had hired Richard Thoma to make the English translations of Proust's letters, but after a disagreement with Caresse he had quit and the Crosbys had finished the translating themselves. As resplendent as the Proust volumes was a large edition of *Alice in Wonderland*, 791 copies, a little over half of which Caresse marked for America. Besides some attractive typography, there were six colored lithographs by Marie Laurencin. The press also issued a collection of photographs of New York taken by Gretchen and Peter Powel, since the mid-twenties close friends of the Crosbys and with whom, as Caresse observed, they shared the secret of being "escapists from a Puritan background." Peter, who took pictures in a "very unprofessional manner," and his wife, who amused Harry by her habit of crouching beside her husband when he photographed (Harry called them the crouchers), had assembled a collection of eighteen pictures with poetic captions and had asked the Crosbys to make up ten copies. Sumptuously bound in red-grain Morocco and multicolored calf, with dark-brown marbled endpapers, and the title *New York* stamped in gold on the spine, the Powels' very limited edition bore the highest price of all Black Sun books: one hundred dollars.

Caresse also oversaw the printing of what would be several posthumous books by Harry. First came *Shadows of the Sun*, the third volume of his diary, which he had finished in New York in December, followed by *Aphrodite in Flight*, a series of sportive reflections on flying and love he had composed while taking flying lessons. Marked *hors commerce* and limited to just twenty-seven copies, it was being printed "six months after the death of the author . . . from the original manuscript without revision." Beneath the whimsical exterior of these "observations on the aerodynamics of love" reside some fundamental lessons in how to succeed in love, and for the aerial-minded, in flying, and the impressive rewards that may await those, like Crosby, blessed with "vigilance and attention to detail." "A love-affair," instructed Harry, "should be [as] delicate and swift as the most modern pursuit-plane." Just as the racing-plane requires "the most high grade oil," so the "chariot of love" needs "the most high-grade champagne." The "three great elements of an air attack are surprise rapidity and manoeuvrability and this applies to an 'attaque d'amour' as well. . . ." The good aviator should have a thorough knowledge of acrobatics so as to be able "to extricate himself from any situation no matter how precarious." Likewise, the expert lover whose acrobatics are conversational will be able "to talk himself out of the most hazardous predicament." After the flight the usual procedure is to switch off the motor, "but it is wiser to leave the motor idling so that one is always prepared to take off again at a moment's notice on a New Flight." For Harry Crosby, the poet-adventurer, love and flying provided the last frontiers, each offering abundant and unknown regions to explore, hazards against which to test one's skill and will and strength, and exquisite moments of pleasure and peril and mystery.

The other two Black Sun publications of 1930 were poetry volumes, both limited editions and both by poets who had long known that a profit could usually be turned on a limited edition of a book scheduled for commercial publication at a later date. In 1927 Archibald MacLeish had gladly let the Crosbys issue a small edition of *Einstein* (one hundred copies at $7.50, fifty at $20.00), assuring them his publisher, Houghton Mifflin, would have no objections. Two years later MacLeish proposed that the Crosbys bring out another limited edition of a new collection entitled *New Found Land,* and look into the possibility of doing a printing for Houghton Mifflin at the same time. Harry had supplied the American firm with a "dummy' of MacLeish's book and a quotation, and it was agreed that Black Sun would print five hundred copies for the Boston publisher. The Black Sun edition of 135 copies appeared in March, several months ahead of the American publication. Besides a dedicatory poem "O Sun! Instigator of cocks!", certainly intended for Harry, several others bore the names of MacLeish's Paris friends—"Tourist Death" for Sylvia Beach, "Land's End" for Adrienne Monnier, and a long reverie on the meaning of being an American ("It is a strange thing to be an American./ It is strange to live on the high world in the stare/ Of the naked sun and the stars as our bones live."). Called "American Letter," it was dedicated to Gerald Murphy, the expatriate painter on whom Fitzgerald based Dick Diver, the deteriorating hero of *Tender Is the Night.*

Caresse and Ezra Pound met for the first time in the spring of 1930 when the poet, "bronzed and negligé," arrived in Paris from Rapallo; the correspondence that followed their meeting, though limited first to matters related to the Black Sun edition of his *Imaginary Letters,* gradually expanded into a general discussion of publishing in Europe and, eventually, to Pound's specific recommendations for a project that would change the direction of the Crosby firm. Though *Imaginary Letters* had been published in 1917 in the *Little Review*, the Black Sun volume would mark the first time the selections had appeared in book form, and, per Pound's instructions, Caresse planned a book that would match any of the deluxe editions of Pound's other works. The deluxe book, Pound told her, could be "useful in breaking the stranglehold that s. o. b. [i.e., commercial publishers] had on ALL publication." Its usefulness, however, he feared might be waning, for already there were signs that large firms like "Random Louse" had made the deluxe book "a trust" and had forced it into a trade channel, with the result that the writer often found himself "tied by what [he] could sell." As for "new writers at any time," Pound thought the deluxe book was "almost worthless." Nonetheless he had found that the deluxe edition, despite the troubles that often accompanied its preparation, was a dependable and relatively uncomplicated way to make a substantial profit on a book that might have a limited appeal as a commercial investment. He recommended that Caresse print an edition of four hundred copies of *Imaginary Letters* (she did) and ask fifteen francs (she charged five dollars), a price he believed would "enable one to distrib. [ute] the edtn. and that a reasonable number of people wd.[would] pay." Of the four hundred, however, fifty were printed on Japanese Vellum, and bore the author's signature (he had suggested thirty). Pound had originally asked Polia Chentoff to make illustrations for the three fantasies that closed the book, but the printing of the text had been done so quickly that the artist had had no time to prepare the illustrations. Since it seemed pointless to keep the "type standing about" while waiting for Miss Chentoff and since the printer had set the book up with such "magistral margins" that even without the illustrations it had reached a "decent size," Pound saw no reason to delay. As soon as he had finished reviewing the proofs and signed the fifty title pages ("most frequent error," he reminded Caresse, was "letter upside down"), he urged Caresse to go ahead with the publication.

More important to Pound than the publication of *Imaginary Letters* was the problem of what to do about his edition of the complete works of Guido Cavalcanti, the friend and correspondent of Dante, which the bankrupt Aquila Press had left unfinished. The difficult part of the composition had been printed (i.e., "the gordorful notes on the Donna mi Prega"), leaving, he estimated, around sixty pages more, which could be done at a cost of approximately £50. The book "ought to command serious attention and have a general value for the press (putting it onto several maps that it hasn't yet been put onto), let alone my personal feelings," he wrote Caresse. Furthermore, should she consent to finish the job, she would find Wyn Henderson, the former managing director of the Aquila, ready to lend the type used to print what already existed of the work ("without extra expense to the Black Sun"). Mrs. Henderson, although then busy overseeing the publication of Nancy Cunard's final Hours Press books, was also willing to work on *Guido* without immediate payment, and her printer at the Hours, John Sibthorpe, who had set most of *Guido*, would cooperate (for "a small sum weekly") if Caresse wanted him. The Black Sun, Pound assumed, would not have to pay up anything to Mrs. Henderson until money from sales began coming in; and forty or fifty sets of what had been done could be used for advertising purposes, thus eliminating waste and sparing Caresse the expense of turning out new advertising materials. The *Guido* text was worth printing, Pound assured Caresse; there was a lot of his work "locked up in the book," a lot that he would like to get unlocked, and he hinted that if Black Sun published it the way he had designed the book, it would serve as a guide for a series of volumes of the "few dozen real authors"—such as Arnaut, Daniel, Corbière and Rimbaud—whose texts under Pound's editorship would be printed as the texts were prepared in manuscript. The series would be valuable "fer the restartin' of a bearable civilization."

To be sure, the proposal was tempting, and Pound, no doubt realizing that it was, kept up the pressure for a quick decision. A month after outlining just how Caresse could take on *Guido* without incurring heavy responsibilities in the process, Pound wrote again, apologizing for "werritin' about this Cavalcanti" but admitting that it had been on his mind so long that it had very nearly driven him "OFF it." He promised that he would "choke off" his London agent and steer clear himself of all undesirable complications if Caresse would publish *Guido* in 1931; and he would also leave to her discretion the decision of whether to take over the fifty-six pages printed by Aquila or to start afresh. He had looked into the possibilities of putting out a cheap Italian edition and reported there was a chance of issuing what he called the "scholastic section," but that it would not appear before the deluxe version had had "ample time to sell to everyone who can afford it." And, finally, he alluded to Rimbaud, a translation of whose works Caresse had asked him to consider undertaking. Guido was as important as Rimbaud, but the former would have to be done first. Not only would the *Guido* serve as a "leverage for the Rimbaud" but it would allow time to try out different sizes of type, formats, and designs. In hesitating before committing himself to the Rimbaud assignment, Pound may not have been merely trying to force Caresse into taking *Guido* in exchange for Rimbaud. The translation assignment of Rimbaud was as difficult a job as she could have picked, he wrote; the best he could do was to give it a try later if there was "a reasonable body of stuff fit to print." Meanwhile, he suggested she approach William Carlos Williams about doing it. The stimulus of "outside attention" might produce results, particularly if she told him that he was "one of the few people [who could] do a few decent licks of work on the job."

Both projects, despite the strong interest each sponsor had invested in them, gradually receded from view. Pound eventually arranged to have *Guido* printed in Italy, and Caresse, having failed to find someone to translate Rimbaud, abandoned the idea, not however without trying to persuade T. E. Lawrence to undertake it. Lawrence sent Caresse a "quite marvelous" version of Rimbaud's "Marine," but then begged off, complaining that he was "out of conceit with writing," and not well enough acquainted with French "to attempt Rimbaud." His suggestion was F. L. Lucas. Caresse had also received sample translations from Emanuel Carnevali ("very good") and a young Frenchman named Roditi. Finally, it was to T. S. Eliot she turned. Would he consent to write an introduction for an edition of Rimbaud? Eliot demurred, recommending Edith Sitwell, with whom he would be glad to discuss the matter of a translation and an introduction, it being better, in his opinion, to have the same person do both. Eliot's kindness was much appreciated, but Caresse replied that she would approach Miss Sitwell herself if and when she decided to proceed. Meanwhile she had undertaken two new projects that would make heavy demands on her time and resources for the next several years. The first was the preparation of four memorial volumes of her husband's work.

VI

By the spring of 1931 Caresse had gathered all of Harry's poetry, published and unpublished, and had set out to find four poets to write introductions. At hand was the Lawrence preface Harry had omitted from *Chariot of the Sun*, which Caresse decided would be the first volume of the collected works, this time with the preface. For the second volume she chose *Transit of Venus*, which Harry had once sent to T. S. Eliot and to whom Caresse now wrote asking if he would consider "writing a few words" for the third volume, the book of dreams *Sleeping Together*, a copy of which she had given to Eliot in London the previous year. Ezra Pound, she informed Eliot, would write a foreword for a collection of Harry's heretofore unpublished prose and poems called *Torchbearer*, and she hoped Hart Crane would do the same for *Transit of Venus*. She explained that since this edition for Harry had to be "something worthy of his memory and of literary importance," she was prepared to pay him (and presumably Crane, Pound, and Stuart Gilbert as well) "five francs a word or seven thousand five hundred francs for fifteen hundred words." By midsummer, Eliot had made up his mind to write an introduction, but for *Transit of Venus* rather than *Sleeping Together*. Crane, perhaps inaccessible somewhere in Mexico, had not answered Caresse's request for an introduction, and so she had asked Eliot to do the introduction for *Transit* and Gilbert an introduction for *Sleeping Together*. Shortly before *Transit* went to press an apologetic Eliot sent his preface. "I am more than dissatisfied with what I have done and enclose, not so much on account of its brevity (I am always shortwinded) but on account of its poverty of ideas; and I am afraid that it will sound rather listless." What disappointed the author delighted the receiver. "Thank you a thousand times for the preface," she replied. "The brevity I approve of. I could not expect Harry to be one of your great enthusiasms but I find what you have written wise and illuminative. . . . I am having it set up at once." Beneath Eliot's cadenced prose exist bafflement and considerable uneasiness. At one point he had to admit he was very far from understanding what Crosby was up to. Nor could he be sure he would like it if he did. What he did like was the "fact that Crosby was definitely going his own way." Even his imperfections were of interest, but less so than his "search for a personal symbolism of imagery." Adventurous, unafraid of failure, impetuous, Crosby, in Eliot's estimate, was a man clearly in a hurry, hurried "because he was aware of a direction, and ignorant of the destination, only conscious that time was short and the terminus a long way off." Crosby's triumph, concluded Eliot, lay in his having fearlessly taken the risk of writing what might not have been poetry at all. He had made an already "adventurous vocation" even more adventurous. It was the same quality Stuart Gilbert accented in his anecdotal and reverential preface to *Sleeping Together*, where he casts Crosby as a poet-adventurer, frustrated by the lack of challenging conditions and dismayed by the absence of mystery and peril, who, in a reversal of the things that send shudders through most men, feared "the *terre a terre*, the normal," and who, through no defect of the imagination, welcomed danger as an antidote to the world of "hollow men."

Of the four poets who contributed prefaces only Ezra Pound had not known Harry Crosby personally, but it was his "critique" that Caresse liked the best. "Notes" was what Pound titled his introduction to *Torchbearer*, a forty-six page miscellany of verses and short prose pieces Caresse assembled in 1931. Breaking a twenty-year vow never to write about religion, and suppressing a fleeting desire to turn his pages on Crosby into a manifesto, Pound flatly announced that Harry Crosby's "life was a religious manifestation," and his death "a comprehensible emotional act (if one separated five minutes from all conditioning circumstance and refused to consider anything Crosby had ever written). A death from excess vitality. A vote of confidence in the cosmos." More important than the verbal manifestations of his work was Crosby's concern for the relationship between himself and the cosmos, which was basically a religious matter. Impervious to "technical pedagogies," Crosby sustained himself and animated his poetry by "immediate contact and not by having his elders tell him." Perhaps he was "too much alive to bother" doing it any other way, "or that there was too much else in living." Anybody except a "blighted pedagogue subsidized to collect washlists and obstruct the on-rush of letters" would feel "an ass in trying to concoct a preface" to Crosby's "magnificent finale."

PREHENDERE TO CATCH HOLD
OF YOUR SOUL AS A TALENT OF
PURE FIRE ENTER INTO ABSOLUTE
POSSESSION OF THIS FIRE MAKE
A CHAIN TO PRESERVE THIS FIRE
ATTACK TO DEFEND THIS FIRE

Toward the end of 1930 Caresse had shut herself away "in the fastness of the mill" and endeavored to capture in poetry the essence of her life with Harry. The poetry flowed, spontaneous and swift, "almost as though some urgent ghost" were providing the guidance. Shortly before she gave the poems to Lescaret, she consulted Stuart Gilbert about the title and asked him to write an introduction. Her proposed title, *Poems for Harry by Caresse*, while perhaps suitable for a book that would be circulated privately, struck Gilbert as inappropriate for one destined, in his opinion, to command the "highest respect and admiration" in the world of letters. Furthermore, he believed a title composed of "two pet names" would be out of keeping with his introduction, in which he intended to maintain a standard of dignity: her title might make his contribution look "absurd and incongruous." If only to discourage flippant critics who might succumb to "ironising about the 'little names' on the title," he recommended that it be changed to *Poems for Harry Crosby*. Caresse acquiesed. In his prefatory remarks Gilbert not only tried to avoid being critical by "moving to and fro . . . between [Caresse] and Harry Crosby and to prepare for that feeling of intimacy" he had found throughout her poems, but to present the author as a "gentle genius" who had successfully recaptured the language as well as the "desire for high adventure." Reading her "fugitive elegies" he had caught accents of Harry's voice "transcribed into a gentler mode"; his spirit (a "very real presence"), living and moving in the elegies, Gilbert concluded, was alive and, remarkably, "inevitably there, as we knew him."

With the memorial volumes and her tribute to Harry behind her, Caresse turned to the second new venture, one destined to transform the Black Sun from a small press specializing in finely printed limited editions into a commercial firm in direct competition with the huge Tauchnitz company. In 1931 she had met Jacques Porel, the son of the French actress Réjane, and together they had mapped out the plan. Since Tauchnitz had made a good profit as the only publisher on the Continent of reprints of the English classics and some moderns (though the Penguin was about to waddle in), there seemed reason to believe that a publisher of cheap reprints of avant-garde literature might succeed as well or better. Porel recommended several recent French novels as starters, including *Grand Meaulnes* by Alain-Fournier and *Vol de Nuit* by Antoine de Saint-Exupéry. Caresse, turning to friends for advice and encouragement, found Ezra Pound bursting with suggestions. Pound listed a score of books he vouched would get the firm off to a successful start. First came stories by Wyndham Lewis. *Dubliners* by Joyce was "out," but his "bad play" *Exiles*, Pound thought, might sell because of Joyce's reputation. Stories by Robert McAlmon and James T. Farrell (with an introduction to the latter by Pound) would strengthen the series, as would Cummings' *The Enormous Room*, Mike Gold's *Jews Without Money*, and "something" by Hemingway. For balance he recommended the "Inquest Series" he had edited for Bird's Three Mountains Press. The six books might be published in one volume. Concerning translations, he suggested Tozzi's *Tre Croce*, which Basil Bunting might translate for her, Frobenius' *Paideuma* (a refreshing book of nonfiction as contrast to the "pewk Tauchnitz supplies the non-fictionalist in way of essays by Chesterton and Northcliffe"), at least two books from Bolshevik Russia, and the Germans Speyer, Krauss Krell, and perhaps Wasserman. He also proposed an anthology of modern American poetry which, if he were not too pressed, he might try and compile himself; it would give him an opportunity "to beat the damn Tauchnitz mortuary," that is, an anthology of "allegedly modern English poetry" that omitted all Americans except Ezra Pound. In case she ran short he had in reserve a volume of his prose, "cut down from *Instigation* and elsewhere"; and, finally, to fill out the series, he suggested grabbing "any damn French or American best sellers" that Tauchnitz or other cheap collections had not yet nabbed.

What the Crosby Continental Editions (the name of the series) needed, however, was a bestselling writer, and the name that came to mind first was Ernest Hemingway, with whom earlier the same year Caresse had discussed the publication of "A Natural History of the Dead" in a Black Sun deluxe edition, but Hemingway had hesitated, uncertain of whether he wanted the story to come out separately or as part of *Death in the Afternoon*. Finally he agreed to let Caresse publish it in an edition of 150 copies (Caresse's request), for which he would be paid seven hundred dollars. But then it was Caresse's turn to demur. Was his story, she wondered, really suitable? Had she, furthermore, perhaps paid too much for it? The exchange of letters that followed brought no resolution, and by early fall Hemingway had apparently decided to include the story in *Death in the Afternoon*. Anyway, he informed Caresse that their agreement was off and that he would gladly return her check in exchange for the manuscript, adding that he was not "a bit angry" but disliked dickering on such things and peddling or defending his writing. While author and publisher had been concentrating on the deluxe book, they had also discussed the Crosby Continental series and Caresse had proposed starting it off with one of Hemingway's books. His two choices, one of which was agreeable to her, were *Torrents of Spring* and *The Sun Also Rises*. Since the latter had been reprinted so often and had probably "lost its interest," she decided to make *Torrents of Spring* the first book in the new series, apparently doing so without being aware that it was a satiric, and to many, an unkind portrait of Sherwood Anderson. To Kay Boyle she wrote of feeling upset when she heard it was "an intended mufflerie," explaining that she had chosen it mainly because it was a book that would "get hold of a public." There were no signs of distress, however, in her "Open Letter to Ernest Hemingway," which served as an introduction to Hemingway's book as well as to the new series. "I wanted to do something as you . . . had done something," she wrote. "I wanted to make something out of all this Anglo-Saxon alertness and zest for discovery of new things in ancient lands. Every American fancies himself a new Columbus rediscovering Europe. And Europe seems to welcome their curiosity with open arms." The Continental editions would try to provide some insight into the "racial consciousness" of both the discoverers and the discovered, some glimpse into the "genius of every country." She had decided to begin with this American book because it was one that she and a "few million others" admired. It would be followed by two French "classics"—*Devil in the Flesh* and *Bubu of Montparnasse*—and then, hopefully, others by Lawrence, Joyce, Colette, Aldington, McAlmon, Kafka, and Maugham. All would be books the publisher liked and believed possessed merit. She would operate on the premise that remaking "really good books" was a high calling, especially if they could be provided at prices that would make them attractive to large audiences tired of expensive reprints and translations.

Soon after returning to Paris in 1930 Caresse had asked Kay Boyle to translate a portion of René Crevel's novel *Babylon*. Long an admirer of his work, Miss Boyle was overjoyed at having been given the opportunity to translate what she considered a modern French masterpiece. In September, she was nearly finished and was more fascinated than ever with Crevel's "emotional imagination." The author raised no objection when Miss Boyle suggested that the title be changed to one of her choice—*Mr. Knife, Miss Fork*, originally the title of the first chapter. To illustrate the "surrealistic" text, Caresse commissioned Max Ernst, whose "photograms" (photographs of heavily-shadowed pencil drawings) elucidated such "Crevelisms" as "What is death?" "What is a whore?" "But at this moment the apocalyptic beast was death . . . it is two little birds she has closed up her dress." *Mr. Knife, Miss Fork*, issued in February 1931, delighted publisher and author (Crevel told Caresse he could only tell from what people said how good it was) and translator, who allowed that Crevel had been "wonderful discipline"; it was the "mystery" in his writing and the "spirit" that was all but untranslatable: "You have written a book that belongs to France," Miss Boyle intoned. "You have revived an aristocracy of the emotions, and if the wind of it blow in a few isolated places, it is enough."

Although Caresse's decision to start the Crosby Continental Editions off with *Torrents of Spring* disappointed Miss Boyle, she was jubilant over her other selections, particularly *Devil in the Flesh* and *Bubu of Montparnasse*, both of which Eliot had also endorsed ("I cannot think of any two modern French novels that I have read, which I should be more interested to see in translation"). Eliot had reservations about how successfully the latter could be translated however, and he suggested it ought to be done by someone who knew something about the underworld of London and Paris. It is unlikely that Laurence Vail knew much about the underworld of either city, but he liked Charles-Louis Philippe's novel and he was enthusiastic about translating it for the new series. As for *Devil in the Flesh*, the Radiguet novel of youthful love had long been a favorite of Miss Boyle's (it was the first book she had read in French after arriving in France) and the opportunity to translate it engendered some strong entreaties to Caresse: "I shall die if you don't let me do this one! It is one of the greatest, simplest books—the most beautiful in that generation of Frenchmen. I have done battle for it—read it a dozen times. Please, take anything else from me, but let me translate that!" Grateful to have two such willing and practiced translators at hand, Caresse happily awarded the assignments to Miss Boyle and Vail; each would receive five thousand francs. Through the fall and winter of 1931 they labored on the texts, occasionally sending Caresse a progress report. The title of Radiguet's book bothered Miss Boyle. *Devil in the Flesh* had a "satisfactory sound" but nothing else; she asked Caresse to consider others—*Limb of Satan* ("less false and more fitting"), *Devil's Spawn* ("not far off, but a little literary"), and *Thorn in the Side*, but in the end both women agreed that the first choice was probably the best. In November she had finished. Vail, after stopping work for a time when it seemed unlikely he would be able to place his translation in America, completed *Bubu* shortly afterward, and it followed Radiguet's novel into print in March 1932.

For each translation Caresse had acquired an introduction. Aldous Huxley wrote a glowing preface for *Devil in the Flesh* in which he acknowledged that Radiguet had all the qualities customarily found in the "ripest and most experienced artists," and T. S. Eliot, guided somewhat by Porel's recommendations, composed a restrained yet appreciative introduction for *Bubu of Montparnasse*—he had first read it 1910, when he had lived in Paris, and for him it had always been a symbol of the city at that time. Eliot quibbled a little over Vail's translation. It was "adequate," he admitted, but "not highly polished" and could probably do with "a little revision." The slang, always a problem, had been particularly mishandled, and he urged Mrs. Crosby to press Vail to make some improvements if there was time. Both novels were printed by Paillart, Paris-Abbeville, in editions of three thousand copies, and like subsequent CCE books, they were bound in soft cream-colored covers over which was laid a clear glassine protective wrapping. All CCE books were distributed by the Paris firm of Hachette, and most sold for twelve francs.

The *Torrents of Spring*, Number One in the CCE series, was published in December 1931. Number Two, *Devil in the Flesh*, appeared in January 1932; Number Three, *Sanctuary* by William Faulkner, and Number Four, *Bubu of Montparnasse*, both arrived in March, and from then on, at the rate of nearly one book per month, followed six more CCE publications: *Lament for the Living* by Dorothy Parker (April); *In Our Time* by Ernest Hemingway (June); *Night-Flight* by Antoine de Saint-Exupéry, translated by Stuart Gilbert, with a preface by André Gide (July); *Year Before Last* by Kay Boyle (September); *Big Meaulnes* by Alain-Fournier, translated by Françoise Delisle, with an introduction by Havelock Ellis (October); and *The Indefinite Huntress and Other Stories* by Robert McAlmon (November). Although all the series books except McAlmon's were reprints, the translations of the novels by Saint Exupéry and Alain-Fournier, having been done especially for the series, could be considered first editions, and Miss Boyle's novel, *Year Before Last*, although published earlier that year by Harrison Smith and Robert Haas in New York, was appearing on the Continent for the first time. In February, when Miss Boyle was struggling to finish her novel, she informed Caresse of her intention to retain continental rights and to give her the "first look at it." She confided, too, that it was "infinitely better" than her other two novels, and that while writing it she had felt very close to Caresse, so much so that it was as though they had gone "through some terrible thing together."

As early as October 1931 Miss Boyle had urged Caresse to include Robert McAlmon in the CCE series, and when she agreed, Miss Boyle immediately undertook the job of sorting out some of the author's best stories. It was a task which she knew was not going to be easy, for if

McAlmon himself were allowed to make the selections "he would naturally leave out all the sentimental, childish ones" which, in her opinion, were among his finest. She agreed with Ezra Pound, to whom McAlmon had written about the CCE book, that the choices would have to be carefully made, and made, if possible, with as little interference from the author as possible. As soon as Miss Boyle had finished the translation of Radiguet's novel, Caresse asked her to assist in compiling the McAlmon volume, and in April she forwarded the stories. She had objected to only one—"the pajamas one"—a story entitled "The Highly Prized Pajamas," which had just appeared in the *New Review*. Katherine Anne Porter had also disliked it and Miss Boyle agreed that it should not be included, but the others she found very good indeed. The first section of "Mexican Interlude," for example, had left her "speechless with enthusiasm and admiration," clearly one of the "most beautiful things" she had ever read; and two others, "It's All Very Complicated" and "New York Harbour," were admirable. Pleased with her report, Caresse left the final selection to Miss Boyle, which as she foresaw eventually led to disagreements with McAlmon. He was upset that Miss Boyle did not want to use "The Highly Prized Pajamas" as well as "Spectators" and "14th of July"; they did agree, however, on most of the others, and after trying out several titles on Miss Boyle, all of which she rejected, he accepted her recommendation: *The Indefinite Huntress and Other Stories*. He also liked how she had arranged the nine stories. Published in November (without the "pajamas story") it was the last CCE book and the only one that contained unpublished work, although the fresh writing consisted only of the title story and parts of another. As in so much of his work, McAlmon returned to his youth and the American West for the subjects of these stories, but it was the author's "stripped sentences" that drew comments from the *Tribune* critic Waverley Root. While Hemingway's spare sentences worked, according to Root, McAlmon's did not, in the sense that by shorning off the "unessentials" he had "cut away all the feeling as well." Resenting the comparison to Hemingway, McAlmon retorted that several of the stories in his book had been written long before Hemingway's books had begun to appear and before he was even aware of Hemingway's existence. Answering McAlmon, Root denied that he intended to stress time relationships, and agreed with him that McAlmon and Hemingway had certainly been influenced by their predecessors rather than by each other. His objective in the review, he continued, was to give some "rough indication" of

Caresse Crosby and Ezra Pound, Italy, 1963.
SOUTHERN ILLINOIS UNIVERSITY LIBRARY

the flavor of McAlmon's style by alluding to Hemingway. Finally, in a letter to Root published in the *Tribune*, Miss Boyle came to McAlmon's defense. If a debt is owed to anyone, she insisted, it was Hemingway that owed it to McAlmon. Quoting from a review she had just finished of McAlmon's book, she contended that at least a half dozen contemporary authors owed McAlmon a "debt of influence." She recognized him as the "sound and almost heedless builder of a certain strong wind in American letters" and Hemingway "as the gentleman who came in afterward and laid down the linoleum because it was so decorative and so easy to keep clean."

Six months after launching CCE, Caresse had taken in profits amounting to only twelve hundred dollars. Discouraged, she turned to Kay

Boyle for advice. The question uppermost in her mind was whether or not to continue the series and, if so, for how much longer? Along with encouragement Miss Boyle offered candid opinions of some of the CCE titles, and a few suggestions that she thought might help to improve the series.

> Consider how many years it takes to build up most publishing houses, and you have started off with an almost unprecedented publicity bang. I do not feel that the circumstances mean that you should either return to de luxe publishing or take up cheap books. I should think you would simply have to give it another year's trial—everyone says that the de luxe book business is shot to hell at this moment, but there's no doubt that such books as 'Sanctuary', 'Torrents of Spring,' 'In Our Time,' 'Devil in the Flesh' (for this has always had a steady though small sale in France in the original) will keep on selling constantly, even to the point of where you may have to get out further editions. Is this sound? Perhaps not, but so it seems to me. I think that such books as 'Night-Flight' (which I am now reading), 'Bubu' (which is a far finer book) and 'Nadja' will never be anything but a loss. Which means that you have to be more ruthless, perhaps. But with such names as Faulkner and Hemingway you cannot have failures. And they are not cheap writers. It seems to me that for the present you should concentrate on names with reclame and yet names that you have respect for. . . . Frankly, I don't see *how* you can make a success, a really big success, of any of the last six titles on your list, including my own. It is too much your own excellent and sensitive taste and not what people are clamouring for.
>
> To my mind, Colette is an excellent bet. She has been little translated and there is constant demand for her work. And there is this man Simenon whose work is *not* cheap—detective stories they are, but with such a fable and atmosphere and youth to them. If you had a handful of steady, if not overwhelming, sellers, then you could afford to take a chance every now and then. I wish to God I had the $5000. to put in with you. I'm sure we could make a go of it.

Still undecided, Caresse traveled to New York, hoping to sell "the idea of paper-covered books" to an American publisher, but the Crosby Continental Editions did not interest Bennett Cerf (Random House) and Dick Simon (Simon and Schuster), and along with other editors and publishers to whom she had shown them, they chorused that the American public simply would not buy paper covers, no matter how cheap. Random House, however, was interested in binding and distributing Black Sun books under a joint imprint, but Caresse, feeling an allegiance to her loyal distributor Harry Marks, quietly dismissed the idea. Simon and Schuster also had a proposal. If Caresse would choose and edit a series of Black Sun modern novels, they would publish and distribute them. Difficulties arose, however, when one of the firm's editors, Clifton Fadiman, discarded all but one of the titles she recommended. She had proposed books by Kay Boyle, René Crevel, and Emanuel Carnevali, but Fadiman, arguing that other titles were needed "to establish" Mrs. Crosby as an editor, insisted that Carnevali and Crevel be replaced with Katherine Anne Porter and Willa Cather. The former authors could be slipped in later. Indignant and determined not to be overruled by Fadiman, who seemed to be intent on establishing himself rather than her, she cancelled the agreement, tore it up, and declared that if Crevel and Carnevali could not be published first there would be nothing at all. As the year drew to a close, despite all the favorable publicity the CCE had received and the encouragement of people like Kay Boyle, only a few of the ten books were selling well enough to convince Caresse that the series ought to be continued for another year; and in May 1933 she told Miss Boyle that the Black Sun had "not one cent working capital" and could not accept any more manuscripts. The only Black Sun book published in 1932 (all ten series books carried the Crosby Continental Editions imprint) was a collection of Harry's war letters, with a preface by his mother. A private edition, limited to 125 copies, it was the last book Lescaret printed and the final Black Sun book published in Paris. It is difficult to believe that the young correspondent of *War Letters* is also the author of *Red Skeletons, Mad Queen*, and *Sleeping Together*. While sun and death fill the latter, the letters Harry wrote his family resound with God and patriotism. Only his faith in God saved him from death. But if he should die he would have no regret in "laying down" his life for America and for those he loved. There would be no "finer, squarer way of dying than getting crowned" fighting in a war that God had ordained.

For three years Caresse suspended all publishing activities, and then, in 1936, from New York, she issued three books: a deluxe edition of the *Collected Poems of James Joyce*, with a crayon portrait Augustus John made of the author in 1930. Although "Chamber Music" had already been published in the United States, "Pomes Penyeach" had not, and "Ecce Puer" had never appeared in any edition. As elegant as any of the limited editions created in Paris, *Collected Poems* was designed and hand-printed (in a blue italic type) under Caresse's direction, and bound in cream-white boards stamped with an "all-over" design of twenty-three floral ornaments within a border of floral decorations and rules—all in blue. There was even a blue silk ribbon place-mark. *Interregnum*, a collection of sixty-four original colored lithographs by George Grosz, was even more impressive than the Joyce book. The artist's satiric and moralistic depictions of obese Germans desecrating themselves in acts of butchery and bestiality prompted John Dos Passos, in an Introductory Comment, to predict that "few complacencies" would be able to withstand the artist's weapons. The third book was *Surrealism* by the artist and art dealer Julian Levy, who had promoted the work of Max Ernst and Salvador Dali in America. Besides illustrations by such surrealist artists as Duchamp, Arp, Chirico, and Ernst, Levy had collected excerpts from surrealist writings, including a portion of Kay Boyle's translation of *Mr. Knife, Miss Fork*, Eugene Jolas' translation of André Breton's *Nadja*, and two short pieces from Crosby's *Sleeping Together*.

The last publications Mrs. Crosby edited or supervised appeared irregularly in the forties and fifties. *Four Poems* by Sharon Vail, designed and edited by Caresse and printed by the Gemor Press of New York, in an edition of one hundred copies, was published in 1942; *Misfortunes of the Immortals* by Max Ernst and Paul Eluard, translated by Hugh Chisholm, and printed by the same press came out the next year; an anthology of drawings by Pietro Lazzari called *Horses* followed in 1945, the same year that the first issue of *Portfolio* appeared. Described as an "intercontinental quarterly," *Portfolio* took over the assignment once held by *transition* (defunct since 1938) of finding and publishing the most important experimental writers and artists in Europe and America. Three of the six numbers were published in Washington, D. C. (1945, 1946, 1947), the others in Paris (1945), Rome (1946), and Athens (1948). Due to wartime paper shortages, the early numbers were printed on odds and ends of paper, printer's remnants. From each capital *Portfolio* provided a "portfolio" of poetry, stories, essays, and art; *Portfolio* II, published in Paris, contained a lithograph of Matisse and examples of the work of Picasso, Sartre, Camus, and Paul Eluard; the Rome and Athens numbers announced new literary and artistic renaissances in both countries, and *Portfolio* V, the last to appear in America, contained a silk-screen holograph by old Paris resident Henry Miller. In 1948 *Manifesto for Individual Secession into World Community* by J. C. and R. G. King appeared in

Paris under the CCE imprint (Caresse was once president of Citizens of the World and Women Against War), and the same year from Washington came a portfolio of poems by Charles Olson titled *X & Y*, with drawings by Corrado Cagli. The final Black Sun books, issued in the early fifties, were Modigliani's *Pencil Portraits* (in facsimile reproduction) and *Pierrots* by Jules Laforgue, newly translated by the American poet William Smith and illustrated by the French artist Willette.

VI

Gertrude Stein's
PLAIN EDITIONS

WHEN GERTRUDE STEIN and Alice B. Toklas decided that the time had come to publish the unpublished works of Gertrude Stein, the author was in her fifty-sixth year, and although many of her writings had already appeared in print, beginning with *Three Lives* in 1909, nearly all had been issued by small presses in limited editions and several of them the author had subsidized herself. The problem, Henry McBride, editor of *Creative Art*, told her, was that she was an author who had a public but no publisher. That was hardly news to Miss Stein, who reminded McBride that while publishers were "awfully fond" of keeping her manuscripts, they also gave them back whenever she asked for them, and, unfortunately, magazine editors very often did the same. In fact, she had learned early that publishers could be annoying even when they were paid to print your book. The owner of the Grafton Press, for example, with whom she arranged to have *Three Lives* published, objected to "some pretty bad slips in grammar" in her text and recommended she correct them before the book went to press or, if she was unwilling to make the changes herself, that she permit him to send someone to her who would. When the "man from the Grafton Press" turned up in the rue de Fleurus, he came face to face with the formidable figure of an outraged author who commanded him to instruct his superior that the stories in *Three Lives* must be printed exactly as she had written them. She did, however, take the publisher's suggestion to change the title from *Three Histories* to *Three Lives*. In 1914, Claire Marie, a small New York publishing firm devoted to "New Books for Exotic Tastes," published *Tender Buttons*. An advance brochure announced that the author "is a ship that flies no flag and

William Aspenwall Bradley, American literary agent, Paris, 1935.
COURTESY OF MRS. WILLIAM A. BRADLEY

she is outside the law of art, but she descends on every port and leaves a memory of her visits." While the author's experiments in getting "the same sort of feeling out of things" that she had "gotten out of people" caused a mild furor, her book received few critical notices and had no discernible influence on writers. Of the many publishers Miss Stein knew, only one earned her everlasting gratitude. He was John Lane, who, at his own expense, published two editions of *Three Lives*, one in England in 1915, the other in the United States in 1920. Mindful of Lane's magnanimous gesture when she wrote *The Autobiography of Alice B. Toklas*, Miss Stein recalled that he alone among publishers ("like Holland he is unique") had chosen to be an adventurer, and for it he had reaped the rewards of living well and dying a "moderately rich" man. The fourth edition of *Three Lives*, brought out under the direction of John Rodker, appeared in 1927, and one admirer, the author's faithful friend, Carl Van Vechten, considered it "more gay than the others and . . . typographically the most beautiful." But by the late twenties compliments like this had become almost commonplace. After the appearance of the American edition of *Three Lives*, she had received congratulations from the greatest writers of England and France but, welcome though they were, the important question for her was always whether or not the book was selling. The difficulty—and it was the same one she had had with the Grafton edition —was getting her work into the hands of booksellers.

Agents were more of an annoyance than a problem, and although there would be one who would serve her devotedly and would arrange for the sale of her one and only bestseller (*The Autobiography of Alice B. Toklas*), her opinion of them probably deviated little from the verdict she set down in *Everybody's Autobiography*: "I don't know that literary agents are anything, that is to say, I have had them but they have never been able to sell anything of mine." Certainly she had reason to be disappointed in the years prior to the First World War when she had asked Van Vechten to show her writing to agents in New York, all of whom complained that they could do nothing with one so advanced. In 1922, without an agent, Miss Stein subsidized the publication of *Geography and Plays* (Four Seas Co., Boston), which, like *Three Lives*, drew the usual parcel of praise from friends but few reviews and no enquiries from publishers. For close to two years in the mid-twenties, the tireless and devoted surrogate agents Jane Heap and Van Vechten labored to place *The Making of Americans*, before Miss Stein herself made arrangements with Robert McAlmon to publish the ill-starred Contact edition of the book in 1925; and the following year, after delivering her successful lectures at Oxford and Cambridge, and again acting on her own, she placed her address, retitled *Composition as Explanation*, with Leonard and Virginia Woolf's Hogarth Press. Finally, at the end of the decade she had arranged to have a small limited edition (two hundred copies) of *An Acquaintance with Description* printed by the Seizin Press operated by Laura Riding and Robert Graves in Majorca.

With the little magazines Miss Stein fared somewhat better, notably in *Transatlantic Review* and *transition*. Earlier in the decade, Harold Loeb had printed her short piece, "Wear," in *Broom*, his international magazine of the arts, and long before that, in 1915, Van Vechten had sold a Stein story ("Aux Galeries Lafayette") to Allen Norton for his new magazine *Rogue*. The *Little Review* printed her shorter pieces from time to time as did *This Quarter* when it was directed by Miss Moorhead and Walsh, but Titus printed nothing by Miss Stein after he took over the magazine. Critical evaluations of her work appeared periodically. American critics were not as unfriendly to her as one might suppose, that is, when they deigned to recognize her. In 1923, both Edmund Wilson and Kenneth Burke wrote serious considerations of several of her books, Wilson in *Vanity Fair*, Burke in the *Dial*, but it was the transplanted American Elliot Paul who provided, in her words, the "first seriously popular estimation of her work." Paul, an itinerant staffer for the Paris *Tribune* who wrote occasional literary and music reviews while working as proofreader and night editor, devoted three long articles to a detailed analysis and explanation of Miss Stein's art and, one gathers, thereafter gracefully assumed the role of her defender and interpreter. According to the young publisher Joseph Brewer the situation in England was dismal. Not only had Stein not yet reached London, but in the few critical notices she had received she was still being "reviewed as though she were mad or a fool." The only remedy Brewer could think of, might be for Miss Stein to spend some time there. Not inclined to go to England to rectify by her presence what Englishmen ought to be able to do for themselves, she remained at home and, in time, Brewer came to her.

When Miss Stein and the publisher met in Paris in 1928, they discussed the "possibilities of his firm printing something of hers." Though Brewer "promised nothing," she told him she had just written a "shortish novel called *A Novel*, and was at the time working at another shortish novel," *Lucy Church Amiably*. She gave him a summary of *Lucy* which, intended as an advertisement, roused so much opposition to the project among the publisher's associates that it was abandoned. Still determined to publish something by Miss Stein, however, Brewer suggested that the first book ought to be a collection of "short things." If that was what he wanted, she replied, then he could have "all the short things she had written about America and call it *Useful Knowledge*." Before the end of the year Brewer had the book out, a stylish volume bound in unfinished black cloth, and bearing the seal "2 Rivers," a snobbish frill of Brewer's making intended to increase sales and offset the absence of the limited-edition designation, which the author had opposed. If, as seems likely, Miss Stein expected Brewer to be at least as adventurous as John Lane, she was disappointed. When she asked him to print still another edition of *Three Lives*, he refused, and after carefully reconsidering *Lucy* concluded that that, too, would be too risky to take on. Sales of *Useful Knowledge* (calculated to the end of 1928), had come to only 226 copies (the printing had been 1500), and despite the fact that the accommodating John Lane had purchased 500 sheets, Brewer's firm had already lost a thousand dollars on her book, and "could easily have lost more without gaining more." To William Bradley, now the author's agent, Brewer confided that though he and his associates would have liked to build up a market for Miss Stein, even if doing so meant breaking even, "we [were] reluctant to sacrifice our desires to our necessities." She was "a pure luxury" they could not afford, and putting out *Lucy* might have meant risking losing another thousand dollars. While at the time Brewer purportedly wept at the "necessity" of letting her go, Miss Stein later wrote resignedly of the matter: "I suppose this was inevitable." Like others, "instead of continuing and gradually creating a public for Gertrude Stein's work he procrastinated and then said no."

While Miss Stein and Brewer had been conferring, William Bradley learned from his friend Ford Madox Ford that Miss Stein wanted to speak with him about her literary matters. What she had finally decided to do was to ask Bradley to become her agent. She had also decided that the time had arrived to make money out of her writings, and that, as she told him, would be Bradley's main responsibility. Hers was a challenge unprecedented in the agent's experience and one that would test both his patience and persuasive powers mightily during the next five years. To discover which publishers might make his new client's work pay, Bradley sent out manuscripts to Little Brown, Macaulay, Viking, and Harper's, all of which, after expressing varying degrees of interest, returned them, with regrets. For a while it looked as though the moribund *The Making of Americans* would be the only one to have an American printing. On a visit to Paris, Lee Furman, president of the small Macaulay Company that had published *The American Caravan* (1927) containing Miss Stein's story, "Mildred's Thoughts," for which she had received $18.70, expressed interest in publishing a shortened version of *Americans*. For many months, however, Miss Stein refused to make revisions, hoping that Bradley would find someone who would take the uncut version. But after three firms had turned it down and Bradley advised her that Furman was still interested, she consented to make some reductions. In mid-1930, a shortened manuscript reached Furman, who speedily returned it, complaining that even revised it was too long—200,000 words—and that the revision was less effective than the first draft. He could not justify putting money into a book on which he was sure there would be insufficient return. Bradley, shaken by the news, commiserated with Miss Stein by saying she should "feel a certain relief at having escaped from the hands of such a crew." And Elliot Paul, who had helped the author and Bradley pare *Americans* to what they considered publishable proportions, observed that what publishers said they would do while they were abroad they very often did not do when they returned home. Of Furman, he had once noted: "It's alright when he is over here, but when he gets back the boys won't let him." Who the boys were Miss Stein did not know. But Paul was right. "In spite of the efforts of Robert Coates and Bradley nothing happened."

It can only be assumed that the disappointment over the collapse of Brewer's plan, and then Furman's, and the trouble Bradley was having placing her work contributed to Miss Stein's decision to start her own publishing company. The chance of somebody else turning up with proposals like Brewer's or Furman's seemed remote, and even if someone had she probably would have greeted them skeptically. Also, the Paris-based publishers she could approach about publishing a book had shriveled to a few. The alternative, of course, she had known about for years: like others, she could publish her own books. Whether the idea first came to Alice B. Toklas or to Gertrude Stein hardly matters, but it was Miss Stein who made the decision to sell a Picasso painting to finance the new enterprise, and after posting an urgent request to Van Vechten to inquire whether his New York "picture man" would consider buying a Picasso ("girl sitting on horse") for twelve thousand dollars, she herself managed to sell the artist's *Woman with a Fan* to Marie Harriman (wife of the future governor of New York) for an undisclosed amount. While the loss of the Picasso made Miss Toklas cry, the proceeds made possible Plain Editions—the name Miss Stein gave their joint business. She could hardly wait to tell her friends the news. "Here we are in business," she wrote Van Vechten, "at least Alice is the imaginary editor and I am the author but then I have always been the author and she has always been the manager but now in despair at using up our energies to shove the unshoveable we have concluded it will take less energy and get more results if we do it ourselves." Despite such optimistic assertions, neither woman knew anything about publishing, a fact Miss Stein admitted in the *Autobiography*: "All that I knew about what I would have to do, was that I would have to get the book printed and then to get it distributed, that is sold." As the news spread that Paris was about to have another publisher, the women were overwhelmed with advice and offers of help. Bradley supplied a list

Gertrude Stein, Paris, 1930s.
PRINCETON UNIVERSITY LIBRARY

of bookstores he had procured from Random House and promised another of college and university bookshops, and suggested they advertise in
Publisher's Weekly and subscribe to the magazine. But while all this was
unquestionably "wise advice," the "real difficulty," as Miss Stein had
discovered many years earlier, would be finding ways to get Plain publications to the booksellers. With the help of Ralph Church and "a kind
friend" who supplied another publisher's list of booksellers, Miss Toklas
began sending announcements to bookshops in England and the United
States containing instructions on how to order Plain books directly from
Paris.

It was decided that the author's most recent work, *Lucy Church*

Title page (*above*) and advertisement (*opposite page*) of *Lucy Church Amiably* by Gertrude Stein (Plain Editions, 1930).
PRINCETON UNIVERSITY LIBRARY

Amiably, would lead off. In this novel, subtitled "A Novel of Romantic beauty and nature and which Looks Like an Engraving," which Miss Stein had composed leisurely in Bilignin in 1927, almost nothing happens, and the impression, finally, is one of joy and contentment in the natural beauties of the pastoral landscape of the region through which the author roamed. Externally, the book resembles a novel—most chapters are of equal length and sentences and paragraphs are recognizable units—but it is little more than what the author herself called it, "a landscape . . . in which there are some people." To do the printing the women sought out Darantière, whose estimate must have been too high, for the contract was awarded to another printer who thought "he could make it pay." Miss Stein insisted that *Lucy* be bound in blue and that the whole book should

238

look like the blue copybooks used by French schoolchildren, and which for some time she had used for her own writing. In late spring, Miss Toklas delivered the manuscript to the Union Printery, 13 rue Méchain, and in June, in Bilignin, author and publisher began poring over the proofs. They found the printing most unsatisfactory, and when the finished book was delivered their disappointment was compounded. Besides the poor quality of the printing and a large number of typographical errors, Miss Toklas complained that the book "would not stay closed" and, when opened, "its back broke." About the only thing that pleased them was its appearance—it did look like a French copybook. And for the author, at least, there was the rare and delightful experience of wandering about Paris "looking at the copies of *Lucy Church Amiably* in the windows and coming back and telling [Miss Toklas] about it." Except for the French translation of *Ten Portraits*, *Lucy* was, up to that time, the only one of her books ever displayed in a bookstore window. Using stationery bearing the letterhead "Plain Editions" boldly printed across the top, Miss Stein announced to friends that the new publishing company had produced its first book and, as usual, asked for any assistance they might be able to give. She told Henry McBride that it would be "more than appreciated" if he would write some of his "deeply appreciated remarks about the book and the edition," and to Bob Brown she sent a packet of subscription blanks and asked for the names of more buyers and booksellers. "Our idea is to grow," she told Brown, and added encouragingly that orders had begun arriving prepaid, an indication, she thought, that "they really do read it."

Six months after *Lucy* had been released (January 1931), Miss Toklas and Miss Stein began preparing the second Plain book, this one a collection of the author's pronouncements on writing composed the same year called *How to Write*. This time she wanted the book to resemble an "eighteenth-century copy of Sterne which she had found once in London, bound in blue and white paper on board," in the form of an Elzevir; and to make sure that the work would be properly done Darantière was hired to do the printing. Meanwhile, Miss Toklas notified booksellers that a second Plain book would soon be on the way, and an assistant, Elem du Pois Taylor, recommended that follow-up letters be sent to booksellers and that renewed efforts be made to advertise Plain books and, if possible, get them reviewed. With most of their money going into printing, however, Miss Toklas had to rule out advertising, especially if she hoped to publish several additional Stein books. Reviews continued to be a troublesome matter. There were plenty of humorous references to Miss Stein's work, but disappointingly few serious evaluations, and although Miss Stein took comfort in the belief that when she was quoted it meant her "sentences get under their skin," such references did little to enhance her reputation. Also, those writers who did admire her work, and said so in congratulatory letters to the author, seldom made an effort to shape their appreciation into a review. One exception was Robert Coates, who wrote a favorable commentary on *Lucy* for the *New Yorker*. Typical of some local reviewing was Waverley Root's estimate of *Lucy*, written in mock-Steinese, in which he commended the Advertisement (close to a blurb) as being "less difficult than all other parts of *Lucy Church Amiably*." After quoting the Advertisement, Root concluded: "This is less difficult than other parts. This is more simple. But then it is all simple. She said by repeating you can change the meaning you can actually change the meaning. Repeat. But then it it it is all simple. It is all simple. It is all simple. It is all. Simple."

When Miss Stein and Miss Toklas saw what Darantière had done with their second book they could not hide their displeasure. Even the masterprinter, it seemed, was capable of faulty workmanship. Although the overall "bookmaking" was acceptable, the binding had been poorly molded. Obtaining a "decent" commercial binding in France seemed to be nearly impossible, perhaps because French publishers covered their books mainly in paper. Moreover, Darantière had not managed to fit the pages together properly. What had gone wrong, Miss Toklas wanted to know? His apologetic explanation did little to mollify her, but it was a "classic answer" both women would long remember: "What can you expect, Madame? It is machine-made, it is not done by hand." As usual, letters praising the new book followed its appearance. F. Scott Fitzgerald wrote that he was halfway through *How to Write* a second time and had learned "a lot as we all do from you." The main business, however, was a vigorous effort to get the book into bookstores, and the means the two women chose was a rather pretentious, if not intimidating, circular letter:

> It is an undisputed fact that the influence of Gertrude Stein upon the generation of young writers of to-day has been the most vital force in American letters. A book from this pioneer on her technical approach to art and theory of writing is at this moment of the utmost interest and significance. This book is now ready. In *How to Write*, Gertrude Stein dramatises, analyses [sic] and gives examples of the modern approach to Grammar, Sentences, Paragraphs and Vocabulary. Copies of *How to Write* are sent on consignment post paid: the book, 395 pages, sells for $3.50, 40% discount, bills to be settled quarterly.

A few booksellers, apparently afraid they might be caught with an oversupply of Plain books, tried to head off shipments before they left Paris. Miss Steloff, whose Gotham Book Mart had kept large stocks of Plain Edition books on hand, made efforts to stem the flow after Miss Toklas informed her that her shop had "by its orders successfully proven the possibilities in the sales of Plain Editions," in appreciation of which she proposed to consign to dealers like the Gotham an undisclosed number of copies of the "books of Gertrude Stein which have so far appeared."

241

Alice B. Toklas, Gertrude Stein, and W. G. Rogers, Nîmes, 1937.
COURTESY OF MILDRED WESTON

Though Miss Toklas and the author had been disappointed with *Lucy* and *How to Write*, there was nothing wrong with the next Plain book, a poem of Miss Stein's pleasingly called "Before the Flowers of Friendship Faded Friendship Faded," a title that came to the author, according to Miss Toklas, "in the dining room of a hotel at Bourg [near Belley] when two guests of the hotel at two different tables were disagreeing." Printed in Chartres, on handmade peach-leaf paper, in an edition of one hundred copies, it was the one Plain book that sold out immediately. Typical of the compliments this time was Lindley Hubbell's appreciation that it was "what a poem should be," and that it had the "loveliest format of any of the [press'] books." Miss Stein's poem had already appeared in the Winter number of *Pagany* (Boston, 1931) under the confusingly alliterative title "Poem Pritten on the Pfances of Georges Hugnet." In the same number was a poem by Hugnet called "Enfances," which he had sent to Miss Stein in the summer of 1930 and, in return, had received a "translation" in Stein English. Astonished and pleased at the same time, he wrote at once that what she had done was not a translation, it was something else, and it was better. "I more than like this reflection, I dream of it and I admire it. And you return to me hundred-fold the pleasure that I was able to offer you. . . ." Around the same time, however, Hugnet confided to Virgil Thomson, who had introduced him to Miss Stein, that he believed he might have friends who were too strong; but to Thomson, Miss Stein explained that her method in "translating" Hugnet's poem was to set down a "mirroring of it rather than anything else, a reflection of each little poem." Hugnet's remark to Thomson presaged the quarrel that would eventually end his friendship with Miss Stein.

Besides being a poet, Hugnet was the publisher of Editions de la Montagne, which had brought out a half dozen volumes of modern prose and poetry, including two by Miss Stein, a translation of selections from *The Making of Americans* (translated by Hugnet), and *Ten Portraits*, printed in English and French, and illustrated by "portraits of the artists and of themselves and of the others drawn by them, Virgil Thomson by Bérard and a drawing of Bérard by himself, a portrait of Tchelitchew by himself, a portrait of Picasso by himself and one of Guillaume Apollinaire and one of Eric Satie by Picasso, one of Kristians Tonny the young Dutchman by himself and one of Bernard Faÿ by Tonny." *Ten Portraits* appeared in the spring (1930) and, as Miss Stein later said, both of Hugnet's volumes "were very well received and everybody was pleased." That fall *Pagany* had accepted Hugnet's "Enfances" as well as Miss Stein's "translation"; she still referred to the poems as the "two Enfances." In Paris, Hugnet was preparing to issue both poems, with illustrations by Picasso, Marcoussis, Tchelitchew and Tonny, in what promised to be another distinguished addition to Hugnet's series of limited editions. But before the project could be finished, a disagreement arose between the publisher and Miss Stein over the layout of the subscription blank Hugnet had designed and sent her for approval. It read: "Georges Hugnet En-fances—Suivi Par La Traduction De Gertrude Stein." According to Virgil Thomson, a witness to the episode, Miss Stein regarded Hugnet's action as disloyal. It was disloyal to print her name in smaller type than his, and it was inconsistent to call her work a translation when Hugnet himself had said it was something more; furthermore, she believed their work should be put forward as a collaboration. Hugnet, stunned and determined not to give in to her, replied that placing her name beside his would "give the impression of a collaboration," which was precisely what their working together had not been. He also feared that if the word translation were dropped in favor of "another term like adaptation, transposition," people might think that his poem was a translation of an original work by Ger-trude Stein. The lines were drawn. Miss Stein refused to accede. Hugnet, with a book in the offing, asked Thomson to intercede as "his agent." Miss Stein, hoping to avoid a face-to-face exposure with Hugnet in *Pagany* (their poems were originally scheduled to appear in the magazine on facing pages), wired Boston to stop the publication of the two "Enfances," but her request arrived too late, and there was only enough time to rewrite the title. Meanwhile, Thomson, learning that Miss Stein would consider as fair a title page on which "the two names were of equal size and no reference was made to 'translation,' " actually worked out such a page and showed it to Hugnet, who, after some negotiations, settled for a revision that would contain the names of both authors printed at the top and at the bottom of the page (his at the top), "with the title centered and equidistant from both." Despite the care with which they were conducted, Thomson's deliberations failed. Looking over the pages he had designed, on which Hugnet had written "I accept," Miss Stein nodded and said, in a businesslike way, "This seems all right to me." Did Miss Toklas approve? Miss Toklas did not. Reading Hugnet's jotting, she merely said: "It isn't what was asked for." And that ended the joint publication Hugnet had planned.

Delighted with the way *Flowers* had turned out, Miss Toklas was determined to maintain the same high quality in the remaining books on the Plain list, and once more she turned to Darantière for help. Would he, she wondered, be able to produce inexpensive but well-printed books that could be sold for low prices in America? Too often Miss Stein's books had ended up in the hands of collectors rather than with students, librarians, and fellow writers. "Gertrude Stein wants readers not collectors" was the sense of what Miss Toklas wanted Darantière to understand, and he could help by telling her how to obtain a good printing for little money. What Darantière proposed was that all future Plain books be set by monotype, a "comparatively cheap" process, after which he would "handpull" the books "on good but not too expensive paper" and have them bound in "heavy paper" like that used for *The Making of Americans*, and then slipped inside little boxes covered with yellow paper of the same shade used on the cover of *Americans*. Would all this, she wondered, mean another expensive book? Not at all, the printer assured her. But here was another promise that could be broken as easily as some had been in the past, and although this good printer had told her not to worry, worry she must until she had proof of what he had promised had actually been done. The next book on the Plain list was *Matisse, Picasso and Gertrude Stein*, to be followed by *Operas and Plays*.

Besides the title essay, the former contained two short stories, "A

MATISSE PICASSO
AND GERTRUDE STEIN

with two shorter stories

by

GERTRUDE STEIN

Title page of *Matisse Picasso and Gertrude Stein* by Gertrude Stein (Plain Editions, 1933). PRINCETON UNIVERSITY LIBRARY

PLAIN EDITION
27 - rue de Fleurus - 27
PARIS

Long Gay Book" and "Many Many Women," both of which dated from the first decade of the century. In the title piece, Miss Stein placed herself in the company of two great artists, but how they related to each other artistically and spiritually was not clear, perhaps because, as the author admitted later in an interview, halfway through the book "words began to be for the first time more important than the sentence structure or the paragraphs." Darantière printed five hundred copies and began distributing them in February. Like other Plain books, this one measured six-by-seven inches, and was bound in plain brown covers, soft, but this time, as proposed, the book was confined in a yellow slipcover, on the outside of which, both on the front and the spine, appeared the full title and the author's name.

The last Plain book was the four-hundred-page volume *Operas and Plays*, which obviously brought Miss Stein immense satisfaction. "I have been agitated for a long time about the problem of narrative," she wrote Bob Brown while still working on the book; it was the only thing she had not been pleased with in *How to Write*, where she had discussed, rather opaquely, the technical problems of grammar, narrative, and vocabulary. In the new book, though, she was almost certain that she had solved the problem in the series of plays. Of the operas included, the most important and successful was unquestionably *Four Saints in Three Acts*, on which her friend Virgil Thomson had set to work in 1927, putting her words to music and receiving in return her encouragement and approval. The theme was the religious life, the "peace between the sexes, community of faith, the production of miracles." Thomson announced the work completed in 1928, and the following year it was published in *transition*, but it was not until 1934 that it would have its first public performance, in the Avery Memorial Auditorium of the Wadsworth Atheneum in Hartford, an event that preceded by nine months the author's triumphal return to America.

In the summer of 1932, while the final two Plain books were going through the press, Miss Stein was at Bilignin working on the book that would have a profound effect on her life and career. Shortly before she died in 1946, Miss Stein admitted that when she had been asked to write an autobiography (probably by Bradley) she had refused, but then "as a joke" had started to write one anyway. She also said that writing it gave her a chance to try out some new theories of narrative, which, unlike poetry and exposition, was "in itself . . . not what is in your mind but what is in somebody else's." What she had done in the amazingly short period of six weeks was to compose an anecdotal history of her life with Alice B. Toklas (or vice versa), using the speaking voice of Miss Toklas and re-creating her point of view. She described it as "her autobiography one of two. But which it is no one which it is can know."* That cryptic description to the contrary, Miss Stein had written to be understood.

Letters from Bilignin kept Bradley informed of the progress of the new book, and the agent, sensing its great commercial possibilities, urged Miss Stein to let him see the manuscript as soon as possible, suggesting in order to save time that she send it to him in two installments. Miss Stein did even better and began forwarding it chapter by chapter. With each, Bradley's enthusiasm increased and when the second installment had arrived he wrote that "wild horses couldn't keep . . . [him] from reading it at once!" When Miss Stein returned to Paris in December, Bradley announced that, if she had no objections, he was ready to send her manuscript to Harcourt Brace; she had none, but if the book had a British publication she wanted the Bodley Head (John Lane's successors), for sentimental reasons, to be the publisher. In mid-January (1933), Bradley heard from Alfred Harcourt. Enclosed with his acceptance were contracts for the author. Harcourt reported he had followed Bradley's injunctions and had read every word of the book. His suspicions concerning the authorship had been "aroused by the extraordinary gifts of style," but he had "played fair" and had not succumbed to the temptation to turn to the end to confirm them. However, he added, at the moment he had reached that point he had been interrupted by his wife who, coming into the room and hearing him cursing under his breath, had asked, "What's that that's so good because when you begin to 'Jesus Christ' it's a good manuscript?" For an hour he had made her stay around while he read bits of it aloud. The *Autobiography* would round out what Harcourt called the picture of an extraordinary group of people, among whom were Lincoln Steffens and Mabel Dodge Luhan, both of whose memoirs his firm had just published. Along with an advance of five hundred dollars for the author, Harcourt advised the agent that the Literary Guild had taken the book and would

---

* The authorship of the *Autobiography* puzzled Bradley. Was she Miss Stein or Miss Toklas? Later, of course, he assumed the book had been written by Miss Stein. Recently, however, George Wickes revealed that Miss Toklas once told him that at Gertrude's insistence she had started to write a book of memoirs to be called "My 25 Years with Gertrude Stein," but had found the writing so·troublesome that she had accepted Gertrude's help in making revisions and later allowed Gertrude to take down her words and revise them as she went along. As far as Miss Toklas was concerned, the *Autobiography* had always been Gertrude's book.

pay six thousand dollars two months after it was published, that sum to be divided equally between author and publisher.

With the publication settled, Miss Stein instructed Bradley to look into the possibility of placing her book with the *Atlantic Monthly* for serialization. In her opinion, the *Atlantic* was the best of the American magazines, and it was also the one that for years had consistently rejected everything she had submitted. Not even sponsors as powerful as Mildred Aldrich had helped her breach the formidable resistance maintained by the *Atlantic*'s editor Ellery Sedgwick. It was time to strike again and now, instead of a piece of hermetic writing, she would advance with a potpourri of anecdotes. In February, the once redoubtable fortress cracked. The *Atlantic*, Sedgwick wrote, would publish Miss Stein's *Autobiography*. "There has been a lot of pother about this book of yours," he told her, "but what a delightful book it is, and how glad I am to publish four installments of it! During our long correspondence, I think you felt my constant hope that the time would come when the real Miss Stein would pierce the smokescreen with which she has always so mischievously surrounded herself. The autobiography has just enough of the oblique to give it individuality and character, and readers who care for the things you do will love it. . . . Hail Gertrude Stein about to arrive!" The triumph inspired Miss Stein to issue more instructions to Bradley. First, he must induce Harcourt to reprint her Plain Editions books. Although she had grudgingly allowed Bradley to exclude from her Harcourt contract a clause that would have bound the publisher to publish *The Making of Americans*, she saw no reason for waiting to press him to print her other books, especially since the *Atlantic Monthly* serials had already stimulated sales of Plain Editions. Harcourt, however, could not convince himself that he could publish more Stein books at a profit. Importing booksellers would no doubt satisfy the demand for the more esoteric Stein, but he told Bradley to wait until the *Autobiography* was out for his final decision. Bradley concurred and urged Miss Stein not to hold the knife to Harcourt's throat, even though the *Autobiography* must have seemed a "virtual godsend to him." The publishing business was insecure, he reminded her, and she might press what she considered an advantage too far. But Miss Stein brushed his admonitions aside, and with the help of Lindley Hubbell arranged to have *Three Lives* published in Bennett Cerf's Modern Library series.

The Autobiography of Alice B. Toklas came out in August 1933. The following month it was published in England. As expected, reviewers and a large audience responded enthusiastically, delighted to discover that Stein could be read and understood and enjoyed, and charmed by the anecdotes and intimate revelations and disclosures. Even the "gnarled and soured" Samuel Putnam, noted Bradley with amazement, confirmed the majority opinion in the *New York Sun*; and, in Paris, Waverley Root heaped honors on the "hometown" author. Miss Stein was at last being read, Root suggested, because she could at last be read, and what readers could now discover was the mystery of Gertrude Stein, the person of the legend so long denied. On this point Miss Stein once told Harcourt that the things people do not understand "attract them the most." Beyond that, Root conceded she had written a brilliant, clever book, a *tour de force,* unambiguous, witty, all told in language simple and precise and devoid of ragged fringes of meaning. Before her book had been out a month, she reminded Bradley of Harcourt's willingness to consider *Americans* once the *Autobiography* had appeared. Bradley sent the revised version to New York in September, and a month later Harcourt sent word back that he would publish it, although not with much enthusiasm, probably in September 1934; he could not, however, give Miss Stein an advance. In view of the record sales of the *Autobiography* (even Harcourt admitted he did not believe Gertrude Stein would be so popular), an advance was probably the last demand she would have made. As of the end of October, 5,900 copies had been sold in America, and 535 in England; besides her accumulating royalties, the author had received her share of the Literary Guild payment (three thousand dollars) and an amount nearly as large had come from *Harper's Bazaar* for the first installment of the *Autobiography*.

Bradley was as jubilant over the success of the book as the author. Handling it, he told her, had given him the "most exciting episode" in his life as an author's representative. Alongside it everything else seemed "a trifle tame by comparison" and probably would continue to do so until she entrusted him with a second book to handle. Of course he was also happy because he had obtained for her what she wanted. Miss Stein, however, was not so sure he liked what she had. Being a success and earning money from her writings had made her happy too, but at the same time everything had begun to change inside her. Success, elusive for so long, had arrived precipitously and had disturbed the pattern of her life. "Suddenly it was all different, what I did had a value that made people ready to pay, up to that time everything I did had a value because nobody was ready to pay." Her old friend Henry McBride had once said he hoped she would never have any success because it spoiled one. Now that she was a success he told her he was pleased, but Miss Stein understood what he had meant. "The thing is like this, it is all a question of the outside being outside and the inside being inside. As long as the outside does not put a value on you it remains outside but when it does put a value on you then it gets inside or rather if the outside puts a value on you then all your inside gets to be outside. I used to tell all the men who were being successful young how bad this was for them and then I who was no longer young was having it happen."

The possibility of going on a lecture tour in America had first been mentioned to Miss Stein sometime before the *Autobiography* appeared, and after its scintillating success the subject came up again. Harcourt told Bradley that several universities and colleges were interested in having the author come to lecture. But Miss Stein was uncertain. She had long believed, for good reason, that Americans would rather see her than read her; it was the personality that interested them, not her work. "After all," she said, "there is no sense in it because if it were not for my work they would not be interested in me so why should they not be more interested in my work than in me. That is one of the things one has to worry about in America." She would postpone a trip for awhile. In the meantime, though still unsettled and easily distracted, she tried to get back to her writing. A *divertissement*, ghoulishly titled "Blood on the Dining-Room Floor," went poorly; however a long, discursive, generally uninformative book she started writing during the winter called *Four in America*, portraying Ulysses Grant, Wilbur Wright, Henry James, and George Washington as Americans who, like herself, had never quite succeeded in accomplishing what they might have done, progressed better and helped divert her attention from the disruptive world of commercial success. Not entirely, however, for she stepped up her efforts to find publishers who would print her other books in the United States, and she urged Bradley to go after Harcourt again. The publisher, however, stood firm. He rejected the Grant section of *Four in America*, saying it was too confusing; he wondered whether Miss Stein could not supply "more open books" like the *Autobiography*. When Bradley went to the United States in the spring (1934), she hoped that the agent would accomplish more in face-to-face discussions with Harcourt and other publishers. But Bradley's reports were hardly optimistic. The sale of *Americans* had been only one-quarter of that of the *Autobiography*. It would be unwise, he advised, to continue pressing Harcourt to take *Four* or *Geography and Plays*, especially since

Americans had actually retarded the sale of the *Autobiography*. Meanwhile, in order to protect her best interests, he had proposed that Harcourt consider a "confession" and a "lecture" book. But Miss Stein would not be placated. Harcourt, she retorted, must understand that her reputation was based on books like *Four* and that what Bradley had called a "confession," the "open and public" books, were really "illustrations for the other books, and that illustrations should be accompanied by what they illustrate." Harcourt, in her opinion, ought to be ready to risk publishing some of her "real kind of books" if he wanted to go on with the volume of essays and later the "confessions." He should be willing to publish both kinds of books. What her writing was, she insisted, was just commencing to be understood and a book like *Four* would help.

While Bradley had been trying to satisfy both his client and Harcourt, Miss Stein had been in touch with Bennett Cerf of Random House, to whom she had already sold *Three Lives* and who, shortly after she had signed the contract with Harcourt for the publication of the revised edition of *Americans*, had cabled he wanted to bring out the unabridged edition in the Giant Series of the Modern Library. It was an opportunity she very much regretted missing. Cerf, however, had other tantalizing proposals for her, the main one being an offer to become her American publisher, and, if she agreed, to begin their association with the publication of the lectures (under "some intriguing title") she intended to deliver on her American tour. Further, Cerf offered to take over Plain Editions and sell all the unsold stock "at the regular published price less the usual 40% discount to dealers," the "entire proceeds" of which would be turned over to the author. All that he had proposed would be carefully reviewed when Miss Stein came to America. Although delighted with these developments, she nevertheless told Bradley she still hoped Harcourt would do what Cerf had promised he would do, and she hoped everything could be settled with Harcourt before her arrival. Cerf's offers and Miss Stein's last charge to Bradley exacerbated relations between her and the agent. Moreover, Miss Stein had complained to Bradley that she felt she was not being well served. Rejecting the assertion that he had done her "publishing programme 'incalculable harm,'" Bradley charged that she had never even had "such a programme—except that which I have sought to establish for you—only the publication of individual books here and there, according to circumstances." If they had reached an impasse, it was of a "strictly personal, i.e., literary, nature" and had "nothing to do with the practical questions involved." Bradley was certain Miss Stein's friends would agree with him that "no necessary relation" existed between the two categories of her work—the "open" and the "real" books—and that "to seek to create a purely artificial one for your publisher would be fantastic, if not fatal."

Three months before Gertrude Stein arrived in America to begin the lecture tour she had all but decided not to make, Bradley, his patience gone, gave up trying to advance Miss Stein's interests. Not only had she continuously found fault with the plans he had made for her tour but she had grown increasingly critical of his work as her literary representative, notwithstanding his success with Harcourt. Each had finally charged the other with bad faith. Miss Toklas, taking over for her friend, asked Bradley to return to her everything belonging to Miss Stein. In reply Bradley instructed Miss Toklas that any future correspondence should be sent to his lawyer. Just before the quarrel that led to the breakup, Bradley had told Miss Stein that by refusing to go to America she was giving up a chance to get rich. Apparently getting rich no longer had the same appeal it had when she first came to him. "I do want to get rich but I never want to do what there is to do to get rich"; and lecturing in America was one of the things she thought she did not want to do, at least not until she had the reassurances of two longtime friends—Carl Van Vechten and William Rogers—that America was ready for her and she for America. The trip to the United States, no doubt undertaken timorously, was a personal triumph that exceeded all her expectations. It rekindled her affection for her native land and capped the success of her bestselling book by reacquainting her with the masses of Americans who, instead of ridicule, granted her the respect due a visiting celebrity. She basked in the adulation. "It is very nice being a celebrity a real celebrity who can decide who they want to meet and say so and they come or do not come as you want them." One who did come was Bennett Cerf. When Miss Stein asked whether he still intended to be her American publisher, he replied that when she decided each year what she wanted published he would "publish that thing." Bravig Imbs, who at one time was part of her inner circle, once observed that Gertrude Stein "never lost hope that one fine day a publisher would come rushing to the salon and carry off her manuscripts." The adventurer John Lane had carried off *Three Lives*. Now another adventurer, the one of her fancy, had materialized and promised to carry off not only everything she had written but everything she would ever write. "Just like that," Miss Stein said. "Just like that," Cerf replied. And so "happily very happily" Miss Stein and Miss Toklas boarded the *Champlain* and sailed for home.

VII

Nancy Cunard's
TWENTY-FOUR HOURS

I

ABOVE ALL, the promise of excitement and the long-awaited chance to realize an old ambition to learn hand-printing prompted Nancy Cunard to buy the equipment and all the accessories of the Three Mountains Press which that older pioneer in the "black art," Bill Bird, had decided to close after seven years. For £300 Bird agreed to let Miss Cunard have everything, and to arrange for shipment of his mammoth Mathieu press to her Norman farmhouse at Réanville, fifty miles from Paris, and to find a French printer, expert in the operation of hand presses, who would introduce her to the secrets of hand-printing. By the late summer of 1928 Miss Cunard, with her companion Louis Aragon serving as interpreter and general overseer, had begun converting the farmhouse into habitable living quarters and the stable, some twenty-five yards away, into a printery. In the midst of the renovation, the printer whom Bird promised to send arrived and, "rather sourly," took stock of the operation, evidently disturbed as much by the location Miss Cunard had chosen for the printery as by the discovery that she and Aragon had already started to work and had turned out a sheaf of Hours Press announcements (the name Hours, "dullish but not unsuitable," came of itself, Nancy once remarked, "and was not only pleasing to me but suggestive of work") as well as several neatly printed stanzas of Lewis Carroll's *The Hunting of the Snark*. It was agreed Aragon would contribute something to the new firm, but exactly what remained vague until he suddenly announced he would make a French translation of *The Hunting of the Snark*. Can the spirit of *Snark* go into another language? wondered Miss Cunard. Aragon insisted it could,

Nancy Cunard and Maurice Lévy, printer, in the Hours Press,
Réanville, France, 1928.

and after a few days of concentrated work—presumably unbothered by
the confusion and noise of carpenters and electricians still swarming over
the place—he produced a translation, which (with Miss Cunard's help)
he had impatiently begun to set by hand. Gradually, it became apparent to
the tyro printers that Maurice Lévy (the printer's name) had come to
Réanville expecting to find a submissive young English woman obediently
awaiting his arrival to begin her studies, and that the sight of the novices
at work, blithely practicing an art he believed could only be mastered after
long and hard training, had rudely shaken his expectations and challenged
his respect for custom. "In France," he counseled Miss Cunard, "one
cannot be a printer unless one has worked a long time." How long? she
wondered. At least seven years. "And what is all that stretch filled with?"

she wanted to know. "First, you are made to sweep the floor and pick up fallen type and pieces. You are only a beginner. You keep the place tidy, run errands and so on. Then, little by little, you are permitted to learn to set type, and all the rest comes later. It depends on your intelligence. It is a lengthy job."

Her reply hardly forecasted a long period of amiable companionship. "Thank goodness there is none of that here, Monsieur Lévy. We are going to forge ahead. My intention is to learn from you everything I possibly can as quickly as may be, so as to be able to work without you as well as with you. Do you see? I like this beginning very much."

Lévy, uncowed but circumspect, cautioned that she and Aragon were about "to fly in the face of accepted conventions and long-established rules—all of them." He could hardly have spoken a greater truth.

The Hours Press, announced Miss Cunard, would favor new vision and innovation, "no matter how non-conformist," since they "made for the individuality" of the non-commercial press. The firm's first offerings, besides Aragon's translation, would be three volumes of "contemporary poetry of an experimental kind": *The Probable Music of Beowulf* by Ezra Pound, *St. George at Silene* by Alvaro Guevara, and a *plaquette* of poems by Miss Cunard's close friend, Iris Tree. What was certainly a brave beginning suffered a setback, however, when friends, having learned of her enterprise, began sending unsolicited manuscripts and books and requests for special printing favors. One of the first—marked "urgent"—came from Norman Douglas, who wanted as "faithful" a reproduction as Miss Cunard could make of a report he had written years before for the British Foreign Office. It would be hard to imagine a first assignment less inspiring than the *Report on the Pumice-Stone Industry of the Lipari Islands*. The dry, conventional style and content of the piece Douglas sardonically referred to as the "only meritorious action in my whole life" did nothing to ease the tedious labor of setting the six-page essay in the small 11-point type, which, in (or out) of the hands of a novice, seemed forever bolting from the composing stick, or lying down in it—"out of sheer fatigue," quipped Lévy. After two weeks of arduous work, eighty copies of the "pesky little piece" were dispatched to the author, a present from the Hours, most of which Douglas sent on to friends and collectors of his works.

No one, Miss Cunard confided to her London friend Otto Theis, had ever launched out on a new endeavor so "sail-less, mast-less, provision-less, uncompassed and abashed" as she had. Though she had long been attracted to the art of printing, not so much from the purely aesthetic point of view as from the sense of "independent creativeness" it might provide, it was, she had soon realized, a back-breaking and wrist-breaking occupation, demanding from one unaccustomed to regular working hours the most rigorous self-discipline. Moreover, she confessed, it was an "introduction to permanent fatigue." Douglas' *Report* (its shortcomings aside), had provided precisely the practice Nancy needed to handle the tricky 11-point type that she was to use again for the first scheduled Hours Press book, a revised edition of *Peronnik the Fool* by her close friend of nearly thirty years, George Moore. In the late nineties the Irish novelist had been a regular visitor at Nevil Holt, the Cunard estate in remote Leicestershire, presided over by Miss Cunard's socially ambitious mother, Maud, or Emerald, as she later preferred to be called, of whom Moore remained a devoted admirer, if not a suitor, for the rest of his life. His attention and affection for Lady Cunard extended to her solitary, precocious daughter, with whom, on rambles through the countryside—Nancy still the frolicsome adolescent, Moore the middle-aged savant—he would discourse on French painting and English poetry; later she would show him her poems and struggle to understand what he meant by "objective" poetry, and, still later, collaborate with him in the search for "objective" poems for his anthology of *Pure Poetry*. In her mid-teens, when she had been sent to Munich to study music, and German, Russian, and Scandinavian literature and (on her own) had found her *"mysticisme"* while wandering in the narrow streets behind the Pantheon, Moore had become her confidant, demanding, inquisitive, and unsatisfied until he was certain she had provided a full description of all her adventures. He insisted she read Turgenev, Dowson, and Morris, ignore Symons (much to her surprise), and show him all her poetry. In 1916, six of her poems appeared in Edith Sitwell's anthology *Wheels*. Of these, her first published poetry, Moore wrote: "I find that you have written much better poetry than I thought. . . . Nature has given you an exquisite ear for rhythm and I think if things go well with you, you may write some poetry that will do you honour and please your friends." In the poems of her first published collection, *Outlaws* (1921), he found his expectations verified. Nancy Cunard, he wrote in the *Observer*, has "more genius . . . than there is in the great mass of her contemporaries, and much less talent. . . . Genius cannot be acquired; we have it or we have it not; but talent can be." Talent and genius joined two years later in a second collection, *Sublunary* (1923), which delighted Moore, but it was *Parallax* (1925), a free-verse poem, that elicited his unalloyed admiration. Though bothered by a certain obscurity, he concluded that "the elusiveness that puzzles today will be tomorrow's delight."

When *Parallax* appeared, Nancy Cunard was already a commanding figure in Montparnasse, raffishly attractive, reckless, talented, and compellingly energetic. Moving to Paris in 1920 had been like being born again. Drawn quickly into the orbit of its seething literary and artistic coteries, she had formed close friendships with the dadaist Tristan Tzara; the surrealists André Breton, René Creval, and Louis Aragon; with American writers Janet Flanner, Solita Solano, Robert McAlmon, and Ezra Pound; and, among her countrymen, with Aldous Huxley, Wyndham

Portrait of George Moore by S. Celia Harrison, Dublin, 1907.

Title page of *Peronnik the Fool* by George Moore (Hours Press, 1928).

Lewis, Nina Hamnett, and Norman Douglas. Her poetry attracted less attention at the time than the art she inspired: sculptures by Brancusi; paintings by Kokoschka, Ortiz de Zarate, and Eugene MacCown; drawings by Wyndham Lewis, and photographs by Man Ray, Cecil Beaton, and Curtis Moffit. Aldous Huxley modeled Lucy Tantamount, in *Point Counter Point*, after Nancy, and she was unmistakably Iris March, the heroine of Michael Arlen's immensely popular novel *The Green Hat*.

As Nancy's "first friend" (her epithet) and longtime self-appointed literary advisor and confidant, Moore insisted that he be granted the honor of being the Hours first author, exclaiming, in rather indecorous language, that he wanted to start her press off "with a good bang!" Even if it promised only "a sort of 1906 bang," Nancy agreed *Peronnik* was an "enchanting book," certain to bring attention to the press, and one she would do her "best to bring out in a dignified and well-balanced manner —paper, type and cover." Nevertheless, for an apprentice, it was an intimidating offer. To relieve his as well as her own apprehension, she assured Moore that with Lévy (an "excellent" printer) she regularly went through "all the phases . . . with unflinching patience," and that the type and format they together had chosen would closely resemble those used in the copy of *Peronnik* he had sent as a model. Nor did disposing of an edition of two hundred signed copies of *Peronnik* seem unrealistic to her, but Moore replied that the book would sell more quickly in his opinion if she wrote a short prefatory reminiscence of their years together at Nevil Holt. The idea made her quail. Writing anything that could accompany Moore's "measured prose" and at the same time earn his high estimate for "personal literature" (it "is the only literature for the age it is written and for the age that follows") was out of the question. Besides with so much of her time and energy already going into printing, there would hardly be any left over for writing. The subject lay tactfully unmentioned in their letters, but the specter of the "sage of Ebury Street" haunted the Hours printery until *Peronnik* was finished. Once, working alone in an intense heat wave, Nancy noticed that the pressure of the old Mathieu press was uneven; the sheets were coming out heavily indented at the top and bottom, and from the direction of the channel she imagined the voice of a distraught Moore, booming: "Come, now! This is not printing. This is Braille." Nothing, however, could be done to correct the problem, and the printed sheets left for London with the hope that the flaw would not cause too much displeasure. If Moore noticed the imperfection he did not mention it, but the wide gutters bothered him, and he wondered whether Nancy should not take a lesson from earlier printers whose "first consideration was beautiful spacing." In the end they were allowed to stand, but Nancy made four revisions of the title page before producing one he approved.

Moore, as expected, fully realized his ambition to launch the Hours "with a bang." Besides the notices his name attracted, *Peronnik*, at £2 a copy, had more than paid for itself ten days after publication in mid-December. But, despite her successful financial debut, nothing changed Miss Cunard's resolve to print experimental verse, no matter how uncommercial; and while she had no intentions of turning Hours into a publishing firm (partly to avoid taxes she did not declare her business to the state), it was not to be just a hobby, either. If she could publish "good work" by the "young people," the "discoveries," she wanted to print and reward them in a manner more generous than that to which they were accustomed, Hours would be a success. Accordingly, she vowed to pay her authors one-third of the proceeds after deducting production costs; and a few like George Moore and Norman Douglas, authors "so famous they could expect higher royalties," would receive fifty percent after cost deductions.

The two books that followed *Peronnik* confirmed the publisher's intention to print "experimental" work. Appearing just ahead of *Snark* was a short poem that the Chilean artist Alvaro Guevara had written especially for Miss Cunard, a "poem-fresco" that reverberated with the color and detail of pre-Raphaelite verse. What impressed Ezra Pound about Guevara's *St. George at Silene* was its "simple ignorance of all criteria of English verse." He commended the artist for writing with "real naiveté at a time when the grovelling English" were breaking their backs to attain the false"; Guevara had made the happy discovery that the discipline he practiced in his own art could provide the fundamentals of an aesthetic in another: clichés and inversions, contended Pound, hardly mattered; unpretentious and unprecocious, *St. George* possessed only the artifice of rhyme, "always very simple, and utterly without inhibition." Composing and printing the four-page *plaquette* fell entirely to Nancy (Aragon had left Réanville and Lévy was working on the next book), a task she welcomed as an opportunity to prove her competence to the still-skeptical Lévy. Often temperamental with *Peronnik*, the old Mathieu behaved admirably with *St. George*; the generous format suited the press perfectly, and the 16-point Caslon type Miss Cunard chose stood out boldly on the heavy Velin de Rives paper. Printing the covers which Guevara had adorned with rows of tiny red leaves and the end papers (where the leaves weep copious tears) tripled the labor and delayed completion of what Nancy had thought would be a "quick job" until a few days before her Christmas deadline, just in time to fill a second "urgent" request, this one from Richard Aldington, for 150 copies of a "special" Christmas message (a jesting squib on the Trinity and Immaculate Conception) entitled *Hark the Herald*, which Aldington later gleefully reported had gotten rid of some "tiresome acquaintances."

Aragon discountenanced the misgivings Nancy had about whether the "spirit" of *The Hunting of the Snark* was "too much of its time" to go

Nancy Cunard and Louis Aragon, Paris, 1920s. Photograph by Curtis Moffit.

into another language. *Snark*, he insisted, was of all time; it could not be dated. Crowded with strange figures, "motivated by no one can tell what springs," wanderers on uncharted seas, adrift on a craft "now led, now driven," it defied classification. It was its own extravagant and unique self, yet uncannily attuned to their own time as well. Aragon was certain Carroll would have understood surrealism perfectly. The proof resided in his writings, in *Alice's Adventures in Wonderland, Through the Looking-Glass*, as well as *Snark*. Nancy had only to wait for his translation ("I can hear it already in my head," he told her) for assurance that the poem's spirit was translatable; and with *Snark* his "terrestrial daily companion" he did not keep her waiting long, completing the transformation with astonishing ease and speed in four or five days. What Carroll would have thought of it Nancy had no doubt. So smooth, authentic, and guileless was the work that his response could only have been one of complete admiration. Stanzas like the following offered proof that Aragon had indeed translated the untranslatable, while retaining the spirit and sense of the original:

> He would answer to 'Hi!' or to any loud cry,
> Such as 'Fry me!' or 'Fritter my wig!'
> To 'What-you-may-call-um!' or 'What-was-his-name!'
> But especially 'Thing-um-a-jig!'

> *Il répondait à Hep ou à n'importe quel cri vulgaire*
> *Comme Mes-puces ou Mes-bottes*
> *A Comment-que-tu l'appelles ou à Au-diable-son-nom*
> *Mais spécialement à Trucmuche.*

Having managed to put the poem into French so felicitously, Aragon was impatient to see it in print, and with the same zeal he had given to the translating, set by hand several lines ("his hands were deft, the printing-stick seemed as if already known to him") and in one, solitary, all-night session composed and printed four intricate cover designs, mosaics of black arabesque motifs, which even Lévy conceded were extraordinary printing "exploits." Before he left Réanville, Aragon accomplished one more "exploit," single-handedly—the composition and printing (only twenty-five copies) of a short poem, *Voyageur*, now among the rarest of his writings. *Snark* was the first Hours book to be printed on a new Minerva press Miss Cunard had purchased to speed up "the tempo of the work." By early winter the Paris binders delivered three hundred copies of the poem, bound in scarlet, with Aragon's ornately tessellated cover designs. Sales, although modest in England, where a critic for the *Times Literary Supplement* acclaimed the translation a "metaphysical poem of the modern school," were gratifyingly brisk in France.

After *Snark*, Nancy's resolve to print mainly unpublished poetry of

an "experimental" kind receded again, as several more unsolicited manuscripts came to the Hours and when two of the books she had announced
in her circular—*The Probable Music of Beowulf* by Ezra Pound and
Poems by Iris Tree—failed to materialize. At the same time, she had
found poets she wanted to publish, for example, Louis Zukofsky and Roy
Campbell (a "discovery"), and perhaps Cummings; and David Garnett
had mentioned that he might have something for her. But on a trip to Italy
that winter, which included a visit with Norman Douglas in Florence, "in
his delicious apartment on the Lungarno," she had accepted his gracious
offer of another "official" essay, this one a "charming" albeit "discursive"
account of Athens which the Greek government had once commissioned

La Chasse au Snark

*une Agonie
en Huit Crises*

par

LEWIS CARROLL

Auteur d'"Alice au pays des merveilles", et "A travers le Miroir".

Traduit pour la première fois en français par

ARAGON

THE HOURS PRESS
Chapelle-Réanville - Eure
1929

Title page of *The Hunting of the Snark* by Lewis Carroll, translated by
Louis Aragon (Hours Press, 1929).

him to write, but which for some "imperceptible" reason had remained unfinished. It was hers if she wanted it. Fragment or no, she did. *One Day* (Miss Cunard supplied the title) is Douglas' account of a day's wandering in Athens, first in the lower city, then as day lengthens, in the hills behind. Partly travelogue; partly treatise on Greek art, philosophy, history, and literature; partly epigrams (they abound after dark and after the author has dined and consumed quantities of wine), *One Day* discloses at least as much about the author as about Athens, and delighted collectors of Douglas' works, who exhausted the Hours supply by subscription before publication and made it Miss Cunard's most profitable book, the entire edition of five hundred copies selling for either £3.3 (signed) or £1.10 (unsigned).

Of the many who offered Nancy encouragement and advice at the outset of her enterprise—Virginia and Leonard Woolf gaped disbelievingly when they learned Nancy had started a press and warned her that her hands would always be covered with ink—few could provide more useful information than Norman Douglas and Richard Aldington. But neither could have buoyed her spirits as much as a black American musician named Henry Crowder, whom she had first seen playing the piano with "Eddie South's Alabamians," in Venice in 1927, and who, after considerable persuasion, had agreed to leave the "Alabamians" to help "in a general way" at the Hours Press. This "enchanting aide and companion," who would be the inspiration of Miss Cunard's monumental anthology *Negro* (1934) and to whom she would dedicate it, had come to Réanville at Christmas, 1928, just as the last pages of *Peronnik* were being pulled from the press, and in a short time had taken over the clerking chores so detested by Nancy and, to her great relief, had quickly learned how to manipulate the press lever of the old Mathieu. Douglas and Aldington, on the other hand, though each visited the press either in Réanville or Paris, never proffered more than advice.

Douglas, by turning himself into a one-man publisher, supervisor, accountant, and packer, had managed to keep a sizable band of loyal admirers supplied with costly limited editions of his books, nearly all of which were published by his friends, the Florentine bibliophile, Pino Orioli, under the Lungarno imprint. For the hours spent correcting the mistakes of Italian typesetters, adjusting accounts, answering correspondence, and even packing and posting bundles of books ("Mind you," he warned Nancy, "never forget to register everything"), Douglas assured Miss Cunard when she visited him that he was at last collecting "reasonable prices." She, too, he told his visitor, could make a decent profit with hard work and good writing for a start. Aldington, although far less experienced than Douglas, urged Nancy to double the number of Hours titles and increase the printings of each, perhaps by as much as a hundred or more. Like Douglas, he also had something for the press, a long philosophical poem entitled *The Eaten Heart*, a seminal work with strong ties to his war novel *The Death of a Hero*, then about to be released. In the medieval legend of love and revenge on which the poem was based, Aldington found the situation which dramatized what he averred was a modern dilemma: within the loneliness of his soul man is forever plagued with a love-sorrow. Early in the poem, the lover Philoctetes, emerging from "a ten years prison," grasps the hand of his friend Neoptolemus, expecting to end his loneliness, only to discover there is no deliverance from solitude. Modern man confronts a similar fate: release from self and solitude can never occur since no one can respond to his wish to communicate. So the "one thing worth achieving"—release from self, escape from the awful loneliness—is unobtainable. And even for those who, like the lovers in the Provence Tale, find release and response, whose natures do combine, the end is death, their fate "the last variety of this tragedy." Even they at last share Philoctetes' fate.

The printing of *The Eaten Heart* passed to Miss Cunard, and in the "hard-come" spring of 1929, remembered for its "sharp, cold sunsets" that marked not the end of her day in the printery, she labored on, unassisted by Lévy, who by now could be "actually laudatory about the look" of her pages. Out of the long communion with Aldington's poem, seeing it materialize letter by letter and line by line, came a satisfying sense of understanding. "I came to feel it," she wrote Otto Theis, "more and more, during the setting and diverse re-readings as it was being done—and it seems to me that I, knowing nothing of Philoctetes' pain and Timon's rage and the relation of Greece to us must just have got (what I have got) through that for me ever-permanent 'reading-in' of symbol, value recognition, with no criticism possible to me but that of actual lines and words and, as it were, gestures." Nonetheless, grateful as she was for her own hard-earned comprehension, she wondered how the "question of fairness towards the reader" would be solved.

There was still one other who, along with encouragement, offered Miss Cunard a manuscript. She had known Arthur Symons ever since "old Café Royal and Eiffel Tower restaurant days," around 1915, when both were "regulars," and when Symons, knowing that Nancy had

Arthur Symons, author of *Mes Souvenirs* (Hours Press, 1929).

settled in Paris, would spend hours telling her about his life there in the nineties. Symons, a lonely defender of the *fin de siècle* in France and England (even his conversation abounded with words like "daemonic," "exotic," "satanic," "macabre"), would appear clothed in the artist's garb of the period—a long Inverness cape and a high wide-brimmed black felt hat—and talk animatedly of the "vitality" of the Decadence and of his dead friends Beardsley, Conder, Whistler, Dowson, Rimbaud, and especially Verlaine, whom he had known in Paris and entertained at Oxford. He had aroused Nancy's curiosity by promising her something "literary yet very personal," a fitting description for the manuscript that arrived in Réanville in the summer of 1929 bearing the French title, *Mes Souvenirs*, and containing three essays, the longest and finest being a sharp visual and psychological portrait of Verlaine. Of the French poet's face, Symons wrote: it seemed to be "without a beautiful line . . . with its spiritual forehead, its animal jaw, its shifting fawn's eyes. But it was genial and it had a singularly manful air . . . the eyes were certainly curious: oblique, constantly in movement, with gestures (there is no other word) of the lids and brows." Verlaine's ills, Symons theorized, resulted from an uncompromising nature. "Never was there a nature more absolutely impelled to act itself out, more absolutely alien to every conceivable convention than that of Verlaine." On the reputed mixture of good and evil in him, Symons was eloquent: "What in Verlaine became soiled with evil might, under other chances and influences, have made part of the beauty of a Saint Francis. He had an inconceivable simplicity of nature, and . . . profound instincts. . . . Whenever he was not under the influence of those drinks . . . he was the most delightful companion. . . . All his verse is a confession of what was beautiful and dreadful and merely troublesome to him in life, at first under courtly disguises, and then, gradually, with more and more sincerity to fact as well as to emotion or sensation, and at the end, in a pitiful enough way, a sort of nakedness in rags."

In the second essay, "Bohemian Chelsea," Symons evoked the Chelsea of Wilde ("reckless, insolent, too certain of himself"), of Augustus John ("the born Bohemian and the born wanderer"), of Conder's Fancy Dress Ball in 1900 at 91 Cheyne Walk, and of the "Chelsea girls," in one of whom, Jenny (after Rossetti's), he discerned "a kind of diabolical beauty" and "something in her regard that was infernal." In "The Magic of the East," the third, Symons wrote movingly of the gypsies of India which the Indian poetess Sarojini Chattopadhya, his confidante in "matters of the heart," had once described.

II

Near the end of her first year as a publisher, Nancy paused long enough to take stock of her enterprise and reached some conclusions which would importantly affect the future of the press. She concluded that whatever success she had enjoyed was the result, first, of having had the good fortune to publish a few celebrated authors; second, of working hard; third, of being ignorant of the customs and practices of printing;

and, last, of having good luck. She also decided that had she consulted more people knowledgeable in the ways of private presses, she might have been put off by what surely would have been recommendations to do things in a conventional manner. They would certainly have told her that, in addition to printing books, she would have to find ways to advertise, distribute, and sell them, all of which she rightly feared would involve volumes of correspondence and bookkeeping. In her surge toward composing and printing, she had scarcely been aware of such matters, and except for the initial circular announcing the first series of Hours Press books and where they could be procured (outside Paris, only at Dorothy Warren's gallery in London), she had done nothing to publicize or extend the distribution of her publications. Still, the Hours had prospered— *Peronnik, The Eaten Heart*, and *One Day* had all sold well, and *Mes Souvenirs* was in heavy demand—and Nancy cheerfully admitted she had doubled her investment and had acquired a new press with part of the profits; moreover, even without the benefit of publicity, the Hours had become quite well-known in England, mostly due to friendly reviews, and was gaining recognition in the United States and France. As comforting as these accomplishments were, however, they could not entirely compensate for certain hardships and strains which had grown increasingly bothersome and which at times had come close to producing serious interruptions in the operations of the press as well as nearly insupportable demands on the patience of its owner. Working and living in the country, no matter how pleasant the old farmhouse and the picturesque Norman landscape, meant putting up with annoyances that often made work at the press an ordeal rather than the pleasure it was intended to be. Supplies, for example, had to be fetched from Paris, fifty miles away, which consumed a day in travel each time; books had to be transported to and from the binderies, either in Paris, Rouen, or Evreux, and when binders became "recalcitrant" they had to be "argued with in person"; moreover, in rural Réanville, one had to be prepared, if possible, for the frustrating delays in the mail and, even more irritating, for the sudden, unscheduled, and always alarming interruptions of the electricity, which would bring the Minerva to an instant halt and plunge the printery into darkness. And for Nancy, personally, despite Henry's assistance, her patience with the detested "packing and clerking" duties had nearly reached the breaking point; and of bookselling and bookkeeping, too, she emphatically wanted "no more." At her lowest point, she would disgustedly dismiss everything as "labor for an oldish solitary person who can't do anything else!"

In less harried moments, however, Nancy confirmed that Hours was still something she was determined to enjoy, and if living in the country had proved to be impractical for the smooth functioning of the press, perhaps moving the Hours to Paris would provide an answer; at least being closer to the sources of supplies and to the other needs of the press might solve some of the problems. So when news reached Réanville from her friend Georges Sadoul that a small shop with an *arrière boutique* had just fallen vacant at 15 rue Guénégaud, a narrow side street near the Seine in Montparnasse, Nancy lost no time in replying that she would take it (she leased the place for nine years on the profits of eight months' work at the press). She also asked Sadoul to help her and Henry make the move to Paris as soon as possible—a task completed without delay (and with surprising ease) in the winter of 1930, and early in the new year, with Sadoul serving as an "elastic secretary and general factotum," the Hours began functioning once more, a bit irregularly, perhaps, but always productively, Nancy insisted. For awhile Sadoul assumed the clerking chores, the packing and posting of books and the maintaining of accounts, leaving Nancy and Henry free for composing and printing (Henry's typographical skills had by now vastly improved) and, at the start, free to redecorate the shop, at the front of which, holding rendezvous among paintings by Miró, Malkine, and Tanguy (the Galerie Surréaliste, in the rue Jacques, was close by), ornamented shields, fetish figures, and pieces of sculpture from Africa and new Guinea—the rakings of "treasure hunts" Nancy and Aragon had made to English and French seacoast towns in the early twenties—were the Hours Press books, neatly arranged in a line of neutral grey bookshelves which contrasted sharply with the black and white linoleum floor. A handsome Boule writing-desk that once belonged to Nancy's father served as the office table. Here and there strong lighting shone on the rich assembly of colorful African beading and the multi-colored Brazilian tribal head-dresses made of parrot feathers. In the *arrière boutique* the two presses resided in the company of other "working furniture." In place of Maurice Lévy, who had left the Hours with his opinions of tyro printers unchanged, was a young printer, "sympathetic" and "progressive-minded," who worked an eight-hour day bothered neither by the crowds of meddlesome visitors who sometimes threatened to overflow into his precinct, nor by the owner's rather erratic working habits.

In the form of an attractive broadsheet divided into three sections—poetry, prose, and music—Nancy announced the Paris, or Second Series, of Hours Press books. Already contracted were poems ("modern, much advanced poetry," as always) by Walter Lowenfels, Robert Graves, Laura Riding, Bob Brown, Harold Acton, Roy Campbell, Ezra Pound, and Brian Howard. From Richard Aldington would come a war story, and from Laura Riding, in addition to the poetry, a prose piece called *Four Unposted Letters to Catherine*; and Henry, the object of some persistent coaxing by Nancy, had agreed to try to set some poems to music. Having decided that the poetry volumes should appear in the same rather large format, Nancy had approached several artists about making the covers. Yves Tanguy agreed to design those for Lowenfels' Apollinaire poem, Len Lye would do the same for the books by Miss Riding and Graves, Man Ray would make a large photomontage for Henry's music book, if it materialized, and Elliott Seabrooke, John Banting, and a printer named John Sibthorpe would create cover designs for the others. The announcement finished with a reminder that all the poetry would be "hand-set" and most volumes "printed on a Hand Press over a hundred years old . . . in 16-point Caslon old-face, on Haut-Vidalon, Canson, and Montgolfier paper," and that the Hours Press was also "interested in Ethnography— African Art, Oceania, and the two Americas—and will always have a few specimens on show, as well as certain modern french pictures, a few english and american books and the Surrealist Series." The news that the Hours Press had moved to Paris and intended to issue a new series of books brought forth well-wishing notices in the *Observer* ("new poems . . . from this house are sure to be agreeably turned out in a large, plain format"), the *Nation*, which called Hours "an interesting experiment in printing and publishing" without any "fussy artiness," and *Everyman*, which complimented Miss Cunard on having the good sense, so often lacking among English private publishers, to issue "her wares at a price . . . the ordinary book collector can well afford." To make certain English customers would know of her inexpensive wares, Nancy hired a book traveler, the "very estimable Mr. Gray," who went the rounds of the London book trade selling the Hours Press productions, and, in her opinion, "very well, indeed."

As had been the case at Réanville with Douglas' *Report*, the maiden Hours publication in Paris turned out not to be the first book listed on Miss Cunard's schedule but another unannounced item requested by a friend at the last moment. Though fortunately a less dreary project than the Douglas essay, the catalogue the American artist Eugene MacCown asked Nancy to produce for his first exhibit (at the Galerie Leonce Rosen-

Hours Press, 15 rue Guénégaud, Paris, 1930.

berg) made uncustomary demands on the still somewhat inexperienced
press. With MacCown, a handsome, boyish-looking midwesterner (he told
Nancy he had been born in a "prairie schooner"), Nancy had traveled to
Italy in the mid-twenties, stopping for visits with Osbert and Sachie Sitwell
and Norman Douglas, of whom MacCown had made a sketch that struck

HOURS PRESS
HOURS PRESS
HOURS PRESS

15 Rue Guénégaud
PARIS 6e
Tel. Littré 50-03

New works by living authors. Signed, numbered and limited
editions privately printed.

POETRY	E	PROSE
	Z	
Walter Lowenfels	R	*Richard Aldington*
Apollinaire. An Elegy	A	A W a r S t o r y
150 signed copies £ 1.10.		300 signed copies £ 2.
	P	
Robert Graves	O	*Laura Riding*
Ten Poems More	U	Four Unposted Letters
200 signed copies £ 1.10.	N	to Catherine.
	D	200 signed copies £ 2.
Laura Riding		
Twenty Poems Less		
200 signed copies £ 1.10.		
		MUSIC
Bob Brown	*	
Words. Cover by Man Ray	C	*Henry Crowder*
150 signed copies £ 1.10.	O	Six Piano Pieces with
		poems by Richard Al-
Harold Acton	L	dington Walter Lowen-
T h i s C h a o s.	L	fels and Nancy Cunard.
150 signed copies £ 1.10.	E	
	C	
Roy Campbell		*Covers by* Frank
P o e m s	T	Dobson, Eugene Mac
		Cown, Man Ray, Yves
Brian Howard	E	Tanguy, Hilaire Hiler,
First Poems	D	Elliott Seabrooke.

C A N T O S
in One Volume
200 Copies £ 2.

Hours Press announcement, 1930.

her as "more of a rendering than a likeness"; he had also done a portrait of Nancy dressed in her father's Ascot garb, including top hat, and with an imperious expression on her face, as well as an abstract design for the covers of her poem *Parallax*, issued by the Hogarth Press in 1925. Mac-Cown's catalogue, "simple yet somewhat deluxe," contained four full-page illustrations and a preface by the artist in which he explained that at his request six friends—Clive Bell, Jean Cocteau, Norman Douglas, Bernard Faÿ, André Gide, and Raymond Mortimer—had agreed, "independently of one another," to provide titles for his titleless paintings, a procedure he believed, perhaps over-optimistically, would provide glimpses into "each man's sensibility" as well as opinions of his work. The results, in practice, were remarkably variegated; for one painting, his friends came up with this medley of titles: "Si Jeuness Savait" (Bell), "Trois Personnes Qui Sont Venues Sans Etre Invitées" (Cocteau), "The Happy Family" (Douglas), "Le Présent (Figure de Pierre entre deux Rêves)" (Faÿ), "The Unhappy Family" (Gide), and "Intrusions of a Dead Morality" (Mortimer).

The first book in the second Hours Press series satisfied all Nancy's criteria—new and old. The work was "modern," the author a self-declared avant-gardist, and the cover artist a foremost surrealist painter. For Miss Cunard, Walter Lowenfels seemed to be the "ideal American," spontaneous, buoyant, and generous-spirited, epitomizing "all the good things in life," besides being a hard worker. Even Douglas, who professed a dislike for "advanced" poetry, liked Lowenfels, as did "various French intellectuals," perhaps because of his "great feeling for France and its writings." What Lowenfels had for the Hours was an *Elegy on Apollinaire*, a section of *The Poem That Can't Be Stopped*, and one of several elegies on celebrated writers that he would complete in the next few years and in which he would refine the "spiritual death" theme first enunciated by Michael Fraenkel. In *Apollinaire*, the great poet's death is mourned by the world as the "world's own death," but dying, according to Lowenfels' vision, is a re-creative spiritual process forever bearing new existences; thus the world dies and, simultaneously, gives birth to its "creation Apollinaire." Nancy discerned in Lowenfels' work a sense of "time and timelessness," of continuity, a linkage between the "accidental, the unknowable, and the foreseen." Some retinal correspondence of her perception Yves Tanguy tried to capture in his cover drawing, a lunar landscape, filled with "dream-inspired" cliffs, disembodied and floating in space, the whole rendered in black on a buttercup-yellow background.

Laura Riding and Robert Graves supplied the next three manuscripts, companion volumes of poetry, *Twenty Poems Less* by Miss Riding
and *Ten Poems More* by Graves, as well as the former's epistolary essay
Four Unposted Letters to Catherine. A New Zealand artist and film-
maker, Len Lye, who occasionally visited the authors at their Seizin Press
at Deyá, Majorca, created the covers for all three books—striking photomontage compositions of stones, rocks, wood, sea life, and wire netting,
which to Nancy suggested the "assembled fragments that might be found
on some exotic or dream strand," and the designs themselves seemed
creations of "nature's world in a sort of petrified permanence." Of the two
authors and fellow printers, Laura Riding and Robert Graves, Nancy had
seen little, though in 1929 she had met both in London. Graves she
thought a "striking personality," one of the most striking "of our time," a
man whose being was "all in nerve," with a suggestion of an "equine
nobility" that evoked "a strong, wilful young horse—and a wild one at
that." Also in him was a "deep, thoughtful strain" that appeared in *Ten
Poems More*, in his eleven poems that had a "look you in the eye"
directness as well as subtlety. For several reasons it turned out to be the
Hours' most successful book. Besides being a "good short collection"
(seventeen pages), the edition of two hundred copies sold almost at once,
and Nancy sent Graves £180 in royalties, "rejoicing in the thought that
fine poems, for once, were paying their author." Reviewers, typical of
whom was the *Observer*'s, admired the poet's "compression of thought,
phrase and fancy," and twenty years later at the Victoria and Albert
Museum in London, Nancy was delighted to discover *Ten Poems More* in
an exhibit of books selected as examples of outstanding book production.

Immediately after the publication of *Ten Poems More* came the
companion volume, *Twenty Poems Less* by Laura Riding, the meaning of
which Nancy moved toward, gropingly, with vagaries like "other world,"
her responses partly inhibited perhaps by the vivid impression she had
retained of the poet and her surroundings in London. "Distinctly supernatural? Is that what she is?" Nancy wondered. "No, indistinctly, vaguely
so. Her personality was very tense, dominating, and quietly American.
Like a brooding, sultry day, there was electricity around, if not visible; a
sense of contained conflict. And there was, on the one hand, the terrific,
clinical tidiness of everything in the London flat—a hand press I remember in particular, with its accessories about it in a way no printer would
take time off to keep so clean, almost as if in a museum. On the other
hand, there was an eerie atmosphere and the sense of distance between us;

there would have to be a key and I should not find it. In this mystified state I could see two things clearly: her quality and her meticulousness." Nancy's search for the "particular symbolism" within Miss Riding's poetry received a welcome assist from Len Lye, whose photomontage covers seemed "in perfect communion" with what she was expressing. With the second Riding book, *Four Unposted Letters to Catherine*, Miss Cunard had far less difficulty, although the simplicity of the author's language had at first confounded her and she had searched fruitlessly for "inner meanings." Rereading the text many times, however, had clarified Miss Riding's intentions, and with further acquaintance she had come to admire the clarity, directness, and the truth of the little volume that Miss Riding had addressed to a child but filled with insights perhaps only fully understandable to adults. Coming on Michael Robert's review in the *Poetry Review*, Nancy was relieved to find her own conclusions confirmed: "Give this volume to a child; it tells so simply, that an adult may find it difficult, how it is good to live straight, independently of the tortuous conventions of others: how there is a difference between the doing which tends towards the general comfort and that which people 'do, not for comfort or fun but in order to prove to themselves and to other people that they are people.' It shows, too, the difference between the knowing which starts with self-knowledge and the learning which is the acquisition of facts."

Perhaps the most rewarding suggestion Nancy ever received and accepted came from Richard Aldington. In the December 1929 number of Edward Titus' magazine *This Quarter*, Aldington had announced the establishment of the "Richard Aldington Poetry Prize of 2,500 francs" to be awarded to the "ablest young American poet" whose work had or would appear in Titus' magazine. Titus explained in an editorial note that Aldington had been "profoundly touched by the whole-hearted appreciation in America" of his novel *The Death of a Hero*, and intended the prize as a "slight expression of his gratitude" to America as well as a means of "attracting attention to the work of poets likely to prove of interest and promise." Although six months later the prize had still to be awarded (when it was, in September 1931, Walter Lowenfels and E. E. Cummings, as previously mentioned, shared the honor), Aldington urged Miss Cunard to launch a poetry contest of her own. Besides serving to "get the press even better known," he advised it might uncover a "new talent," perhaps even sooner than his own contest seemed capable of doing. On what subject should contestants be asked to write? wondered Miss Cunard. "Let us make it a poem on time," suggested Aldington, "on any aspect of time." As for the length of entries, both agreed that one hundred lines would be a "good, generous" limitation and would hopefully discourage any that might otherwise run to "half the length of the *Iliad*." An announcement, attractively printed in red ink on a small square card and sent to literary reviews in England and France, read: "Nancy Cunard, Hours Press, in collaboration with Richard Aldington, offers £10 for the best poem up to 100 lines, in english or american on TIME (for or against). Entries up to June 15, 1930." Admittedly, a prize of £10 was not large, yet Miss Cunard reflected that it might be won by "four perfect lines" or an "exquisite rhyming epigram." However paltry her reward, it was attractive enough to set off an avalanche of entries descending on the rue Guénégaud, reaching nearly one hundred in a few weeks, and ranging from "doggerel to a kind of sham metaphysics," few of which were by anyone recognized as a poet or, in the opinion of the judges, who deserved to be. "God Almighty! The things that come in," Miss Cunard complained to the *Everyman* editor, Louise Morgan. "I'm going to keep all or copy all: one about 'two little toadstools' . . . is Henry's favourite; and [another] on Time truly enough, an immense letter about the spawning and respawning of insects. . . . You see the link." A few days before the contest ended, Nancy and Aldington traveled to Réanville and stoically read the poems to each other (they later reread them alone). Disappointed, they agreed that from the whole assortment only two or three deserved to be considered for the prize and that even those could only be described as mediocre; they concluded, sadly, that the award would have to go to the "best" of the mediocre entries, unless by some miracle a really first-rate poem should turn up by the fifteenth.

And a miracle there was, although slightly behind schedule. No last-minute entries of importance had arrived during the closing hours of the contest, and on the fifteenth Miss Cunard left the Hours shop resigned to giving the prize to one of two or three poems that she and Aldington had sieved from the mass of entries. The next morning, however, on opening the shop, she spied a small folder tucked beneath the door, presumably deposited there sometime during the night. Written on the cover was the word *Whoroscope*, and beneath, a strange name—Samuel Beckett. It meant nothing to Nancy, nor did Aldington know anything of the author, but the poem, "even on the first, feverish read-through," meant a very great deal. "What remarkable lines, what images and analogies, what vivid coloring throughout; indeed, what technique! This long poem [ninety-eight lines], mysterious, obscure in parts, centered around Descartes, was clearly by someone very intellectual and highly educated." There was no doubt that they held the winning poem in their hands, and the fact that it had arrived at the last moment, technically even after the deadline had passed, made "it all the sweeter." Immediately summoned, Beckett told his astonished listeners how he had composed *Whoroscope*. From a friend he had learned about the contest on the day it ended. That evening he had written the first half of the poem; then after "a guzzle of salad and Chambertin at the Cochon de Lait," he had returned to his room and worked on it until about three in the morning. Close to dawn he had walked down to the rue Guénégaud and slipped the finished poem under Miss Cunard's door. "What other words exist for this," raved Nancy, "but inspiration and virtuosity?"

Beckett, the judges learned, was twenty-four, had lived in Paris since 1928, and shared with them a friendship with James Joyce, for whom he, like so many others, had performed various research chores relating to Joyce's writing. Beckett's appearance—"tall and slim to leanness, of handsome aquiline features"—as well as his personality fascinated Nancy. "He is a man of stone, you think until he speaks, and then is all warmth, if he be with someone sympathetic to him. He is fair, with a direct gaze at times coming to pinpoint precision in his light blue eyes. . . . There is . . . a feeling of the spareness of the desert about him. . . . He is very self-assured in a deep, quiet way, unassuming in manner, and interested in mankind. . . . One would not call him aloof but very self-contained. If you think he is looking slightly severe, this may be because he is assessing what has just been said, and his laughter and ease of manner are frank and swift. He is enchantingly Irish, and . . . on first seeing him, I thought there was just a touch here of the silhouette of James Joyce."

Because *Whoroscope* contained so many remarkable images and analogies which for most readers, including herself, Miss Cunard believed would remain obscure and unintelligible, she asked Beckett to append a few clarifying notes to his poem before it was printed. Soon after reading *Whoroscope* for the first time, Nancy reported to a friend that she and Aldington had just read "an extraordinary poem so learned that even Richard is half-baffled, and I, aghast (if temporarily) at my complete lack of allusive learning." After Beckett supplied the notes a few days later, *Whoroscope* was hand-set and published (in Caslon 11-point with notes in smaller type) and placed on sale for five shillings. A narrow band attached to the cover explained that, besides being the Hours Press contest winner, *Whoroscope* was the author's first separately published work—a scoop the publisher forever after recalled with as much delight as she and Aldington had felt when they gratefully gave Beckett the £10 award.

After enduring several exasperating delays caused by laggardly binders, Miss Cunard was finally able to issue the long-awaited poetry volumes of Ezra Pound and Roy Campbell, both of which appeared about the same time as *Whoroscope*, midsummer 1930. Pound she had first met in 1915, when the poet had often called on Lady Cunard, whose influence and support he rightly believed might further his efforts to acquire financial aid for James Joyce and a less dangerous military assignment for Wyndham Lewis. For the nineteen-year-old Nancy his appearance on such occasions evoked the dramatic figure of Rodolfo in *La Bohème*: "He was of middle stature, with green, lynx-like eyes, a head of thick, waving red hair and a pointed red beard. He was dressed . . . in black and white check trousers, a black velvet jacket, [and] a large-brimmed black felt hat. He wore a sweeping black cape and carried yellow chamois leather gloves and a cane." She also noted that Pound's personality, hardly less dramatic, could be alarming to some, "difficult" to others, but to her it was "vibrating and dynamic" always, and even "ecstatic" at times. He was a "thorough revolutionary, intellectually and artistically, and an intensely creative man, preeminently a maker, entirely personal." Nor could she overlook his prodigious knowledge of various exotic literatures and cultures, although his penchant for learned allusions had once infuriated her to the point of forcing him to admit that only an "old Turkish scholar" could ever possibly recognize all the esoteric references in the cantos. Despite this bothersome matter, however, she had always been an appreciative and admiring reader, impressed by the enormous scope of his cantos as well as by the beauty of his poetry. Pound had proposed that Hours should publish an edition of his thirty finished cantos, half of which Bill Bird had already printed at the Three Mountains in 1925, and the other half John Rodker had printed the following year at his Ovid Press in London; both were sumptuously turned out in a large, gracious format. Pound proposed that the Hours book, in ordinary format, would combine the contents of the two earlier books, and would therefore be the first printing of all thirty cantos.

Having absorbed at least the fundamentals of printing while serving as editor of the Three Mountains series, Pound had become accustomed to keeping a close watch over the production of limited editions of his books, wherever they had been printed, and he was not about to turn the entire responsibility of publishing *XXX Cantos* (the full title is *A Draft of*

XXX Cantos) over to Miss Cunard; and when they both agreed that the length of his book (142 pages) would make printing it at the Hours a rather complicated matter, Pound (with Nancy's encouragement) had quickly found a Paris firm—Maître-Imprimeur Bernouard—to print the volume exactly as he wanted it done. Technically impressive and, in Miss Cunard's opinion, "perfect in taste," *XXX Cantos* featured among its many embellishments handsome initials drawn expressly for the book by the poet's wife, Dorothy Shakespear. The following year, the bibliophile Herbert L. Rothchild, one of Miss Cunard's best clients, honored the production by reproducing the first page of Canto Four in his study of private presses in America, England, and Europe.

Meeting Roy Campbell in London for the first time around 1919, in the brasserie of the celebrated Café Royal, was the fulfillment of a promise repeatedly made to Miss Cunard by the poet and critic T. W. Earp, who had tirelessly praised the "wonderful new poet" he called the "Zulu." Not quite as impressed by the "Zulu" as was Earp, Nancy found something imprecise in his nature, "amounting to 'this is something of a dark horse.'" Yet she saw charm in his quiet manner, and vigor concentrated in his dark eyes, and he could be alternately vivacious and shy. By the time the Hours Press edition of Campbell's *Poems* was published, the prediction Earp had made many years before that Campbell would "turn into someone to be reckoned with" had clearly been verified. In the intervening years he had developed into the "swinger of powerful lines, full of rhyme and fire and color, and rich in ornament and imagery," and, at thirty and at the height of his career, he was awaiting the publication of six books, one of which was the satirical collection of verse called *The Georgiad*, two sections of which he gave Miss Cunard for her Hours Press volume. *Poems* (there were but twelve) was oversubscribed before publication, and, as in the case of Graves, Campbell received generous royalties of £80 or more. A particularly handsome book, *Poems* was bound in vermilion paper boards, with drawings by the author on each cover—on the front, an armed cavalier charging a bull; on the back, an olive tree caught by the wind—simple yet effective evocations of the milieu out of which the poems had emerged.

In August the last book of the several originally scheduled for spring publication appeared. It was also the sixth volume of poetry the press had issued and the only Hours book not printed in France. The author, John Rodker, with years of printing and publishing experience behind him, supervised the production of his *Collected Poems* at the Curwen Press in

England and sent the edition of two hundred books to Miss Cunard. With cover designs by Len Lye—"striking compositions . . . with a graceful, semi-Egyptian influence"—and initial lettering by the English artist Edward Wadsworth, it possessed what an *Observer* critic called "a fastidiously elegant habit." In 1919, Rodker had founded his own press, the Ovid, in order "to bring before the public work that was considered advanced," and among his first publications were *Ara Vus Prec* by T. S. Eliot (264 copies with initials and colophon by Wadsworth) and *Hugh Selwyn Mauberley* by Ezra Pound (two hundred copies with initials by Wadsworth), followed by volumes of drawings by Gaudier-Brzeska, Wyndham Lewis, Wadsworth, and a collection of the publisher's poems, *Hymns*. A few years later Rodker founded a second publishing firm, the Casanova Society, which specialized in lavish editions of Casanova's *Memoirs* (translated by Arthur Machen) and *The Arabian Nights* (translated by William Powys Mathers), both of which became famous among collectors and bibliophiles. Introspective, thoughtful, analytical, Rodker was one of the "most self-critical people" Miss Cunard had ever met. From the work of fourteen years, he had selected twenty-one poems, all of them, he stated in his preface, influenced by the French poetry of 1850–1910—through which he had come to write his own poetry—and, however palely, by his troubled state of mind ("I was, as it were, hanging in the void, and these poems are my efforts to establish contact") and by his conscientious effort to shock. That they had somehow retained their power to shock him in 1930 was "a sufficient comment on their author." Though disinclined to join those who found Rodker "too much a poet of despair," Nancy nonetheless granted that the sincerity and individualism of his poetry tended to reaffirm one's convictions that "even utter blackness may be a thing of beauty."

Ever since the late spring and continuing through the summer the pace in the rue Guénégaud shop had grown steadily more hectic, and with the accelerating "rhythm of production" Nancy was more than ever aware that the operation of a press could not be handled alone, or almost alone. It demanded more surveillance and attention to business than she had expected, and probably more than she had wanted to give to it, and although moving to Paris had eliminated most of the "driven work" (Henry's description of what had gone on at Réanville), maintaining the Hours had nevertheless remained an exhausting and trying occupation. By late summer a near-prostrate Nancy, her patience worn thin by the protracted delays at the binders and her energies depleted after publishing six books of poetry, one volume of prose, MacCown's catalogue, and *Whoroscope*, was ready for more than a vacation away from Paris. She had decided to take leave from the press as well and to turn it over to a temporary manager, an Englishwoman named Wyn Henderson, who, in 1929, with the poet James Cleugh and three others, had founded the Aquila Press, in London, to print responsibly edited, handsomely bound, hand-printed limited editions of "rare or unobtainable classics," and which after eight publications, including Nancy's *Two Poems* (1930), had come to an inglorious end in bankruptcy. Mrs. Henderson, whose duties at the Aquila included those of managing director, production manager, secretary, tea-maker, and stamp-licker, arrived in Paris with the former Aquila printer and typographer John Sibthorpe, both ready to assume their new assignments. It was agreed that on a budget of £300 she would oversee the publication of four books Nancy had already contracted—a short story by Aldington and three volumes of poetry by Harold Acton, Brian Howard, and Bob Brown—after which a decision would be made whether to close the Hours permanently.

With the new manager and her printer in charge and fully instructed, Nancy and Henry headed south ("very fast in Crowder's small dark blue car, the 'Bullet' ") in search of "shade and green fields," traveling as far as the fringes of the Pyrenean Andorra and then doubling back to the Dordogne before installing themselves in the "half-crumbling village" of Creysse, where they lingered a month, living like peasants. For the curious and suspicious villagers they soon became an inexhaustible topic of conversation. Why had two such different people—"one, a tall, imposing handsome man of color, beautifully dressed, who spoke very little French; the other an obvious English woman for all her Parisian accent and vocabulary"—come to Creysse? To live the simple life, perhaps? (They had taken a "dear little place," with no water or cooking facilities, for £1.) To enjoy the beauty of the Dordogne? Nothing really satisfied their curiosity until they saw an ox-drawn farm cart carrying a piano arrive at the visitors' cottage, and a short time later heard the first notes of Henry's playing pealing forth and watched Nancy, alone, walking in the fields with books and "some writing." All speculation ceased with the unanimous decision that they had in their midst *des intellectuels étrangers.*

At Réanville, Nancy had often listened, charmed, to Henry improvising at the piano, and she had long believed his original "musical thoughts" and "harmonies and progressions" should be set down, but Crowder, modest and unassuming, as always, had found reasons to postpone doing

281

it. In Paris, the idea of a music book had suddenly come to her. Why not make one of the Hours publications a collection of songs for which Henry would write the music? And after Henry's usual round of procrastination, Nancy had got her way. Henry agreed to try, provided suitable lyrics or poems could be found, and immediately the search for "poems that would inspire" Henry had begun, spurred greatly by Nancy's hastily composed "battle hymn," "Equatorial Way," describing a Negro's fierce farewell to the United States as he sets out for Africa. Henry had also approved of Nancy's poem "Blues" ("with the Boeuf-sur-le-Toit cabaret in mind"), which he would later sing at various Left Bank clubs. But when four poets, all of whom "much appreciated Henry as man and musician," came forth with a bounteous offer, Nancy and Henry's search had ended suddenly and promisingly. The four—Richard Aldington, Walter Lowenfels, Harold Acton and Samuel Beckett—had told Henry that he could choose whatever he wanted from their works. After four weeks of concentrated labor at Creysse, sometimes working through the "velvet-dark" nights, Henry had composed scores for each poem—"moving" for Acton's "Tiresias," "light" and "pretty" for Aldington's lyric, slow and sonorous for Lowenfels' "Creed" and Beckett's "From the Only Poet to a Shining Whore," which the author marked "For Henry Crowder to Sing." At the end of a month both agreed Creysse had been an inspiration (Nancy had written some poems), and with regret shared by the villagers, *des intellectuels étrangers*" packed up the "Bullet" and headed for Paris.

To make the covers for Henry's book (now titled *Henry-Music*), Nancy at once thought of the photographer Man Ray who, besides having a "strong appreciation" of Crowder, valued the excellence of African art. Since several poems in the collection contained references to Africa, she suggested that he photograph an arrrangement of African artifacts selected from her collection. Entirely in black and white, the *Henry-Music* covers disturb at the same time they please. Cascading across the front cover and over to the back are dozens of bracelets, varying in size and shape; above, suspended before a grey backdrop, stand pieces of sculpture and a crude stringed instrument; at the top, pictured full-faced, is Crowder, dressed entirely in black and wearing a black fedora; on his shoulders, looking like out-sized gold braid, are rows of thin, ivory bracelets, standing rigidly upright and held in place by Nancy's arms, around which they had been tightly twisted.

All the Hours Press books Nancy entrusted to Wyn Henderson's care, excepting a last-minute addition the manager had contracted, ap-

Nancy Cunard and Henry Crowder in the Hours Press, rue Guénégaud, Paris, 1930.

peared the same month, January 1931. Meanwhile Nancy, her indignation stirred by Henry's vivid accounts of racial discord and injustice in America, had announced her intention to compile an anthology that would encompass the whole complex history of Negro culture, and with Henry serving as a rather dawdling assistant, had thrown herself into the toil of collecting material and handing out assignments and duties to interested friends, and, when in Paris, pausing in the rue Guénégaud just long enough to answer the most urgent correspondence. On one brief stopover Mrs. Henderson handed her a letter from Richard Aldington, whose bitter war story, *Last Straws*, had been the first Hours Press book published under her direction. Like *Death of a Hero*, it portrayed a group of doomed veterans protesting against the hypocrisy of victory which their experiences in and out of the military system verify. Advance orders for the book had arrived in gratifying numbers (Hours now had two book travellers in England) and almost the entire edition of five hundred copies, the largest of any Hours Press book, had been ordered before publication day. Mrs. Henderson selected the bindings for both editions—jade-green suede cloth boards with gilt lettering for the two hundred signed copies, and light-brown paper boards with designs by Douglas Cockerell for the three hundred unsigned—and, with both editions selling well, had sent the author an advance royalty payment. To Nancy's great surprise, however, Aldington had returned the check, along with an angry note stating he refused to recognize Wyn Henderson as the director of the Hours Press, and that Nancy should not have given to her manager a story he had written for her. Efforts to mollify Aldington failed. More expostulations followed and finally a real row by correspondence, which subsided only after Nancy consented to make out another check which Aldington retained. Whatever had been the cause of his peculiar action remained a secret, but when told of what had occurred Norman Douglas offered a wry opinion: "Why *do* authors have such difficulties with each other? I'm sure *grocers* don't behave that way among themselves!"

The slim companion volumes of "first poems" by Harold Acton and Brian Howard that Mrs. Henderson issued next rejoined friends who, while students at Eton, had edited the *Eton Candle*, a sprightly collection of prose and poetry; and, later, as Oxonians, had developed into rivals— rebellious, innovative, critically and aesthetically sophisticated. Both, in Nancy's opinion, epitomized the twenties: They "were aesthetes, and how much more. For both there was the same kind of enquiring restlessness, set on and directed against the background of English ease, which they could all the same enjoy. . . . Both were *jeunesse dorée*; good conversation, often sparkling and most original, was theirs, and both possessed quick minds, knowledge and perception of art." The sixteen poems in Harold Acton's collection, to which he had given the title *This Chaos* and dedicated to Miss Cunard, who had proposed its publication, were anything but chaotic, being in style and content tidy, well-written lyrics, learned and also playful, touching on a variety of subjects, including several espousing the joys of regular bathing. While *This Chaos* seems a somewhat inappropriate title for Acton's concise poetry, it suggests perfectly the vision Brian Howard sought to convey in his Hours Press book, *First Poems* (originally the volume bore the ironic title *God Save the King*). In Howard, Miss Cunard had always recognized an "element of extraordinariness." Though "most sane" he could be "literally dominated" by fantasy. Like many he had the faults of some of his qualities: "he could be intensely kind, appreciative, generous, and his exuberance, his violence, even, of heart could overflow, and then he could set to work all attired in arrogance and provocativeness. His sharp likes could vie with his trenchant hatreds, and his often very outspoken contempt for fools and the second-rate earned him many an enemy, whose least word against him might be 'dilettante.' How his personality could swing about on occasion!" The "ring" of Howard's poems, Nancy concluded, was "most true" to the poet's personality, but in the mixture of extremes the heaviest accent fell on his sense of tragedy, his anguish, and his apocalyptic vision of collapse.

By early 1931 compiling the *Negro* anthology had displaced the press as Nancy's abiding interest, and she realized that at least another year would be needed to collect and edit all the material she had been promised. To Louise Morgan and other friends who had often inquired about the fate of Hours, she confirmed what they had already concluded, that the press would definitely not continue after April, and might close even sooner if George Moore refused her permission to print a two-page *plaquette* she still hoped he would allow. *Words*, the last scheduled book and one of several the author Bob Brown had hastily assembled as part of a campaign to announce his Reading Machine, strained the ingenuity and perseverance of both the Hours manager and its elusive owner. To dramatize the revolutionary change Brown predicted his Reading Machine would produce in the printing industry, he proposed that his poems be set in the customary 16-point type, slightly to one side of the page, and that in one corner, on the same page, a poem of the same length be printed in

Cover design by Yves Tanguy for *Apollinaire* by Walter Lowenfels
(Hours Press, 1930).

microscopic type (a mere breath on the page), too small to be read
without a magnifying glass or, as Brown recommended, without the aid of
his invention. Trying to find type small enough for the midget poems
(though at first a search that promised to end happily when Caresse
Crosby assured Mrs. Henderson that the Black Sun could supply as much
as she needed and then did not deliver) turned into an exasperating chase
that ended in disappointment as, one by one, printers in London and Paris
sent word that they could provide nothing under 3- or 6-point type, neither of which came close to meeting Brown's "microscopery" specifica-
tions. The only solution, a costly one, was to print the miniature poems
from specially engraved plates, the whole to measure not more than one-

eighth of an inch when completed. With the covers for *Words*, Brown had even less luck. All hopes of photographing a large slab of ivory came to an end when the proofs revealed that the subtle shading and colors could not be reproduced. As a substitute the Hours printer John Sibthorpe quickly devised intricate, skillfully planned arrangements of type which formed the title, the author's name, and the Hours imprint.

The last book to appear under the Hours Press imprint before the press closed down came as a complete surprise to Nancy. Seeing an opportunity to produce at least one additional book, and one almost certain to turn a profit, Mrs. Henderson procured from Havelock Ellis an essay of forty pages entitled *The Revaluation of Obscenity*, which the author had completed only a few months before. Although perturbed that Wyn had not told her of the acquisition, Nancy responded enthusiastically to the book's attractive format and binding, and with considerable relief when she learned that the edition of two hundred copies had sold out. The real excellence of the book, however, lay in its content. With Ellis' ideas Nancy could not have been in greater harmony, particularly with his contention that censorship was not only bad in itself but frequently defeated its own supposed ends. A "premium is put on things that are dirty and worthless," he argued, largely because the law prohibits their sale on the grounds that they are pornographic. Why not end the secrecy that makes pornography attractive and thereby close the artificial market for pornography that the law creates? As numerous examples have proven, concluded Ellis, there are few who will read a book "because the Home Secretary recommends it; there is a vast public to read it because he condemns it."

Closing the press turned out to be a far more disruptive event than opening it. Among other things, Nancy had looked forward to ending her press by issuing a "small fantasy" by the author who had started it off with such a pleasant "bang," George Moore, and she had ordered five hundred copies of the two-page *plaquette*, a charming dream sequence entitled *The Talking Pine*, that Moore had told her one morning in his "breakfast room" in Ebury Street and had later written down for her. It was "like a small piece of folklore connected with ancient seas and man's agelong business with ships, and trade, and travel, all spoken in the simplest terms, and yet mysterious." Beautifully set and printed on fine paper, it awaited only the author's signature before being placed on sale for ten shillings, a not excessive price, in Nancy's opinion, considering that his name alone would fetch more. But without warning Moore had decided not to sign the copies. It would make him as well as Nancy look ridiculous, he said, and furthermore, as he later told Lady Cunard, he could not resign himself to making money out of such a trivial scrap of literature. Certain that he could be made to change his mind, however, Nancy pointed out that selling the *plaquettes* should be viewed as part of the Hours business, or if he preferred to see it another way, as a "favour" to her, the only one she had ever asked of him or ever would. Moore, however, remained steadfast and volunteered that he never would have allowed Nancy to carry the "prose-poem" away with her if he had known she intended to print it. There was nothing to do but respect the old man's decision (he was then eighty), however unfair it might seem. Angered by what she regarded as a serious breach in their long relationship, Nancy asked the editor of *Everyman* to consider printing a note on the matter, "not particularly nasty . . . just an item on how authors behave." Confidentially she added that Moore's behavior was "monstrous" after all his avowals of "life-long devotion," and, besides, it meant the "loss of a good many pounds." Eventually, Moore returned the copies of *The Talking Pine* to Mrs. Henderson, unsigned.

If Wyn Henderson had been counting on the sales of *The Talking Pine* to bring in enough money to pay off the debts the Hours had incurred under her management, she must have been disappointed by Moore's refusal to permit its publication. Fortunately, however, Ellis' essay was selling briskly, as predicted, and if it continued to do so, perhaps the proceeds would be sufficient to offset the debts. Meanwhile she estimated that the outstanding printing costs came to 13,223 francs, against which, however, 9,400 francs in unpaid accounts could be subtracted, leaving a deficit of 3,823 francs. Though the manager claimed that Hours was far from being bankrupt ("On paper," Wyn wrote Nancy, "we are solvent but of course that does not give us immediate cash for creditors."), Nancy thought otherwise. In her opinion, Mrs. Henderson had turned out to be a "shocking businesswoman" who had left the Hours with a "dead loss of three-hundred pounds." That was a very high price, she wrote Louise Morgan, "to buy my freedom, fool that I was."

Just before Nancy made her final decision to shut the press, Wyn had suggested that she should consider continuing it a while longer. But Nancy's reply left no doubt as to her intentions or to what had contributed to her decision. "Do you really think I ever want to have anything [to do] with publishing again? You must be crazy! I despise the whole thing and am disgusted, thoroughly and permanently. . . . Damn all business!" It was, finally, the "business side" of publishing that had become her neme-sis. In contrast to the first year at Réanville, when she had prospered by doing things in a simple way and as many of them as possible herself, the second year, though prosperous at the start, had seen the introduction of "all the usual business ways, overheads, and who knows what else" under Mrs. Henderson's direction, and the inevitable complications, loss of prof-its, and finally debt and harassment of creditors. Moreover, by the spring of 1931 the new project, *Negro*, had so completely engulfed her that any attempt to combine printing and publishing, either alone or with the as-sistance of a manager, and the tremendous amount of research and editing necessary for *Negro* would certainly have ended in failure. Yet, in replying to her own question on whether the press had come to a timely or un-timely end, Nancy ventured that if she had been able to pass it on to the "ideal partner," if such a person existed, it might have continued for a while. There is no doubt though that the "ideal partner" would have had to look after the *business* of publishing alone—"the publicity and ledger-keeping side of it all"—leaving Nancy unencumbered to concentrate on the hand-setting, choice of paper and bindings, and of course the printing. But in the absence of such a person there was nothing else to do but close the Hours. Shortly after *Negro* appeared in 1934, Miss Cunard gave up the rue Guénégaud shop too, selling everything (the Minerva press, in-cluding all its furnishing and type, was purchased by the "rising French publisher" Guy Levis Mano) save a few books, one case of type, and the great Mathieu press which, out of sentiment and a "nebulous feeling that . . . there might yet be some other kind of printing in the unpredictable future," was returned to its former home in the converted stable at Réan-ville. Three years later, in Spain, the seemingly unpredictable future had become shockingly predictable, and Miss Cunard, by then deeply com-mitted to the Republican struggle for survival, found "some other kind of printing" to do on the old Mathieu. With the help of the Chilean poet Pablo Neruda, and later alone, she printed six *plaquettes* of poetry, which were sold for Spanish Republican relief in London and Paris. Included in the poems by new and old friends like Nicolas Guillen, Langston Hughes, Tristan Tzara, Rafael Alberti, and Neruda, was one destined to be among the few great poems inspired by the Spanish conflict—"Spain" by W. H. Auden. This, nearly the last piece to come from the press, was the first printing of Auden's poem.

VII

FOUR NEW DIRECTIONS

THE NEED FOR ANONYMITY: CARREFOUR

O F ALL THE SMALL presses and publishing firms that operated in Paris between wars, only one—Carrefour—still exists. Based now in London, it functions primarily as an outlet for the almost forgotten writings of Michael Fraenkel who, along with Walter Lowenfels in the early 1930s, founded Carrefour as an instrument to advance the notion of complete anonymity in the arts. Not only did Fraenkel and Lowenfels agree to keep their identity a secret, but they vowed to issue their books unsigned. The only identification would be the Carrefour imprint. They set forth the new credo in a pamphlet titled "Anonymous: the Need for Anonymity," which, being unsigned, naturally became the first Anonymous publication. The "need for anonymity," they claimed, had never been greater; it had grown proportionately to the steady downward process they labeled the "despiritualization" of the world, a process which denied man participation in the "myth, magic and supernatural" of the natural world around him. "Economic needs," along with business and the competition for material comforts—all co-conspirators to keep man separated from the world, even from himself—were responsible for this unfortunate divorce. To restore the lost unity was the responsibility of Anonymous. Working from within to activate man's creative resources (described as imagination, wonder, and magic), Anonymous would help the artist merge his "creative consciousness into the total creative consciousness of the world," thus giving him access to the fund of "creative vitality" undistracted by economic concerns, as well as the opportunity to become a part of a "joint manifestation" incorporating all artists of all

290

time that sought to restore the bond between man and the universe. What might seem an uncertain and rather frothy reward for relinquishing the solid satisfaction of being acknowledged as the creator of something was really not at all insignificant. Besides the personal unity the artist would share with the "world and with his art," he would also be making "an active effort to shape the destiny of that world, and to contribute to world unity," by contributing to and thereby participating in the "universal sources of creation," not single-handedly, but as a member of the vanguard actively "remodeling the world." With Shelley's famous dictum the Anonymous statement shared the belief that the artist and his words possessed revolutionary power.

Aside from the metaphysical considerations and rewards, the Anonymous creator could strike a blow against one arm of "mechanical and industrial civilization"—the acquisitive commercial publishers who degraded art by classifying it as a salable or an unsalable commodity and the artist as a businessman with a product to sell. Too often, argued the editors, the artist had had to bow to the demands of the marketplace, and in order to survive had turned out "what he [could] sell rather than sell what he [could] produce." Anonymity would end this distortion as well as the enervating competition among artists (a natural ingredient of large-scale publishing) and restore the stress to where it belonged: "on the work, on creation." Thus free to concentrate on his art rather than the advancement of his name, freed from even inadvertently becoming a leader to a band of worshipers and collectors, the Anonymous writer could function as a moral force. Anonymity offered him an opportunity to circumvent the "mob mind or the necessity for the cryptic"; and in Paris, where adulation for the few (e.g., Joyce, Stein, and Pound) could inhibit as well as inspire the writer, particularly the novice, it provided at least a theoretical way out of the romantic cul-de-sac. By being denied an audience, in the sense that he no longer had to compete for its attention or even to regard it as "significant" or "important" to him, the Anonymous writer had to concentrate on his work, aware that it would be judged apart from him, the creator, almost as though it were posthumous. As an added inducement the editors conjectured that the Anonymous artist would be able to experience immortality—not just once, but many times over. They explained that, since the Anonymous artist "dies" so that he can live as an artist and individual, that is, in the sense that he snuffs out his ego by deciding to remain anonymous, the public for his work will actually be posterity. He could share in his own objective immortality; in fact, by stopping and starting afresh at any time he could experience one immortality after another. Dedicated to those for whom "disintegration in the modern world is stubborn fact," the Anonymous pamphlet alerted readers to the first two Anonymous publications, and, in theory, at least, prefigured what the editors hoped might be their first experience in immortality.

Michael Fraenkel and Walter Lowenfels both arrived in Paris in 1926, Fraenkel after a meteoric career as an encyclopedia salesman (he realized his pledge to save enough money by his thirtieth birthday to quit work and go to Paris to write), and Lowenfels after an unpleasant tryout in the family butter business and the almost unnoticed publication of a first book of poems, *Episodes and Epistles*. Both expected Paris to be the talisman that would transform aspirations into art, and, in time, with the help of Carrefour, it did seem to perform that magic. Except for a brief meeting in 1928, Lowenfels and Fraenkel did not see each other again until they became neighbors at the Villa Seurat in 1929. By then Fraenkel had composed *Werther's Younger Brother*, a seminal statement of his ideas on death, and had begun looking for a publisher; Lowenfels was doing the same, hoping to find someone to take his play *USA with Music*, which had narrowly missed being produced in the Berlin Shiffbauerdam Theatre. (It was scheduled to follow the Weill-Brecht production of *Die Dreigroschenoper*, but at the last minute had been cancelled as a play politically "too dangerous.") For both, forming a publishing company would meet a mutual need. The costs, though, would have to be assumed by Fraenkel alone, since Lowenfels had nearly exhausted the six thousand dollars he had brought to Europe. There was at least the likelihood of some return, however; if only as a novelty, Anonymous was bound to receive publicity, and regardless of what service it might be to the arts, it would have the immediate practical function of serving as a distinguishing trademark. By early fall, 1930, notices of the new firm had appeared in Paris, London, and New York; shortly after, the first two Carrefour publications were ready for distribution. Both had been printed in Bruges, on heavy Kingsway paper, in 12-point Garamond type, each in editions of four hundred copies. Neither bore the author's name, the only identification mark being the Carrefour imprint and Fraenkel's address, 18 Villa Seurat.

It is a pity *USA with Music* did not follow the Weill-Brecht production into the Berlin theatre. Lowenfels' kaleidoscopic picture of America's disintegration would have perfectly extended the theme of the new world. Based on an Associated Press report of the slaying of several miners during a strike in a small town (Herrin) in southern Illinois, *USA with Music* presents a multitude of events—a man is entombed alive in a cave-in, a Chicago political convention is invaded by the KKK—which embodied and simultaneously enlarged the "spiritual idea" Lowenfels found in the tragic events at Herrin. It is death that haunts America in this "non-literary, non-realistic, purely theatric" operatic tragedy: it is the death of the inner life which has been "muted" and "mutilated" by a powerful "outer life," raucous, glib, commercialized and painfully superficial, but potent and attractive enough to destroy the significance of death and to transform existence into a blaring operatic spectacle. The victim of the cave-in, like the men killed at Herrin, provides a whole population with an

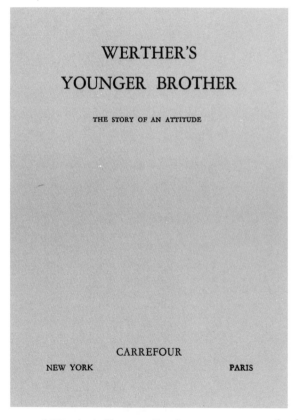

Title page of *Werther's Younger Brother,* an anonymous book by
Michael Fraenkel (Carrefour, 1930).

Walter Lowenfels and Norman Douglas, Menton, France, early 1930s.

irresistible "sales opportunity"; imagination parlays another's misfortune into dollars, and eventually into death as well. The result is that the nation's ability to feel humanely, and its capacity for inner and outer experience, are corroded along with its sense of mortality, the sense of death. The loss will reduce human behavior to a "purely physical" level; and so it is in *USA*, brutally physical. Assaulted by pitches shouted by opportunistic barkers as well as by the acrobatics performed by excited cheerleaders and con men, the inner life—the conscience—even the word, must succumb, opening the way for violence in which "human death loses significance." *USA* revealed Lowenfels was as much obsessed with death as Fraenkel, but his treatment was decidedly political. The actual physical death of the "old ruling order," the demise of that part of the world, corrupt and corrupting, which Marx predicted would precede social change, was what concerned him.

To Henry Miller, who gladly accepted space in Fraenkel's Villa Seurat flat in 1931, Michael Fraenkel was a man who "glowed inwardly with a white flame," a man possessed and absorbed by the idea of dying.

294

As Boris in *Tropic of Cancer* Fraenkel is only slightly less wild-eyed and woolly than Miller's other eccentric creations. It was Lowenfels who brought the two men together. For Miller, still homeless, there would be shelter, and for Fraenkel, Lowenfels reckoned, Miller would be "just the sort of person to whom Fraenkel could sell a creation of himself." The union, as Fraenkel described it, was an immediate success. The moment they met they dispensed with preliminaries and started talking. When Fraenkel showed Miller the manuscript of *Werther's Younger Brother*, Miller diplomatically commented that he "would dearly love" to say such things himself—which is what he eventually did—but before that happened they had begun a "dialogue on death" which would last for nearly ten years and would be preserved in a collection of correspondence called *Hamlet*.

Although Lowenfels admitted that he and Miller often joked about Fraenkel's death business and turned "it into something else, something we could use in our business, which was, say what you like, writing," Fraenkel's theories were nonetheless the cement that held together what Lowenfels called the "avant-garde of death"—the triumvirate of Miller, Fraenkel, and himself. But they could be baffling, too, as *Werther* proved. Even Lowenfels could not understand it. "Don't you see," Fraenkel protested, "it is the inner counterpart of World War I." But where was the war, Lowenfels wondered? "It's implicit," Fraenkel replied. Whether moved by pique or the recognition that Lowenfels had spotted a flaw, Fraenkel hastily consulted a few war novels—mainly Richard Aldington's *Death of a Hero* and Erich Remarque's *All Quiet on the Western Front*— and reworked *Werther*, creating scenes that resembled some of those in the novels. In Remarque, Fraenkel found the situation that perfectly embodied the message of *Werther*: annihilation of self is a prerequisite to fulfillment and happiness. Fraenkel adapted the scene in *All Quiet on the Western Front* in which the young German volunteer, Paul Baumer, destroys his French counterpart in what seems to be an act of self-defense. Baumer, however, later realizes he has actually committed suicide by proxy. Fraenkel interpreted it as an act of spiritual suicide which illustrated the point he wanted *Werther* to make, namely, that by means of spiritual suicide one can destroy the self, transcend self-consciousness, expel pain and fear, and survive as part of an "external pattern." Werther, like Baumer, was a suicide "who lived to tell the tale." His act is a last desperate "act of creative will," a final and necessary effort to triumph over the sickness of death.

The few favorable notices *USA* and *Werther* received encouraged the partners to expand their series, and among the first they asked for manuscripts was Kay Boyle. Though she had nothing for them, she confirmed that the idea of anonymity had come at the right time, that is, at a time when "few Americans . . . felt the necessity of being anything else." She disputed the editors' claim that Anonymous could "assert a high and lovely thing"; there, she felt, it might fail. On the other hand, if Anonymous had been created to make money, it seemed to be "a working scheme." Without being asked, F. Scott Fitzgerald wondered if Carrefour could handle a book he wanted to write about his father, one which he would prefer not to sign. Lowenfels, jubilant over the prospect of adding so prominent a name to their list, hurried off to confer with Fraenkel, who quickly quashed his enthusiasm by demanding: "How much does he want?" When Lowenfels recovered and replied he had not asked, Fraenkel gave him the "pitying look" he reserved for his follies and explained that even to publish a book by Fitzgerald anonymously "would take a couple of hundred thousand dollars" and a lifetime "to promote and sell it and get your money back." When Lowenfels gave Fitzgerald an account of his discussion with Fraenkel, he "understood right away." Another celebrated novelist, Michael Arlen, asked if Carrefour could print an "intimate story of London" to which he did not care to affix his name; but like Fitzgerald he had to be turned away, too. Lowenfels also approached Tom McGreevy (then barely making a living escorting tourists around the Louvre and Versailles) and Samuel Beckett for manuscripts, but neither responded with any enthusiasm. It was evident that Anonymous had generated more theoretical interest than practical support; and, anyway, in the spring of 1932, when Lowenfels rather quixotically drew up a lawsuit that required identifying himself as the author of *USA with Music*, Anonymous suddenly came to an end. Lowenfels charged that George Kaufman and George Gershwin, the authors of the hit play *Of Thee I Sing*, had plagiarized the plot of *USA*, at least its conception and general treatment. However, as Waverley Root noted, his case against Kaufman and Gershwin lacked proof that they had done more than "borrowed" a few ideas from his play. The suit was dropped, and Lowenfels quipped that Anonymous was the first movement in the arts ever to sue itself to death. In a hastily written statement issued in May, he announced that although the experiment with anonymity had ended "in order to seek redress against piracy," the principles Fraenkel and he had set out to advance would not be discarded; they would simply be organized under another name. Hereafter, although Carrefour books would be signed, their merit would be "under more scrutiny than ever," since one of the purposes of Anonymous —to stress work rather than authors' names or reputations—had already been achieved. The first non-Anonymous publication, Lowenfels' elegy in memory of D. H. Lawrence, was, in fact, already in the press.

Despite the death of their idea, Lowenfels and Fraenkel remained as strongly attached to the death nodule as ever. As announced, the *Elegy in the Manner of a Requiem in Memory of D. H. Lawrence* appeared in the fall of 1932, nearly two years after Lawrence's decease in southern France, and unlike his *Elegy for Apollinaire* which Nancy Cunard had published in 1930, the Lawrence elegy aspired to achieve through "verse, music, moving design, synchronized on a recording instrument" a new form the author called an "operatic poem." Voice markings indicating points of emphasis and stress suggested that the poem was to be delivered as a "choral service, in the manner of a Requiem for a dead man." The poem is really a double elegy: one for the dead Lawrence, another for the poet's own dead past, a past he destroyed with the help of Lawrence, whom he viewed as a "symbol for creative vitality undergoing sacrificial death" and depicted as one who survived the disintegrative process whole ("oneness in death") and shared his creativeness with the living. Dominating Lowenfels' middle-class background was a thriving family business in which he was expected to assume a place. His refusal to remain in the family firm past his thirtieth year (like Fraenkel he exchanged business for poetry in 1926) was the first of many deaths and succeeding "presents," each of which had to be killed off to give birth to another: "By continual suicide/I escaped being similar to myself." To Waverley Root, who had praised the opening lines of the elegy but found the rest a "morass of uneven poetry," Lowenfels explained that it was part of a long and as yet unfinished work entitled *Reality Prime*, one other section of which appeared in 1934 under the title *The Suicide*: another elegy, this one inspired by the death of Hart Crane, it explores the three levels of experience remembered by the dying poet: "a bundle of fears; a rock of faith; and anemia of reason"; as the final culminative wave sweeps him away, "his old self" expires.

By the end of 1932, Fraenkel's fortune, once rumored to be near $100,000, had almost vanished. To replenish it he announced that he would leave Paris to make a second fortune selling books, this time in the palmy new territory of the Philippines, where a "two-dollar set of books [could] be sold for $40.00 quicker and more often than at home." For the next couple of years, Fraenkel immersed himself in the profitable but stultifying routine of bookselling—the venture made tolerable only by the time he could devote to making his "death jottings" and the certainty of quick and generous rewards. On schedule, at the end of the second year, he returned to France, bringing with him $50,000, quite enough, he estimated, to support himself and cover the costs of publishing a few more books, the first of which would be a volume of his own poetry, *Death in a Room*. Brief evocations of disintegration, this collection of fifteen poems written between 1927 and 1930 rhapsodized once again his passionate attachment to death. "I have met death too many times single/ I should

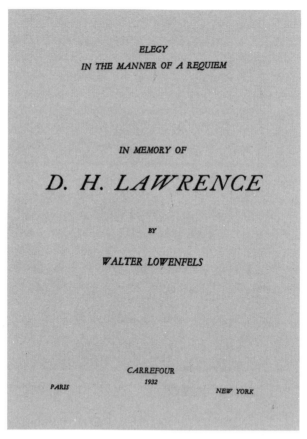

Title page of *Elegy in Memory of D. H. Lawrence* by Walter Lowenfels (Carrefour, 1932).

not know how to do without him/ He gives my days number and purpose." Later the same year (1936) he issued a second book, *Bastard Death* (sub-titled *The Autobiography of an Idea*); in an introductory letter to Henry Miller, Fraenkel described his evolving conception of death "on the poetic and metaphysical plane." Imagining himself a man straddling two shores, one foot in Life, the other in Death, Fraenkel submits that only by taking both feet in his hands and leaping to the farther shore can he commence to live. The leap is tantamount to dying and being reborn at the same moment, the dying being the death of the "old self," the birth being that of the "new self which is dead, dead, of course, in life, which is a bastard death, or, if you like, alive in death, which is a bastard life." Fraenkel, of course, had attempted the leap, but whether he succeeded in planting both feet firmly on the farther shore was a matter for Miller and others to decide.

Miller's reply, printed immediately after Fraenkel's letter, masterfully reduces his friend's claim to the "bastard life" to the level of a Pyrrhic victory. He agreed that Death had given Fraenkel the "universal frame" (the "Egypt of your despair") within which he could move with every semblance of life. On the nether shore, outside life and death, a free creative spirit, empowered at last to act and to destroy, Fraenkel, wrote Miller, engaged in a titanic struggle to destroy "both the mask and the wearer of the mask." From out of the apocalypse, out of the "body of the book," emerged Fraenkel, naked, revealed, saying: " 'I am the person, the One and Only One.' " But if he had succeeded only in jumping farther than "any other man in our time," as Miller believed he had, then his mighty achievement would probably attract few admirers and even fewer followers. It was Fraenkel's old nemesis—neglect—that would obviate what he had done: "Your book will enjoy an obscurity which is not inherent in the content," Miller foretold, explaining that Fraenkel's ideology can be "accepted and understood . . . only [by] those endowed with a heightened consciousness. . . ." Privately, perhaps, he had been brought into a union with an evolving universe, undivided, always dying and becoming, and perhaps even restorative to his "power of action." As though reluctant to desert him on the farther shore, Miller assured his fellow mythmaker in Death that he, too, would descend into the tomb with him "to await the hour of resurrection."

The countless letters that the "avant-garde of death" exchanged can scarcely be labeled conscious experiments in a literary form. Lowenfels called them necessities, the "medium of desperation," transcripts of the

Villa Seurat discussions sent to the only people capable of understanding them. One evening, following a particularly exhaustive discourse on the "death of the world," Miller, still elated by the conversation, suggested that there was no reason to go on talking about death when "it was just as easy to write about it." They "might as well kill two birds with one stone," have their fun and "write a masterpiece at the same time." He guessed that "in no time" the three of them (Perlès was the third) could turn out a one-thousand-page book which would be the "longest funeral sermon in history." The only way to do it successfully, Fraenkel advised, was in the form of letters. He offered to "kick off the ball" by writing the first letter to Miller, "with a carbon" to Perlès, and they, in turn, would reply to his letter independently, and in less than a week, Fraenkel estimated, they would be "grappling with the essence of the subject." Only Fraenkel knew what that essence would be, however. Perlès objected to Death. It was too abstract. What they needed was a "concrete theme, around which death [could] creep up, like ivy around a tree." Perlès suggested that perhaps the Merry Widow would be "concrete" enough, and for the moment even Fraenkel agreed, adding that the "very name exhales the stench of death." Miller countered with Hamlet. He was composed of tougher stuff. Why not "track Hamlet down and see if [they] could finally lay the Ghost"? Under a merciless inquisition the Merry Widow gradually faded, her character considered insufficiently neurotic to survive any sort of harsh treatment. A quick burial would be a blessing. Hamlet survived.

Miller "rose full-armed to the battle," but from the start (their first letters were exchanged in November) he regarded the "whole affair [as] a grand game, a joke of immense energy and size." Perlès, who dropped out at the end of the first month, watched, transfixed, from the sidelines as Miller turned out ten-page letters to Fraenkel, sometimes two a week, warming-up exercises before going to work on the *Tropic of Capricorn*. While Miller parried and thrust, pranced around playfully, unwilling to view Hamlet's predicament seriously, Fraenkel grew increasingly irritated with his friend's refusal to live up to their bargain. Miller accused Fraenkel of being obtuse and too sensitive.

Often their letters did not make contact on the matter under discussion, or, if they did, there was a misunderstanding about what Hamlet represented. Once, after Miller had written that he was trying to dispossess himself of Hamlet and that such a thing was probably beyond his friend's power, Fraenkel ruefully replied that he was not ashamed to admit that Hamlet was Michael Fraenkel and that Michael Fraenkel was the modern

300

sick man. There it was, almost as Perlès had predicted; Fraenkel, the death-obsessed man, had found yet another objectification, this time in Hamlet. Miller neither accepted nor rejected the notion. For Fraenkel, death would always be the topic of their correspondence, but for Miller something had intervened, and that was "life"—by which he meant the "creative compromise between the imaginative and the actual." What they had projected the night the Hamlet idea was born was bound to change as time passed—and that, Miller contended, was exactly what was happening.

If their correspondence had a unifying subject (one hesitates to say concrete), it was Michael Frankel. It was a discovery he himself made after their correspondence had gone on for just over a year; disturbing it was, because in shifting the argument to "Michael Fraenkel the private person," Miller might be more apt to ridicule his work. A portent of the abuse Frankel feared came in Miller's letter of September 7, 1937, in which he contended Fraenkel had made a fetish of death because he feared it.

Fraenkel's replies to outbursts like this were surprisingly well-tempered and mild. Of course Miller had erred, again; and, of course, he had, again, fallen victim to inconsistency; and, of course, as was increasingly the case, he had written nothing but words and more words; words that proved he wanted neither honest communication nor understanding. Nonetheless, if he deigned to remain outside Fraenkel's system of death, he could not be extricated from Fraenkel's human system, his own consciousness; for whatever the consequences might be he was there to stay.

Miller's final letter to Fraenkel, written "with a most solemn realization" of the impending debacle, amounted to a repudiation of Fraenkel's theories and some of his own. Depressed by the outcome of Chamberlain's meeting with Hitler in Munich ("To send an Englishman with a codfish smile and an umbrella to deal with the passionate Adolf is suicidal."), and convinced that nothing now could prevent the coming war, Miller renounced any claim that he (and Fraenkel) foresaw the struggle emerging. "I renounce the pleasure of saying: 'I was right.'" But, beyond that, he was also ready to declare an armistice from death.

Miller's defection was too much for Fraenkel, though by now he was used to disappointment and inured to ridicule. It confirmed what Miller had said about himself—that he was irresponsible and even treacherous. The Hamlet correspondence would have to end, Fraenkel declared. Miller had broken all the rules, leaving Fraenkel no choice but withdrawal.

Short of the thousand pages they had envisaged as the appropriate length for the "longest funeral sermon in history," the combined Hamlet correspondence nonetheless had swelled to the impressive bulk of nearly 450 pages. Seven months after Fraenkel posted his final message to Miller, in June 1939, the first volume of *The Michael Fraenkel–Henry Miller Correspondence Called Hamlet* was published in New York. Filling 234 pages, it bore the Carrefour imprint and was issued in an edition of five hundred. A second volume, printed in Mexico, came out in 1941, and two years later Fraenkel reissued a revised edition of volume one, again from Mexico, where he passed the war years. It was almost as though he had decided to ignore what Miller had foreseen—a Europe collapsing into war—and had sought the sanctuary of a neutral nation where, undisturbed, he could go on nurturing his death philosophy. There he could still be death's spectator, even its confrere, but not its physical victim. Death in the abstract was quite potent enough. Following the bombing of Hiroshima, Lowenfels asked Fraenkel if it was the death that would "make people whole again—not half-dead inside?" Not even Lowenfels could have foretold his reply: "Not enough," answered Fraenkel. "I expected it would be on a grander scale." When he died in 1957 he was as obscure a writer as he had been in Paris thirty years earlier. Today, those aware of him at all are attracted to his ideas, not to his idiosyncratic personality. His thoughts on death, the fixations of an obsession rather than ideas in evolution, provide the only substance of an intensely private man—an Anonymous man.

FOURTH-DIMENSIONAL WRITING: THE ROVING EYE

No one who saw the 1913 Armory Show was ever quite the same afterward. Certainly a free-lance writer named Bob Brown was not. Like most others who went to the Armory exhibit unprepared for that upheaval of European modernism, Brown came away shaken and excited by the work of the new, radical thinking, unacademic artists, some of whom, like Marsden Hartley and Jean Cocteau, combined painting and free verse, or, like Marcel Duchamp (*Nude Descending a Staircase* instantly became the stormy centerpiece of the exhibit), seemed both to exemplify and solve all the problems of the artist in a technological society. "In Paris," Duchamp told Brown, "some of us decided to paint the first thing we saw every day, an axe, a bidet, a baby, and naturally in our own way." For Brown, anxiously looking for a way to end a career of monotonous hack work, Duchamp's resolution had the force of a command. The morning after he had absorbed "eyefuls of Armory pictures and a mindful of Marcel's exciting art talk," he put the method to a test. Using his own medium rather than painting, he drew in words the first thing he saw: a red geranium on the fireplace. What he showed Duchamp the next day at lunch was his first "optical," or, as Duchamp might say, retinal poem:

```
       red                        red
              my potty
              geranium
       red                        red
              my nooky
              chimney pot
       red                        red
       red      rectangular       red
```

Already impressed by the skill and alacrity with which his friend had translated theory into practice, Duchamp was amazed when Brown unexpectedly turned out a second example of retinal art. Struck by the similarity between his own "big oystery eyes, as protuberant as Man Ray's," and the oysters on his plate, Brown snatched up a paper napkin and drew, in rapid sequence, four sets of eyes, each one progressively larger, and circled by a fifth set with the eyes turned in toward the center, between which he jotted the words: "Eyes! My God! What Eyes! Eyes on the Half Shell." Duchamp printed the "Eyes" poem in *The Blindman*, the little magazine he prepared for the Independents' Show, and hailed Brown as a fellow avant-gardist with an unholy tendency to deny words their customary places in familiar patterns.

Brown credited "Eyes" with transporting him through and beyond every art movement of the time and away from a career that had made him a virtual writing machine. According to his own figures, he had, before his thirtieth birthday, written "1000 short and long fiction stories, one every three and 6/10th days, counting 100,000 word typewriter busters and 3000 word playful finger-tip type-ticklers." Pulp magazines sometimes printed his stories in batches of five or six in a single issue, either under his own name or any of a dozen nom de plumes. In addition, he had produced a bestseller, *What Happened to Mary*, later a successful motion picture, and a popular book of detective stories, *The Remarkable Adventures of Christopher Poe*. Moreover, he had turned out "jokes, poems, epigrams, novelettes, anecdotes, articles, jingles, sketches, monologues, serials, digests, slogans, advertisements, *feuilletons*, reports, memoirs, confessions, tales, narratives, guides, monographs, descriptions, obituaries, wise-cracks, legends, journals, lives, plays, adventures, experiences, romances, fairy tales, parables, apologues, circulars, doggerel, sonnets, odes, episodes, lyrics, thrillers, dime novels, nickel novels, society verse, essays, rondelets, biographies, codexes, broad-sheets, fly-leaves, pages, quires, and reams." After ten years of functioning as a "writing factory," disgorging in that time an astonishing ten million "multi-colored words," for fees ranging from one-tenth of a cent to ten cents a word—and earnings that occasionally reached fifteen thousand dollars a year—Brown, understandably, concluded he had just about written himself out. He chronicled the labors of a decade in a six-thousand-word peroration, which, at ten cents a word, brought in a final six hundred dollars.

Along with the Armory Show and Marcel Duchamp a third new force suddenly entered Brown's life: Gertrude Stein. In 1914 his friend Donald Evans published Miss Stein's *Tender Buttons*, and for Brown—regardless of what it was supposed to be about—*Tender Buttons* was an "optical" book, the first he had seen (he would not know of Apollinaire's "optical poetry" until he reached Paris in the late twenties). Gertrude Stein "gave me a great kick," he rhapsodized. "Her formula, whatever it is, interested me . . . I began to see that a story might be anything. Hurrah! Writing wasn't just Hart, Shaffner, Marx and Arrow collars after all. . . . Suddenly it was something else. A story didn't have to be a tangible hunk of bread interest." *Tender Buttons*, like Duchamp's *Nude*, was another revolutionary exemplar, liberating and instructive. "Thank God for Gert Stein," Brown roared. "I threw my typewriter into the air and huzzaed. That's the way you feel when you're tired to death finishing up the final paragraph of a three-hundred-page thriller and some blonde angel slips in on a pink cloud with a cooling case of champagne. Sprays your scorched writing tonsils with it. Stein's book sprayed mine. It was a case of champagne to me in a time of dire need."

Despite the stimulating new forces that had invigorated his creative life, Brown spent a large portion of the next dozen years making and losing a fortune on the New York Stock Exchange, publishing magazines in South America, and perfecting an invention he called a Reading Machine, a precursor of the microfilm reader. In 1916, however, with H. L. Mencken's help, he published a small collection of verse, *My Margonary*. As individualistic as the author, it hardly brought him any closer to experimentalists like "Others" and the "Imagists," with whom, except for

Mina Loy, he admitted he could not "affiliate" and whose "interest in words seemed sophomoric." To be sure, he wrote no better than any of them, but he could write "different" (i.e., "Eyes"). Having emerged from Wall Street "badly bent" and temporarily unmoved to write, sell, or even read a story, he tried magazine publishing, first in Rio de Janeiro and afterward in Mexico City and London, earning between fifteen and thirty thousand dollars a year, and, at his peak, producing a sixty-page magazine every six days. But after a few years—and some six hundred issues later —he had again reached the same conclusion about free-lancing: even in the comparatively stable world of magazines, it was "more than ever the bunk"; and this time, determined to carry out his creative pursuits fully, he renounced all business affiliations and left for France.

Brown's stint on Wall Street produced more than a transitory fortune. As he passed the hours watching the ticker disgorging paper ribbons filled with figures like BS–1000–608–½, he often wondered why there "wasn't a man-made machine like the running tape-of-thought device in the mind which would carry words endlessly to all reading eyes in one unbroken line," a reading machine that would be as rapid and refreshing as thought which could take the place of the antiquated word-dribbling book. Years earlier, Stephen Crane's "dingy" volume of poems, *Black Riders*, had given him a first inkling of type in motion. The title, especially, had suggested that printed words were like "romantic knights galloping across white pages, astride inky chargers." The kinetic and retinal effects produced by his own "Eyes" poem were its main source of pleasure. Looking at it, merely sitting and looking at it, taking it all in without moving an eye, he wrote, "gives me more than rhymed poetry. It rhymes in my eyes. Here are 'Black Riders' for me at last actually galloping across a blank page." Would it be possible to make the "Black Riders" gallop faster if they appeared on the moving tape of a Reading Machine?

In the little runaway colony at Cagnes-sur-Mer, where Brown settled, he met several people who would contribute to the development of the Reading Machine, among them two young American artists, Hilaire Hiler and Ross Saunders, who fashioned a crude but working model of the machine out of a cracker box, and Harry Crosby, a temporary resident, who agreed to publish at the Black Sun Press a short book Brown had written to announce his invention. Called *1450–1950*, it was a fanciful history of innovative printing in which Brown placed himself at the end of the line that began with Gutenberg. Conceived in a playful spirit, the book brought a playful and enthusiastic response. Mencken and Williams sent

A page from *Readies*, compiled by Bob Brown (Roving Eye Press, 1930).
PRINCETON UNIVERSITY LIBRARY

their blessings. Manuel Komroff called it a "scream," and an anonymous critic proclaimed it "an excellent symbol of what symbolism is trying to do." Encouraged, Brown wrote a second book to amplify and illustrate his theories. This one, entitled *The Readies*, was the first Roving Eye publication (the imprint had obvious associations with the "Eyes" poem) and, appropriately, was dedicated to "all Eye-writers and all Readers who want an Eyeful." What they could anticipate was an "optical" revolution: "The written word hasn't kept up with the age. The movies have outmanoeu-vered it. We have the talkies, but as yet no Readies. I'm for new methods of reading and writing and I believe the up-to-date reader deserves an eye-ful when he buys something to read. I think the optical end of the written word has been hidden over a bushel too long. I'm out for a bloody revolution of the word." As one who believed he could "regurgitate with Gert" and "Proustly rejoice in Jamesre" and who felt at home in the company of Hemingway, Williams, Harry Crosby, Link Gillespie, Charles Henri Ford, and Norman MacLoed, Brown demonstrated how far he could go, or had gone, in hastening the disintegrative processes some of his contemporaries had already set in motion. A sample:

———

oo

———

.

(Explain yourself)

(Title)

———

(Hyphen) o (Head)

———

oo (heads)
Bullet = Heads

———

oo

———

The Readies concluded with a description of the Reading Machine and another a specimen of Brown's writing, this time a few lines of prose—looking rather like cablese—designed to be read at unprecedented speeds: "Harry—virtuoso—born—musical—mid—midwest—mellow—moving—farm—milky—mooey—farm—; lullaby—mother."

As soon as *The Readies* appeared, Brown announced he would publish an anthology of writings (now called "readies") specially suited for his Reading Machine, and he invited contributions from the entire expatriate colony. In the meantime, he issued a second Roving Eye book, *Globe Gliding*, a collection of sprightly free-verse descriptions of various cities he had lived in or visited, and, almost immediately, a third, *Gems: A Censored Anthology*, an amusing reminder of the baleful effects that censorship could have on writing and publishing. *Gems*, which Brown had offered to the Hours Press, where he had just placed another book, *Words*, carried a dedication to the owner of Hours, Nancy Cunard, who had encouraged the project: "Permit me, Madame, in the words of former light-fingerers of 'Gems from the Poets' to dedicate to you a book which, I hope, may be found a life-long fountain of innocent and exalted pleasure; a source of animation to friends when they meet, a book of beauties which the eye cannot see but may easily imagine. If this collection proves a storehouse of delight, if it teaches those indifferent to the Poets to * * * them, and those who love them to * * * them more, the aim and the desire entertained in framing it will be fully accomplished."

Gems is an insider's guide to the business of selling "dirty" books to unwary customers who believe they are purchasing high-class pornography. Masterminding the operation, according to Brown, is the "booklegger," an unread, unprincipled, shrewd businessman who prospers by practicing such trade secrets as always covering forbidden books in plain wrappers ("virginity belts"). Envious of Paris-domiciled books like *Ulysses* and *Lady Chatterley's Lover*, the "booklegger" dreams of matching their success, meanwhile freely turning out "lickerish books badly printed in English," scarcely worth the attention of a "healthy prying mind." To England and America go thousands of these "adolescently lewd and unimaginative" creations every year, there to be sold under the counter. As for the "book of proportions" (i.e., *Ulysses*), unjustly banned, it becomes the bread-and-butter item of the "publishing mites on the edge of things" who scurry around "getting out nasty parodies of the original which is usually pure in purpose," and selling their facsimiles to the "chance curious" who are thus denied the genuine article. Pirates, of course, thrive on the misjudgments of censors, as the plethora of pirated editions of *Lady Chatterley*, *Jurgen*, and *The Painted Veil* demonstrated. Censorship, contended Brown, was largely a matter of "pure taste, personal taste, good or bad (some like it hot, some like it cold, some like it in the pot)"; and there was always the danger that the censor's taste would turn out to be capricious. To illustrate the point that censorship often made the wholesome and the innocent look pornographic, Brown used the whimsical device of placing a "black blot" over three or four words in a familiar quotation, which gave even nursery rhymes a salacious look:

> Old Mother Goose, when
> She wanted to * * *
> Would * * a fat goose
> Or a very fine gander.

Wordsworth's pristine lyric, interlarded with "black blots," takes on a decidedly obscene appearance:

> My * * * leaps up when I behold
> A * * * in the * * *

So was it when my * * * began,
So is it now I am a man,
So be it when I shall grow old
Or let me die!

Though overshadowed by the widely publicized *Readies* anthology, issued later in 1931, a small collection of verses Brown published at the beginning of the year called *Demonics* contained some of his best poems; for example, the one to Stuart Davis, to whom Brown dedicated the book:

Clean-cut color strokes
over under through
vivid lightning flashes
tipsy street scenes
with wicked windows
all brunettes
winking devilishly
Surfaces to feel and fondle
concrete samples for contractors
houses wrecked and rebuilt
closer to the please of
far-away nature's inward eye
gables for cat-ghost prowling.
To music
his French urinals sing
hum like hurdygurdys
on shabby-shouldered
shrugging cafe corners.

The main event of the year was the publication of the last Roving Eye, the anthology of "readies" now called *Readies for Bob Brown's Machine,* to which over forty of Brown's friends* had contributed poems and prose pieces heavily interlarded with dots and dashes, or unusually large gaps between words and phrases. Since Brown had asked for writing as different from a book as the "talkies were from the stage, most contributors apparently assumed he wanted something in which the number of words one would have to read in order to discover what an author was

---

* Among the best known contributors were Hilaire Hiler, Laurence Vail, James T. Farrell, Kay Boyle, Peter Neagoe, Samuel Putnam, Walter Lowenfels, Paul Bowles, Gertrude Stein, Manuel Komroff, Ezra Pound, William Carlos Williams, Alfred Kreymborg, Nancy Cunard, Charles Henri Ford, Eugene Jolas, and Robert McAlmon.

getting at would be drastically reduced. Foremost among those considered expendable were articles, followed by pronouns, connectives, and adjectives. Typical of most readies was Kay Boyle's "Change of Life":

> "Sat smoking cigarettes thinking change coming over him—interest where was it in slipping lace bolts off counters—diamonds green ice rubies gone stale—watches in gentlemen's vests no longer tempted—playing gigolo paled like conversation of fat behinds who fell for it—not that he had done much—one two little things not very much but better Paris police didn't know where he was awhile—took overcoat off hook in restaurant—couple of fox hides slipped off counter —enough to keep him sitting out of sight—hotel room smoking cigarettes Maman brought him—Maman doing well now on boulevard Clichy—no time to herself night-work extra—"

James T. Farrell "readified" a story by John A. Farrell called "One of the Many," which began—"Miss Ryan . . . keen dress model from work . . . walking . . . stark naked . . . into his dreams . . . her face beams . . . smiles . . . a comeon daddy . . ."

Brown followed the 150 pages of specimen "readies" with an explanation and defense of the Reading Machine. The "Airplane age," he contended, was vital and dynamic. Nothing stood still. Radio urged television into being, and change in the arts was ubiquitous. Painting had Picasso, sculpture Brancusi, music Antheil, drama O'Neill, and writing Joyce, Stein, Cummings, and Hemingway. Only reading, the "reading half of literature," lagged behind. In an age of accelerated speed and men with "reading minds" capable of reading faster than ever before ("quickened from centuries of practice") and demanding "fourth-dimensional writing," the old-fashioned book was an anachronism, no longer capable of meeting the demands. What could was Bob Brown's Reading Machine, a device as compact as a portable radio or phonograph, containing a "tough tissue roll" no larger than a typewriter ribbon, on which could be printed the entire contents of a book and which could be unrolled beneath a magnifying glass at any speed the reader selected. What he would see would be a single moving line of type before his eyes, not blurred by the presence of lines above and below, which he could read as fast through the eye as through the ear (Brown claimed the eye was faster than the ear). The material advantages of the Reading Machine were manifold: since entire books would be printed on tiny paper ribbons, enormous quantities of paper and ink could be saved; the magnifying glass would multiply both paper and ink at no additional cost; in place of expensive bindings, small paper boxes could be produced at a fraction of the cost of large cloth covers; manual labor would be minimized; and for the consumer, reading would be less costly and, as an added bonus, perhaps forever independent of advertising.

Unfortunately, publicizing the Reading Machine turned out to be easier than selling it to a manufacturer. Brown assured book lovers afraid that the invention might eventually replace books entirely that he never intended to take away their books, only augment their scope, liberate them. A few publishers expressed mild alarm. One told Brown that if his idea "ever gets over," a lot of expensive machinery would have to be scrapped. Their fears, however, were needless, for after several unsuccessful efforts to market the invention and secure a patent for it, Brown tried to give it away to the Russians, only to learn in Moscow that the "comrades were way ahead" and had already hitched up "their own machine to go with television boxes." And by the late thirties, at least six different models were being peddled about, the best a "one-eyed stereoptican, a sort of prehistoric sterespondylian lorgnette" called the Fiskeoscope, named for the inventor, Admiral Fiske. Competition of course reduced the chances of selling the Reading Machine, and, resignedly, Brown concluded that he would rather write for a "readie machine" than try to sell or patent one.

THE REVOLUTION OF THE WORD: SERVIRE

The Servire Press was located in The Hague, a day's journey from Paris, but the books that bore its imprint were created in Paris, sold there, and read there. Already on the Servire list in 1932 were *Front*, a trilingual anthology of writings by a score of European, American, and Russian authors dedicated to literature that would arm the "workers against the bourgeoisie"; a play by the Irish writer Charles Duff entitled *Mind Products Limited* ("probably the most original melodrama ever written"), and a book of twenty poems and fourteen sketches "in polyphonic prose" called *Cross-Country* by Solon R. Barber, with forewords by Nelson A. Crawford and Richard Thoma. Also scheduled to appear later the same year were two sizable issues of the newly revived magazine *transition*; a book on "metaphysical language" by *transition*'s founder, Eugene Jolas;

and an anthology of American writing collected and edited by the assistant editor of Samuel Putnam's *New Review*, Peter Neagoe.

Americans Abroad, the Neagoe anthology, was Putnam's idea. Putnam, a man of indefatigable energies, was himself in the midst of amassing a huge compilation of modern European writing which he would publish the same year in New York under the title *European Caravan*. To one used to doing several projects at the same time, it must have seemed natural to Putnam to consider assembling another anthology, one that would bring together the "best work" done by Americans who had presumably been stimulated by residence in Europe. Far too busy himself to do more than outline the project, he had urged Neagoe to take it on, and as early as September 1931 Wambly Bald reported in the Paris *Tribune* that it was nearly ready for publication; it was not, however, until December 1932 that *Americans Abroad* finally appeared. Putnam was pleased with the book. It showed "a great deal of industry" on Neagoe's part, he wrote, and "I am glad I didn't appoint someone else who might have bungled it." The *Tribune* book critic, Waverley Root, pleased and relieved to find that the contributions were of such a "high quality" and that there was little of the "merely freakish and the out-and-out idiotic," pronounced it a "good value for one's money." But when George Jean Nathan saw a copy in New York he summarily dismissed it as "the worst book of the year."

Perhaps one reason Neagoe found theorizing on the problems American writers had faced at home and the reasons for their exile in Europe a rather intimidating task was because he himself was a recently naturalized American. He argued that, whereas young writers on the Continent had found in the middle class a target against which to rebel, the young generation in America had had no such opportunity. Their revolt had instead to be directed against the "rule of industry through standardization," a foe "subtler than old age and the middle class, but no less oppressive and insidious." The great problem for Americans was compromise, leveling down, and gradually conforming to values of standardization. Against those writers he had gathered in *Americans Abroad*, however, the conformist charge could not be made. They comprised a group of Americans who had not become "weighted down in the balance of utility." What art America could regard with respect had been done by them, the "undaunted non-conformists—the Young America of today." Not everybody in Neagoe's anthology could be called young—for example, Ezra Pound, Gertrude Stein, and Emma Goldman—but they were all, in the editor's opinion, serious creators. The list was remarkably complete (the only conspicuous absentees were Hart Crane, Elliot Paul, and R. C. Dunning) and included Conrad Aiken, Djuna Barnes, Kay Boyle, Bob Brown, Emanuel Carnevali, Malcolm Cowley, the Crosbys, E. E. Cummings, John Dos Passos, James T. Farrell, Ernest Hemingway, Eugene Jolas, Robert McAlmon, Henry Miller, Samuel Putnam, Ezra Pound, Gertrude Stein, Laurence Vail, Ernest Walsh, and William Carlos Williams. As for the contributions, Hemingway sent "Big Two-Hearted River"; Miller, "Mlle Claude"; McAlmon, "Leavetaking"; all of which had already appeared elsewhere. There were poems (also mostly previously published ones) by Cummings, Harry Crosby, Walsh, Pound, and Cowley; and two "Readies" (composed for Bob Brown's anthology) by Kay Boyle and Link Gillespie. Neagoe even published Laura Riding's explanation telling why she would not contribute. As readable as the contributions themselves, and in some cases more important, were the biographical sketches writers submitted with their work and which appeared at the beginning of each contribution, sometimes with a photograph of the author. Pound, for example, requested that the following appear in place of a sketch: "The reader wishing information re Mr. Pound's bio-bibliography will have to consult the English 'Who's Who' as his name has been removed from the American one." And Kay Boyle took the opportunity to announce that she was working on an epic poem for which she needed "funds for research and quiet in which to write it."

Americans Abroad, Neagoe contended, showed "the influence of Europe and European culture on American literature." While the work of a few writers might support his claim, say, that of Stein, Jolas, and perhaps Henry Miller, in most cases there was little or nothing to indicate that European influences had contributed importantly to the writing. Also, rather than being experimental, most contributions were examples of finished work, much of it already in print, which had come to be identified with the authors. Even Neagoe seemed aware that the European influence might be a little difficult to find. In one of the announcements he admitted that whatever the impress of Europe on American writers they were still distinctly American and would carry home the results of arduous work.

After suspending *transition* in 1930 and devoting himself to tasks related to the magazine for two years, including editing a volume of *transition* stories with associate editor Robert Sage, Eugene Jolas revived his magazine in 1932 and in rapid succession brought out two hefty numbers. The same year he also issued a sixty-page pamphlet under the

Servire imprint called *The Language of Night,* in which he once again discussed the attitudes toward language which had so often been advanced —and sometimes rejected—in the pages of *transition.* Having introduced the early work of the surrealists in *transition* (Jolas printed interviews with Breton and others in the late twenties), he had long been aware of what the surrealists called the "night mind," and in the final number of the magazine (June 1930) he had tried to explain both its meaning and value. The "wisdom of the ages," his theory went, can be counted on to reveal itself only occasionally and always through the dream, hypnosis, automatic writing, and in half-waking states. The "night mind," then, corresponded to the revelations of the dream and the borderline experiences of half-sleep, which, Jolas maintained, were the proper subjects of art. Through dreams man can awaken within himself the sense of the wonderful and miraculous which will make life rich and complete. The "language of night" was the language not only of the surrealists but of the contributors to *transition*—the "Revolutionists of the Word"—who believed that reality existed in the realm of dream, magic, and the unconscious.

From 1924 to 1926 Jolas was literary critic for the Paris *Tribune.* After leaving the paper he kept up a close relationship with the staffers, of whom several contributed to *transition* and two, Elliot Paul and Robert Sage, helped to operate it. Unsurprisingly, he had come to expect favor-

Eugene Jolas, author and editor
of *transition,* Paris, 1931.
COURTESY OF MRS. MARIA JOLAS

able notices of the magazine in the *Tribune*, but in the person of his successor, Waverley Root, Jolas found an antagonist, although a kindly one, who viewed the self-consciousness of *transition* (as well as its contributors) as a signal that the arts under Jolas' direction were likely to become even more obscure than they were already. The artist, Root complained in "An Open Letter to the Editor," was too self-conscious; for no reason should he be encouraged to become any more so. By all means he should be inspired to create by "instinctive and automatic processes," Root continued, for, after all, the work he does is part of him in the sense "that any other excretion is a part of him"; however, he argued, the artist has as little to do with its quality, "except in being what he is, which is an accident," as with the quality of any other excretion. "Hence, when the artist with good work behind him, lacking the urge to get something off his chest, stands back and regards his opera with calculating gaze in order to discover what he did and do the same thing again, the result is lifeless and uninteresting. We do not know enough about our automatic instinctive selves to reproduce their work. We will never know enough because the part can never know, in its entirety, the whole. The more we pry, the more of our work will be conscious, the less instinctive and automatic. Let us, then, cease prying, cease joining movements, cease crusading, and write, paint, compose, eat, drink, sleep, make love and attend to all other metabolic necessities when we feel like it. And for heavens sake let us have no more fine talk about it."

Predictably, Root's letter failed to make much of an impression on Jolas, who accused him of "playing with words" himself and "ignoring and confusing the categories of the instinctive being as such and the expression of the instinctive being in us." All *transition* was trying to do, replied Jolas, was to help writers "get away from the boredom of external description and to see the twentieth-century world more in relation with the eternal values of our being." By 1932, however, Root was more than ever convinced that Jolas had gone astray and that he was leading others astray too. The main problem was that Jolas, who was really a poet, was trying, unsuccessfully, to be a professor of aesthetics, a shift that his mind simply would not permit. *The Language of Night* provided all the evidence Root needed to prove that, although Jolas might feel he knew what he was doing, he actually did not. Challenging his thesis that language must be revolutionized ("We are tired of the word that does not express the kinetic and subconscious"), Root proposed that the problem might lie in the writer rather than the language. And as for his contention that new word forms and patterns would give birth to new ideas, there certainly was no assurance or proof of that. But what brought the critic's fault-finding to a head was Jolas' insistence that Joyce and Stein were the symbolic figures of the "Revolution of the Word." Jolas, of all people, Root chided, should know that they were "complete antipodes." One trouble with citing Joyce and Stein as representatives of the avant-garde was that both were already old-fashioned. Echoing Samuel Putnam's views then appearing in the *New Review*, Root explained that the battles successfully fought by Joyce and Stein had ended, and while the former had long had a place reserved for him in English literature, the latter had ceased to amuse even the "ephemerally clever persons who at first liked to talk about her because her particular brand of nonsense was at least a change from the sort of nonsense to which they had previously listened." At best, Root admitted, *The Language of Night* would push readers to seek answers to worthwhile questions, questions, however, which Root doubted Jolas could answer himself. The book was "a remarkable stimulus, and capable of leading almost anyone (except Mr. Jolas himself) to the brink of new esthetic discoveries."

In 1932 Servire issued two thick volumes of *transition* (Number 21, published in March, ran to 350 pages; Number 22, published nine months later, came to 200 pages). Contributors, many of whom were perhaps chosen to illustrate Jolas' theories, included Gertrude Stein, Kurt Schwitters, Hans Arp, Philip Soupault, H. L. Mencken, Peter Neagoe, Bob Brown, Kay Boyle, and Stuart Gilbert, but the principal attraction was a new installment of *Work in Progress* by James Joyce, the mainstay of *transition* almost from its inception. Both numbers instantly reactivated Root's campaign against *transition*'s excesses. Number 22 was the worst the reviewer had ever seen; it had gone "completely haywire." Jolas, "in his frantic attempt to abandon logic and reason and to be guided only by the more unthinking sections of his being," had unhappily succeeded in "getting rid altogether of those contributions which pleased him instinctively, and in filling his review only with such matter as his reason tells him ought logically to be printed by a gentleman holding the theories which he professes to hold." Except for the extract from Joyce, there was nothing of value in the entire issue.

Besides several more numbers of *transition*, issued biannually until the magazine suspended publication in 1938, Servire published two special projects for Jolas, the first a fragment from Joyce's *Work in Progress* entitled *The Mime of Mick, Nick and the Maggies* (1934). Joyce's daughter, Lucia, designed initial letters, a tailpiece, and the covers. Twenty-nine copies were printed on Simili Japon of Van Gelder Zonen and bound in parchment; numbers five to twenty-nine were signed by Joyce and Lucia. Another one thousand copies were printed on Old Antique Dutch paper and distributed in England and America. The following year Servire issued as a *transition* supplement (the only one the magazine ever published) *The Testimony Against Gertrude Stein*. A refutation of Miss Stein's recently published *Autobiography of Alice B. Toklas*, the supplement had already appeared in *transition* (Number 23). In reply to what they considered Miss Stein's misstatements and irresponsible accusations, the contributors to the *Testimony*—Braque, Matisse, Tristan Tzara, André Salmon, and Eugene and Maria Jolas—set out to straighten the record and divest the presumptuous Miss Stein of a few of her pretensions. Their rejoinders all made the point that Gertrude Stein had no understanding of the time in which she lived or the movements that went on around her. She had entirely misunderstood cubism, Braque claimed, because she insisted on seeing it "in terms of personalities." Matisse asserted that Sarah, not Gertrude, was "the really intelligently sensitive member of the family." Agreeing with Robert McAlmon, Tzara called Miss Stein (as well as Miss Toklas) a megalomaniac, and Salmon used his allotted space trying to correct Miss Stein's account of a banquet at which she claimed Salmon had suffered an attack of delirium tremens and, after being locked in a cloakroom, had devoured Alice B. Toklas' hat. That Jolas had succeeded for so long to print Miss Stein's work in the same issues with installments of Joyce's *Work in Progress* seemed nothing less than a remarkable instance of editorial legerdemain to some observers. But that Miss Stein had smarted over that fact as well as a number of other things the *transition* editor had done there was little doubt. For example, she strongly implied that co-editor Elliot Paul had not only had more to do with the founding of the review but had been of more assistance to her than Jolas. "Elliot Paul," she wrote in the *Autobiography*, "slowly disappeared and Eugene and Maria Jolas appeared. Transition grew more bulky. At Gertrude Stein's request *transition* reprinted Tender Buttons, printed a bibliography of her work up to date and later printed her opera, Four Saints. For these printings Gertrude Stein was very grateful. In the last numbers of *transition* nothing of hers appeared. *Transition* died." In her "testimony" Maria Jolas refuted Miss Stein's account of the founding and death of *transition*, charging that Gertrude Stein was incapable of writing objectively about either because she was jealous of the attention the magazine paid to Joyce. The *Testimony* made good reading, and in some respects at least seemed to verify what Waverley Root had written about Miss Stein a few years before. Certainly she had ceased to amuse the editor of *transition.*

CONTENT OVER FORM: NEW REVIEW

Samuel Putnam's short-lived magazine *New Review*, hastily created after Putnam broke with Edward Titus and *This Quarter*, was one half of an always precarious publishing business Putnam maintained for a few years in the early thirties. Under his direction and with some help from associate editors Ezra Pound and Richard Thoma and contributing editors George Antheil and Hilaire Hiler (who also served as art director), the *New Review* offered what Putnam called "an international reportage for the arts, the higher journalism of ideas." In 1930 he set forth the policies of the review in a manifesto entitled "Direction," co-signed by Thoma and Harold J. Salemson, the latter the former editor of another little magazine, *Tambour*, which appeared off and on in Paris in 1929 and 1930, and the author of a widely circulated series of articles about Americans in Paris, which *transition* editor Robert Sage labeled "lurid and distorted." "Direction" was really a broadside leveled against *transition* and the program Jolas and Sage had advanced in their own manifesto, the "Revolution of the Word." Like Waverley Root, Putnam and his co-signers believed Jolas had gone too far. For example, the excesses he and *transition* encouraged, particularly the exaggerated stress placed on form at the expense of content, were already having deleterious effects upon contemporary writing. What was needed, and at once, was the development of a "realistic intelligence and a spiritual order." Literature over the previous ten years had been invaded by "pretenders, corpse-raisers, and cheap miracle-men," and although Putnam and the others stopped short of accusing Joyce and Gertrude Stein of being mainly responsible for the situation, they nonetheless declared that a "Joycean-Stein stutter" had become the "Shibboleth of the Gileadites," not just a fashion but a snobbism. *Ulysses* was "essentially an end-of-before-the-war book," and Joyce, although an enormous figure, was out of his time, and his influence on the new writing generation was deplorable. Whatever could be learned from him as well as from Gertrude Stein might of course be of value. But the group gathered beneath the banner of the "Revolution of the Word" was nothing more than a collection of parasites fastened to the French and coming at the end of a long history of "revolutionary" writing found in Aristotle, Quintilian, Horace, and Castiglione. In a sense, they were revolutionaries without a revolution.

Having aired their complaints and, incidentally, identified the high priest and priestess of the "Revolutionists of the Word," both of whom would soon descend on America with the publication of *Ulysses* and *The Autobiography of Alice B. Toklas* in the same year, 1934, the "Direction" signers turned to more positive matters. "Good writing does exist," they agreed, and there would be more of it if authors could overcome certain obstacles—for example, "lack of knowledge, of orientation, of critical and esthetic background; lack of feeling for the standard of writing, style (not to have 'a style' but to have style); fruitless groping for the sake of novelty; failure to achieve a synthesis of the unreal and the real; lack of technical equipment, *métier*, which any effective craftsman must possess." It was an American art Putnam and the others wished to see flourish, not a "badly translated and badly garbled European carry-over." In the second number of *New Review* Putnam emphasized that writing must be disciplined and clear, the accent must be on the "object" and the "sacramental significance of reality." Content over form, fewer tricks and devices to capture the eye, more substantial material to engage the mind were the goals of the *New Review* editors, but most of all they urged "a return to content."

In the two years (five issues) it lasted, *New Review* published the work of longtime residents of the Quarter—Ford Madox Ford, Jean Cocteau, and Ezra Pound—as well as newcomers such as Charles Henri Ford, Henry Miller, James Farrell, and George Reavey; of the Europeans who appeared in *New Review* the most prominent were Filippo Marinetti, Emanuel Carnevali, Boris Pasternak, and Yuriy Olesha. Aside from the financial uncertainties that made the appearance of each number a miracle, Putnam was constantly attending to other matters which often necessitated turning over the job of putting the magazine out to his wife, or, on one nearly disastrous occasion, to Alfred Perlès and Henry Miller, who took the opportunity to fill the number with obscenities as a protest against two authors Putnam had printed—Pound and Farrell. Delegating responsibility to Perlès and Miller was a perilous thing to do, Putnam wrote later, for what they did was to set out "to steal" the issue and run it into the ground, a fitting end for a magazine that had paid too much attention to their enemies. Fortunately, Putnam's wife learned what was going on just before it went to press, discarded what she termed offensive, including a spoofy "manifesto" Perlès and Miller had written about something called the "New Instinctivism," and managed to put out a rather thin but readable issue.

As an associate editor of *New Review* Pound remained a somewhat inactive member of the staff. Even his reaction to writers Putnam introduced could not usually be predicted. Farrell, who appeared in the first number, was the "real thing," but when Miller came along Pound was silent, "too contemptuous," according to Putnam, "even to discuss it." On such occasions Putnam noticed Pound would take "refuge in a noncommittal say-little attitude; he was not invariably the bold and slashing warrior that he gave the impression of being." When Peter Neagoe bought a half interest in *New Review* early in 1932 and became a co-editor, Pound was demoted to advisory status; at the same time there occurred a shift of "editorial policy and orientation." Neagoe, Pound knew, was aligned with the Jolas-*transition* group, who had always been hostile to him and, moreover, had often been abusive toward Cocteau, a Pound favorite. Nonetheless, Neagoe's presence and the policy shift were not serious enough to bring about his resignation, but a poem by Kay Boyle did. Entitled "In Defense of Homosexuality" it was accepted by Neagoe and approved by Putnam. Unbeknownst to Putnam, however, it revived an old quarrel between Pound and Miss Boyle and Ernest Walsh, with whom Miss Boyle worked on *This Quarter* just before his death. Shortly after the issue appeared Pound wrote Putnam and requested that his name be dropped from *New Review*'s "editorial supports."

During the two years he ran *New Review* Putnam published seven books under the same imprint. His own translation of Georges Hugnet's poem *Enfances*, over which the poet and Gertrude Stein had quarreled, and H. J. Salemson's translation of Cocteau's *Angel Wuthercut* (a poem "without a blot," Cocteau called it) both came out in 1931. The same year associate editor Richard Thoma issued his volume of poems *Green Chaos* in an edition of one hundred numbered and signed copies. Thoma dedicated poems to everybody, including Ezra Pound, Aldous Huxley, and Harry Crosby. The one to the latter began: "Nothing is so rapid as transition,/ and black suns die as quickly as gold,/ but you can't buy death at the price of a pistol/ and a few drinks." Thoma had managed to crowd into one stanza the name of the magazine Crosby had attached himself to (*transition*), his press (Black Sun), a reference to the Morgan fortune, and a blunt comment on Crosby's recent suicide. In 1932, Putnam edited the "Direction" statement and issued it under the title *Direction, A Symposium*. After Neagoe joined *New Review* as part owner, he published a new edition of *Storm*, his collection of short stories which Jack Kahane's Obelisk Press had printed the previous year. The New Review edition contained an introductory letter by Jolas, Neagoe's discoverer, who had accepted his first story, "Kaleidoscope," for *transition*. Jolas found much to praise in Neagoe's work. Among modern authors writing in English Neagoe was one of the few in whom there was such a "complete balance between a sincere telluric sense and its expression." Neagoe had the courage in an age that "regards literature as a result of social environment" to create "very personal abstractions and to give us the elemental functions of living." In a long review of *Storm* published in the swan number of *New Review*, Putnam mildly rejected Jolas' "rather big and perilously frightening words" and stressed Neagoe's "immigrant" quality, the characters in his stories being peasant-immigrants who had seen America and who, in broken English and with almost Sophoclean wisdom, tell about their experiences and about the old country they left for the new. "And it was for this reason," Putnam predicted, "that they will come as a tonic in an era of crashing stocks and currencies and a seeming deep-settling world's night."

Title page of *Storm* by Peter Neagoe (New Review Press, 1932).
PRINCETON UNIVERSITY LIBRARY

The final New Review publication was George Reavey's first book of poetry, *Faust's Metamorphoses*, for which Putnam wrote an introduction and S. W. Hayter made six "original engravings." Six months after Reavey's book appeared, early in 1933, Putnam returned to America. Reavey, however, stayed on in Paris until 1936, starting his own press called Europa a year or so before he moved to London, and bringing out under that imprint two more volumes of his poetry, *Nostradam* and *Signes d'Adieu*, and Samuel Beckett's first book of poems, *Echo's Bones*. In London, Reavey published five more books, including *Thorns of Thunder* by Paul Eluard, with a drawing by Picasso; *The Garden of Disorder* by Charles Henri Ford, with a drawing by Tchelitchew; and another collection of his own poems, *Quixotic Perquisitions*.

322

IX

Harrison
OF PARIS

I

ABOUT THE TIME the tremors created by the Wall Street crash began reaching the exile colonies abroad, one brave little Paris press announced its existence in a sumptuously designed prospectus which, if the tastefulness of the typography betokened the quality of the books it would produce, heralded what many must have believed would be a latter-day Kelmscott, the renowned private press of William Morris long respected for its idiosyncratic but typographically exquisite publications. While many expected worsening economic conditions to produce serious upheavals on both sides of the Atlantic, if not worldwide turbulence, there were no signs in the prospectus issued by the new firm—Harrison of Paris—that the founders believed their enterprise was in the least threatened by financial collapse. The Harrison announcement assured prospective subscribers and readers that the press intended to publish limited editions in English which, "whenever appropriate," would be illustrated by "brilliant draughtsmen," executed by the "chief European presses," and printed on "durable and in some instances precious papers, variously cased or bound, at remarkably low prices." Each publication, moreover, would represent "the finest of contemporary craftsmanship and the best modern taste." Harrison, continued the prospectus, had adopted "the French system of printing a few copies on China or Japan Vellum, richly bound; a few more on Holland or Madgascar or hand-made Auvergne or the like; and a principal edition of a few hundred and in rare instances a thousand copies on one of the French or Dutch all-rag papers." Lest it be assumed that the new firm would cater primarily to the bibliophile with

Barbara Harrison and Monroe Wheeler, Davos, Switzerland, 1934.
COURTESY OF GLENWAY WESCOTT

typographical interests, the founders added that they would stress not just the "artistic interest of [the] illustrations [but also] their technical execution and their close marrying with the printed page," as well as the "suitability of both to the literature in question." The Harrison "texts" would avoid both the "beaten paths" and what was "merely in fashion, curious, or pedantically important," and each would fall into one of four classifications: great popular stories; poetry, including collections of "little lyrics" as well as major works; human documents on the order of Rousseau's *Confessions* and Franklin's *Autobiography*; and "original writing of extraordinary quality, or of special or intimate interest."

The supervisor of the Harrison firm was Monroe Wheeler. If Wheeler's name meant little to those who saw the 1930 prospectus, the technical expertise reflected in its format and typography revealed at once how talented a designer the press had found and furthermore, how deserving he was to have his work known by the widest possible audience. Ten years earlier Wheeler had printed his first book, a collection of twelve poems called *The Bitterns* by Glenway Wescott. The booklet, only twenty-four pages, was dressed in a black paper cover, with a design by Fredrik Nyquist, and issued in an edition of two hundred copies selling for seventy-five cents. Wheeler and Wescott, who would become lifelong friends, had met while students at the University of Chicago, where they were members of a lively Poetry Club. For each, *The Bitterns* was a maiden publication, and, in a sense, it formalized their independent yet complementary careers, Wheeler's as typographical designer and printer, Wescott's as writer; and except for one other combined effort their ascendant talents would remain unjoined until 1930 when the Harrison press would reunite them. Wescott dedicated *The Bitterns* to his friend and fellow poet Yvor Winters, and it was Winters' small volume of poetry (sixteen pages) *The Immobile Wind* that Wheeler published a year later, along with *The Living Frieze* by Mark Turbyfill, another friend and member of the coterie, whose collection, at eighty-six pages, was the longest book Wheeler issued, and, at twenty-five cents, one of the cheapest. In 1922 Wheeler published two more books of poetry, *The Keen Edge* (with a foreword by Yvor Winters) by Maurine Smith, who with Turbyfill had appeared in the *Little Review*, and *Poems* (*The Indians in the Woods*) by Janet Lewis, whom Winters would marry in 1926. By 1923 Wheeler had temporarily settled in New York (the first three books had been printed in Evanston, Illinois, the fourth and fifth in Germany, where Wheeler and Wescott lived and traveled during the early twenties), where he issued another two volumes of poetry. In answer to a request to Marianne Moore for a "poem of some length," Wheeler received one of her longest, *Marriage*, to which Wescott contributed a four-page foreword. The other volume was *Go Go* by William Carlos Williams. Finally, from Villefranche, in 1926, Wheeler printed a second book by Wescott, a small "presentation" book (no copies for sale) entitled *Like a Lover*, which Wescott later included in *Goodbye Wisconsin*.

What Wheeler was able to contribute to the press in typographical know-how, the firm's patron, Barbara Harrison, provided in financial support and security. Relieved from the usual impositions of costs and expenses that plagued most small presses, Wheeler was free to consign the Harrison publications to the best European printers he could find and commission the most "brilliant draughtsmen" available to illustrate them. In return for her expenditure, Miss Harrison could look forward to seeing Harrison books assume a lofty rank among the work of publishers of limited editions. To Wheeler she entrusted all decisions of book design and production, and to both Wheeler and Wescott the choice of selections. Although technically the press was composed of the partnership between Miss Harrison and Wheeler, Glenway Wescott must be considered the firm's third, albeit unofficial, member, whose friendship with the partners naturally made him privy to all their activities. Acquainted with the little magazines and presses both as a contributor and reviewer, he became an indispensable co-partner.

Harrison's first four publications, all issued on schedule in October and November 1930, admirably fulfilled the promises announced in the prospectus. Besides bearing the stamp of a leading European printery, each one represented one of the four classifications, and all benefited greatly from Wheeler's designing skills. Even the pledge that Harrison books would be modestly priced was realized, with none exceeding six dollars. The first of the two October releases, *Venus and Adonis*, the partners defended as one of Shakespeare's "most generously pleasure-giving poems," an "abandoned masterpiece," simpler than the sonnets and more "realistic" and "touching" and, above all, a work in which Shakespeare had accomplished what contemporary writers lacked the courage to attempt: the exploration of the timeless psychological problem of the "inability to love." It was Glenway Wescott who had strongly urged that Shakespeare's poem be the first Harrison publication, and it was he who created the cover design consisting of a fusion of the letters V and A. The trade edition (440 copies), printed by a Paris firm on heavy Arches vellum, was bound in boards hand-decorated by Suzanne Roussy, with black parchment backs and aluminum tops. Wheeler chose moderately sized type (14-point), which, on pages measuring 6½ by 10 inches, allowed for the placement of three six-line stanzas per page and resulted in a pleasing balance of text and space.

The other October publication was *The Wild West*, a collection of seven Bret Harte tales, including the popular *The Luck of Roaring Camp* and *The Outcasts of Poker Flat*, which the editors described as superbly and artfully composed "literary" stories celebrating America's most magical historical and legendary setting. Harte, they contended, was the Old West's "particular prodigy, its spokesman and laureate," to whom countless cowboys "with Greek profiles," maidenly and sturdy heroines, and "poetical platitudinous films" owed their existence. That the work of this illustrious laureate should be relegated to cheap popular editions printed on "muddy-looking paper" amounted to premature literary extinction.

Mr. Thompson's
Prodigal

WE all knew that Mr. Thompson was looking for
his son, and a pretty bad one at that. That he
was coming to California for this sole object was
no secret to his fellow-passengers; and the physical
peculiarities, as well as the moral weaknesses, of
the missing prodigal were made equally plain to
us through the frank volubility of the parent.

Page from *Tales of the Wild West* by Bret Harte, illustrated by
Pierre Falké (Harrison of Paris, 1930).

Harrison would repair the damage done to the "good and handsome Californian" by turning out a volume technically worthy of him. Determined
that it should be "no less than the most virgin of contemporary texts,"
Wheeler selected a large 11-point Bodini type, a sturdy vellum paper, and
covers bound in rough Hessian cloth (coarse to the touch and suggestive
of Western garb). To make the illustrations he commissioned a young
French artist named Pierre Falké, heretofore unknown to English and

American collectors, whose eight watercolor drawings (in the words of the announcement) were "vivid, simple, and surprisingly well-suited to the time and place of Bret Harte's inspiration"; regrettably, however, they also showed a penchant for endowing the American West with a pictorial imagery of rather spurious historical reliability. Nonetheless, *The Wild West* was an effective example of the "close marrying" of pictorial and typographical ingenuity and the "printed page."

The two November publications, Thomas Mann's *A Sketch of My Life* and Glenway Wescott's *The Babe's Bed*, could almost qualify as examples of "human documents" and "original writing of extraordinary quality, or of special or intimate interest." Though of different genres, both were documents of decided human interest, and both were certainly original in scope and quality. Harrison announced it was publishing them for the first time (since Mann's book, however, had had a German publication earlier the same year, the Harrison edition must be considered the first published English translation, the translating having been done by H. T. Lowe-Porter—very poorly, according to the partners, who spent long hours trying to improve it). Both books of course were the work of renowned writers whose fame had spread far beyond their native countries. Mann's short autobiographical account of his life up to 1929 and Wescott's story, which he once called "a melancholy fantasy upon western themes" with significant autobiographical overtones, were both "summing-up" statements, punctuation marks that came, if not exactly in mid-career, then close to it. For both writers the decade just ended had been marked by considerable writing activity and production as well as critical acclaim, perhaps more than they would ever again undertake or experience. Mann, who was Wescott's senior by twenty-six years, had begun his long literary career in 1901 (the year Wescott was born) with the publication of the remarkable *Buddenbrooks*; by 1930 (he had received the Nobel Prize in 1929) he had become the celebrated author of *Tonio Kröger*, the masterly short novel *Death in Venice, Reflections of a Non-political Man*, and *The Magic Mountain*. Ahead lay the long tetralogy, *Joseph and His Brothers, Doctor Faustus*, and *Confessions of Felix Krull, Confidence Man*. In 1930, at the height of his career, Mann could look with pride and equanimity on past accomplishments and his emergence and stature as a great writer; he was, in the opinion of the Harrison partners, the "ideal great writer."

A Sketch of My Life made clear that Mann's life had been almost entirely devoted to writing. The genesis of each new book, its composition, and critical reception (Gide's appreciation of *The Magic Mountain* was a moving experience for Mann) are carefully recorded. The few glimpses he provides of his personal life recapture dramatic, often troubled, events: an attempted suicide at twenty (Wescott tried to commit suicide at the same age), his reaction to sudden fame at twenty-six (Wescott had a similar experience at the same age when *The Grandmothers* became a popular and critical success), his marriage, and the death of his sister and mother. He admitted that the Nobel Prize found him "not unprepared: It lay upon my path in life—I say this without presumption, with calm if not uninterested insight into the character of my destiny, of my role on this earth. . . ." In a brief recapitulation, he suggested how much longer he expected to fulfill that role. After noting that his life had been as ordered and dependable and exact as a formula, he predicted it would end in 1945, "at the same age as my mother." That he missed by a decade (Mann died in 1955) is less a rebuke to his powers of prescience than one more example of the extraordinary power he believed was his to order and control his life.

Though acclaim of the magnitude that had come to Mann had not yet been conferred upon Wescott, his work had nonetheless been the subject of an unusual amount of favorable critical attention during the previous decade. Of the dozen books Wescott has published to date, the most recent being *Images of Truth* (1962), the Harrison publication, *The Babe's Bed*, was the sixth. Behind him, in 1930, were probably his greatest successes, beginning with his first novel, *The Apple of the Eye* (1924), the Harper's prize novel *The Grandmothers* (1927), and *Goodbye Wisconsin* (1928). In 1929 Wescott had written *The Babe's Bed* with the understanding that Random House would publish it, but the American firm demurred, and rather than submit it to another publisher he had turned it over to Harrison.

Dedicated to Barbara Harrison, *The Babe's Bed* was the last work of fiction Wescott would publish for ten years. A watershed in Wescott's career, it holds an important position, both as it relates to his output of the previous six years, and to several of the stories in *Goodbye Wisconsin*. Since 1921, except for a brief hiatus in 1923–24, when he lived in New York and wrote reviews for the *Dial* and the *New Republic*, Wescott had been ceaselessly locomoting between Europe and America. In 1925 he settled permanently in France, living mostly at Villefranche, near Nice, and Paris, interrupting his exile from America only long enough each year for brief visits with his family in Wisconsin. Like catalysts the home trips stirred and sharpened his recollections of the American Midwest, from which flowed the materials for his novels and stories. In each Wescott examined and re-examined the Midwest, and in each his revolt against the region intensified. What emerged as an overriding resolve to disassociate himself from his midwestern heritage, or from the part of himself which maintained roots in that soil, reached its height in *Goodbye Wisconsin* and *The Babe's Bed*, the first being a public statement of rejection (a long autobiographical essay, it appeared originally in the New York *Herald Tribune*), the second a private and deeply personal analysis of the reasons for rejection. Both can be regarded as termination points in Wescott's life and literary career, ideological adieus to Wisconsin, the Midwest, and the 1920s. At the beginning of a new decade, with Wisconsin publicly and perhaps privately expunged from his psyche and his art, Wescott looked forward to a new career, unhampered by ties to home or to Europe, at the start of which, he hoped, might come a book "out of which myself, with my origins and my prejudices and my Wisconsin, will seem to have disappeared." *The Babe's Bed* was to be that book, but like Bret Harte's stories, with which it was ironically paired, the myth of the American West resists all efforts to dislodge it. If the substance of place disappeared from the printed page, as indeed it did, the concept remained. In the end Wescott reveals that he himself is the maker of fantasies about the Midwest, and concludes that it may be his fate to live all or part of his life "in an ephemeral western town in himself, in his mind."

II

Included in the Harrison prospectus for 1931 was a page of critics' comments praising the first four publications. The two English-language newspapers in Paris found Harrison books far more impressive than the publications of most little presses; Waverley Root, the Paris *Tribune* critic, wrote that he had "rarely seen such uniform good taste, intelligence and artistic sensibility displayed by any publishers of limited editions." If the firm could maintain its high standard, he predicted, "there need be no hesitation in accepting this imprint as a guarantee of an important book perfectly printed." The Paris *Herald* called *The Babe's Bed* "really inspiring" and "far superior to anything" Wescott had yet written. The London *Observer* admired Harrison's "bold and courageous fanfare," and the London *Times Literary Supplement* proclaimed Mann's book "a little

Barbara Harrison and Monroe Wheeler, Coux, Switzerland, 1931.

masterpiece of its kind." *The New York Times* described the format of *The Wild West* as "decidedly attractive."

The favorable critical notices and what was described as "satisfactory distribution" of the four Harrison books gave the partners a sense of optimism and economic security sufficiently encouraging to prompt drawing up "ambitious plans" for the coming year, in the process of which they admitted having been tempted to increase the number of publications. In

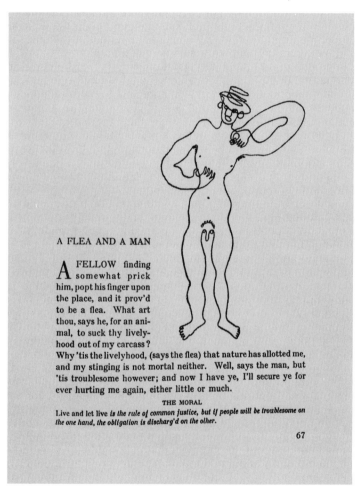

A FLEA AND A MAN

A FELLOW finding somewhat prick him, popt his finger upon the place, and it prov'd to be a flea. What art thou, says he, for an animal, to suck thy livelyhood out of my carcass? Why 'tis the livelyhood, (says the flea) that nature has allotted me, and my stinging is not mortal neither. Well, says the man, but 'tis troublesome however; and now I have ye, I'll secure ye for ever hurting me again, either little or much.

THE MORAL

Live and let live *is the rule of common justice, but if people will be troublesome on the one hand, the obligation is discharg'd on the other.*

67

Page from *Fables of Aesop*, according to Sir Roger L'Estrange, illustrated by Alexander Calder (Harrison of Paris, 1931).

the end, however, they had resisted the temptation, explaining that more publications might endanger the "one excellence which the book-buying public" had welcomed; "the individuality of each volume, all the slight but so perceptible effects of spontaneous impulse and personal care." Still, in 1931 there would be five instead of four titles. The main innovation, though, would be the introduction of the work of four new illustrators. Since the press was, after all, located in Paris, the partners considered "it . . . almost a duty to specialize in the pictorial aspects of book-making," and, furthermore, book-illustration, in their opinion, had lagged far behind "modern taste in printing." Harrison subscribers and readers could be certain that the four artists were "already well-known to perspicacious collectors on the continent," although three had never before illustrated a book, and the fourth had not been published in America and England. To be sure, there was a chance conservative bibliophiles might find the illustrators' "different originalities" startling or even displeasing at first sight, but the editors guaranteed that they would not "cloy, weary, or irritate," as "pretty book-decorations do." Whatever happened, they felt satisfied that the "necessary affinity between the artist's imagination and the text in question [and] between the various harmonies of pictures" and the printed page would be achieved. For the collector with investment interests, Harrison promised to continue the policy of printing limited editions, thus assuring the bibliophile of "genuine rarity within a short time." On the "finest items" genuine bindings would still be substituted for pseudo-bindings; precious papers, "made to last for centuries without decay or discoloration," would continue to be used instead of the "attractive modern substitutes"; and, as in the past, the "moderate European wage-scale" and the European artisan's "unambitious love of his work" would permit setting prices "considerably below those of our competitors." The Harrison partners confidently looked forward to bettering the "more than sufficient success" of the previous year.

October was once again the first publication month, and the *Fables of Aesop* (the Sir Roger L'Estrange translation), the second in Harrison's "great popular stories" series, was the first to appear. In many ways it was a remarkable volume, one of the most attractive and entertaining the press produced. Much could be said for the juxtaposition of Aesop's "desperate mysticism" (the "primitive Greek mind") and the "outbursts of the rough and sparkling genius" of the witty Elizabethan translator. But the fifty drawings Alexander Calder made to accompany Aesop's tales, audacious in their simplicity and revelation, provided an even more explosive and expressive contrast. Next to the fabler's quiet humor, delicate and never perverse, Calder's linear interpretations often gave the stories a bittersweet, if not outrightly, demoniac meaning. For the fable entitled "A Man with Two Wives" Calder pictures the unfortunate victim standing—in shocked immobility and entirely naked—between two women (his wives, also nude) who are gleefully plucking the last two hairs from his head. The scene might have been staged by the Comte de Sade or Aleister Crowley. Shortly before the Harrison publication appeared, the Galerie Percier had held a first exhibit of Calder's art objects, most of which he had made out of wire, wood, tin cans, sheet zinc, whitewash, house paint, and other assorted materials. An impressed Leo Stein had been moved to comment that Calder's abstractions were more complete and satisfying than Picasso's. A few months later, in Montparnasse, the artist's circus went on exhibit. Composed entirely of puppets assembled out of wire, cardboard, and other odds-and-ends (the resemblance between the wire and string figures and the drawings in the Aesop book is striking), it brought him even more acclaim.

Besides the type—12-point Old French Face—even the paper Wheeler selected for the *Fables* helped to convey the sense of antiquity. Named Auvergne, after that region of France, it was a hand-made pure-rag paper that Wheeler discovered was still being made, "just as in 1326, in the morning by farmers who [worked] in the fields all afternoon: the pulp beaten by water-driven hammers in stone vats, the great sheets, as soft as old handkerchiefs, dried in the open air." Louis XIV had written his memoirs on Auvergne, and it had served for the first editions of Molière. To the touch the paper felt coarse but its texture was uniform and smooth. The edges, slightly irregular and ragged, maintained a striking unevenness when piled one on the other in the bound volume, rather like a sheaf of bleached tobacco leaves. The covers, a soft, pale blue, possessed the same smooth-yet-coarse texture as the pages and had the appearance of old cloth worn into shape by long usage. Though the prospectus made no mention of it, the covers had been made from discarded blue aprons worn for years by the Auvergne schoolchildren, all no doubt admirers of Aesop's wisdom and humor. It was a book in which the physical, the aesthetic, and the philosophic could hardly have been more felicitiously blended.

Harrison's sixth book, unclassified but representative of either a "great popular story" or a "human document," was obviously intended to revive interest in the original text of Prosper Mérimée's opera *Carmen*, which the editors rightly noted had been generally ignored and transmuted into something quite unlike the original by the librettists who prepared the story for Bizet. In addition to providing a new and more faithful translation of Mérimée's text "than any previously published," the Harrison volume included a series of travel letters that Mérimée had addressed to the *Revue de Paris* fifteen years before writing *Carmen*, in which he had created preliminary sketches of his characters and the "final love-story." Thus the editors claimed, by joining the finished masterpiece and the seminal sketches from which the opera grew, the book would possess a special literary interest and value. Responsible for the new translation were the partners themselves who, although they remained anonymous, described Mérimée's prose as "intimate, cruel in its precision, very poignant with a sort of civilized restraint, very elegant in the way of a gentleman who does not deign to be a dandy." The tale, too, they discovered, contained little of the popular myth. "Everything in it is explained, everything is realistic, simple, almost prosaic, everything except the play of fever and of fate in the soldier's heart and the gypsy's, her ugly loveliness or beautiful baseness, infinitely exciting, and the cold grandeur of their end." In an allusion to contemporary realists, the translators observed that many owed their "colloquial style" and "stoic sensationalism" to Mérimée, never, however, surpassing him.

For the illustrations Wheeler commissioned the Swiss painter, Maurice Barraud, who had just ended a long sojourn in Spain. Barraud's ten monochrome watercolors, all done in white and varying shades of brown, evoke perfectly the arid, dusty, sun-baked atmosphere of Spain, an effect enhanced by the light-beige cover and the dark-brown slipcase. Fifty copies (twenty-eight for America) containing original proofs colored and signed by Barraud and printed on Imperial Japan vellum were offered for $25.00; but a trade edition of 595 copies (425 for America) on Rives pure-rag vellum were available for $5.00.

The Death of Madame by Madame de La Fayette, Harrison's third October publication, was the press' shortest and smallest book. Only twenty-five pages (the pages measured 3½ by 5 inches), it was printed in 7-point Ehmcke Medieval on Iridescent Imperial Japan vellum in an edition of 325 copies (195 for America) and bound in parchment by a Darmstadt professor. Boxed, it sold for $2.50. Translated by Monroe Wheeler, *The Death of Madame* was Madame de La Fayette's account of the death of Charles I's daughter (Louis XIV's sister-in-law), which the author had witnessed. Madame de La Fayette's poetic powers, contended

335

Wheeler, were equal to those of Racine and Corneille, who had also successfully elevated the previous "tribulations of the unlucky princess far above the level of royal intrigue."

As poignant as *The Death of Madame* was the first November publication, Fyodor Dostoyevsky's *A Gentle Spirit: A Fantastic Story*, in the Constance Garnett translation, with original drawings by Christian Bérard —a full-page frontispiece and a very small tailpiece, in dark-brown wash, both of the unfortunate heroine. Bérard, like Calder and Pavel Tchelitchew, had begun to make an impress on the Paris art world in the mid-twenties. With the Berman brothers and Tchelitchew, he had exhibited at the Pierre Loeb Gallery and thus had become identified with the group rebelling against the cubist vogue. Bérard and Tchelitchew, who the following year would make the illustrations for Wescott's *Calendar of Saints*, often joined the company of the Harrison partners.

A Gentle Spirit was still another account of a disastrous human relationship, or, more exactly, another demonstration of the failure of love. *The Babe's Bed, Venus and Adonis, Carmen,* and *The Death of Madame* all offered varying commentaries on the subject, and *Childe Harold's Pilgrimage*, Harrison's second November book, and *A Calendar of Saints for Unbelievers* would expand it. Dostoyevsky's unhappy couple, a regimental officer turned pawnbroker and the sixteen-year-old girl he subdues but loses, both fall victim to a love they cannot control or comprehend. The officer, haunted by inadequacy, survives an ordeal in which his wife nearly destroys him; and although he manages to regain his self-respect (presumably his wife can no longer regard him as a coward) he cannot rewin her affection, even after promising her a fabled trip to Bologna and kissing her feet. Her long self-imposed silence, symbolic of her lack of love, is interrupted only briefly before she jumps from a window and dies, leaving the aggrieved widower to contemplate an empty future and the ways reconciliation might have been achieved.

The final Harrison book of 1931 was the second to be suggested by Wescott, an edition of *Childe Harold's Pilgrimage*, which the partners hoped would "attract those who [had] not up to date been able to grasp the poet's unique greatness," no matter how charming they may have found him as a man. Assuming that prospective readers of Byron had often been intimidated by the learned notes found in many collections of the author's work, they decided to discard the "brackets and asterisks" and the "unsightly storehouse of fine print," the dense commentaries, and retain only Byron's own notes, which would be conveniently located as close as possible to the passages they explained or supplemented. Of additional assistance would be a "series of mere indications," or short annotations regarding the poet's subject or a sudden change of his thought, which would be placed between the number of the stanza and the first line. The result, they promised, would be a "clear view, a legible revelation of Byron's dual intellect; the humane, casual, supremely sincere commentator in one column, the haughty and sumptuously gifted rhapsodist in the other."

Deciding to join text and notes created some formidable problems

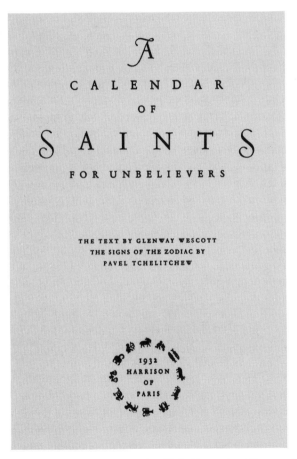

Title page of *A Calendar of Saints for Unbelievers* by Glenway Wescott, with signs of the Zodiac by Pavel Tchelitchew (Harrison of Paris, 1932).

for Wheeler, chief of which was the difficulty in placing both on a single page without causing crowding or a look of overabundance. The solution, which produced an amiable blending of space and the printed word, came in the use of 12-point Didot roman for Byron's text, and 9-point Didot italics for the notes, on an 8- by 9-inch page. The choice of the English painter Sir Francis Cyril Rose to make the illustrations for *Childe Harold* enhanced Harrison's reputation as a press dedicated to putting forward the work of young artists. Rose's twenty-eight wash drawings, printed in collotype by Daniel Jacomet, marked his first appearance in book form, and gave the volume a peculiarly static visual dimension.

Wheeler ordered 660 copies of *Childe Harold* (425 for America) on Montgolfier vellum and bound and boxed in pink cloth; thirty-five copies (twenty for America) on Maillol hand-made paper, in three-quarter Morocco bindings made and signed by Huser of Paris (the "dean of the French school of binding"); and five copies (three for America) on Imperial Japan vellum, in full Morocco bindings by Huser, each containing four of the artist's original drawings. The usual twenty-five copies were put aside and marked Not for Sale. The large edition sold for $7.50, the edition of thirty-five for $25.00, and the five copies for $100.00. However, despite the obvious riches of the Byron volume the book sold poorly.

The Harrison offerings for 1931 received the applause of critics on both sides of the Atlantic. The London *Times* man called *The Fables of Aesop* "a pleasant book," and *Carmen* "a translation worthy of the elegant frame in which it appears"; *A Gentle Spirit* brought the highest praise: "an extremely elegant piece of book-production. It is a pleasure to contemplate the pages." The London *Observer* urged "all lovers of good clean pages, square printing, and spirited drawing [to] possess themselves" of *Childe Harold*. And the *New Yorker* appraised Harrison publications as "the best of the year's issue" and added that "for paper, print, and price, they are extraordinary as collector's items in any land." It is doubtful whether such exuberant citations had any influence on the ingenious typographical experiments that characterize Harrison's two publications in 1932, the first, *A Typographical Commonplace-Book*, compiled by Monroe Wheeler; the second, *A Calendar of Saints for Unbelievers* by Glenway Wescott. In both, Wheeler executed a printing tour de force. His aim in the *Commonplace-Book* was "to exploit the possibilities of certain European type-faces" [i.e., types], rarely on view, and "for the most part unsuitable for book-printing," but very likely "enchanting" when viewed in a paragraph or two. Using as his text a "series of brilliant passages and

touching anecdotes from literature of various sorts and different epochs"
—so as not to disappoint those "insensitive to typography"—Wheeler
arranged each page individually, using a different type face each time, and
thus making the volume a "little exhibit of printing" as well as literature.
The book was printed in three colors and, like *A Calendar of Saints*, was
bound by Huser, whose craftsmanship, already a vanishing art, made the
inferiority of machine-made casing done in a shop or studio by many
hands depressingly obvious.

A Calendar of Saints for Unbelievers might have been the costliest
publication Harrison ever produced. Besides running to 293 pages, making it the longest book the press issued, it was set entirely by hand by
printers at the Enschedé foundry in Haarlem. The 12-point Romanée type
designed by J. van Krimpen, which Wheeler was using for the first time,
seemed to possess a natural dignity, simple yet appropriately aristocratic,
as seen in such touches as the hairline curlicues connecting the letters C
and T. The partners' friend, Pavel Tchelitchew, described in the prospectus as the "truest draughtsman among the younger European artists" and
"one of the best known Russian painters in Paris," created highly individualistic signs of the zodiac to accompany the calendric arrangement of
Wescott's book; it was as though "he had just seen them," the editors
noted.

If Wheeler and Wescott indulged their special interests and pastimes
in those two books (*Calendar* was the "author's pastime for many
months"), they managed to produce exquisite volumes while doing so.
Beginning with its intriguing title, *Calendar* is a collection of saucy, ir-
reverent portraits of saints *qua fools*. Perhaps written in some haste (one
source said six weeks; the announcement suggested many months), the
book may have served as an anodyne for the author, whose collection of
intensely serious truth-bearing essays, *Fear and Trembling*, critics had
either ignored or harshly condemned earlier in the year. It was with a
sense of urgency (following a trip through Germany) that Wescott had
composed the book, and collectively the essays were a warning that Western civilization was on the verge of destroying itself, probably in another
war. The near silence that followed publication, along with the hostility of
those who deigned to review it, shattered the expectations he had had for
the book, and it is quite possible, as has been said, that he turned to
A Calendar of Saints to compensate for the "failure of that book."

The apocalyptic view expressed in *Fear and Trembling* is replaced in
Calendar by a witty rendering of the foibles and failures of those "peers of

Left: Katherine Anne Porter,
Paris, early 1930s.

Below: Barbara Harrison and
Monroe Wheeler, aboard the
S.S. *Conta Rosso,* 1932.
COURTESY OF GLENWAY WESCOTT

heaven"—more than four hundred of them—who have been immortalized by canonization. Who are they? ". . . ragamuffins, kings, maiden aunts of monks who wrote well, blessed degenerates, mere sportsmen of asceticism, man-sized infants, a demi-god or two, politicians, fearful beauties, awful fools, and, of course, those for whom there simply would have to be some such word as 'saint,' even if Christianity had not come to pass." What makes them a company, besides their common beatification, is their common love of God, a love expended entirely upon Him and divorced totally from the practical world. Together they comprise a calendar for unbelievers (i.e., for those unable or unwilling to accept "the creed and its corollaries"), because, like all who succumb to love, these venerables in the end are victimized, reduced to fools by their own love. "Perhaps love is always sexual," Wescott wrote in the foreword. "And it is usually hopeless, sooner or later; ignorant, from first to last; thankless, too soon." The author's view of love, which had important precedents as well as auguries for the future (for example, in *The Pilgrim Hawk*), may have been formulated by 1926, when Wheeler published, privately, Wescott's *Like a Lover*, where love is depicted as a wild, powerful madness, quite beyond the control of reason or knowledge, and capable of bringing one to destruction. The bachelor figure in *The Babe's Bed*, "like a lover," gives himself up to "his distant ambitions—the necessary infatuation with himself" and wonders what will result from self-infatuation. In a sense that answer appeared in *Calendar of Saints*; although the saints are enamored of God, their affections, in Wescott's opinion, are drastically restricted—confined to God and the Church—and therefore separated from most of humanity. Love, whether directed outwardly or inwardly, toward God or self, may lead one away from the truths of human existence, even if it does not entirely strip one of dignity.

III

Katherine Anne Porter and I "made friends in Paris in 1932," Wescott wrote in an appraisal of her writing. It was in the same year that Harrison announced it would bring out Miss Porter's *French Song-book*, the first of two books by the author it would issue in the next two years. A *French Song-book*, certain to appeal to typophiles and bibliophiles, combines poetry and printing as well as music in a pleasing and complementary harmony. In a note on the composition of the book, Miss Porter explained her selections: "My choice of these particular songs for a small collection is neither arbitrary nor casual. First, I wished to make a singing version in English of French songs ranging over a period of about six hundred years; second, each song should be fairly representative of its time, and there should be only one song of a kind, such as a Carol, a Ballad, a Complaint, a Legend, a Brunette. Among these kinds I chose first for musical beauty, next for poetical and historical interest. In the end I chose always the special song that most appealed to me. This is the peculiar happy privilege of the collector, without which no one would ever be tempted to such an enterprise. The book is therefore a medley of the familiar, the famous, the popular, the obscure, the almost lost: but there is no song here that has not at one time or another been greatly known and loved; not one that has lost its meaning in spite of the differences of their luck in the mysterious chances of human favor. There was no searching of the archives for recondite treasure. I consulted only a half-dozen song-books such as are published in France, a rich and wonderful jumble of songs meant to be sung and enjoyed, usually somewhat disfigured by trite accompaniments meant for the family piano." Since Miss Porter made rhymed verse transcriptions of each song (there are seventeen), following the French syllable by syllable, the problems of translating must have been formidable, infinitely more difficult than her free-flowing English verses would suggest. That she was able to preserve the original rhythms (the French originals appear nearby), and at the same time manage to make the English version "singable," was an achievement which supported the belief that her absorption in French culture was both comprehensive and spiritual, an observation further borne out by her informative and entertaining accounts of the authorship or origin of each song.

What to do with the musical examples (a problem that must have deterred others from making similar volumes) was solved by a specialist in musical calligraphy named Paul Koch, who made new transcriptions of each melody which, in simple unharmonized form, appear at the beginning of each song; staves of Koch's music recur throughout the book as designs, and two staves embrace the author's name and title on the spine.

Instead of ending its activities in Paris in the first months of 1934, the Harrison of Paris press survived a transatlantic journey to New York, where it operated long enough to issue a final book, Miss Porter's *Hacienda*, its thirteenth publication. Among the last of the longtime American residents to leave Europe—Wheeler and Wescott had lived abroad for eight years, Miss Harrison a shorter time—the partners shared the feeling that Europe had gradually come to hold less interest for them (Wescott called

342

it a "rat race"); moreover, each had reasons for returning to the United States. Miss Harrison, engaged to Wescott's brother, would marry in 1935; Wheeler, settling in New York, would soon become Director of Exhibits at the Museum of Modern Art; and Wescott, also settling in New York for a while before moving permanently to the family enclave in rural New Jersey, would go on writing while undergoing the throes of repatriation, a process which finally ended, he admitted, in 1939.

With the partners relocated in America and about to assume new personal and professional responsibilities, the likelihood of continuing to operate the press on anything close to the scale on which it had functioned in France was at best uncertain. However, since it had been agreed that the press would bring out Miss Porter's short book, the partners decided to keep it going at least until *Hacienda* had appeared, which turned out to be in December 1934. With *Hacienda* Harrison was of course adding another important title to its list (the author's collection of short stories, *Flowering Judas*, had "established her overnight as one of the great contemporary masters of English prose," the Harrison brochure reminded readers), and Wheeler, anticipating that it would perhaps be the press' liveliest seller, ordered an edition of 895 copies. There was also another advantage in continuing Harrison. It provided an opportunity to dispose of the stock of unsold books, many of which, despite the services of the American agents, Minton, Balch and Company, had not found their way into the American market. Brochures issued from the Harrison's new address—362 Fifth Avenue, New York—listed all the previous publications, and one "broadsheet" announcement bore the heading: "Offerings for the person of taste who has everything (else), from Harrison of Paris (with your collaboration)." Mentioned along with illustrations by Calder and Tchelitchew, were *French Song-book*, *A Calendar of Saints for Unbelievers* (each ordered copy to bear the author's signature), *Carmen*, and the *Fables of Aesop*; the latter, prospective buyers were informed, contained fifty drawings by the same artist (Calder) whose wire sculptures were currently being exhibited at the Museum of Modern Art.

To print *Hacienda* Wheeler contracted the Haddon Craftsmen at Camden, New Jersey, and, as always, he selected the type, a 12-point Baskerville italic; the paper, Arnold English unbleached pure-rag; and the binding, a claret balloon-cloth, with apple-green slip case. The price Wheeler set at three dollars.

Miss Porter's ability to absorb the quality of a new and different culture, noted previously in the example of the *French Song-book*, was again evident in *Hacienda*. The location this time is a Mexican hacienda where a "corpse-white liquor" called *pulque* is produced, which the peasants consume in large doses to fortify themselves against the suffering and boredom that blight their lives. To the company of film-makers who have come to Mexico to make a motion picture about the revolution, however, the liquor is anathema; nonetheless, they have devised their own ways to transcend reality (besides the obvious one of making a film). At the center of Miss Porter's story is the Russian director Kennerly (modeled after Eisenstein), whose obtuseness blinds him to the values of Mexico and begets a shocking moral insensitivity. And the company over which he presides, a strange collection of Russians, Mexicans, and Americans, exude a pervasive immorality, animalism, and decay, which are perfectly embodied in the timeless place of oppressiveness and death, the hacienda. As in Wescott's stories, love once again fails, and again it is not because it is misplaced, or too tenuous, but because it is, or appears to be, obsessive, mad, abnormal, and doomed to fail out of frustration. The host at the hacienda escapes his wife by infidelity, or believes he does, for she, in turn, enters a liaison with her husband's mistress. And the murder that temporarily halts the filming (a young Mexican shoots his sister) may have been prompted by incest. From this unhealthy and unsavory Buñuel-like environment everyone seems powerless to escape. Only one does. At the end of the story as members of the company begin drifting off, knowing they will return later to film "some of the best scenes over again," the narrator, Miranda, decides she can no longer bear the "deathly air"; even the prediction made by the Indian who drives her to town that the hacienda will be a "different place . . . in about ten days" fails to arrest her departure.

Although the Haddon Craftsmen produced a distinctive edition of Miss Porter's book, the partners agreed that the superb printing facilities as well as the reasonable costs that existed in Europe could not be duplicated in the United States, and that to invest what would have to be a large outlay in future publications would not be feasible. *Hacienda*, Miss Porter's "nouvelle in memoir form," was an impressive last publication, however. Not only did it have the largest printing of any Harrison book, but it was one of the press' best sellers, and, of course, it brought the partners the honor of publishing a second book by one of America's foremost writers.

X

Jack Kahane
AND THE GUARDIAN OBELISK

I

IN HIS BUMPTIOUS autobiography *Memoirs of a Booklegger*, completed shortly before his sudden death in 1939, Jack Kahane divulged in a slightly modified adage what lay behind the success of his Obelisk Press: one publisher's poison, he explained, was often another publisher's meat. For more than a decade as the Paris-based publisher of books no other publisher in the English-speaking world dared to issue, Kahane had been gathering evidence to support that observation. Elsewhere in his memoir he decried the practice too often followed by responsible English publishing firms of abandoning books they had commissioned at the first sign of censorship trouble. As distasteful as it was bewildering, it was not exactly unwelcome, for waiting just a few miles away, across the English Channel, alert and eager, was Kahane, prepared to rescue the beleaguered books, rush them to the printers, and release them to the Paris bookshops—all within a few weeks. Only war and the publisher's death finally toppled the Obelisk, but by the time those calamities occurred Kahane's Obelisk logo had been affixed to some of the most controversial books of the past half century, many of them branded as pornographic and obscene or serious or all three, depending upon the tolerance and understanding with which one could view works that were ofttimes abrasively forthright in style and subject.

Like most Montparnassians, Kahane venerated James Joyce, but he admired Sylvia Beach almost as much as the writer she had published. "How's God?"—meaning Joyce—he would inquire when he visited her shop. The fact that she had found and then printed a book as "obscene"

345

Jack Kahane, author and publisher of Obelisk books, and friend, France, 1930s.
COURTESY OF MR. MAURICE GIRODIAS

as *Ulysses* was as mystifying as it was admirable, and Kahane never quite lost hope that someday he might convince the redoubtable Miss Beach to let him take over the publication of Joyce's book. That day never came, but with her help he did obtain two short manuscripts from Joyce: an extract from "Work in Progress" entitled *Haveth Childers Everywhere*, which nearly plunged him into bankruptcy, and a new edition of *Pomes Penyeach*, already published by Shakespeare and Company, which he reissued with lettering and decorations by Joyce's daughter Lucia. That was as close as he ever got to *Ulysses*. For D. H. Lawrence he held the same admiring respect, but since Lawrence had died before Kahane had become an independent publisher, there had never been an opportunity to petition him for a manuscript, although in the early thirties Kahane arranged to

346

take over the publication of *Lady Chatterley's Lover* from the local Pegasus Press, thereby becoming its third Paris publisher. Along with all the other magazine editors and small publishers, Kahane shared the hope that some day he would discover a new genius—a Joyce or a Lawrence—on his own, and for him that wondrous day finally came. The "new genius" turned out to be Henry Miller, and after 1934, when Kahane belatedly published *Tropic of Cancer*, he liked to believe that he had "discovered" the American Céline. Before Miller had emerged as the Obelisk's *grand vedette*, however, Kahane had prepared the stage for him by acquiring two of the most celebrated "forbidden" books of the time: Radclyffe Hall's lesbian novel *The Well of Loneliness* and Frank Harris' gargantuan sexual confessions *My Life and Loves* (in four volumes).

Kahane ended his *Memoirs* with a tribute to himself. It had taken him, he wrote, less than the two decades that separated world wars to move from a "dirty little office in a Manchester back street to a 'posh' establishment in the Place Vendôme." He had gone in that time from "dealing in cotton to dealing in the products of some of the finest brains in existence"; and, of hardly negligible importance, he had exchanged a room in a Manchester boardinghouse for a flat in Neuilly. The Horatio Alger guise in which he invested his career is scarcely diminished by the fact that, at the time of his birth in 1888, the Kahanes of Manchester were a prosperous middle-class family, and although the death of the publisher's father resulted in the family fortune being thinly distributed among a dozen children, it does not appear that young Kahane began life in anything close to a destitute state. Forsaking the university for the Manchester mills and for a life of thrift, industry, and shrewdness, he managed to acquire "quite a bit of money" by the time the First World War erupted, by which time he had also developed a taste for the theatre, music and writing—practicing each with an amateur's enthusiasm—as well as a fondness for elegant living. (At one time he owned seven bulldogs and fifty pairs of trousers.) All these pleasures suddenly stopped, however, with the outbreak of war in Europe, an event that coincided with "a great emotional catastrophe" in his life. Giving away all he owned, he volunteered to die, presumably somewhere on the western front, but, instead, he survived and emerged from the "hell of Ypres" with a revived interest in living as well as a French war bride—a "bubbly, charming, piquant young French bourgeoise" named Marcelle Eugenie Girodias. The war had nonetheless taken a toll. Gassed in one of the battles, he contracted tuberculosis, and following a crisis that nearly took his life, retired to the French country-

side for an extended convalescence. But the compulsory rest only produced an explosion of creativity which first materialized in the form of a
light, breezy novel, consciously imitative both in style and content, but
mainly in spirit, of the work of several popular French writers. It was the
Gallic sexual morality that animated Kahane. How much more reasonable
it was—and how much more tolerant too—than the Englishman's recal-
citrance to sex, a condition for which he held Queen Victoria responsible.
It was regrettable that the overwhelming preponderance of women in
England made anything like the French openness unlikely, for, he supposed, since sex was necessarily a woman's "chief stepping stone to comfort and success" she certainly would not want to divulge its secrets. While
not exactly a new genre, Kahane had produced a Gallic novel in English,
to which he gave the whimsically prophetic title *To Laugh and Grow
Rich.* Lowell Brentano, manager of the bookstore's publishing department, agreed to print a small edition. Later, after sales had reached an
impressive volume, the English publisher Grant Richards brought out
another edition, which was promptly banned by the powerful circulating
libraries. In his *Memoirs,* Kahane claimed he did not realize the "commercial advantages of that . . . abominable and arbitrary act," at least not at
the time. Yet it is hard to believe that the practical benefits of having a
book condemned or banned, both for author and publisher, were lost on
the convalescent, who, flushed with success now that his first book had
gone into a third printing, had already started a second, this one the story
of a woman trying to preserve her youth, an unoriginal but, in his opinion,
"a worthy undertaking." Few, unfortunately, realized that he had tried to
write a tragedy. The book flopped, Richards went into bankruptcy, and
Kahane vowed never again to write a "serious comedy with a tragic under-
tone." In his third book, *The Gay Intrigue,* he prudently repeated the
successful formula of the first. The events dramatize the conflicting aspirations that encumbered his career as author and publisher. On the one
hand, he wanted to make money: for a publisher it was a responsibility,
for an author a necessity. At the same time he wanted to be known as a
publisher of "serious books," if not his own, then those of others. "Serious
books," however, seldom made money. It was a dilemma from which he
would never succeed in extricating himself.

Several more years invested in writing novels and in frustrating bouts
with publishers convinced Kahane he was pursuing a "fruitless occupation." An unexpected release from his bondage mercifully materialized in
1928, however, in the person of a dapper French publisher of deluxe

editions named Babou, whose trim beard, high heels, and fashionable suits must have impressed Kahane almost as much as the books he printed. Babou had just issued the first three volumes of a limited edition of French illustrators, and Kahane, certain the series would have a large sale in America and England, offered to make an English translation. Lowell Brentano encouraged him to begin at once, but since neither he nor Babou wanted to pay for the translation, Kahane's interest in the venture quickly faded. Still hoping somehow to escape from the boring routine of turning out potboilers for skinflint publishers, he proposed that Babou consider selling him a share of his business. Negotiations could not have been easy, but after lengthy discussions and even longer silences, Babou announced, in a letter of "dazzling eloquence," that he would be flattered to acquire his collaboration, that is, if he was willing to invest 300,000 francs. Joining Babou as a business partner gave Kahane the title of publisher but none of the privileges. Babou remained in complete control, allowing Kahane to take his share of the profits but none of the responsibilities of operating the business. Reduced to the "most somnolent of sleeping partners" was a situation almost as intolerable as the one he had left. Determined to be a full-fledged publisher, despite the noxious restrictions, he turned to the one person who might come to his rescue—Sylvia Beach. Like other Paris publishers, Kahane explained to Miss Beach, he had long wished to print something by James Joyce ("the greatest expatriate"); he had come to see her, he continued, to ask for help in procuring a Joyce manuscript, a request which he remembered brought a look of faintly humorous incredulity to the face of Joyce's conscientious protector that was almost as disquieting as the reproachful glance she gave his eye-glass, a dandyish prop he had perhaps worn to impress her. In the end, whether convinced by his sincerity or worn down by his persistence, she agreed to conduct him to "the Master."

Meeting Joyce was like an audience with the Pope. After being led into the "Presence" by Miss Beach, Kahane clasped Joyce's tenuous hand, looked into the almost sightless eyes, and nearly swooned with an excess of reverence customarily foreign to his nature. Commanding and gracious, Joyce solemnly introduced the publisher to the people who formed his court while Nora Joyce, pouring tea, disturbed the "cathedral calm" with a "touch of boisterousness." "I drank and ate and listened to the Master and his disciples, and when the feast was done and the libations poured, repaired with him and Miss Beach to another room, where after a short discussion I respectfully handed to her for his account a cheque for fifty thousand francs in payment of the right to publish a fragment of five thousand words from the work he had in progress in an edition de luxe to be entitled *Haveth Childers Everywhere*."

Kahane expected to have no trouble convincing his partner that in signing up Joyce they would be adding the "greatest writer" of the time to their list. But Babou, more fearful than proud, and understandably curious to see what such a large sum had purchased, plied Kahane with tough questions. What was *H.C.E.* all about? What exactly did it say? Embarrassed, Kahane admitted that he did not know, but that they should consider it a privilege to be publishing anything by Joyce, even if it could not be understood. But why, Babou persisted, since Joyce's work was in English and Kahane had read it, could he not tell him what it said? Because, Kahane stammered, Joyce's language was too abstruse. Impossible, retorted Babou. True, insisted Kahane. Despite the contretemps, the partners agreed to produce a volume that would be worthy of such a distingushed writer and, hopefully, one that would bring at least a partial return on their investment. At a cost of nearly 100,000 francs, they turned out an edition of six hundred copies, five hundred printed on "a gorgeous Vidalon vellum" and the other hundred, signed by Joyce, on "iridescent" (Kahane's coinage) Japon Nacre, "literally mother-o'-pearl Japanese vellum paper." The outsized volume delighted Joyce, but the partners, though of course pleased with their work and the pleasure they had given the author, were soon once again having misgivings. Subscription orders for the opus had barely reached a trickle before they had stopped, and Babou's fears now included financial ruin. The situation looked ominous when, by the most unlikeliest chance, Kahane met an American visitor in Paris named Elbridge Adams, the owner of the Fountain Press (New York) and a great admirer of Joyce. Would he, Kahane queried, be interested in bringing out *Haveth Childers Everywhere* in America? He would, indeed, Adams replied, and their meeting (Kahane understandably called it historic) ended with Adams agreeing to pay for the privilege of taking over half the edition. Kahane's performance brought tears to Babou's eyes. Catastrophe had been averted, and in the end they actually made "a handsome profit."

The book that set Kahane's publishing enterprise on the course it would follow till its dissolution in 1939 was the first novel by a young English writer named Norah James. Indebted to Hemingway and particularly to *The Sun Also Rises,* Miss James' novel, *Sleeveless Errand,* presented a brazen picture of dissolute Bohemians in London, too brazen for "a lady of great political importance" who had considered herself maligned in Miss James' book and had used "her subterranean influence" to have the book banned. Responding to pressure the London police confiscated copies and halted further publication. The episode amazed Kahane. How could a book containing only the minutest amount of offensive material (he found a few words "provocatively taboo") outrage authorities and produce such determined repression? More important, how could a publisher like Eric Partridge, who had taken the James' book on the recommendation of Edward Garnett (a man of "flawless" discrimination), make the error of printing it without first taking the precaution of expunging the objectionable words that might alarm the censors and evoke the ban? Such rashness was incomprehensible. Publishing a book that ran even a remote risk of being banned seemed totally unrealistic both commercially and legally. Breaking the law, even in the interest of defending a controversial principle—a defense used by several British publishers such as Heinemann and Cape—was pure defiance; it would do nothing to change the law, and commercially the errant publisher stood to lose his investment. Furthermore, Partridge, who normally published books of serious nature, was bound to suffer damaging publicity.

The circumstances that led to the suppression of Miss James' book emboldened Kahane. If British publishers preferred to continue the "hypocritical nonsense" of trying to publish sure-to-be-banned books in defiance of the law in order to advance a principle, let them, but there would be no need for that in France where books like *Sleeveless Errand* could be published with impunity. Full of moral rectitude—and certainly not oblivious to the possible financial windfall that lay ahead—Kahane telephoned Miss James, arranged to buy her beleaguered book, and had a large edition printed in Paris. Put on sale in a little over a month, it sold, in the publisher's words, like "mitigated wildfire," at a hundred francs a copy.

For Partridge, the James book had been a dead loss; for Miss James, however, there was at least the possibility of some remuneration; and for Kahane an exciting and potentially lucrative vocation had emerged. If, as the law stood (so Kahane's reasoning went), it was illegal to publish books like *Sleeveless Errand* in England, "it was not so in France, and if the law was respected as it should be, many fine books which would therefore be lost to the world might be saved by the creation of a vehicle for their publication in a country where it was legal." As long as the restrictions remained in effect in England (as well as in America), and as

351

long as the law was applied to violations, Kahane reckoned that a publisher might actually thrive in France on a steady supply of banned books. At the very worst, he had only harassment to fear from French detectives who, either on their own or prompted by pressure from British or American officials, might occasionally meddle in the affairs of a foreign-language press. Thus, supported by legality in what would be his campaign to preserve books threatened with extinction, Kahane blandly announced in a statement issued to the London press that he was prepared to publish in Paris, "within a month," any book of "literary merit" which had been banned in England.

Before Kahane had a chance to realize his expectations, however, he suffered a series of disappointments which nearly ended his publishing career before it started. Besides an unexpected paucity of banned or likely-to-be-banned books, Babou, "flushed with success," suddenly began expanding the business in all directions and losing money on "everything he touched." Then Kahane, already horrified by his partner's extravagance and helpless to do anything about it, was stricken with illness and forced to retire once more to the countryside, losing almost all touch with the business. So bleak, in fact, did the situation look that he felt obligated to reject an offer from D. H. Lawrence, for whom, aside from boundless admiration, he had an "abundance of sympathy" and a sense of kinship based on their common interest in free expression. Turned down by Sylvia Beach, Lawrence had extended his search for a publisher for *Lady Chatterley's Lover* to Edward Titus and Kahane. Although taking on the Lawrence book would be "a huge step in the direction" Kahane wanted to follow, he could not in good conscience accept the novelist's offer in view of Babou's unreliable, wasteful, and, at times, even wanton conduct. He had to be protected for his own sake. Understandably, however, Lawrence assumed Kahane had refused his book out of fear that he might be prosecuted, an assumption scarcely commensurate with what actually nagged him—the fear that his partner's profligate spending would sooner or later ruin both of them. When Kahane finally returned to Paris, weak but at last recuperated from his illness, he discovered his worst fears confirmed. His entire investment as well as the profits from the Joyce book and *Sleeveless Errand* had vanished, a total loss of nearly 400,000 francs. The same year (1929) Kahane's wealthy father-in-law lost heavily in the Wall Street crisis, and thus, with his own fortune gone and now that of his father-in-law as well, he had reached bottom.

Despite the desperate situation, Kahane resolved to remain a publisher, hopefully, however, one without encumbrances, and he set down what he regarded as "an impeccably logical conception." He would start a publishing business that "would exist for those . . . writers, English and American, who had something to say that they could not conveniently say in their own countries." He would be ready for the next Lawrence or Joyce who came along, and in the meantime he would "automatically" print any books that had run into censorship trouble. Finding money to fund the new project turned out to be no problem at all. From Lowell Brentano, now in New York, came news that a movie company had named one of their films *To Laugh and Grow Rich*, the title of Kahane's first novel, and although the film had no resemblance to the novel, Brentano was ready to sue the company and go "halves" with Kahane. Since this was too tempting an opportunity to pass up, Kahane wired his friend to proceed. What eventually reached him, far from the paltry fifty dollars he expected, if anything at all, was a check for a thousand dollars, his half of the sum Brentano had settled for. With money in hand, Kahane set out to find a printer. And it was to the dignified Herbert Clarke, of the rue Saint-Honoré, that he turned. Clarke patiently listened to Kahane outline his plans, agreeing with all he proposed except the rather fatuous declaration that his enterprise would "in its more serious aspect" be an instrument for the advancement of literature. That, coming from the author of *To Laugh and Grow Rich, The Gay Intrigue*, and a new one he had dashed off during his illness called *Daffodil*, struck Clarke as slightly preposterous. Nonetheless he agreed to go along, bridling a little, however, at Kahane's insistence that the partnership would work only if he had "complete literary control," a stipulation which probably explains why Clarke delayed signing an agreement of partnership. His enthusiasm for *Daffodil*, however, was unbounded. Similar to the light, amoral trifles the author had composed during his earlier convalescence, this one about a young lady losing her virtue by stages seemed perfectly suited to the tastes of the Anglo-American visitors who, Kahane always assumed, came to Paris to do what they would not or could not do at home and to procure books not likely to be found in England or America. If risqué, slightly naughty novels added spice to their visit, Cecil Barr or Basil Carr, the two pseudonyms under which Kahane wrote, was only too willing to provide them, stopping short, of course, of explicitness and always suggesting—often with the aid of dots and dashes—more than was actually said.

Clarke rushed *Daffodil* into print, and as the author had predicted, it was soon in heavy demand, selling, reported Kahane, "like the tastiest and hottest of hot cakes." Five years later it had reached eighteen editions.

Exuberant and confident that he had at last found the right combination—the "flower" books, as he called *Daffodil* and the others, would pay for the serious ones he intended to publish—Kahane moved into finer quarters to await the arrival of the new Joyce or Lawrence. Before then, however, and even before he had time to publish a second book, Clarke died, and with unpleasant memories of the partnership with Babou still vivid, Kahane was once more forced to strike an agreement with another French printer, this one Clarke's partner, Servant, who had acquired the business. Servant's offer, unsurprisingly, differed from what Clarke and Kahane had agreed on, but lest he endanger the future of *Daffodil* by any hard bargaining that might end in an impasse, Kahane agreed to the printer's terms, hoping that their relations would at least be amicable. The agreement stated that Kahane would be allowed to publish two or three books a year, but that one was expected to be by him.

II

Kahane's reluctance to be rejoined to a French printer notwithstanding, his new associate, besides being an eminent gastronome whom clients often relied on for advice on good eating and drinking, was a superior printer with an impressive reputation. Kahane could hardly have done better. With the agreement signed, he christened the press the Obelisk, thus distinguishing it from Servant's printery known as the Vendôme Press, and probably mindful of the "phallic implications" of the Egyptian obelisks in nearby Place Vendôme and Place de la Concorde, designed a colophon for the new press that consisted of an obelisk standing on a book, which, seen in perspective, assumed a vaguely yoni-like shape. Besides the Joyce book, his stock included *Sleeveless Errand, Daffodil,* and a "very mediocre novel" he had inherited from Clarke, probably *The Lamb* by Philippe Heriat, which Kahane had translated and tried to polish up. The expected inundation of banned books, however, had still not come, nor had he received manuscripts from the Quarterites whose work one heard discussed so heatedly in the cafés. Why were not the "café geniuses" who had so often "bemoaned the lack of a publisher broad-minded enough to understand their aspirations" knocking down his door? Could it be that now that they knew there was a publisher ready to read and possibly publish their work they could only retreat to their Pernods, shamefaced, unable to admit that there never was a "great unpublished novel" back in their room? Kahane tried Hemingway, who, though friendly, did not have anything for him at the moment, and, besides, was just shoving off for Havana. Kahane tried Ford, who introduced him to several "budding" writers whose buds "obstinately refused to flower." Ford took Kahane to see Gertrude Stein, whom he instantly revered for her excellent business acumen, but not for her writing, which he could not understand. There was nothing of Stein's for Kahane either. But by this time the search was nearly over, and it ended one day at Sylvia Beach's shop when he picked up a copy of Sam Putnam's *New Review* that contained a short story by an unknown writer named Peter Neagoe.

Peter Neagoe was himself attached to the Paris publishing trade, having joined Putnam at his New Review Publications, which earlier that year (1932) had issued Neagoe's first book, a collection of short stories called *Storm*. Neagoe, whom Kahane described as looking like a "solid countryman who had done a hard day's work in the fields and had fed well after it," had arrived in Paris with his wife, an artist, in 1926. In New York, where he had lived for twenty years after leaving Romania, he had studied art (at the National Academy) and begun to read in American literature, an experience which gave him an American identity that probably had its fullest expression in the mammoth anthology *Americans Abroad*, which he was editing for Putnam the same year he met Kahane. Already in his mid-forties when he moved to Paris, he had waited several years before the little magazines began taking his stories; then, at fifty, Putnam had issued *Storm*.

Neagoe looked as though he had stepped right out of one of his own stories: rugged features, untidy hair, a "taking" smile, a solid build, a peasant with a literary gift. The stories Kahane admired as "masterpieces of their kind" (they had already received the blessings of Jolas, Mencken, Edward J. O'Brien, and Conrad Aiken) celebrated the peasant's inherent qualities of joy, stability, resignation, satisfaction with the things available, and pride in work. Neagoe's was essentially a folk literature. The New Review edition of *Storm* that the author showed Kahane in 1932 contained ten stories, filling 180 pages, and an eulogistic introduction by Jolas. Although Neagoe hardly qualified as "a great writer," Kahane urgently needed a book that would represent the "type of literature that *Daffodil* was supposed to finance." To his delight, in addition to the considerable merit the book possessed, it had just had the unexpected good fortune to be condemned in America. Shortly after copies had been shipped to the United States, Putnam heard that the U. S. Customs Service in Chicago had declared the book obscene and that shipments were being held up and returned to Paris. New York officials had also banned it. The American Civil Liberties Union, notified by Putnam of the situation, agreed to bring the matter to court, and with impressive speed he and Neagoe assembled a sheaf of protests from "leading men of letters." Indeed, as Kahane appreciatively noted, they saw to it that the indignation over the banning of *Storm* remained an issue for some time. Putnam rushed into print a facsimile of the customs department's letter, across the top of which appeared the notice: "Banned in America by the U. S. Customs Officials." The halo of banning was a welcome bonus to Kahane. Here was an opportunity to demonstrate that the Obelisk Press would publish books denied publication or circulation elsewhere, and it appeared he had also selected a book likely to make money.

Storm (the New Review edition) had been execrably done. Misprints abounded on nearly every page and the printing throughout was generally sloppy. Also, the organization displeased Kahane. By rearranging the order of the stories and adding six new ones, promptly supplied by Neagoe, Kahane expanded the Obelisk edition to 306 pages. It appeared in the fall of 1932, dressed in a bold black-and-white jacket, on the back of which appeared the same letter Putnam had circulated earlier. A satisfied Kahane noted later that the "first duty of American tourists of a literary turn of mind, when in France, was to buy *Storm*, and thanks to my unremitting efforts to ensure that the book should be prominent in every appropriate shop window, the appropriate tourist could not miss it." *Storm* soon went into a fourth edition, the money rolled in, and Neagoe, if not the Obelisk Press, began to be noticed.

A second Joyce book, this one a deluxe boxed edition (twenty-five copies, numbered and signed, and priced at a thousand francs) of the already published *Pomes Penyeach* (Shakespeare and Company, 1927), contributed little to the reputation Kahane was anxiously trying to build. The edition the author asked Kahane to do in conjunction with the British publisher Desmond Harmsworth ("an untidy exquisite," Kahane said of him, "dreadfully elusive, and as unlike as possible to what I imagine must be the popular conception of a Harmsworth") was Joyce's gift to his daughter Lucia who, the victim of a nervous breakdown for which physical therapy had been recommended, had created decorative letters for each of her father's poems—extraordinary, multi-colored designs, but unrelated to anything Kahane had ever seen, and even allowing for their "strangely attractive" nature, hardly suited for a book "as it is usually conceived." He solved what he called a "complicated problem" by making a sort of album on precious paper, with Joyce's actual handwriting being reproduced and Lucia's letters copied identically by the *pochoir* method, which he had learned from Babou. The book, or "sub-book," as Kahane described it, "was a curiosity rather than a real book, and although it was pretty to look at," he was never really proud of it. Far from being an "original discovery," the best it could do was satisfy the publisher's love of "fine trappings of literature."

By the end of 1932 (Obelisk was officially founded in the summer of 1931) Kahane had more to worry about than the caliber of the books he had published. England had gone off the gold standard the previous year, and in Paris the pound, which had formerly fetched 125 francs, was now worth only 75. In dollars, for Obelisk books priced at 50 francs, it meant an increase of over a dollar, from $2.00 to $3.30. Furthermore, with fewer tourists in Paris, fewer books were being sold. There were, however, some compensations. From America came Charles Henri Ford, who brought with him the manuscript of *The Young and Evil*, a novel on which he and Parker Tyler had collaborated, amiably, for close to two years, and which, despite the fact that the authors lived in widely separated parts of the country—Ford in Mississippi and Tyler in New York— had developed into an integrated work. At the outset each author would post to the other chapters for completion or revision, with Tyler supplying material on the underground homosexual world in Greenwich Village and Harlem (the novel couples two white and two black heroes), and Ford devising the narrative structure. To their immense delight, Gertrude Stein proclaimed that *The Young and Evil* had created the authors' generation as authentically and exactly as Fitzgerald had created his in *This Side of Paradise*. Publishers, however, seemed unimpressed; Liveright, Cape, and Gollancz all rejected it, and in mid-1932, Ford, acting on the advice of Miss Stein, delivered the manuscript to William Bradley, who quickly passed it on to Kahane, who accepted it, paid the authors a small advance (three hundred dollars) and issued it in August 1933 (the edition may have numbered twenty-five hundred copies). Prominently displayed on a band wrapped around its middle was Miss Stein's proclamation, which Bradley, rather optimistically perhaps, thought might help to carry Ford "on to victory." Not long after the book appeared, however, British customs seized and burned five hundred copies, and American officials fol-

Above: Parker Tyler, co-author of *The Young and Evil* (Obelisk Press, 1933), England, 1933.
COURTESY OF MR. PARKER TYLER

Left: Charles Henri Ford, co-author of *The Young and Evil* (Obelisk Press, 1933), England, 1933.
COURTESY OF MR. PARKER TYLER

lowed suit and turned back several large shipments. And in Paris there was more trouble. One of the local reviewers, Waverley Root, who had received a report on the joint work two years before, stirred up a brief and noisy debate by criticizing the authors for failing to show any understanding of homosexuals and how they live. Those looking for dirt will find it, Root warned, but it will be "very dull dirt" and certainly not new. "The authors have patched incoherently together all the well-known tags that are bandied coyly back and forth by the elfin voices of their fairyland, but if they have added anything original, I fail to find it." Enraged by such temerity (How could a mere journalist set himself up as a critic?) and furious at his fault-finding, the authors' friends rushed to defend the maligned book and repudiate the impudent attacker. Who understands Messrs. Ford and Tyler's work better, Richard Thoma and Bart Anderson demanded in a letter to the *Tribune*, Gertrude Stein, Bernard Faÿ, Djuna Barnes (whose words of praise appeared on the cover flap), Stuart Gilbert, Kay Boyle—or Waverley Root? And from New York, Parker Tyler recommended, softly, that what Root deserved was "simply an old-fashioned thrashing."

In addition to consolidating his reputation as a publisher of "serious" books, the other titles Kahane added to his list in 1933 practically assured the solvency of the Obelisk. *Boy* by James Hanley, *The Well of Loneliness* by Radclyffe Hall, and *My Life and Loves* by Frank Harris had all been ceremoniously banned in England and America. In spite of Richard Aldington's assertion that it had "poetic sensibility achieved by nobody since Lawrence," Hanley's book was charged with possessing pederast tendencies. Miss Hall's novel, although it had acquired battalions of literary, religious, and even medical defenders, had never been out of trouble since 1928 when it was first published in England and banned almost at once. That same year the Paris-based Pegasus Press, operated by C. Holroyd Reece, who also founded Albatross Books in Paris, a paperback reprint house that competed with Tauchnitz, took over the publication of Miss Hall's novel and printed several editions until Reece closed the Pegasus in the early thirties. Kahane grasped at *Well* "with joy," although he correctly guessed that there would be little profit in it and, in fact, after the franc fell the book lost money. Its controversial history alone, however, made it an almost obligatory addition to the Obelisk list. Though he admitted that "in a literary sense" the novel had certainly been overrated ("For all the masculinity of its spirit, its style is intensely feminine"), he nonetheless admired it as a courageous, "if long-winded," defense of a forbidden subject. Frank Harris' four-volume autobiography had had an even more calamitous history for the first ten years of its life. Forced to print the volumes privately at his own expense and to distribute them himself—assignments demanding the utmost ingenuity—Harris had just barely survived a decade as author-publisher. Besides seeing his profits drastically reduced by pirates whose clandestine editions of the books he was powerless to halt, he had watched, with alarm, the steady depletion of his capital, the decline of his reputation, the loss of his friends, and the erosion of his once-substantial reading public. Moreover, he lived under the constant threat of being prosecuted for obscenity. That charge in fact had been brought against him after the release of the second volume by a Nice court, presumably at the instigation of the British Embassy, but it was dropped on the recommendation of, among others, Henri Barbusse and Romain Rolland. By 1931, a weakened, dispirited, ailing Harris agreed to sell the publishing rights to Kahane, offering besides the four published volumes, a heretofore unmentioned fifth installment, which presumably he would be allowed to publish with the others. But Harris' death later the same year ruled out that possibility. (In 1958, Maurice Girodias published Harris' fifth volume, as well as the original four, after paying the author's widow one million francs.)

III

Henry Miller once said that one of the luckiest days of his life was the day he delivered the manuscript of *Tropic of Cancer* to the American literary agent William A. Bradley. Miller did not remember how he happened to meet Bradley, but since the agent was well known throughout the Quarter, any of Miller's acquaintances could have suggested his name. Anyway, sometime during the middle of 1932 the two men met. Miller left two typescripts with Bradley, a novel on which he had labored in the United States (*Crazy Cock*), and a new one he would call *Tropic of Cancer*, which he had written since returning to Paris in 1930. In August, Miller heard from Bradley. The agent had been through both books, and had found *Cancer* "magnificent." For another week he would be in Paris. Could Miller come again to his office? Across the bottom of Bradley's message, the author scribbled: "First good news about *Tropic of Cancer*."

It would not be the last good news Miller would receive about *Cancer*. Bradley wasted no time sending the manuscript to Kahane, who, with just a hint of trepidation, agreed to publish it. But Miller would spend the next two years impatiently waiting for his novel to appear. In fact, the period between the time Kahane accepted *Cancer* (October 1932) and when he finally published it (September 1934) outlasted the time Miller had spent writing it. Soon after his rearrival in Paris, Miller had met Michael Fraenkel, a better critic than he was poet or philosopher, who, along with other bits of advice, urged him to write more spontaneously, "red-hot," to let himself go and not try and write for the critics. After a year and a half of floating around Montparnasse, cadging meals and drinks and slowly finishing *Crazy Cock*, in which he had lost interest, Miller decided to take Fraenkel's advice. That was in August 1931. Letting it all go meant writing the way he felt, lived, and thought. "I start tomorrow on the Paris book: first person, uncensored, formless, fuck everything." What came out was a phantasmagoria of scenes and impressions and episodes, a synthesis of his experiences in Paris. In October, he sent Anais Nin a few pages of the new book, warning that they might displease her, but adding he did not care much whether they pleased or displeased, "since (for the time being) it gives me some joy or satisfaction." Displeased Miss Nin was not, and what followed was a long and fruitful collaboration. As Miller finished sections of *Cancer* he would send them to Miss Nin, inviting her comments and criticism. When she learned Miller had already finished *Crazy Cock* and had not been able to place it, she asked to see it, too, and later reported she thought the book might be "doctored" and "made publishable." Delighted, Miller invited her to prune it. "Even if only a hundred pages remain and they are good, why O. K. . . . Nothing but good can result. I can always trim down to French proportions. I think too I would agree with you on whatever you wanted to cut. And after you get through with it I believe I would have sufficient enthusiasm to make further revisions myself." Her offer brought a return invitation from him: "Perhaps I could reciprocate some time by doing the same for you." Miss Nin did not forget the offer.

Besides Anais Nin, Miller's other helpmates were all friends he had made in Paris: the young American lawyer-turned-banker, Richard Osborn, who sequestered him in his apartment during Miller's first winter in Paris; Alfred Perlès, with whom he lived for two years in Clichy, and who introduced his friend to the world by slipping Miller's writings into the Paris *Tribune* under his own by-line, for which Miller collected the few francs the newspaper paid, and on one happy occasion, a bouquet of compliments from Cyril Connolly, who, of course, mistakenly addressed his appreciation to Perlès; Samuel Putnam, the tireless, scholarly editor of

Right: Henry Miller, Paris, 1932.
PRINCETON UNIVERSITY LIBRARY,
SYLVIA BEACH COLLECTION

Below: Title page of *Black Spring*
by Henry Miller (Obelisk Press,
1936).
PRINCETON UNIVERSITY LIBRARY

BLACK SPRING

BY

HENRY MILLER

AUTHOR OF

TROPIC OF CANCER

THE OBELISK PRESS
16, PLACE VENDOME,
PARIS

the *New Review*, who printed Miller's first signed piece of writing done in Paris, an essay on Buñuel's then-controversial film *L'Age d'Or*, and later the oft-reprinted story, "Mlle Claude"; Wambly Bald, the *Tribune* staffer, who, in one of his columns, gave Miller the first publicity he ever received, and who unknowingly also supplied the raw sexual stuff he used in *Cancer* —rather fancifully, according to Bald, whom Miller immortalized as Van Norden; Walter Lowenfels, the poet, publisher, playwright, publicist, and occasional real-estate agent, whose claim to have been the one who introduced Miller to "modern" writing may well be disputed, but whose stimulation, Miller confided to Miss Nin, was like the irritation caused by the mucous membrane that creates the pearl in the oyster; and Michael Fraenkel, who, as the senior "death" ideologue of the group and the prod behind *Cancer*, did more than anyone else perhaps to integrate Miller's disparate creative energies and impulses and help him find the direction he lacked. All except Miss Nin turned up as characters in *Cancer*, the novel they had encouraged, supported, and defended.

When Miller went to see Bradley the agent told him that "only one man in the whole world" would dare publish his book—Kahane. That one existed was enough for Miller. Bradley forwarded the manuscript to Kahane, with "his cautious and non-committal blessing," and one weekend late in the summer of 1932 the publisher took it with him to the country. His description of that weekend, set down several years later, conveys all the intoxicating joy of making a long-delayed discovery. "I began it [*Cancer*] after luncheon in the shadow of the great copper beech tree . . . and the twilight was deepening into night when I finished it. 'At last!' I murmured to myself. I had read the most terrible, the most sordid, the most magnificent manuscript that had ever fallen into my hands; nothing I had yet received was comparable to it for the splendour of its writing, the fathomless depth of its despair, the savour of its portraiture, the boisterousness of its humour. Walking into the house I was exalted by the triumphant sensation of all explorers who have at last fallen upon the object of their years of search. I had in my hands a work of genius and it had been offered to me for publication."

For all his enthusiasm and gratitude, however, Kahane could not convince Servant that he had at last made the discovery he had been waiting for, that he had finally uncovered a "great literary piece of work." To the practical-minded Servant, "literary" connoted "obscurity and unsaleability." What people wanted, he instructed Kahane, was "a clever description of underclothes . . . with plenty of spicy references to their contents." Sex, "dressed up or in the gradual process of being undressed," had after all been the sine qua non of every book on the Obelisk list. Furthermore, *Tropic of Cancer* sounded like a medical treatise. Kahane could hardly find fault with Servant's objections. Contending that it was the "good book that paid" was hardly convincing, coming from the author of *Daffodil*. Nor could he ignore Servant's prediction that *Cancer* would be expensive to produce, that publishing it would involve a considerable risk, and that the market for the book hardly showed signs of improving. Furthermore, Servant went on, Miller was unknown and probably a "down-and-out Montparnasse reject" who would demand advances on royalties and make scenes because his book was not selling a thousand copies a week.

Hoping to confirm his own beliefs rather than contradict Servant's, Kahane asked his friend, Michael Bogouslawski, head of the foreign-books department in the huge Hachette firm, to read the manuscript and give him an opinion as soon as possible. Bogouslawski's report extinguished any doubts Servant's complaints might have sired. Miller was unquestionably "a powerful and formidable" writer, and *Cancer* made *Ulysses* and *Lady Chatterley* seem like lemonade. If he could be sure there would be no danger of prosecution, Hachette itself would publish a French edition of the book. Meanwhile, he advised Kahane to take every precaution with the first printing, and to avoid attracting attention and announcing himself as the publisher, he suggested that instead of the Obelisk colophon the words "Privately Printed" ought to be used on the title page and that Obelisk Press (in tiny letters) should appear on the next to the last page.

In October (1932) Kahane joined Bradley, now acting as Miller's agent, and the author to draw up an agreement, the principal contents of which Miller described to Miss Nin. "I agreed to the option on the next two books; Kahane seemed quite fair and his courage improves as he goes along. I don't remember the exact terms any more (too many figures!) but in substance I am to get $12\frac{1}{2}\%$ up to 5000 and 15% over 5000 copies on the next two books, plus an advance of $\frac{1}{2}$ the amount represented by the sales on the preceding books at time of acceptance. Is that clear?" As for the proceeds of an American sale, if any could be arranged, the figures were simply too confusing for Miller to remember.

It is a little ironic that he should have been satisfied with the explanation Kahane gave for putting off the publication of *Cancer* until after Christmas (it would "hardly make a good Xmas gift"), since, as he would soon learn, it was the first of many delays that postponed its appearance until September 1934, a period filled with increasing frustration for Miller and agonizing indecision for the publisher. That Kahane wanted to put *Cancer* over with a bang, without errors or fumbling, certainly not "sneaked over," as Joyce and Lawrence had been, was admirable. But Kahane's recommendation that Miller should establish himself as a "literary figure" by writing a second book on D. H. Lawrence was one Miller angrily dismissed as an impertinent attempt to direct his career, and, in retaliation, he launched against the publisher an attack that was originally intended to be a brochure to precede the publication of *Cancer*; rather than annoying Kahane, this only whetted his curiosity to learn more about his "new discovery." Disregarding the publisher's wishes as well as his intrusions, Miller drew up plans for a mammoth study of Lawrence, one which would absorb him for the rest of the decade and which he would finally abandon only after admitting to be hopelessly confused. At one point (February 1934) Miss Nin, fearing he was drowning in gigantism, suggested that he throw the "unessentials overboard . . . so things will become transparent." But neither her rescue efforts nor Miller's detailed sketches, plans, schemes, projects, and lists helped. Lawrence, he finally had to admit, was as full of contradictions as he. If the experience taught him anything, it was that, while he was a "writer of tales" and a "man who gets electrified by ideas," he was also one who could be derailed by them.

Being absorbed in the Lawrence book and in the new novel he had started, *Black Spring*, did little more than provide temporary relief from the anxiety over the delayed publication of *Cancer*. One year after he had signed the contract with Miller, Kahane complained that the printing business at the press (Servant's department) had been so overburdened that he had had no opportunity to go ahead with the book. Skeptical but also confident that the publisher had his best interests in mind, Miller reported to Miss Nin that everything seemed to be in order, that Kahane had assured him he would soon have his turn, and that when he had asked the publisher if he wanted to renege he had protested "quite positively," assuring him that, if necessary, they would both go to jail together. To Bradley, Kahane confirmed he had not brought *Cancer* out "within the contracted time" (that is, one year) and asked for a six-month extension (subject to Miller's approval), within which time he promised to publish the book; Bradley advised Miller to join him and allow the publisher the additional time. But six months later (March 1934), when there was still no sign of

Cancer, Miller again demanded an explanation. This time Kahane protested that as long as the world financial crisis lasted he could not publish any books; moreover, "his buying public" had "temporarily vanished." Satisfied that he was still being "reasonable, sympathetic, and sincere," and that his intentions were good, Miller bided his time, but not for long. For nearly two years, ever since signing the contract with Kahane, he had been tinkering with the text of *Cancer*. In mid-1934, he told Miss Nin he had gone over it again "with a fine comb" and had found it on the whole good. He had made "big alterations," cutting out "all the extraneous stuff," rewriting weaker sections, and accelerating the pace of the story, the latter problem one that both Bradley and Kahane had mentioned. The time to publish had arrived. "There's a time for everything—and this is the time!" Further delay, he feared, would make *Cancer* outdated.

Miss Nin, who had shared Miller's frustration from the start, agreed that the time had come to do something about publishing *Cancer*. Neither Bradley nor Kahane, in her opinion, had done all they could for Miller. Bradley, she believed, had lost interest in him, and Kahane had not only failed "in business" but also "in true loyalty." Convinced that the publisher had already made up his mind not to publish *Cancer* at all, or at least not to do it if doing so meant risking his own money, she went to see him, and, "full of courage and determination," delivered a "marvelous speech," which, since it included an offer to pay for the publication of Miller's book, successfully cleared the way for the long-awaited event at last. Her belief that that was the only argument strong enough to dispel his fear might explain her observation that Kahane saw Miller only as a pornographic writer.

The publication of *Cancer* in September 1934 coincided with Miller's return to the Villa Seurat, where, at Fraenkel's urging, he had started the novel four years before. It was a joyous occasion. He was moving into his first real home, an apartment Anais Nin had found and paid for, and he was at last the author of a published book, also thanks partly to Miss Nin. Kahane ceremoniously delivered one of the first copies of *Cancer*, on the jacket of which appeared a quote from Miss Nin's preface that left little doubt about its content.

> In a world grown paralyzed with introspection and constipated by delicate mental meals this brutal exposure of the substantial body comes as a vitalizing current of blood. The violence and obscenity are left unadulterated, as manifestation of the mystery and pain which ever accompanies the act of creation.

366

Elsewhere on the jacket readers learned that *Cancer* was "the first full-length work of an American writer of genius, comparable to Céline's *Journey to the End of the Night*. . . . In no work hitherto has been seen such an entire laying bare of body and spirit, such a remorseless description of thwarted appetites and unappeased desires." Directly beneath, printed in bold type, appeared this warning: *"Ce volume ne doit pas être exposé en vitrine"* (This book must not be displayed in the window), an admonition clearly intended for French rather than English or American booksellers. Alfred Perlès wryly noted that, in his efforts to assure that the appearance of *Cancer* would be a quiet affair, Kahane succeeded so well that "it almost seemed as if he didn't want to sell it at all." In fact, what he had rather disdainfully referred to as the "sneaky" publication of *Ulysses* and *Lady Chatterley* now seemed to be happening to *Cancer*. Not only had he followed Bogouslawski's advice to avoid all advance publicity, but he also appeared to be trying to keep the very existence of the book a secret. Oblivious to the concerns that kept his publisher on guard and eager to proclaim *Cancer* a reality at last, Miller launched a publicity and selling campaign intended to carry the news of his book far beyond Montparnasse. (In his memoir, Kahane, with a feeling of genuine thankfulness, recalled that Miller was the "most useful collaborator a book publisher ever had.") Even in the Quarter, however, where under-the-counter copies of *Cancer* could always be found, Miller's friends helped him publicize the event, and one of them, a café regular named Eve Adams, even went along the boulevards selling copies Miller had procured from Kahane at the author's rate. Soon after the book appeared, a friend at Brentano's told him he sold one or two copies a day, despite very slow business, and a bookseller named Tschann on the Boulevard Montparnasse, near the Dôme, tore off Kahane's warning and, to Miller's delight, actually put the book in the window. For awhile it was the only place in Paris where it could be seen. Miller also kept depositing circulars and announcements at various bookshops and circulating copies to critics and writers, whose comments, if complimentary, he later intended to print and circulate in England and America. A copy of *Cancer* sent to Ezra Pound brought a reply scrawled on two postcards: "Great deal more to the book than I thought when I wrote you yester/ after reading about 40 pages." Pound, however, seemed more interested in what Miller had said about money. "NEVERTHELESS, though you realize the force of money as destiny, the one question you haven't asked yourself is: What IS money? who makes it/ how does it get that way?" Pound's final question provided Miller with the subject as well as the title of an essay he would write in 1938. As for an American outlet for *Cancer*, Pound could only suggest *Esquire*. Katherine Anne Porter tersely praised the author's "gorgeous madness," which "only a very sane imagination" could produce. Though welcome, these and other accolades could hardly take the place of reviews and two months after publication none had appeared. In December, however, Miller ran into Marcel Duchamp, who promised to do what he could to place a review in a small French quarterly called *Orbes*. A few days later, a stranger called on Miller, introduced himself as Blaise Cendrars, and exuding a vitality and enthusiasm that left him awed, expatiated on Miller's connection to the "best [French] tradition" stemming from Rabelais. Before leaving, Cendrars promised to have *Cancer* translated into French, and his review of the book, the first to appear and as full of fervor as its author, promptly came out in the next issue of *Orbes*.

Having launched *Cancer* with the caveat that it was "strong meat [and] not meant for the unripe intelligence," Kahane spent the post-publication months in a state of unrelieved apprehension. He would recall later that the trade received *Cancer* with "cold hostility" and that wholesalers would have nothing to do with it. Bookshops that stocked the book handled it as though it were a "lump of gelignite." Reacting to every murmur as a possible danger signal, he cautiously began circulating copies to selected friends such as Hope Richardson, who agreed that while *Cancer* was "amazing," Kahane had probably "ruined" himself as a publisher. However, from the Countess Edith Gautier-Vignal (another "dear friend") came word that *Cancer* was "wonderful," and that her neighbor, Somerset Maugham, agreed completely. As he expected, general opinion was mixed and confused. "Some thought it great, some thought it vile; some thought it mortally dull, others wildly exciting."

Kahane did not publish another Miller book until *Black Spring* in May 1936, by which time Miller had either finished or was in the midst of completing several projects. With Michael Fraenkel (and for a short time with Alfred Perlès) he had started the Hamlet correspondence, he had finished sections of *Tropic of Capricorn*, and he had worked on several stories and essays Kahane would issue in 1938 under the title *Max and the White Phagocytes*. For his friend Perlès, ostensibly short of funds to finish a book, he wrote a "touching and humorous" pamphlet called *What Are You Going to Do About Alf*, in which he asked readers to send donations to his needy friend. Also, in 1935, he had begun corresponding with a young Englishman living in Greece named Lawrence Durrell, whose

Miller-inspired novel, *The Black Book,* he would soon preside over with the devotion of a foster parent.

Anaïs Nin was almost as productive as Miller. In the early thirties when he began showing her sections of *Cancer,* she had started sending him portions of a novel called *House of Incest* that contained strange, mysterious evocations of June Miller (the author's second wife), of her "unconscious self," as Miss Nin perceived it. Her beautiful language, the abstract, dream-like treatment of June, whom Miller had described so realistically in *Cancer,* and the amorphous structure of *Incest* he found disconcerting and at the same time fascinating. When Miss Nin explained what she was trying to do, Miller was convinced she was a surrealist (it was as far as he would go toward classifying her work) who was perhaps closer to realizing a "deeper intention, direction, a more determined attitude" than even the surrealists. When he learned she had been keeping a diary for several years that already numbered several volumes and had seen some sections, he suggested she show it to Bradley, whose report (the volumes were actually read by Bradley's wife Jenny, according to whom the volumes had already attained a towering five feet), while mostly positive, nonetheless left her unsettled. Ironically, it was his enthusiastic response to her "naiveté, charm, and depths" as well as his kindness and thoughtfulness that caused the disturbance. "Before such people as Bradley," she complained, "I begin to imagine that I am also a fake—that maybe all my journals, books, and personality are fakes. When I am admired I think I am duping the world." She sensed Bradley saw her as "a discovery" and that he intended to act as her advisor and director. When he sent a report to Miller there was more trouble. Out of the five-foot stack, he told Miller, perhaps two or three books might be extracted. Obviously the diaries would have to be drastically cut. Shocked, Miller sent the agent a searing reply. "You asked her to obliterate what there is of art in her work in order to reveal her personality. I simply don't follow you at all. . . . Let me tell you what I, an author, an impractical person, think ought to be done. I say after mature deliberation—*print the whole god-damned thing*! If there must be any alterations let it be in the nature of excision only, and that after great deliberation. You pick up one volume and find it fascinating. The next one you throw down in boredom and disgust. But you are an individual, not the public, not posterity. . . ." Tampering with the diaries would be like trying to excise Dante's cantos, a blasphemous and futile exercise. Bradley, wisely, returned the volumes to Miss Nin, and a short time later Miller announced that he would issue the first volume of the diaries himself under the title *Mon Journal*, in a limited edition of two hundred and fifty copies, for a hundred francs. A poor response to a subscription-blank mailing forced him to abandon the project, however. Despite the wrangling over the diaries, Bradley continued to advise Miss Nin. Regarding *The House of Incest*, he recommended she write out the big, obsessional theme, the love for her father, and reduce the "poetry," the stylization of the book. He urged her to be more egotistic, to live more for herself, and to live and write for herself. He complained that her "humanity" was her weakness. Though she sometimes seemed to resent Bradley's heavy slices of gratuitous advice, her response to him remained positive; he "was humorous, quick, and stubborn too."

While still working on *Incest*, in the last months of 1933 Miss Nin started a second novel she would call *Winter of Artifice*. Everything she wrote Miller read. He liked his portrait in *Winter*, and the "pictorial passages" of *Incest* inspired him to write a scenario which would begin, he told her, with a scene of a "gigantic fish bowl." *Scenario*, as it was called when published in 1935, started as a collaboration with Miss Nin— ("Henry would compose a scene, I another. We enlarge, expand, probe my sketchy material. He wants to pour into it his notes on a scenario. He would create the universe of the dream, I the details. He drags in cosmic symbology, and I the individual. We get intoxicated with our inventions.") —but before it was finished Miller had injected so many of his ideas and so much of his own language that it seemed, at least to her, to be close to "a parody of the original" (i.e., *Incest*). In February 1934, she completed *Winter of Artifice*, which Miller praised for its "depth and sincerity"; it was a "terribly human and more than human" book, and, more than any book he had ever read it "revealed woman, a feminine attitude." A year later, having also finished *Incest* with the help of Otto Rank, she approached Kahane and Fraenkel about having the two books published, and although in June Kahane agreed to bring out *Winter*, it did not appear until August 1939, and only then because Lawrence Durrell paid for its publication. *Incest*, presumably more difficult to place, became one of the books in a publishing enterprise founded by Miss Nin and supported by Fraenkel and Perlès. At the outset, her idea to start a press at Louveciennes was warmly received by her friends, but when Fraenkel nearly "appropriated" the project and threatened to dominate Louveciennes, she hastily transferred the headquarters to Villa Seurat. Perlès provided a name for the new press—Siana—Anaïs reversed, and Fraenkel, the publisher of the group, got out a list of books starting with Miller's *Scenario* and *Aller Retour* and Miss Nin's *House of Incest*, the latter mysteriously omitted from the first listing. *Aller Retour*, issued in a limited edition of 150 copies and, like *Scenario*, paid for out of royalties earned by *Cancer*, was Miller's account, cast in the form of a letter to Perlès, of a return visit he had made to America from December 1934 to May 1935. Only 140 pages, it was printed on thin India paper and sent to subscribers by first-class mail. *House of Incest* appeared in May 1936, nearly a year after *Aller Retour*. Fraenkel, in addition to lending the author funds for print-ing, had promised to take over the distribution, but he soon lost interest and did nothing about circulating it, leaving Miss Nin to do what little she could to distribute copies. Although there were no reviews, friendly letters like that from Stuart Gilbert offered some compensation. Gilbert likened her book to music: ". . . it is a symphony. And I love the irony. A unique use of language. Like Scriabin."

Black Spring, Miller's long-completed second novel, also appeared in May. Begun over a year before *Cancer* was published, *Black Spring*, or *Self-Portrait* as Miller called it up to the time of publication, had gone through several transformations before taking final form. Kahane thought it "better written" than *Cancer* but "less homogeneous." As he had done with *Cancer*, Miller showed the parts of *Black Spring* to Miss Nin, who recognized in their collaboration important mutual benefits, which she described in her diary entry for January 1933: "The first half of his novel [*Black Spring*] is all incident; the second is all ecstasy, rivers of poetry and surrealism issuing from the adventures, explorations, a fascinating completion. When I praise his writing for its power and explosiveness, he says he thinks the same of mine. A feminine revolution. We have much influence over each other's work, I on the artistry and insight, on the going beyond realism, he on the matter, substance, and vitality of mine. I have given him depth, and he gives me concreteness." She often accused him of being too uncritical of his work, however, too unwilling to "evaluate, or throw out" what was unnecessary. Later the same year she commented on the enormous task of "creative synthesis of his fragments," the "struggle for unity" in which Miller was constantly locked. As he neared the end of *Black Spring*, he informed her that he thought he could recapitulate the themes of the book in a dream sequence; the section became "Walking Up and Down in China." In March 1935, when he had written the "Burlesk" and the "City Man" sections, he still had not shown the manuscript to Kahane. Observing that Miller seemed filled with an obsession that he was writing in a void, that he was "like a rat caught in a trap," she tried to boost his spirits by pointing out that even D. H. Lawrence had seen his books burned. Apparently, however, her efforts failed to relieve his gloom, for later she recorded that he "cannot bear rejections, the silence of conventional publishers, formal rejection slips from magazines, obtuse comments of people." Sometime in mid-1935 Miller took his manuscript to Kahane. It was, indeed, a self-portrait: there was Miller the "patriot of the 14th Ward" in Brooklyn; Miller working in his father's tailor shop, Miller the painter; Miller the creator of hilarious caricatures of his Paris friends, and Miller the synthesizer of dreams. *Black Spring*, he wrote in 1952, "came nearer to being myself . . . than any book I have written before or since." He dedicated it to Miss Nin. Kahane, encouraged by unexpectedly brisk sales, published a second edition before the year ended. But the publisher was still unhappy. It was not that he objected to the enlargement of Miller's reputation, which he claimed had increased "by leaps and bounds" after the appearance of *Cancer* and *Aller Retour*. Rather it was that Miller was still unknown among the general public in England and America, partly because travel to Europe had declined. Furthermore, since France was still on the gold standard, everything had become terribly dear for both publisher and buyers, a fact which even Miller's rising reputation among the intelligentsia could hardly alter.

IV

As much as Kahane would have liked to improve the distribution of Obelisk publications, there was really very little he could do. Not only had Miller's books been banned in America and England, but the other titles on the Obelisk list had also run into trouble with postal authorities in both countries, and one new book, Wallace Smith's *Bessie Cotter*, had recently been prosecuted, too. Smith's book, which Kahane described as the "best story of a prostitute ever written in English," had actually been published in England by William Heinemann, but the London firm had been taken to court, found guilty of publishing obscenity, and fined. Kahane, who promptly took over publication, again wondered why reputable firms took risks when they knew the uncertainties of printing a book that might be construed as obscene. He himself found no harm in Smith's work; it was a "humorous and sentimental description of one of those houses that are not supposed to exist in England, and in its way and within its limits a little masterpiece."

Another book that might have run into trouble with British censors came to Kahane partly because Hanley's *Boy* and Smith's book had already caused such a stir. In England to confer with the daughter of Ralph Curtis about publishing the letters Henry James had written to her father, Kahane had been given Cyril Connolly's name as one who might undertake the job of editor. A visit was arranged, the two men discussed the project, but then abandoned plans when it was discarded for want of a publisher. Before Kahane returned to Paris, however, Connolly confided that he had written a "forbidden" book, which after having been accepted by one publisher and then rejected by the partners of that publisher, had been rejected again by a second firm on the grounds that it was too dangerous to be brought out of England. Kahane, whom Connolly remembered as a "charming and faintly Mephistophelean" man waging a "lonely guerrilla war against English prudery," offered to look over the persecuted book, and much to his pleasure found *Rock Pool* to be a "sweet piece of writing," the "work of an exquisite, steeped in the classics, and in certain ways a model of impropriety." (Kahane once jokingly complained that *Rock Pool* was so little salacious that it was "a disgrace to his list.") The book had a fault, however, a fault the author himself explained in the preface, a letter addressed to Peter Quennell. His narrative of a group of expatriates summering along the Riviera in the "raffish days of 1919" had certainly dated, because, as Connolly put it, the "life it deals with has almost disappeared." Like most first books *Rock Pool* had an account to settle with the past; Connolly's was in debt to the 1920s. In his hero, a "young man flying from the Hercules of modern civilization," he had tried to objectify a "certain set of English qualities, the last gasp, perhaps, of rentier exhaustion." The young man in flight bends over the "glassy pool of the Hamadryads" and is dragged to the bottom. Kahane agreed with the author that there was less interest in the decade just ended than he had expected, but nonetheless he drew comfort from being responsible for bringing out a work of "such wit and distinction." Lagging sales were a disappointment, however, and the only tangible return was a two-column review by Desmond MacCarthy in the *Sunday Times*, which, considering the paucity of reviews inspired by Obelisk publications, was probably the best kind of publicity the press could receive.

When France finally abandoned the gold standard in 1936, the sales of Obelisk books, as Kahane had predicted, went up; production, however, did not, and in the following year, the worst the press had yet had, Kahane issued only the minimal two titles, *Uncharted Seas* by Eric Ward, advertised as a full presentation of gynandrous love, and another Cecil

Barr epic called *Lady, Take Heed!* Perhaps it was the nadir itself that prompted the usually circumspect publisher to act. Always unhappy with the arrangement that bound him to the cautious Servant and more determined than ever to become an independent publisher, he suddenly bought the stocks of all the unsold Obelisk books, thereby relieving Servant of any liabilities, and capped his dramatic maneuver by moving into the plush offices recently vacated by the Paris branch of Curtis Brown, in the Place Vendôme, fashionably positioned between Morgan's and the Westminster Bank, opposite the Ritz, from where—and from the nearby Castiglione Bar as well—he would conduct his business for the next two years. It was in the Castiglione (where Kahane had arranged to have the Obelisk book list placed beneath the glass tabletops) that he met the author of the first book he would publish independently. Informed by a waiter (a whispered message) that a lady waiting in the bar wished to see him, Kahane presently found himself in the company of Princess Paul Troubetzkoy, who disclosed she had written a novel about a famous scandal that had shaken

Mrs. William Aspenwall Bradley, literary agent, Paris, 1960.
COURTESY OF MRS. WILLIAM ASPENWALL BRADLEY

London a year or so before "involving a murder or at least some form of homicide or suicide." Would he care to read it, she wondered? Gallantly, he replied that he would, noting later in his memoir that just as he had never refused to meet a lady so he had never refused to read a manuscript. Probably contrary to all his expectations, what the Princess had done surprised him. Quite brilliantly written, her story had enough authenticity to titillate readers into figuring out who the real-life characters were. Published under a title of Kahane's making, *Half O'clock in Mayfair*, it sold sufficiently well for Kahane to congratulate himself "on the assiduity of [his] visits" to the Castiglione. The publications that followed all seemed certain to be banned in England and America and thus to become slow but sure money-makers. First came *Through the Ark* by Olga Martin, an animal allegory depicting "moderns and their absurd illusions of life," followed by *Starborn* by "Arion," a study of homosexuality "unprecedented in the frankness of its naive confession"; *Love Counts Ten* by Theodor Zay, a Hungarian nobleman's description of the secret resorts of pleasure and vice in the Berlin underworld; and *Dark Refuge*, a "memorable novel" by Charles Beadle showing the "effect of hashish on the individual, its annihilation of all conventional taboos, social and sexual. A symphony of lusts and hates, fears and loves." Fortunately, before the year ended, besides the lascivious ones, Kahane brought out two books which enormously bolstered the Obelisk's reputation: one was Miller's *Max and the White Phagocytes*; the other, Lawrence Durrell's *The Black Book*.

V

In Henry Miller, Lawrence Durrell found a kindred spirit and a mentor with powerful and persuasive qualities. In Durrell's opinion the older writer's *Tropic of Cancer* (Durrell was twenty-three, Miller forty-three, when they began corresponding in 1935) was an epic-making book, one that turned a corner "into a new life" that had at last "regained its bowels." He believed Miller had outdone all his contemporaries, including Eliot and Joyce, in presenting the gutsy reality of life. "I salute *Tropic*," he wrote, "as the copy-book of my generation." Tributes like this could hardly be ignored. Miller replied at once and, in time, the exchange of letters between him and his admirer developed into an engrossing record of their writing activities. Ever-curious and encouraging and prodigal with ideas and suggestions as to how Durrell could best advance his career,

Miller learned in a short time that Durrell had been rereading a manuscript called *The Black Book* and marking "with a blue pencil" all the echoes to him. When he asked the author to send it to Paris, Durrell replied in the letter accompanying the manuscript that he had already published a novel under a pseudonym (Norton) called *The Pied Pipers of Lovers* ("A cheap romance, wishy-washy stuff. Sheer lochia"), adding that his contract with Faber and Faber included options on his next two books. He was certain, though, that the firm would never consent to publish *The Black Book*. His "little chronicle of the English death, done in a sort of hamstrung tempo, with bursts of applause here and there," he considered a "book Huxley could have written if he were a mixture of Lawrence and Shakespeare." It dated, he went on, "from that insomniac day when I felt a sort of malaise, and began to wonder if I would really be content as a bestselling novelist (once my ideal)." He advised Miller to "pitch it in the Seine" after reading it. Miller's response to *The Black Book* matched Durrell's reaction to *Tropic of Cancer*. "I read [*The Black Book*] goggle-eyed, with terror, admiration and amazement. I am still reading it—slowing up because I want to savor each morsel. . . . You are the master of the English language. Stupendous reaches, too grand almost for any book. . . . You have written things . . . which nobody has dared to write. It's brutal, obsessive, cruel, devastating, appalling. I'm bewildered still. So this is no criticism. . . . No, this is a salute to the master!" Of course Faber and Faber would never publish it, nor in his opinion would any other American or English firm. *The Black Book* would end Durrell's commercial career. An "outlaw," like him, he would have to find an outlaw publisher, and as far as Miller knew there was only one man who could do it: Jack Kahane. But persuading him to take it on might be a problem. It was almost a case of professional jealousy. Kahane had reacted spitefully to Durrell's admiration for the publisher's "star author," Miller explained, and had obdurately set himself against Durrell. He confessed that he might have been partly at fault by passing along Durrell's appreciation to Kahane, but with no one in sight who could possibly publish *The Black Book* (Fraenkel had to be discounted because of a lack of courage and initiative), he was prepared to do battle with the whimsical publisher. "I will wheedle and cajole and jig for him, if necessary, because I believe in it [*The Black Book*] wholeheartedly."

Miller and Durrell spent part of the six months before they met in Paris in September 1937 hatching a scheme to sell more copies of *Tropic of Cancer*. Mostly Durrell's idea, it involved printing a circular containing excerpts from letters Miller had received from admirers of his book. Aldington, Lewis, Campbell, Huxley, Shaw, Morgan were all names Durrell wanted to include in the anthology, as well as Stein, Joyce, Pound, and Williams. Miller replied that he had once tried to put together a collection of excerpts himself from reviews and letters and would go after more. Meanwhile, he sent Durrell copies of all those he and Kahane had received, noting that the ones from Stein and Pound were "absolutely imbecilic," as were the ones from Dos Passos, Dreiser, and Max Eastman. But he agreed the scheme was worth trying. Durrell's recommendation that additional review copies be sent to prospective contributors brought a warning from Miller that Kahane would more than likely bridle at sending out many free books, if only because he liked doing everything himself.

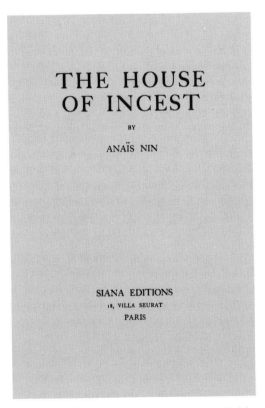

THE HOUSE
OF INCEST

BY

ANAÏS NIN

SIANA EDITIONS
18, VILLA SEURAT
PARIS

Title page of *House of Incest* by Anais Nin (Siana Editions, 1936).

What others advocated made him suspicious, and to get anything across to him required the support of several people. Unfortunately, that was the case with Durrell's book. With any other man, Miller continued, "I would already have sold your book—with him I have to proceed like a tortoise. I have to get other people to back up my opinion—for he is like a weather-cock and has no opinion of his own at all. I don't give him the least bit of credit for having published me. He was forced into it!" Durrell assured Miller that however many copies of *Cancer* he could wheedle out of Kahane would be husbanded and would go only to those from whom some statement of value could be expected.

Miller's next letter to Durrell contained a catalogue of good news. First, after a single whisky at the Castiglione, Kahane was "most eager to see . . . *The Black Book*," and Eliot (at Faber and Faber) was also "waiting impatiently for it." Miller had already had copies made in Paris (Durrell had sent him his only copy) and would forward one to Eliot. He also reported that Kahane was "vitally interested" in the scheme to adver-tise *Cancer* and had promised to print the testimonials in brochure form and distribute them gratis. And for the second time *Cancer* was on display in Paris. Brentano's ("still very conservative") had begun to put copies on view, which, for Miller, was "a big step forward."

Shortly before arriving in Paris, Durrell heard from Faber and Faber, who, to his surprise, had liked his book and wanted to publish it if he would consent to do "an altered edition" for England. Without consulting Miller, he agreed, so long as it would not block later publication of an expurgated edition in Paris. Obviously uncomfortable about the situation, however, he tried to explain his decision to Miller. The British and Amer-ican editions, he contended, "would contain enough jewelry to give the Paris edition *réclame* and movement," assuming Kahane would agree to give up exclusive rights to the book and put out the unexpurgated edition anyway. If, however, Kahane refused to settle for the unexpurgated book, then he hoped Miller would see it was better "to castrate for Faber and wait until [he had] money enough to do the full version." The real bind, of course, was trying to figure out what would happen if he refused Faber and then found that Kahane refused him, too. "I'll be left with my first real book on my hands. No money. No edition. Nowt." In his reply, Miller not only solved the author's dilemma, he lectured Durrell on the meaning of integrity and success. Faber's plan was a "pis aller," he began, an offer that demanded conformity, and one certain to end with his being "fucked good and proper." As soon as Durrell said no to that plan he would find someone to sponsor him, maybe even Kahane the "weather-cock," who, allowing for a certain stubbornness in his nature, might eventually decide to publish the book and "blow you to the skies, because a few others have seen merit in your work. One never knows with such guys." Meanwhile, his problem was an affair with his conscience. "On that grain of faith on which you built your book you must rest. You stand firm and let the world come round. No, it won't be Faber's and so on, but always someone, something unexpected, something from the blue. It may even be me! In other words [Miller concluded], forgive my advice, but I would say you can't look two ways. You've got to accept the responsibility for your actions." When Durrell reached Paris Kahane was still reading *The Black Book*. He would give his answer as soon as he could, and he also understood that Faber would not publish the book in its present form. Thus, if he decided to do it, there would be no possibility that Faber would come out with an unexpurgated edition.

VI

Henry Miller remembered that Durrell's appearance in the Villa Seurat circle was "truly sensational," He was "electrifying [and] only too eager to throw himself into what he thought was the 'decadent' life of Paris." Instead of debauchery, however, he found a "world of Rabelaisian jollity . . . an endless three-ring circus," one of the funniest acts of which had to be the shenanigans inspired by the unexpected bequeathing to Alfred Perlès of a staid house organ, colorlessly named *The Booster*, which he had lackadaisically edited for the American Country Club of France, and which the manager, after firing him, had decided to award "as a parting gift." As long as Perlès ran "a couple of pages of club news," it was his to do with as he wished. He even innocently suggested Perlès might get his "writer friends" to contribute and turn *The Booster* into "something really good." That he might have had in mind letting Henry Miller "go haywire" in the pages of the magazine would have filled him with horror. What Perlès and Miller saw was a second opportunity to run a little magazine "into the ground" (their first attempt, the intended victim Putnam's *New Review*, had miscarried) and to make a "spot of literary history while doing so." Administered by a protean staff headed by Perlès as managing editor, Miller, Durrell, and William Saroyan as literary editors, Anaïs Nin as society editor, Nancy Myers, Durrell's wife, as art editor, Michael Fraenkel as chief of the Department of Metaphysics and

379

Metempsychosis, and Walter Lowenfels as head of Butter News (Lowenfels forsook the family butter business to become a poet), the first *Booster* appeared in September 1937. The transformation from country-club sheet to dadaist anthology was breathtaking. In an "*étalage* of pernicious sentiments," the editors vowed to eschew all "fixed policies" as well as politics and to be "eclectic, flexible, alive . . . fluid, quixotic, unprincipled." Even the noisy rumblings of war did nothing to extinguish the belief that they were living in the "Golden Age," golden since it was the only one they would ever know and intended to make the most of it. After all, they wrote, "The world is what it is and not what we like it to be." The next five issues would confirm that they intended to fulfill their vows. But a contribution in the second number (Perlès' former employer had actually praised the maiden issue, his only complaint being about a certain directionlessness) brought the tenuous alliance between the American Country Club manager and the new administration of *The Booster* to a sudden and disagreeable end. It was Durrell's little story, an Eskimo legend recounting the blissful disappearance of an old bachelor inside a beautiful girl during the sexual act and the expelling of the old man's skeleton by the girl days later, that outraged the Club's manager, who, besides condemning the issue as "repugnantly filthy and pornographic," threatened the editors with legal actions if they did not immediately drop the *Booster* name. Money difficulties rather than the threat of "judiciary pursuits" delayed the publication of the third number, still called *The Booster*, but beginning with the fourth the magazine was rechristened the *Delta*, the first issue of which (April 1938), edited mainly by Durrell, was devoted entirely to poetry and included works by Dylan Thomas, Kay Boyle, Roger Burford, David Gascoyne, Nicholas Moore, Fraenkel, and, of course, Durrell. The "best number," according to Perlès, came next, around Christmas 1938, and was appropriately called "Special Peace and Dismemberment Number with Jitterbug-Shag Requiem," and featured excerpts from Miller's soon-to-be-published *Tropic of Capricorn* and Miss Nin's *Winter of Artifice*, also then close to publication, as well as contributions by Dylan Thomas ("Prologue to an Adventure"), Antonia White ("The House of Clouds"), and Durrell, who wrote an appraisal of the still unpublished Miller-Fraenkel correspondence, *Hamlet*. The last *Delta* appeared shortly before the outbreak of war, its size emaciated by lack of money and the general malaise of the time.

What had been facetiously undertaken in the case of *The Booster* was seriously formalized in the creation of the Villa Seurat Series. Organized by Miller and the Durrells as an adjunct of the Obelisk Press, the Series was intended to supply Kahane with new books of their choosing—as well as the money with which to print them—in exchange for the distribution and circulation facilities at his disposal. By the end of the year (1937) Kahane had told Durrell that he would publish his book, but he had also asked the author to pay the printing costs, which Durrell agreed to do not only for his own book but for Miller's *Max and the White Phagocytes* and Miss Nin's *Winter of Artifice* as well. Kahane, who later usurped credit for starting the Villa Seurat Series, was delighted when Miller agreed to serve as editor. He was certain that under Miller's direction manuscripts would flow in, and he generously prophesied the Series would play an "important part in the literary history of our time." With the Durrells in England collecting contributions for *The Booster* and reacquainting themselves with London literati, Miller settled down to his new editorial duties. The Villa Seurat Series, he announced, had been "formed in answer to a contemporary demand for greater freedom of expression in literature," a demand more strongly felt by the author than by the public. The Series would search for the one book every writer wants to write, that is, the book "nobody understands," which no "publisher wants to print," the "hypothetical book . . . your writer never writes, because there would be nothing left to do with it when written—except perhaps burn it." The Villa Seurat Series was "the only home in the world for such a production. Its interest is not in the merely unprintable book, but in the unwritable book . . . and . . . for those authors whose work does not derive from, or cater to, the commercial standards of the day it exists as an incentive to write the books which lie on the side of the precipice." In January he sent Kahane's contract for *The Black Book* to Durrell, noting that all seemed in order, and only getting the money to Kahane remained to be done. He also mentioned he had sent Kahane a prospectus for Durrell's book. As for proofreading and any last-minute alterations (Durrell had already made "nearly a hundred excisions" which reduced the typescript only a dozen pages), Miller recommended that the author ought to have the last word.

The summer and fall of 1938 were crammed with frustrations and a few unexpected joys for Miller and his Villa Seurat associates, Anais Nin and Alfred Perlès, to whom, with the Durrells now once more in Greece, fell the editing chores and other tasks related to the publication of *The Black Book*. In May, Miller reported to Durrell that they had reread the proofs of his book for the third time and that it was "still not right." The writing, however, sounded "swell," even in proof. He assured him Kahane would take the book away from the printer if he had any more trouble with proofs. The good news was that Kahane had received "more and more" orders for the Series. Miller wrote again in late June to say that Kahane and he had had "a devil of a time" with the printer and that he (Miller) had had to make changes in the text. But despite the delay he still expected to have the book out in July, ahead of *Max*, the first proofs of which he was just starting to read. He had gone over *The Black Book* for the sixth and final time ("still magnificent") and, regrettably, several pages had to be reset. Durrell, it seemed, had had the misfortune to have the "worst printer." For Miller's troubles, Durrell had only condolences: "I feel so bad about all the trouble over *The Black Book*; I feel it really should be dedicated to you. You have done everything for it, except actually write it." In August, after publication, Miller wondered if Durrell had received copies of his book, and added that he had just finished *Capricorn*; in another letter posted a month later, he told Durrell he was leaving Paris for a vacation, and had packed up all his belongings and turned the manuscript of *Capricorn* over to Kahane to "put in the vault of his bank." For months after the publication of *The Black Book* Miller apologized for the faulty workmanship. Some pages had been misarranged, and Kahane, he told Durrell, had decided to print an errata slip to be inserted in outstanding copies. It was all the printer's fault, not his, and not Kahane's. "I would a thousand times rather that your book had had the workmanship of the *Max* book [*Max* had been printed in Bruges by the St. Catherine Press]—I flushed when I saw my book. I never wanted this, and told Kahane so. I told him the preference should go to yours. But I can't make any headway with him. He's a fish, that's all I can say. Since I have no other prospect of being published elsewhere, I tolerate him." Still, in spite of the disappointments, he repeated his earlier prediction that *The Black Book* was "going to be recognized" and would make Durrell's reputation.

With *The Black Book* and *Max and the White Phagocytes* behind him, Miller turned to the neglected Hamlet correspondence with Fraenkel, which he hoped Kahane would publish, and to another scenario tentatively named "The Sleeping Sleeper Asleep," and, when he could manage, to the rather dusty Lawrence study, still unfinished. At the same time *Capricorn* and *Winter of Artifice* had to be readied for publication. In January (1939) he and Miss Nin were poring over the proofs of their books, and the same month Kahane arranged to have *Capricorn* printed in

Bruges by the same firm that had done *Max* and for the same price: eleven thousand francs. The cover design Kahane had ordered for *Capricorn*—an astrological sun and a Neptunian goat—"was just what he would have asked for," Miller informed Durrell. The book was ready in April, and, disappointingly, it contained so many errors that Kahane would again have to draw up an errata slip. He confided to Durrell that *Capricorn* would not sell any better than *Cancer* or *The Black Book*, both of which, as well as *Max*, were moving slowly. It would therefore be foolish for Durrell to expect any payment from Kahane. Their only hope, Miller thought, now that the ban had been lifted from both books, lay in an American sale, maybe through the Gotham Book Mart. As for Durrell's suggestion that they consider reorganizing their business and look around for another publisher—a change so drastic was nearly useless. "Business," Durrell had to understand, was at a "standstill. . . . People are not buying, nor living, just holding their breath for the expected catastrophe." The only man they could appeal to was Kahane, and Miller had accepted him "as one accepts the cross. . . . He symbolizes the world for me, and in a way, I think it is better it is concentrated thus in one individual. When the world at large gets their grappling hooks into us it's going to be hell to pay. We are tolerated now, because we are unknown. . . . I have had many a talk with Kahane, good and bad ones, and I see into the whole situation quite realistically, I think. You couldn't do much better yourself. His way, which is the cunning English way of watching and waiting and nibbling off a piece here and there, is perhaps the only way in these times."

The demise of the Obelisk Press was foreshadowed, first, in the scattering of the people around Miller, and then in Miller's own departure from France. Nervous and restless after months of tedious work as editor of the Seurat Series and worn down by the frustrating labors connected with the publication of *Capricorn*, he suddenly left Paris early in the summer of 1939 on a long-delayed trip to Greece, to Corfu, to visit the Durrells. Perlès had already relocated in London, Lowenfels had returned to the United States and was editing a political newspaper, Fraenkel had moved to Mexico, where he was preparing to publish the Hamlet correspondence. Only Anaïs Nin remained in Paris. Miller had just reached Corfu when a copy of *Winter of Artifice* arrived. He at once wrote to Miss Nin to report how delighted he and the Durrells were with the book, the last in the Seurat Series and the last Obelisk publication, and that the response she had received, especially from Rebecca West, augured well for the future. He guessed that Americans, critics, that is, would like it too, and if so, the Series "will have had a 100 percent success in time." A few days later he sent her a more personal estimate of *Winter*, saying that what seemed to move and affect people was its "humanness." Everyone, he went on, "finds it so—and discovers too that you are a great personality. That the women, especially, should think thus is a great tribute to you. They find it rich and varied—but above all, true, precise, definite, penetrating. And unique!"

Perhaps because he had a premonition of his own perishability, or perhaps because he thought the time had arrived to set down the story of the Obelisk Press, Kahane devoted the few remaining months of peace—and of his life—to writing his autobiography. In addition to the Miller and Nin novels, he had seen one other book through the press in 1939, Sheila Cousins' *To Beg I Am Ashamed*, still another that an "old and respected firm" had announced for publication and had withdrawn after it had been attacked by a "couple of popular dailies temporarily short of head-line subjects." As with other unfortunate books of the same kind, hers "was a great success," with orders pouring into Paris from all over, and it had gone into an eighth printing just before the press closed, at which time three titles, all scheduled for release in the spring of 1940, remained on the publisher's list. Two days after the war that had threatened Europe for so long at last erupted, on September 3, Jack Kahane was found dead, stricken, as his son Maurice Girodias wrote, "by the sheer horror of it all." The same month, William Aspenwall Bradley, the agent who brought Kahane his "greatest writer" and his "pet genius," also died. The Obelisk had fallen.

Appendix 1

The Seizin Press*
HUGH FORD

THE Seizin Press began life with the lively conjunction of writers intent upon learning the art of hand-printing and an experienced instructor willing to teach them. The writers in this case were Laura Riding and Robert Graves, and the instructor of the novice printers was Vyvyan Richards, himself a press owner who had just produced an edition of Caxton's *Prologues and Epilogues*—the year was 1927—and who at one time had planned to print books with his friend and fellow undergraduate at Oxford, T. E. Lawrence. Though probably not to be included among the small company of fine printers working at the time, Richards was nevertheless a knowledgeable and skilful craftsman and teacher, and after a few instructions the Seizin partners, who had had no previous experience in hand-printing, managed to proceed unaided, gaining in competence and confidence with practice. Richards also advised them as to a source for suitable paper, and as to the matter of type. It has been said that the partners bought their large Crown Albion press (1872)—which they used from the start and later had crated and shipped to them after they had made Majorca their working-ground—directly from Richards. But there seems to be a difference of recollections on this matter; one of the former

---

385

partners[1] has clear recollections of the inspection of an available press, at Richards' recommendation, in the "printers' section" of London, and has in retrospect assumed this to be the press that was installed in the second-story room overlooking St. Peter's Square, number 35a, in Hammersmith, which was to be the press's home for the next two years. That dependable machine was of a model that served more than a few apprentice printers.

Selected to be Seizin One (all subsequent hand-printed Seizin books bore a number) was Laura Riding's *Love as Love, Death as Death*, the author's first book of poetic work published since *The Close Chaplet*, and *Voltaire*, a slight-sized production (a long poem, biographical, in a frame-work of fantasy). A supply of Batchelor hand-made paper had been procured. Their type, until printing activities were shifted to Majorca, was procured from a Monotype firm: that is, the lines were set up in Mono-type by the firm according to supplied text; the partners altered the com-position as judgment suggested, with the help of an extra stock of type. (After the shift to Majorca, a permanent stock of type was acquired, all the composition being done there. The fount used both in England and in Majorca was, uniformly, of Caslon type.)

One can imagine these new-made printers going to work at their first book. What work it was! Besides the readying of the type for page-produc-tion, there was the difficult and demanding procedure of dampening the paper to just the right point of saturation so as to obtain a uniform impression on each printed page—no easy accomplishment for even the most experienced printer. Scrap sheets, always ready at hand, served for trial-run purposes—one thinks of these beginners as perfectionist in their attitude. Despite the imaginable disappointments, setbacks and re-runs however, Seizin One steadily took shape. The partners pulled sheets for an edition of 175 copies, which attained the rather considerable length of 64 pages, making *Love as Love, Death as Death* the longest book Seizin published in its hand-printing career, and somewhat longer than the aver-age private press publication. Arrangements were made with a London firm for binding the pages in linen buckram, a choice that pleased the author, and was repeated with other books.[2] The complete edition (signed

---

[1] That partner is Laura (Riding) Jackson, for whose patient and generous assistance in the preparation of this report on the Seizin Press the author extends sincere and lasting gratitude.

[2] The title page bore a line-formation design, originating with the author, "an illus-tration of certain relation-principles." (Letter: January 19, 1972, Mrs. Jackson to the author.)

by the author) was placed on sale at 11s. 6d; a London bookseller named Bain undertook to stock and distribute the publications of the new press.

In 1929 Will Ransom (that observant and conscientious historian of little presses), writing on the Press, cited its policy "to print necessary books by various particular people." In addition—and here Ransom quoted from an early announcement or prospectus—Seizin editions were "decidedly not addressed to collectors but to those interested in work rather than printing—of a certain quality. That is as far in prophecy as we care at the moment to go. You must take our word for it that our reticence is due to something more than an uncertainty of standards. Quite the contrary."[3] Since it was made clear that content would be valued above the niceties of fine printing—though, as it proved, this was never to be to the point of tolerating avoidable imperfections—the selections from the Seizin partners' own work as well as those from "various particular people" would have to meet the criteria the Press intended to uphold. And, while the prospectus statement denied that "reticence" implied uncertainty in critical standards, it nevertheless withheld instruction as to the nature of those standards. However, for any whose acquaintance with the partners' work extended from their first publications, probably some notion of Seizin's purpose was immediately grasped; for there were controlling ideas which guided the partners in selecting all Seizin publications.

A clue to the spirit of Seizin Press aims may be found in the Preface to Miss Riding's *Collected Poems*, published eleven years after the publication of *Love as Love, Death as Death*. Her poems, she explained, formed "a record of how . . . existence in poetry becomes more real than existence in time—more real because more good, more good because more true." Identifying "the good existence" with poetry, she continued: "Literally I mean: our own proper immediacies are positive incidents in the good existence which is poetry. To live in, by, for the reasons of, poems is to habituate oneself to the good existence. When we are so continuously habituated that there is no temporal interruption between one poetic incident (poem) and another, then we have not merely poems —we have poetry: we have not merely the immediacies—we have finality. Literally."[4] An early vision of possibilities of going beyond the merely

---

[3] Will Ransom. *Private Presses and Their Books*, New York, Philip Duschnes, 1963, p. 182. For other accounts of the Press, *see* James Moran, "The Seizin Press of Laura Riding and Robert Graves," *The Black Art*, vol. 2, 1963, pp. 34–39; Roderick Cave, *The Private Press*, New York, Watson-Guptill, 1971.

[4] Laura Riding. *Collected Poems*, New York, Random House, 1938, xxvi–xxvii.

LOVE AS LOVE,
DEATH AS DEATH

BY

LAURA RIDING

Printed and published at The Seizin Press
Hammersmith London 1928

Title page of *Love as Love, Death as Death* by Laura Riding
(Seizin Press, 1928).

literary in expressiveness entered into the founding ideas of the Press. She describes her contribution to them as the conception that objectives in writing should transcend the boundaries of "literary objectives as traditionally, and also modernistically, understood," and that standards of a "goodness exceeding literary notions of goodness" should be the critical guide.[5]

What Miss Riding has written in the past on linguistic standards, and what she has responded to my consulting her in the course of my preparation of this account of the Seizin Press, helps to clarify its peculiar char-

---

[5] Letter: October 9, 1971, Mrs. Jackson to the author. The English edition of *Collected Poems* was published in the same year by Cassell and Company, and like the American edition, carried the notice that it had been published "by arrangement with the Seizin Press."

acter as a little press of the period; its orientation was not to a kind or kinds of writers, but to questions of word-use—the kind of use writers made of words. I find the intense editorial concern with verbal proprieties evident in everything that bore the Seizin imprint brought to mind by a description of her poetic work by Miss Riding (now Mrs. Jackson) and her late husband (Schuyler B. Jackson), quoted in a publication of 1970, in which emphasis is on the impediments to the perfect realization of truth—to linguistic perfection—that she eventually decided were irremovably present in poetry. "Her objective in poetry may be said to have gone beyond the poetic as a literary category and reached into the field of the general human ideal in speaking. . . . She tried to find in poetry the key to a way of speaking that would realize this spiritual ideal . . . looking to an eventual solution in poetry of the universal problem of how to make words fulfil the human being and the human being fulfil words."[6]

Seizin Two, *An Acquaintance with Description* by Gertrude Stein, would perhaps seem a random choice, one not especially reflective of the standards or tastes of the young Press, sharply selective by critical policy. Speaking of her own attitude of that time, and later, to Gertrude Stein and her writing, Miss Riding has said that, despite there being strong differences between Gertrude Stein's and her own conceptions of the functions of language and "the spiritual significances of humanness," and an awareness in her of a destructive purpose in Gertrude Stein's use of words (to have language on the page and yet nothingness), she read into this wordplay a therapeutic intention and potential. She says, quoting from unpublished reflections on Gertrude Stein, "Something of her personal pathos came through—literarily and in personal contact: she wanted to be successfully human, and yet, oh, so much, successfully, pragmatically, a creature of her time." I reproduce some further related comment as of special interest here as a view of Gertrude Stein and the time retrospectively associated with the Press. Miss Riding describes the implied paradox as being in the inhuman fascination with the disintegrative "that became ascendant in the world of art and literature of the time, in which Gertrude Stein sought to be (according to Miss Riding's estimate) a rallying point at the center of its incoherences." But she holds that, whatever one may think of Gertrude Stein's peculiar human and literary and artistic position as manifested in her work, one must allow that there was expended in it a forceful and dogged will to record exactly how words took

---

[6] Laura Riding. *Selected Poems: in Five Sets*, London, Faber & Faber, 1970, p. 15.

their way in her mind, as she let them, so far as possible, take their way there. *An Acquaintance with Description*, is, indeed, a very clear example of this procedure: the Press can be seen to be paying respect to an effort of extraordinary sustainedness, in which words were the subjects of attention.[7]

An Acquaintance with Description, also set by Monotype, assumed a more "commercial" look than Seizin One. The format remained the same —demy octavo—and the covers were again plain. The title, the author's name, and Seizin appeared in gold lettering on the spine. A small piece of paper stating that the book had been "printed and published at Seizin Press in an edition of 225 numbered copies" and bearing the signature of Gertrude Stein was pasted in opposite the title page.[8] These announcements had been sent to Paris for Miss Stein's signature and then returned for insertion. Seizin Two, a small, handsome volume of fifty pages, went on sale in 1929 for 11s. 6d.

How many acquainted with Seizin Press must have puzzled over its name! Obviously, the point of the name must be presumed not to be contained within the narrow boundaries of the legal sense—which the dictionaries provide—of possession of landed estate by due title. A full explanation has been provided by Miss Riding, who found the name for the Press. The notion of possession was central in her mind as the problem of finding a name for the Press presented itself, but not merely in connection with the fact of ownership of the instrument of a new activity —that of actually printing books—and identification with that activity; attitudes and ideas on a befitting spirit of possession were involved, though not in explicit form. Relevant to this theme is what she wrote on it in *The World and Ourselves* (1938), enunciating what might be described as a morality of possession. "It is a general good effect of life to be able to possess things which are one's very own by their difference from what others would want to possess; and to have the power to care for them so well that one can feel a free agent of control over the domain of one's possessions. . . ."[9] She associated possession and the consequence of proprietory devotion with the principle of hospitality as a new (potential) dynamics of general human behavior, extending from the field of personal

---

[7] Letter: October 10, 1971, Mrs. Jackson to the author.
[8] A small design by Len Lye adorned the title page.
[9] Laura Riding. *The World and Ourselves*, London, Chatto & Windus, 1938, p. 377.

possession. One may, hence, read back into the launching of the Press with "Seizin" for its name a spirit of moral resolve to use it well.[10]

Only one additional Seizin publication appeared before the Press ceased to be domiciled in England. This was Robert Graves' *Poems 1929*, a short (the shortest thus far) collection of 34 pages, issued in the by now customary edition of 225 copies, put on sale at 8s. 6d.

The year held personal circumstances for both partners that inclined them towards a choice of a new seat of activity; and the decision to seek one climaxed, besides personal wishes, a trend towards finalistic thinking to be noted in Miss Riding's work up to this time, and found reflected in opinions and attitudes in Mr. Graves' writing (in emphatic personal strokes in his autobiographical *Goodbye to All That*, which was written before the move from England and published after it). After some prospecting, the partners chose the Spanish island of Majorca as their working-ground. With 1930 a new period of the Press' existence began.

For a number of years, the Press retained the simple identity and limited publication programs characteristic of the London period. In both periods, the submitted manuscript was a rarity. After a time, in the Spanish period, with a broadening of writing activities, which culminated in the critical miscellany *Epilogue*, of which Miss Riding was editor and Mr. Graves the associate editor, the Press underwent a transformation, or rather, from being a "private press," it became a nucleus of plans for the publication, on a larger scale, under commercial conditions, of work of size and varied kind, that might exhibit a common bond in the temper of the writing; in this enlarged course there was intimate editorial presence to every production. The name "Seizin Press" itself came gradually to have a public identity suggestive of the critical values embodied in *Epilogue*; the imprint was combined with that of Constable & Company Ltd. on all books of this later Seizin regime.

In the period of expanded publishing activities in which the name Seizin signified editorial sponsorship rather than direct printing and publishing processes, almost all the books published that bore the name, apart from those of Miss Riding's and Mr. Graves' authorship, came to be

---

[10] Mrs. Jackson, who kindly discussed the origins of the Press's name and the thinking behind it, noted that, while all the later ideas could not have been specifically in her mind at the time the name was fixed upon, "its connotations were generally benign." (In its association, she means, with the anticipated character of the future Press.) Letter: July 24, 1969, Mrs. Jackson to the author.

chosen in consequence of relations with writers centered in the preparation of the make-up of *Epilogue*—of which three volumes were published (1935, 1936, 1937). All contributions to that were by co-operative arrangement between the editor and the writers, with the editor participating variously, both in plan and execution, as the governing policy of coherence in thematic concerns and in standards of writing made appropriate.

Epilogue provides suggestions of the atmosphere in which the later Seizin Press functioned. It had the subtitle, for the three volumes, "A Critical Summary," and the sense of the title and the subtitle was that the time had come for a new critical orientation, a post-historical re-evaluation of human experience, a new finality in the definition of values. The editor declared in her preliminary remarks in the first volume that the time brought within the compass of living understanding "a final law of relation . . . a law in immediate effect . . . We affirm a consciousness of the immediate effectiveness of value, as the consciousness of an event. And our purpose is to create in others a cognizance . . . of this event; to release it to all its implication. . . ."[11] There is to be seen here a thought-development that "gathered together all the various aspects of that concern with objectives transcending the literary" to which I have already made reference.[12] Miss Riding's *The World and Ourselves* was described by her in an introductory note—this being the fourth *Epilogue*. "I have thought it important . . . to suspend the work of general criticism begun in the first three volumes, and to make a special inquiry into the state of the world today in relation to ourselves."[13] An *Epilogue V* was forecast but it never appeared.

The first Seizin of the Spanish period, which was number Four, had for author a New Zealand friend of the partners, Len Lye, who was working to develop forms, patterns of arrangements, structures of experimental make-up, for a primitivistic alternative to the visual experiences afforded by conventional art, and conventional film. The book was called *No Trouble*. It was made up of a group of personal letters, addressed to various people, written in a style that was an informal verbal version of his technique of construction in the visual field, the words being arranged

---

[11] Laura Riding. "Preliminaries," *Epilogue I*, Seizin Press, 1938.
[12] Letter: June 23, 1969, Mrs. Jackson to the author.
[13] Laura Riding. *The World and Ourselves*, London, Chatto & Windus, 1938, a quotation from an announcement on forepage left-hand to title page of book. The fourth *Epilogue* did not bear the name "Seizin." It was published by Chatto & Windus.

for stimulating effects. Seeing some of his letters, Miss Riding thought there was in them, in their energetic simplicity, and their writer's refusal to let the intricacies of language stop him from saying *something*, proper material for a Seizin; this being decided on, she began working editorially, with Mr. Lye's co-operation, on the forming of a book of selected letters, aiming at the least revision "consistent with comprehensibility."[14] There was in Len Lye himself an instinctive sympathy with the devotion to chosen standards that was a strong component of the Press' critical atmosphere. In the sense that both books were uncompromisingly what they were, neither deviating anywhere from the adopted compositional "line," *No Trouble* was not a strange successor to *An Acquaintance with Description*. But it had a very different personal character; for one thing, it produced excitements, and there was evident excitement in the writing. As Miss Riding has expressed it, "There was a greatly appealing, lovable, good-feeling freedom in his letters."[15] Among the titles of the letters are "Linger Longer Laura," "Fried Eggs and Friends," "Mixed Drinks," "Lumpy Words," "Tusalava," "In Grim Determination." The latter two are longer pieces; in them there are glimpses to be had of Len Lye's work and thinking of the time, his absorption in film-making, and generally in the experimental treatment of shapes and forms.

Len Lye fashioned the cover designs of several Seizin Press books, that for his own *No Trouble* being the first.[16] He also created those for two books of Miss Riding's and a book of Mr. Graves' published by the Hours Press.[17] His designs combined strength and delicacy in the use of imagined forms, drawn, or of concrete forms of miscellaneous sort, collected oddments, things of natural origin, arranged into a "construction"

---

[14] Letters: June 23, 1969; October 23, 1971, Mrs. Jackson to the author.

[15] Letters: June 23, 1969; October 23, 1971, Mrs. Jackson to the author.

[16] One other who contributed to the physical appearance of Seizin publications has kindly been described by Mrs. Jackson. (Letters: May 24, July 9, 1969; November 19, 1971, Mrs. Jackson to the author; I reproduce what she has communicated to me.) This was a young German who had taken up residence in Majorca, Karl Goldschmidt. A talented draftsman, he fashioned the title-page design, employing the antique insignia of the village of Deyá, which all the later Seizin Press publications bore; he also drew designs for some of the jackets of the later London-produced books. Meeting Miss Riding and Mr. Graves in the latter part of the Majorcan period, he became increasingly involved in their working operations, assisting with printing work, and taking on all secretarial duties. Leaving the Island with the partners in 1936, he continued his association with them in London, as helper and friend.

[17] The titles of the Hours Press books, all published in 1930, were: *Twenty Poems Less* and *Four Unposted Letters to Catherine* by Laura Riding, and *Ten Poems More* by Robert Graves.

and photographed. All his cover productions were eloquent of his sense of an almost automatic fitting of things to one another, both sympathetically and accidentally. While maintaining contact with Mr. Lye on an intimate plane over cover-design matters, the partners left much to his choices, confident of his sensitivity, trusting his instinct and taste. They had much interest in Len Lye's work in general—which comprised, besides the making of experimental films, an incidental making of designs for textiles, Mr. Lye himself executing the designs. Miss Riding wrote with him an essay on film-making for *Epilogue I*, and wrote separately a pamphlet explaining his ideas on and procedures in filmmaking.[18] The partners exerted themselves to foster attention to the first film their friend completed for public presentation.

In *No Trouble* one finds an outline of the content of the film *Tusalava*; and the description he gives of the component images, figures, and forms that are as the film's characters show a correspondence of imaginative workings in covers and film. He tells how the three sections of the film explore the beginnings of organic life, then the geological ages, the drama of land and water, and then the time of "humanized shapes." In the motifs used on the covers one sees tiny dots spotting larger amorphous shapes; and in his account of his film he speaks of dots "used to convey organic life in a primary stage." Also in one of the letters of the book, written during a while spent in Majorca, he reveals in his joyful report of his findings of things there "unequalled"—"plants, rock formations, shapes of twigs, pebbles on beach"—his personal visual sensitivity at work, gathering the stuff of his art. The covers are remarkably suggestive of the scope and trend of his visual predilections and conceptions. One can imagine him at work on them, from his further expression of his pleasure in his Majorcan findings: "One could easily go on forever choosing arrangements of fissured rock, plant or waterflow or whichever, then to take cement, wire, wood or whichever and make a construction of the natural formation. . . ."[19]

The meeting point between Len Lye's experiments in visual forms and the dominant intellectual trend in the Seizin Press course of publication was (Miss Riding suggests) in an independence, in each part, of association with period groups or "movements"; the writing she did on the

---

[18] The title of the pamphlet was "Len Lye and the Problem of Popular Films," Seizin Press, 1938, 46 pp.
[19] Len Lye. *No Trouble*, Seizin Press, 1930, p. 24.

film ideas and film work of Len Lye, and his manifestations of appreciation of fine processes of thought, exemplified in his letter to her in "Tusalava" and other letters, show, as she describes it, "sparks of sympathetic, mutual recognition of an integrity of independence across an enormous dividing distance." The quality of arresting strangeness that all the covers must have for viewers—characterized by Miss Riding as that of a credo of visual elementalism—is brilliantly present in those of *No Trouble*, and is in active harmony with the text. In the case of the other Seizin covers, the harmony is more formal; Mr. Lye (again, as Miss Riding puts it) "pays each book the friendly compliment of believing there must be some sort of relevance between his visual terms and its interior terms."[20] Yet the *Laura and Francisca* cover designs differ from the rest of these others in their exuberant delicacy, there seeming to be worked into the traceries the notation of a pleasure in doing these particular ones.

When the Press was put into action again in Majorca, some of the facilities of the London printing operations were lacking. But an orderly procedure was soon established; the printing labors and the conduct of the affairs of the Press were essentially simple in character. In the second year of the Majorcan life of the Press, the old Albion was moved from a house in a low-lying part of the village of Deyá to a house at a higher level, which remained the home of the Press until the outbreak of the Spanish Civil War and the forced discontinuance of the life of the Press as a producer of privately printed books. In the life of the Press as such, production remained slow, limited, adapted to the allowance of time and energy the partners could spare from their own work as writers. This was altogether a modest procedure. Expenses were low, sales were low, the printing program was kept within the bounds of a secondary interest. That satisfaction was taken in the labors involved can be deduced from the evidences, in the volumes published, of care exercised in the features of production. A glimpse of their labors is provided in *Laura and Francisca*, Seizin Seven, which suggests the hard work, steady application, and necessary preparedness for incidental difficulties attendant on hand-printing generally:

> How's that? How's anything you know or don't?
> You can't believe . . . on ordinary paper . . .
> Printed by myself, and Robert . . .
>   .   .   .   .

---

[20] Letter: January 1, 1972, Mrs. Jackson to the author.

> Yes, I ink, he pulls, we patch a greyness
> Or clean the thickened letters out . . .[21]

Miss Riding's volume of prose and poetry, *Though Gently*, was the second Seizin to appear in 1930. The format assumed the same generous proportions as *No Trouble*. The cover, again by Len Lye, once more presented forms inspired by conceptions of natural processes, but the coloring here was in tints of subdued grey and blacks, against a quiet beige background. Like *No Trouble*, the book included a half-title page bearing the words "A Seizin," followed by the title page, and another which bore information on the number of copies printed, the Seizin number, and the fact that the book had been hand-printed "by themselves." It may be presumed that by the indirectly clarifying phrase the printers wished to bring a touch of intimacy to the book without self-advertisement; the touch is perhaps mannered, but it leaves the book the center of importance—one thinks of the pure emphasis on the book of Carrefour's "Anonymous Editions," also perhaps mannered, in another way.

Though Gently, Seizin Five, might be described as a hand-printer's dream. The poems were mostly short, allowing the placement of one and sometimes two on a page, and the prose passages, which alternated with the poems, were likewise brief. Seeing them thus arranged, printed on opposite pages measuring $8\frac{1}{4}$ by $11\frac{1}{2}$, and set in columns of only three inches, and framed by spacious white borders, is to appreciate one of the privileges available to the private press printer: the controlled arrangement of space so as to enhance the appearance of the printed word.

Though Gently continued the characteristic preoccupation of its author with the matter of truth in the practicalities of expression. How little expressed may be called truth?

> And how much may we omit without not telling the truth? Depending on how slow we go. Going as fast is if everything were being

---

[21] Laura Riding. *Laura and Francisca*, Seizin Press, 1931. The partners, in their new location, Mrs. Jackson tells, "decided to provide themselves with type for doing their own composition." (Letter: October 31, 1971, Mrs. Jackson to the author.) The paper on which *Laura and Francisca* was printed bore the watermark "Guarro," a supply of which, Mrs. Jackson suggests, "may have been procured, instead of directly from Barcelona," where the paper was manufactured, "by the agency of a printer's shop in Palma de Mallorca that did various services for the Press." (Letter: December 20, 1971, Mrs. Jackson to the author.)

TO WHOM ELSE?

BY

ROBERT GRAVES

The Seizin Press
Deyá, Majorca
1931

Title page of *To Whom Else?* by Robert Graves (Seizin Press, 1931).
COURTESY OF SOUTHERN ILLINOIS UNIVERSITY LIBRARY, RARE BOOK COLLECTION

omitted, nothing may be omitted without not telling the truth. Going as slow as if nothing were being omitted, everything may be omitted without not telling the truth. Gently omitting, though gently.[22]

Seizin Six, Robert Graves' *To Whom Else?*, a book of poems, and Seizin Seven, Laura Riding's *Laura and Francisca*, a single long poem, both appeared in 1931. They were the shortest books thus far published, numbering 20 and 22 pages respectively, and were placed on sale for 25s., which was the price set for all Seizins published during the Spanish period. Two hundred copies of each were printed. The covers of *Laura and Fran-*

---

[22] Laura Riding. *Though Gently*, Seizin Press, 1930.

Front-cover design (faded) by Len Lye of *Laura and Francisca*
by Laura Riding (Seizin Press, 1931).
COURTESY OF SOUTHERN ILLINOIS UNIVERSITY LIBRARY, RARE BOOK COLLECTION

cisca are distinguished by a color treatment different from that employed
in any of the others. The background is a clear mid-blue; the design is an
intricate tracery in white, on both covers, consisting of characteristic Lye
motifs.[23] The covers of *To Whom Else?*, colored in shades of brown, blue
and silver, presented an arrangement of conical, circular, and diamond-
shaped designs.

---

[23] Mrs. Jackson, in commenting on the design, has referred to it as "a mapping of
interconnected forms and movement-paths that could be thought of as a microscopic
field of natural energy, and on the back cover, of the play of released forces in
spacial extension." (Letter: March 31, 1972, Mrs. Jackson to the author.)

Arranged in three parts, *Laura and Francisca* offered glimpses of life in Majorca, "not heaven, but the smallest earth," of its inhabitants, native and alien, and particularly of the village of Deyá, the choice of the partners for a working place—the "island of an island." The theme of the poem, as its author has defined it for me, is "the attainment, in the busy isolation of this miniature world, of a state of suspension in which a close view is to be had of the possibilities and impossibilities that time secretes." The living atmosphere of the poem is compounded of "practical alertness and visionary deliberation." Francisca is a little girl of the village who has a part in the poem of "sharing, in her child's way, the author's course of keeping much of her seriousness to herself."[24]

> And so Francisca sails her boat
> (I gave it to her, she found it by the door)
> Down the slow *siqui* by the wall,
> Looking up only not to talk.
> She lets it ride, then catches up
> By scarcely walking, teasing along
> Until the boat at any moment
> Might play the fool and drop into the hole.
> Enough danger for a short voyage.
> Then she turns out her basket.
> Three cards to laugh at? someone else.
> A sprig to smell? not now.
> Has anything dropped out? perhaps.[25]

I have already, here, given a general view of the course of the Seizin Press from its beginnings in London to its continuation in Majorca and the expansion of its publishing program in its last two years there with conventionally produced books, by co-operative arrangement with Constable & Company of London—these books bearing the imprint of both the Seizin Press, as of Majorca, and that of the English firm. The first book produced under this arrangement was the first volume of the critical project *Epilogue*, already described; this was in 1935. In this year came also, as a Seizin Press–Constable & Company book, a volume of poems by James Reeves entitled *The Natural Need*, the only book of poetic work

---

[24] Letter: December 6, 1971, Mrs. Jackson to the author.
[25] Laura Riding. *Laura and Francisca*, Seizin Press, 1931.

to bear the Seizin imprint besides the four presenting poetic work of Laura Riding and Robert Graves (two by each). This book, unlike the others bearing the double imprint, which were all printed in England, was printed in Majorca, but by commercial printers, not by hand. The title comes from a poem of Laura Riding's written especially as a preface for the book. A passage in the account of the book given on the jacket reads "A poet should not be especially commended for the enjoyment he takes in being a poet, since . . . he is, presumably, satisfying a natural need. But . . . this element . . . is the clue to [these poems'] serenity, and the background of their intelligence." Miss Riding's *Progress of Stories* was a 1935 Seizin–Constable book. The Seizin Press—itself alone—issued in this year two hand-printed productions, at separate times. These were unbound slender sheaves having the titles "The First Leaf" and "The Second Leaf," and presenting two parts of a long poem, reproduced in Miss Riding's *Collected Poems*, three years later, under the title "Disclaimer of Person." Nothing further of Seizin Press workmanship was to come after those two issues.

To be added to the 1935 publications bearing the Seizin–Constable imprint is *A Mistake Somewhere* (Anonymous), a novel. *Convalescent Conversations* by Madeleine Vara, a contributor to *Epilogue*, and Robert Graves' novel *Antigua, Penny Puce* (dedicated "To William Fuller, in gratitude") were 1936 publications. Also of the Seizin–Constable series were the novels *The Moon's No Fool* by Thomas Matthews and *The Heathen* by Honor Wyatt (both contributors to *Epilogue*), and an autobiographical work, *Almost Forgotten Germany*, by Georg Schwarz, translated from the German by the partners. Volumes II (1936) and III (1937) of *Epilogue* were central items among the various others. As in the case of contributions to *Epilogue*, Miss Riding worked closely with the writers of Seizin–Constable books, upon their texts; the publication of *The Natural Need* was preceded by a long and painstaking correspondence between Miss Riding and Mr. Reeves on his poems (made publicly available by Mr. Reeves under the title "Advice to a Young Poet").

I have already referred to two Seizin Press pamphlets, one pertaining to the film work of Len Lye, and another called "Pictures," both written by Laura Riding. The latter, which did not, in fact, bear the Seizin Press imprint, explored the nature of picture-making, giving examples of three contemporary kinds, the work of Picasso, Ben Nicholson, and John Aldridge; then it considered the differences between these moderns, and

THE SEIZIN PRESS

Deya   Mallorca   Spain

These books have been printed by us since the summer of 1930:

> Seizin 4: *No Trouble*, by Len Lye.
> Seizin 5: *Though Gently*, by Laura Riding.
> Seizin 6: *To Whom Else?* by Robert Graves.

NO TROUBLE consists of letters from a film-maker to friends about his film Tusalava and other simple ways of looking at things.

THOUGH GENTLY consists of statements in prose and poetry all leading as gently as possible to annihilation and the rest.

TO WHOM ELSE? consists of poems and as it were poems in which the problem of dedication is treated without poetic ambiguity.

We shall have ready for the summer of 1931:

LAURA AND FRANCISCA, by Laura Riding, a poem-miniature.

OF OTHERS, by the Seizin, an appreciative inventory of whatever others.

═══════════

All these books are hand-set and hand-printed on hand-made paper in editions of 200 numbered and signed copies, quarto.

Their covers are designed by Len Lye.

The price of each is 25 shillings. Of earlier Seizins copies may still be had of *LOVE AS LOVE, DEATH AS DEATH*, by Laura Riding, and *AN ACQUAIN-TANCE WITH DESCRIPTION*, by Gertrude Stein. These are octavo volumes bound in plain buckram; signed, numbered and similarly printed by hand on hand-made paper. Their price is 10 shillings and 6 pence.

Laura Riding
Robert Graves

For immediate enquiries:
BM/SZP London, W. C. 1.

A Seizin Press announcement, 1931.

between modern and historical picture-making generally.[26] There is a third incidental publication of pamphlet-form to report; it was commercially printed in England with the imprint of the Press, in 1938, and was copyrighted. This, however, was a booklet of private status concerned with a project of Miss Riding's for the literal practice of certain values by people privately and concertedly committed to attempting this. The possibility of a gradually widening participation (the beginning number of participants being by purpose small) was envisioned, but the initiator of the project came to view it as too experimental in its personal aspects for principles of value of the kind animating it, and discontinued furthering it.[27]

I close my account of publications bearing the Seizin Press imprint with a reference to Laura Riding's *A Trojan Ending*, not yet mentioned. This was, as I understand the record, the last of the Seizin–Constable publications—and, thus, the nineteenth book bearing the name "The Seizin Press." If perchance *Epilogue III*, published also in 1937, was of later issuance, in that year, *The Trojan Ending* can still be regarded as the last book of "Seizin" identity, in the sense of having an independent book status—and as such the last of historically authentic "Seizin" identity.[28] So one can think of an arc reaching from the inaugural Seizin volume *Love as Love, Death as Death* to the final one, with the same author at the points of opening and close.

As I have described, the Majorcan life of the Press had been terminated by the outbreak of the Spanish Civil War, in mid-1936. (Foreigners were advised by their governments to leave the island, and most did, with British and American naval assistance; the partners, though without polit-

---

[26] Although "Pictures" did not bear the Seizin Press imprint, it can, according to Mrs. Jackson, "reasonably be included in the roll of things of Seizin connection." The omission of the imprint was, as she remembers, intended to give the little pamphlet an informal character, suitable to intimate circulation of it in a particular quarter of interest. "But, though it is an isolated, special case as a publication, it was of the general kind of writing-production and writing interests to which Seizin Press issues, so denominated, belonged. Further, it is very close in construction to an essay of mine entitled "Picture-Making" that was published in *Epilogue I*, with illustrations by John Aldridge, one of the three painters treated of in both (not identical) pieces of writing." The pamphlet "Pictures" bears no date. (Letters: February 16, March 27, 1972, Mrs. Jackson to the author.)
[27] Letter: February 17, 1972, Mrs. Jackson to the author.
[28] Eighteen years later there appeared a pamphlet-like production of poems bearing the Seizin Press imprint, but there was then no surviving entity to make it a Seizin.

ical involvements, were natural objects of suspicion for the Francoist occupiers of the island, as possessors of a press, but they departed by free choice, envisaging the possibility that the conflict, already appearing likely to become acute, would be a prolonged one.) The general course of activity with which the name "Seizin Press" was identified continued in various forms into 1939. In that year, the association of the two partners was dissolved. The partners entered upon separate courses; and the Seizin Press was no more.

Appendix 2

List of Press Publications, Periodicals, and Newspapers

NEARLY all the books, periodicals, and newspapers listed below were published in Paris. In the few instances when they were not, I have supplied the location of publication.

PRESS PUBLICATIONS

SHAKESPEARE AND COMPANY

1922

Ulysses by James Joyce. (Subsequent editions of *Ulysses* published by Miss Beach appeared in 1924, 1925, 1926, 1927, 1928, and 1930.)

1927

Pomes Penyeach by James Joyce

1929

Our Exagmination Round his Factification for Incamination of Work in Progress. Studies of James Joyce's "Work in Progress" by Samuel Beckett, Stuart Gilbert, Eugene Jolas, Robert McAlmon, William Carlos Williams, Elliot Paul, and others

CONTACT EDITIONS

1922

A Hasty Bunch by Robert McAlmon

1923

A Companion Volume by Robert McAlmon
Post-Adolescence by Robert McAlmon
Two Selves by Bryher
Lunar Baedecker by Mina Loy
Three Stories and Ten Poems by Ernest Hemingway
Twenty-five Poems by Marsden Hartley
Spring and All by William Carlos Williams

1924

Village: as it happened through a fifteen year period by Robert McAlmon

1925

Contact Collection of Contemporary Writers
Ashe of Rings by Mary Butts
My First Thirty Years by Gertrude Beasley
A Hurried Man by Emanuel Carnevali
The Making of Americans by Gertrude Stein

1926

Palimpsest by H. D. (Hilda Doolittle)
The Portrait of a Generation by Robert McAlmon
The Eater of Darkness by Robert M. Coates
Ladies Almanack written & illustrated by a lady of fashion (Djuna Barnes)

1929

North America, Continent of Conjecture by Robert McAlmon
Sailors Don't Care by Edwin M. Lanham
Quaint Tales of the Samurai by Saikaku Ibara, translated by Ken Sato

1931

The Dream Life of Balso Snell by Nathanael West (New York)

THREE MOUNTAINS PRESS

1923

Indiscretions or, Une Rèvue de Deux Mondes by Ezra Pound
Women & Men by Ford Madox Ford
Elimus: a story by B. C. Windeler
The Great American Novel by William Carlos Williams
England by B. M. G. Adams

1924

in our time by Ernest Hemingway
Antheil and the Treatise on Harmony by Ezra Pound

1925

A Draft of XVI Cantos by Ezra Pound
Distinguished Air (*Grim Fairy Tales*) by Robert McAlmon

1926

The Herdboy by H. Krebs Friend

BLACK MANIKIN PRESS

1926

Rococo by Ralph Cheever Dunning, with illustrations by Howard Simon
The Case of Mr. Crump by Ludwig Lewisohn
The Frog by Virgil Geddes

1927

First Fruits by Thelma Spear, with an introduction by Ludwig Lewisohn
The Cheese Girl in New Bench by Agatha Itchwyrth
Asbit Omen by Kenneth McNeil Wells
An Original Cartoon by Hendrick Van Loon
Couples (*Der Reigen*) by Arthur Schnitzler, translated from the German
  by Lily Wolfe and E. W. Titus
Little Poems in Prose by Charles Baudelaire, translated from the French
  by Aleister Crowley
The Voice of Fire by Manuel Komroff, with engravings by Polia Chentoff

1928

Circoncision du Coeur by Pierre Minet
Imaginary Letters by Mary Butts, with copperplate engravings from the
  original drawings by Jean Cocteau
Some Gentlemen of the Renaissance by William Van Wyck

1929

Lady Chatterley's Lover by D. H. Lawrence
Windfalls by Ralph Cheever Dunning, with a portrait of the author by
  Polia Chentoff
The Legend of Ermengarde by the Troubadour Uc Saine, translated into
  modern verse from the fourteenth-century Provençal by Homer Rignaut

406

1930

Kiki's Memoirs translated from the French by Samuel Putnam, with an introduction by Ernest Hemingway, with portraits by Man Ray, Foujita, Kisling, Per Krogh, Hermine David, and reproductions of twenty paintings by Kiki

On the Terrace by William Van Wyck, with two illustrations by Margery Nahl

Une Saison en Enfer by Arthur Rimbaud, translated from the French by Ramon Guthrie

1931

There Is a Door by Kathleen Coyle

The Romantic. A Contemporary Legend by Ludwig Lewisohn

No Man's Meat by Morley Callaghan

The Case of Mr. Crump by Ludwig Lewisohn, with a preface by Thomas Mann

Old Prairie du Chien by Laura Sherry, with an introduction by Zona Gale

1932

D. H. Lawrence: An Unprofessional Study by Anais Nin

BLACK SUN PRESS

1925

Crosses of Gold, a Book of Verse by Caresse Crosby, with illustrations by Daniel-Girard. (Printed by Léon Pichon)

Sonnets for Caresse by Harry Crosby. (Printed by Herbert Clarke)

1926

Sonnets for Caresse by Harry Crosby

1927

Painted Shores by Caresse Crosby, with three illustrations by François Quelvée

Red Skeletons by Harry Crosby, with illustrations by Alastair

Sonnets for Caresse by Harry Crosby

The Stranger by Caresse Crosby, with a portrait of the author by May den Engelsen

1928

L'Anniversaire de l'Infante by Oscar Wilde, with illustrations by Alastair and a preface by Harry Crosby

The Birthday of the Infanta by Oscar Wilde, with illustrations by Alastair and a preface by Harry Crosby

Chariot of the Sun by Harry Crosby, with a portrait of the author by Polia Chentoff and an engraving by A. E. Marty

The Fall of the House of Usher by Edgar Allan Poe, with illustrations by Alastair and an introduction by Arthur Symons

Git le Coeur by Lord Lymington

Impossible Melodies by Caresse Crosby, with a portrait of the author by Angelès Ortiz

Letters of Henry James to Walter Berry

The News Letter of the LXIVMOS

Moon Letter. A reproduction of an ancient manuscript found in Damascus, with twenty-six miniatures, hand-colored

Shadows of the Sun by Harry Crosby (First Series)

Sun by D. H. Lawrence, with one drawing by the author

Transit of Venus, Poems by Harry Crosby

1929

Einstein by Archibald MacLeish, with a drawing of the author by Paul Emile Bécat

The Escaped Cock by D. H. Lawrence, with decoration in color by the author

1450–1950 by Bob Brown

Les Liaisons Dangereuses by Choderlos De Laclos, translated by Ernest Dowson, with illustrations by Alastair

Mad Queen: Tirades by Harry Crosby, with a drawing by Caresse Crosby

The Rubaiyat of Omar Khayyam

Secession in Astropolis by Eugene Jolas

A Sentimental Journey Through France and Italy by Laurence Sterne, with illustrations by Polia Chentoff

Shadows of the Sun by Harry Crosby (Second Series)

Short Stories by Kay Boyle

Sleeping Together, A Book of Dreams by Harry Crosby, with a drawing by Caresse Crosby

Spring Song of Iscariot, Poem by Lord Lymington

The Sun by Harry Crosby

Tales Told of Shem and Shaun, Three Fragments from Work in Progress by James Joyce, with a preface by C. K. Ogden and a portrait of the author by Brancusi

Transit of Venus, Poems by Harry Crosby

1930

Alice in Wonderland by Lewis Carroll, with six colored lithographs by Marie Laurencin

Aphrodite in Flight: Being Some Observations on the Aerodynamics of Love by Harry Crosby

The Bridge, A Poem by Hart Crane, with three photographs by Walker Evans

Forty-seven Unpublished Letters from Marcel Proust to Walter Berry, published in French with an English translation by Harry and Caresse Crosby

Imaginary Letters by Ezra Pound

New Found Land, Fourteen Poems by Archibald MacLeish

New York: 1929, as photographed by Gretchen and Peter Powel, edited by Harry and Caresse Crosby

Quarante-sept Lettres Inédites de Marcel Proust à Walter Berry, published in French with an English translation by Harry and Caresse Crosby

Shadows of the Sun by Harry Crosby (Third Series)

1931

Chariot of the Sun by Harry Crosby, with an introduction by D. H. Lawrence

Mr. Knife, Miss Fork by René Crevel, translated by Kay Boyle and illustrated by Max Ernst

Poems for Harry Crosby by Caresse Crosby, with an introduction by Stuart Gilbert and a photograph of a bronze of Harry Crosby made by Caresse Crosby

Sleeping Together, A Book of Dreams by Harry Crosby, with a memory of the poet by Stuart Gilbert

Torchbearer by Harry Crosby, with notes by Ezra Pound

Transit of Venus by Harry Crosby, with a preface by T. S. Eliot

1932

Big Meaulnes by Alain-Fournier, translated by Françoise Delisle

Bubu of Montparnasse by Charles-Louis Philippe, translated by Laurence Vail, with a preface by T. S. Eliot

Devil in the Flesh by Raymond Radiguet, translated by Kay Boyle, with an introduction by Aldous Huxley

In Our Time, Stories by Ernest Hemingway

Indefinite Huntress and Other Stories by Robert McAlmon

Laments for the Living by Dorothy Parker

Night-Flight by Antoine de Saint-Exupéry, translated by Stuart Gilbert

Sanctuary by William Faulkner

The Torrents of Spring, A Romantic Novel in Honor of the Passing of a Great Race by Ernest Hemingway

War Letters by Henry Grew Crosby

Year Before Last by Kay Boyle

1936

Collected Poems of James Joyce, with a crayon portrait of the author by Augustus John (New York)

Interregnum by George Grosz, with an introductory comment by John Dos Passos and sixty-four drawings and a hand-painted lithograph by George C. Miller (New York)

Surrealism by Julien Levy, with sixty-four illustrations (New York)

PLAIN EDITIONS   (*All books by Gertrude Stein*)

1931

Lucy Church Amiably, A Novel of Romantic beauty and nature which Looks Like an Engraving

How to Write

Before the Flowers of Friendship Faded Friendship Faded

1932

Matisse, Picasso and Gertrude Stein

Operas and Plays

HOURS PRESS

1928

Report on the Pumice-Stone Industry of the Lipari Islands by Norman Douglas

Hark the Herald by Richard Aldington

Peronnick the Fool by George Moore

1929

St. George at Silene by Alvaro Guevara

La Chasse au Snark by Louis Aragon

One Day by Norman Douglas

The Eaten Heart by Richard Aldington

Mes Souvenirs by Arthur Symons

1930

Catalogue of Paintings, Drawings and Gouaches by Eugene MacCown
Apollinaire by Walter Lowenfels
Ten Poems More by Robert Graves
Twenty Poems Less by Laura Riding
Four Unposted Letters to Catherine by Laura Riding
Whoroscope by Samuel Beckett
A Draft of XXX Cantos by Ezra Pound
Poems by Roy Campbell
Collected Poems by John Rodker
Henry-Music by Henry Crowder

1931

Last Straws by Richard Aldington
This Chaos by Harold Acton
First Poems by Brian Howard
Words by Bob Brown
The Revaluation of Obscenity by Havelock Ellis
The Talking Pine by George Moore

CARREFOUR

1930

Anonymous: the Need for Anonymity
USA with Music by Walter Lowenfels
Werther's Younger Brother by Michael Fraenkel

1932

Elegy in the Manner of a Requiem in Memory of D. H. Lawrence by Walter Lowenfels

1936

Bastard Death, the Autobiography of an Idea by Michael Fraenkel
Death in a Room, Poems, 1927–1930 by Michael Fraenkel

1939

Hamlet by Henry Miller and Michael Fraenkel (New York)

ROVING EYE PRESS   (*All books by Bob Brown*)

1930

The Readies (Bad-Ems)
Globe-Gliding (Diessen)

1931

Gems: A Censored Anthology (Cagnes-sur-Mer)
Demonics (Cagnes-sur-Mer)
Readies for Bob Brown's Machine (Cagnes-sur-Mer)

SERVIRE PRESS

1932

Cross-Country by Solon R. Barber, with forewords by Nelson A. Crawford
    and Richard Thoma
Mind Products Limited by Charles Duff
Front by various contributors
Americans Abroad edited by Peter Neagoe
The Language of Night by Eugene Jolas

1934

The Mime of Mick, Nick and the Maggies by James Joyce

NEW REVIEW PRESS

1931

Green Chaos by Richard Thoma
Pass to the Stars by Emlen Pope Etting

1932

Storm by Peter Neagoe, with an introductory letter by Eugene Jolas
Faust's Metamorphoses by George Reavey, with an introduction by Samuel
    Putnam and illustrated with six original engravings by S. W. Hayter
Direction, a Symposium by Samuel Putnam
Enfances by Georges Hugnet, translated by Samuel Putnam

HARRISON OF PARIS

1930

Venus and Adonis by William Shakespeare
The Wild West: Stories by Bret Harte, with eight illustrations by Pierre
    Falké
A Sketch of My Life by Thomas Mann
The Babe's Bed by Glenway Wescott

1931

Fables of Aesop, with fifty drawings by Alexander Calder

Carmen and Letters from Spain by Prosper Mérimée, with ten illustrations by Maurice Barraud, stencil-colored by Eugène Charpentier

The Death of Madame by Marie Pioche de la Vergne, Comtesse de La Fayette, translated by Monroe Wheeler

A Gentle Spirit: A Fantastic Story by Fyodor Dostoyevsky, translated by Constance Garnett, with a frontispiece and tailpiece by Christian Bérard

Childe Harold's Pilgrimage by Lord Byron, with twenty-eight wash drawings by Sir Francis Cyril Rose, Bart.

1932

A Calendar of Saints for Unbelievers by Glenway Wescott, with illustrations by Pavel Tchelitchew

A Typographical Commonplace-Book: Quotations and Anecdotes Variously Printed

1933

French Song-book. Famous old French songs in the original and with new English rhymed translations by Katherine Anne Porter, a musical example of each melody drawn by Paul Koch, and introductions giving the origin of each song

1934

Hacienda by Katherine Anne Porter (New York)

OBELISK PRESS

1930

Haveth Childers Everywhere by James Joyce. (Published by Henry Babou and Jack Kahane)

Death of a Hero by Richard Aldington. (Published by Henry Babou and Jack Kahane)

Sleeveless Errand by Norah C. James, with a preface by Edward Garnett

1931

Daffodil by Cecil Barr (Jack Kahane)

The Lamb by Philippe Heriat, translated by Jack Kahane

1932

Storm by Peter Neagoe

Pomes Penyeach by James Joyce, with initial letters designed by Lucia Joyce

1933

The Young and Evil by Parker Tyler and Charles Henri Ford
Boy by James Hanley
The Well of Loneliness by Radclyffe Hall
My Life and Loves by Frank Harris
Amour French for Love by Cecil Barr (Jack Kahane)

1934

Tropic of Cancer by Henry Miller
Easter Sun by Peter Neagoe
Bright Pink Youth by Cecil Barr (Jack Kahane)
The Gentle Men by Marika Norden
Star Against Star by Gawen Brownrigg

1935

Aller Retour by Henry Miller (Siana Series)
Bessie Cotter by Wallace Smith
Scenario by Henry Miller

1936

House of Incest by Anais Nin (Siana Series)
Black Spring by Henry Miller
Rock Pool by Cyril Connolly
Lady Chatterley's Lover by D. H. Lawrence

1937

Uncharted Seas by Eric Ward
Lady, Take Heed! by Cecil Barr (Jack Kahane)

1938

Half O'Clock in Mayfair by Princess Paul Troubetzkoy
Through the Ark by Olga Martin
Starborn by "Arion"
Love Counts Ten by Theodor Zay
Dark Refuge by Charles Beadle
Max and the White Phagocytes by Henry Miller (Seurat Series)
The Black Book by Lawrence Durrell (Seurat Series)

1939

To Beg I Am Ashamed by Sheila Cousins
Tropic of Capricorn by Henry Miller
Winter of Artifice by Anais Nin (Seurat Series)

SEIZIN PRESS

1928

Love as Love, Death as Death by Laura Riding (London)

1929

An Acquaintance with Description by Gertrude Stein (London)
Poems 1929 by Robert Graves (London)

1930

No Trouble by Len Lye (Majorca)
Though Gently by Laura Riding (Majorca)

1931

To Whom Else? by Robert Graves (Majorca)
Laura and Francisca by Laura Riding (Majorca)

1935

The First Leaf by Laura Riding (Majorca)
The Second Leaf by Laura Riding (Majorca)
The following books were published under a double imprint: Seizin Press
and Constable and Company, Ltd., London:
Progress of Stories by Laura Riding
The Natural Need by James Reeves
A Mistake Somewhere (Anonymous)

1936

Convalescent Conversations by Madeline Vara
Antigua, Penny Puce by Robert Graves
The Moon's No Fool by Thomas Matthews
Almost Forgotten Germany by Georg Schwarz, translated by Laura Riding
and Robert Graves

1937

The Heathen by Honor Wyatt
A Trojan Ending by Laura Riding

PERIODICALS

1914

The Little Review, 1914–1929 (Chicago, New York, Paris). Editors:
Margaret Anderson and Jane Heap

1921

Broom, 1921–1924 (Rome, Berlin, New York). Editors: Harold A. Loeb, Alfred Kreymborg, Slater Brown, Matthew Josephson, and Malcolm Cowley

Gargoyle, 1921–1922. Editor: Arthur Moss

1923

Manikin, 1923 (Bonn, Germany). Editor: Monroe Wheeler

1924

Transatlantic Review, 1924–1925. Editor: Ford Madox Ford

1925

This Quarter, 1925–1927 (Paris, Milan, Monte Carlo). Editors: Ernest Walsh and Ethel Moorhead

1927

The Exile, 1927–1928 (Dijon, France). Editor: Ezra Pound

Boulevardier, 1927. Editor: Erskine Gwynne

transition, 1927–1938. Editors: Eugene Jolas, Elliot Paul, and Robert Sage

1929

Tambour, 1929–1930. Editor: Harold J. Salemson

This Quarter, 1929–1932. Editor: Edward Titus

1931

New Review, 1931–1932. Editors: Samuel Putnam and Peter Neagoe

Story, 1931–1941. (Vienna, Majorca, Spain) Editors: Whit Burnett and Martha Foley

1934

Caravel, 1934–1936 (Majorca, Spain). Editors: Sydney Salt, Jean Rivers, and Charles Henri Ford

1935

Epilogue, 1935–1937 (Majorca, Spain). Editor: Laura Riding

1937

The Booster, 1937–1938. Editors: Alfred Perlès, Lawrence Durrell, Henry Miller, William Saroyan, and others

NEWSPAPERS

Paris *Times*, 1924–1929

Paris *Herald* (European edition of the New York *Herald Tribune*) 1887–1940

Paris *Tribune* (*Chicago Tribune*, European Edition) 1917–1934

Acknowledgments

Grateful acknowledgment is made to the following for material included in this book:

From *The Selected Letters of William Carlos Williams*. Copyright © 1957 by William Carlos Williams. Reprinted by permission of Astor-Honor, Inc. Quotations from the unpublished correspondence of Kay Boyle. Permission granted by A. Watkins, Inc. Quotations from the unpublished correspondence of William Aspenwall Bradley. Permission granted by Mrs. William Aspenwall Bradley. Quotations from Caresse Crosby's *The Passionate Years* published by Dial Press. Permission granted by Bertha Klausner International Literary Agency, Inc.

From *Being Geniuses Together*, 1920–1930 by Robert McAlmon. Revised and with supplementary chapters by Kay Boyle. Copyright © 1968 by Kay Boyle. Reprinted by permission of Doubleday and Company, Inc.

From *Lawrence Durrell and Henry Miller, A Private Correspondence*, edited by George Wickes. Copyright © 1962, 1963 by Lawrence Durrell and Henry Miller. Reprinted by permission of the publishers, E. P. Dutton & Co., Inc.

Grateful acknowledgment is extended to the Harvey S. Firestone Library, Rare Book Collection, Princeton University, for the use of material from the Sylvia Beach Collection.

Quotations from the unpublished correspondence of Edward Titus. Permission granted by Mrs. William Friedman.

Grateful acknowledgment is extended to Donald Gallup, Curator, Collection of American Literature, Yale University, for permission to reproduce excerpts from the letters of Gertrude Stein to Robert McAlmon and from "The Making of *The Making of Americans*" (Reprinted in *Fernhurst, Q.E.D. and Other Early Writings by* Gertrude Stein, Liveright Publishing Corp., New York), and for authorization to quote from the letters of Gertrude Stein to Carl Van Vechten.

From *Shakespeare and Company* by Sylvia Beach. Copyright © 1956, 1959 by Sylvia Beach. Reprinted by permission of Harcourt Brace Jovanovich, Inc.

From *The Diary of Anaïs Nin,* edited and with an introduction by Gunther Stuhlmann. Copyright © 1966 by Anaïs Nin. Reprinted by permission of Harcourt Brace Jovanovich, Inc.

Quotations from the unpublished correspondence of Manuel Komroff. Permission granted by Manuel Komroff.

Quotations from the unpublished correspondence of Edwin Lanham. Permission granted by Edwin Lanham.

From *The Life of Fraenkel's Death* by Walter Lowenfels and Howard McCord (Washington State University Press, 1970), *Anonymous,* and "The Paris Years, 1926–1934" by Walter Lowenfels (*Expatriate Review,* No. 1, Summer 1971). Reprinted by permission of Walter Lowenfels.

Quotations from the unpublished correspondence and papers of Robert McAlmon. Permission granted by Mrs. Grace Marissael.

Grateful acknowledgment is extended to Kenneth Duckett and David Koch, Morris Library, Special Collections, Southern Illinois University, for the use of material from the Black Sun Press archives.

From *The Selected Letters of Ezra Pound,* edited by D. D. Paige. Copyright © 1950 by Ezra Pound. Reprinted by permission of New Directions Publishing Corporation.

From *The Autobiography of William Carlos Williams* by William Carlos Williams. Copyright © 1951 by William Carlos Williams. Reprinted by permission of New Directions Publishing Corporation.

From *Henry Miller Letters to Anaïs Nin,* edited by Gunther Stuhlmann. Copyright © 1965 by Anaïs Nin. Reprinted by permission of the publishers, G. P. Putnam's Sons.

From *The Autobiography of Alice B. Toklas* by Gertrude Stein. Copyright © 1933 by Gertrude Stein. Reprinted by permission of the publishers, Random House, Inc.

From *These Were the Hours* by Nancy Cunard, edited with an introduction by Hugh Ford. Copyright © 1969 by Southern Illinois University Press. Reprinted by permission of Southern Illinois University Press.

Grateful acknowledgment is extended to the Collection of American Literature, Yale University, for permission to reproduce excerpts from the letters of Gertrude Stein and Alice B. Toklas to Carl Van Vechten and Ellery Sedgwick (*The Atlantic Monthly*).

From *Madame; an intimate biography of Helena Rubinstein* by Patrick O'Higgins. Copyright © 1971 by Patrick O'Higgins. Reprinted by permission of the publishers, Viking Press.

I wish to express gratitude for the valuable assistance provided by the following excellent studies: *Robert McAlmon, Expatriate Publisher and Writer* and *McAlmon and the Lost Generation, A Self-Portrait,* both by Robert E. Knoll; *Americans in Paris,* 1903–1939 by George Wickes; *Paris Was Our Mistress* by Samuel Putnam; *Exile's Return* by Malcolm Cowley; *Paris Was Yesterday* by Janet Flanner; *Voyager, A Life of Hart Crane* by John Unterecker; *Ladies Bountiful* by W. G. Rogers; *Memoirs of Montparnasse* by John Glassco; *Ernest Hemingway: A Life Story* by Carlos Baker; and *My Friend, Henry Miller* by Alfred Perlès.

BIBLIOGRAPHY

Aldington, Richard. *Life for Life's Sake: A Book of Reminiscences.* New York: Viking, 1941.

Anderson, Margaret. *My Thirty Years' War.* New York: Covici, Friede, 1930.

———. *The Fiery Fountains.* New York: Hermitage House, 1951.

———. *This Thing Called Art.* New York: Horizon Press, 1970.

Antheil, George. *Bad Boy of Music.* Garden City, N.Y.: Doubleday, Doran, 1945.

Arlen, Michael J. *The Green Hat.* New York, Doran, 1924.

———. *Exiles.* New York: Farrar, Straus & Giroux, 1970.

Bainbridge, John. *Another Way of Living.* New York: Holt, Rinehart & Winston, 1968.

Baker, Carlos. *Ernest Hemingway: A Life Story.* New York: Scribner's, 1969.

Barney, Natalie Clifford. *Actes et Entr'Actes.* Paris: Sansot, 1910.

———. *Adventures de l'Esprit.* Paris: Emile-Paul, 1929.

———. *Pensées d'une Amazone.* Paris: Emile-Paul, 1920.

Barry, Joseph. *Right Bank, Left Bank, Paris and Parisians.* New York: Norton, 1951.

———. *The People of Paris.* Garden City, N.Y.: Doubleday, 1966.

Beach, Sylvia. *Shakespeare & Company.* New York: Harcourt, Brace, 1959.

Beaton, Cecil. *The Wandering Years: Diaries: 1922–1939.* Boston: Little, Brown, 1961.

Biddle, George. *An American Artist's Story.* Boston: Little, Brown, 1939.

Boyle, Kay. *Year Before Last.* New York: Harrison Smith, 1932.

———. *Being Geniuses Together: An Autobiography.* Revised and with supplementary chapters by Kay Boyle. New York: Doubleday, 1968.

Brown, Frederick. *An Impersonation of Angels, A Biography of Jean Cocteau.* New York: Viking, 1968.

Bryher. *The Heart of Artemis: A Writer's Memoirs.* New York: Harcourt, Brace, 1962.

Callaghan, Morley. *That Summer in Paris.* New York: Coward-McCann, 1963.

Charters, Jimmy. *This Must Be the Place.* London: Herbert Joseph, 1934.

Cowley, Malcolm. *Exile's Return.* New York: Viking, 1951.

———. *A Second Flowering: Works & Days of the Lost Generation.* New York: Viking, 1973.

Crosby, Caresse. *The Passionate Years*. New York: Dial, 1953.

Croy, Homer. *They Had to See Paris*. New York: Harper, 1926.

Cunard, Nancy. *Grand Man: Memoirs of Norman Douglas*. London: Secker & Warburg, 1954.

———. *GM: Memories of George Moore*. London: Rupert Hart-Davis, 1956.

———. *These Were the Hours*. Edited by Hugh Ford. Carbondale: Southern Illinois University Press, 1969.

———. *Nancy Cunard, Brave Poet, Indomitable Rebel*. Edited by Hugh Ford. Philadelphia: Chilton, 1968.

Davidson, Jo. *Between Sittings: An Informed Autobiography*. New York: Dial, 1951.

Dos Passos, John. *The Best Times*. New York: New American Library, 1966.

Douglas, Norman. *Looking Back: An Autobiographical Excursion*. New York: Harcourt, Brace, 1933.

Duncan, Isadora. *My Life*. New York: Horace Liveright, 1927.

Durrell, Lawrence and Miller, Henry. *A Private Correspondence*. Edited by George Wickes. New York: Dutton, 1963.

Ede, H. S. *Savage Messiah: Gaudier-Brzeska*. New York: Literary Guild, 1931.

Ellmann, Richard. *James Joyce*. New York: Oxford, 1959.

Fenton, Charles. *The Apprenticeship of Ernest Hemingway: The Early Years*. New York: Farrar, Straus & Cudahy, 1954.

Fitzgerald, F. Scott. *The Letters of F. Scott Fitzgerald*. Edited by Andrew Turnbull. New York: Scribner's, 1963.

Flanner, Janet. *An American in Paris*. New York: Simon & Schuster, 1940.

———. *Men and Monuments*. New York: Harper, 1957.

———. *Paris Journal: 1944–1965*. Edited by William Shawn. New York: Atheneum, 1965.

———. *Paris Was Yesterday*. Edited by Irving Drutman. New York: Viking, 1972.

Ford, Ford Madox. *It Was the Nightingale*. Philadelphia: Lippincott, 1933.

———. *Return to Yesterday*. New York: Liveright, 1972.

———. *Letters of Ford Madox Ford*. Edited by Richard M. Ludwig. Princeton, N.J.: Princeton University Press, 1965.

Ford, Hugh. *The Left Bank Revisited*. University Park: Pennsylvania State University Press, 1972.

Friede, Donald. *The Mechanical Angel: His Adventures and Enterprises in the Glittering 1920s*. New York: Knopf, 1948.

Gilliam, Florence. *France*. New York: Dutton, 1945.

Glassco, John. *Memoirs of Montparnasse*. New York: Oxford, 1970.

Goldring, Douglas. *South Lodge: Reminiscences of Violet Hunt, Ford Madox Ford and the English Review Circle*, London: Constable, 1943.

———. *The Nineteen Twenties: A General Survey and Some Personal Memories*. London: Nicholson & Watson, 1945.

———. *The Last Pre-Raphaelite: A Record of the Life and Writings of Ford Madox Ford*. London: Macdonald, 1948.

Guggenheim, Peggy. *Out of This Century: The Informal Memoirs of Peggy Guggenheim.* New York: Dial, 1946.

———. *Confessions of an Art Addict.* New York: Macmillan, 1960.

Hamnett, Nina. *Laughing Torso: Reminiscences of Nina Hamnett.* London: Constable, 1932.

———. *Is She a Lady? A Problem in Autobiography.* London: Wingate, 1955.

Hapgood, Hutchins. *A Victorian in the Modern World.* New York: Harcourt, Brace, 1939.

Hassall, Christopher. *A Biography of Edward Marsh.* New York: Harcourt, Brace, 1959.

Hawkins, Eric and Sturdevant, Robert N. *Hawkins of the Paris Herald.* New York: Simon & Schuster, 1963.

Hemingway, Ernest. *A Moveable Feast.* New York: Scribner's, 1964.

———. *By-Line: Ernest Hemingway: Selected Articles and Dispatches of Four Decades.* Edited by William White. New York: Scribner's, 1967.

Hoffman, Frederick J.; Allen, Charles; and Ulrich, Carolyn F. M. *The Little Magazine: A History and a Bibliography.* Princeton, N.J.: Princeton University Press, 1947.

———. *The Twenties: American Writing in the Postwar Decade.* New York: Free Press, 1962.

Huddleston, Sisley. *Paris Salons, Cafés, Studios.* Philadelphia: Lippincott, 1928.

———. *Back to Montparnasse.* Philadelphia: Lippincott, 1931.

Hunt, Violet. *I Have This to Say: The Story of My Flurried Years.* New York: Boni & Liveright, 1926.

Imbs, Bravig. *Confessions of Another Young Man.* New York: Henkle-Yewdale House, 1936.

Jolas, Eugene *et al. Testimony against Gertrude Stein.* Paris: Transition Pamphlet No. 1 (February 1935).

———. *I Have Seen Monsters and Angels.* Paris: Transition Press, 1938.

Josephson, Matthew. *Life Among the Surrealists: A Memoir.* New York: Holt, 1962.

Joyce, James. *Letters of James Joyce.* Vol. I edited by Stuart Gilbert; vols. II and III edited by Richard Ellmann. New York: Viking, 1957, 1966.

Kahane, Jack. *Memoirs of a Booklegger.* London: Michael Joseph, 1939.

Knoll, Robert. *Robert McAlmon: Expatriate Publisher and Writer.* Lincoln: University of Nebraska Studies, No. 18 (August 1957).

Kohner, Frederick. *Kiki of Montparnasse.* New York: Stein & Day, 1967.

Kreymborg, Alfred. *Troubadour: An Autobiography.* New York: Liveright, 1925.

Laney, Al. *Paris Herald: The Incredible Newspaper.* New York: Appleton-Century, 1947.

Lawrence, D. H. *The Letters of D. H. Lawrence.* Edited by Aldous Huxley. New York: Viking, 1932.

Lawrence, Frieda. *The Memoirs and Correspondence.* Edited by E. W. Tedlock, Jr. New York: Knopf, 1964.

Le Gallienne, Richard. *From a Paris Garret.* New York: Ives Washburn, 1936.

Lewis, Wyndham. *Rude Assignment: A Narrative of My Career Up-to-Date.* London: Hutchinson, 1950.

———. *The Letters of Wyndham Lewis.* Edited by W. K. Rose. New York: New Directions, 1964.

Loeb, Harold. *The Way It Was.* New York: Criterion Books, 1961.

Longstreet, Stephen. *We All Went to Paris.* New York: Macmillan, 1972.

Lowenfels, Walter. *Poetry of My Politics.* Homestead, Fla.: Olivant Press, 1969.

——— and McCord, Howard. *The Life of Fraenkel's Death.* Pullman: Washington State University Press, 1970.

Luhan, Mabel Dodge. *Intimate Memories.* New York: Harcourt, Brace, vol. I, *Background,* 1933; vol. II, *European Experiences,* 1935; vol. III, *Movers and Shakers,* 1936; vol. IV, *Edge of Taos Desert,* 1937.

McAlmon, Robert. *Being Geniuses Together: An Autobiography.* London: Secker & Warburg, 1938.

———. *McAlmon and the Lost Generation: A Self-Portrait.* Edited by Robert E. Knoll. Lincoln: University of Nebraska Press, 1962.

MacShane, Frank. *The Life and Work of Ford Madox Ford.* New York: Horizon, 1965.

Marsh, Edward. *A Number of People: A Book of Reminiscences.* New York: Harper, 1939.

Mellow, James. *Gertrude Stein and Company.* New York: Praeger, 1974.

Miller, Henry. *Remember to Remember.* New York: New Directions, 1947.

———. *The Books of My Life.* New York: New Directions, 1952.

———. *Quiet Days in Clichy.* New York: Olympia Press, 1956.

———. *Stand Still Like the Hummingbird.* New York: New Directions, 1962.

———. *Henry Miller's Letters to Anaïs Nin.* Edited by Gunther Stuhlmann. New York: Putnam, 1965.

Mizener, Arthur. *The Far Side of Paradise, A Biography of F. Scott Fitzgerald.* Boston: Houghton Mifflin, 1951.

———. *The Saddest Story. A Biography of Ford Madox Ford.* New York: World, 1971.

Monnier, Adrienne. *Rue de l'Odéon.* Paris: Editions Albin Michel, 1960.

Moore, George. *Conversations in Ebury Street.* New York: Boni & Liveright, 1924.

———. *George Moore: Letters to Lady Cunard.* Edited by Rupert Hart-Davis. New York: Macmillan, 1958.

Moore, Harry T. *The Intelligent Heart: The Story of D. H. Lawrence.* New York: Grove Press, 1962 (orig. pub. by Farrar, Straus, 1955).

Neagoe, Peter, ed. *Americans Abroad: An Anthology.* The Hague: Servire Press, 1932.

Nin, Anaïs. *The Diary of Anaïs Nin.* 1931–1934. vol. I; 1934–1939, vol. II. Edited by Gunther Stuhlmann. New York: Harcourt, Brace, 1966, 1967.

Norman, Charles. *Ezra Pound.* New York: Macmillan, 1960.

———. *E. E. Cummings: The Magic Maker.* New York: Duell, Sevan & Pearce, 1964.

Parry, Albert. *Garrets and Pretenders.* New York: Covici, Friede, 1933.

Patmore, Brigit. *My Friends When Young.* Edited by Derek Patmore. London: Heinemann, 1968.

Paul, Elliot. *The Last Time I Saw Paris.* New York: Random House, 1942.

———. *Springtime in Paris.* New York: Random House, 1950.

Perlès, Alfred. *My Friend, Henry Miller.* London: Neville Spearman, 1955.

Poli, Bernard. *Ford Madox Ford and the Transatlantic Review.* Syracuse, N.Y.: Syracuse University Press, 1967.

Pound, Ezra. *The Letters of Ezra Pound: 1907–1941.* Edited by D. D. Paige. New York: Harcourt, Brace, 1950.

Putnam, Samuel. *Paris Was Our Mistress: Memoirs of a Lost and Found Generation.* New York: Viking, 1947.

Quennell, Peter. *The Sign of the Fish.* New York: Viking, 1960.

Rascoe, Burton. *Before I Forget.* New York: Literary Guild, 1937.

———. *We Were Interrupted.* Garden City, N.Y.: Doubleday, 1947.

Ray, Man. *Self Portrait.* Boston: Atlantic, Little, Brown, 1963.

Rogers, W. G. *When This You See Remember Me: Gertrude Stein in Person.* New York: Rinehart, 1948.

———. *Ladies Bountiful.* New York: Harcourt, Brace & World, 1968.

Ross, Isabel. *The Expatriates.* New York: Crowell, 1970.

Ross, Lillian. *Portrait of Hemingway.* New York: Simon & Schuster, 1961.

Saarinen, Aline B. *The Proud Possessors.* New York: Random House, 1958.

Sarason, Bertram D. *Hemingway and the Sun Set.* Washington: Microcard Editions, 1972.

Stearns, Harold. *Rediscovering America.* New York: Liveright, 1934.

———. *The Street I Know.* New York: Furness, 1935.

Steegmuller, Francis. *Apollinaire: Poet Among the Painters.* New York: Farrar, Straus, 1963.

———. *Cocteau.* Boston: Little, Brown, 1970.

Stein, Gertrude. *The Autobiography of Alice B. Toklas.* New York: Harcourt, Brace, 1933.

———. *Everybody's Autobiography.* New York: Random House, 1937.

———. *Paris France.* New York: Scribner's, 1940.

Stravinsky, Igor. *An Autobiography.* New York: Simon & Schuster, 1936.

Thomson, Virgil. *Virgil Thomson.* New York: Knopf, 1966.

Toklas, Alice B. *What Is Remembered.* New York: Holt, Rinehart & Winston, 1963.

———. *Staying On Alone. Letters of Alice B. Toklas.* Edited by Edward Burns. New York: Liveright, 1974.

Tyler, Parker. *The Divine Comedy of Pavel Tchelitchew.* New York: Fleet, 1967.

Unterecker, John. *Voyager. A Life of Hart Crane.* New York: Farrar, Straus & Giroux, 1969.

Van Vechten, Carl. *Fragments from an Unwritten Autobiography.* New Haven, Conn.: Yale University Library, 1955.

Walsh, Ernest. *Poems and Sonnets.* New York: Harcourt, Brace, 1934.

Wescott, Glenway. *Good-Bye Wisconsin.* New York: Harper, 1928.

————. *Fear and Trembling.* New York: Harper, 1932.

Wickes, George. *Americans in Paris.* Garden City, N.Y.: Doubleday, 1969.

Williams, William Carlos. *The Autobiography of William Carlos Williams.* New York: Random House, 1948.

————. *The Selected Letters of William Carlos Williams.* Edited by John C. Thirlwall. New York: McDowell, Obolensky, 1957.

Wilson, Edmund. *The Shores of Light: A Literary Chronicle of the Twenties and Thirties.* New York: Farrar, Straus and Young, 1952.

INDEX

Abbott, Berenice, 28

Absit Omen (Wells), 128

Acton, Harold, 270, 281, 282, 284–285; writings of: *This Chaos*, 285, *Tiresias*, 282

Adams, B. M. G. (Mrs. Scratton), 98, 104, 106; writings of: *England*, 103, 104, 114

Adams, Elbridge, 350

Adams, Eve, 367

Adams, Franklin P., 75

Aiken, Conrad, 194, 313, 355

Alain-Fournier, 220, 224

Alastair, 173, 175, 179, 180, 184

Albatross Books, 359

Alberti, Rafael, 289

Aldington, Richard, 139, 150, 195, 222, 264, 265, 270, 277, 281, 282, 284, 359, 377; offers Richard Aldington Poetry Prize, 150–151, 163, 275; selects Lowenfels winner, 163; suggests Hours Press poetry contest, 275–277; writings of: *The Colonel's Daughter*, 164, *The Death of a Hero*, 265, 275, 284, 295, *The Eaten Heart*, 265, 268, *Hark the Herald*, 260, *Last Straws*, 284

Aldrich, Mildred, 248

Aldridge, John, 400, 402*n*

Alice in Wonderland (Carroll), 213, 262

All Quiet on the Western Front (Remarque), 295

Allégret, Marc, 28

Almost Forgotten Germany (Schwarz), 400

American Caravan, The, 153, 187, 210, 235

American Civil Liberties Union, 356

American Mercury, 127

Americans Abroad (Neagoe), 61, 91, 312–313, 355

Anderson, Bart, 359

Anderson, Margaret, 5, 40, 89, 108

Anderson, Sherwood, 75, 108, 221; visits Gertrude Stein, 12–13; mentioned, 55, 62

Angel Wuthercut (Cocteau), 321

Anonymous Editions (Carrefour), 290–297

Antheil George, 51, 96, 136, 310, 318; praises Ezra Pound, 109, 111; works of: *Bad Boy of Music*, 111, *Ballet Mécanique*, 109; mentioned, 27

Apollinaire, Guillaume, 243, 304

Aquila Press, 215, 216

Aragon, Louis: at Hours Press, xvi–xvii, 253, 255, 257, 260, 269; writings of: *The Hunting of the Snark*, xvi–xvii, 253, 260–262, *Voyageur*, 262; mentioned, 7, 10, 74

Arlen, Michael, 162, 296; writings of: *The Green Hat*, 258

Armory Show, 302, 303, 304

Arp, Hans, 229, 316

Asch, Nathan, 28, 60

Asch, Sholem, 150

Atlantic Monthly, xvi; publishes *The Autobiography of Alice B. Toklas* (Stein), 248

Auden, W. H., 289

Babou, Henry, 348–350, 352, 354, 357

Bald, Wambly, 123, 145, 312, 363; describes Dunning, 123; describes Kiki, 149; and Henry Miller, 363

Bandy, W. T., 139

Bankhead, Tallulah, 30

Banting, John, 270

Barber, Solon R., 311

Barbusse, Henri, 360

Barnes, Djuna, 131–132, 136, 313, 359; and James Joyce, xii; writings of: *Ladies Almanack*, 131–132, *Nightwood*, 131; mentioned, 27, 60, 61

Barney, Natalie Clifford, 28, 29, 132, 150

Baudelaire, Charles-Pierre, 174

Beach, Cyprian, 17

Beach, Sylvia, 42, 49, 51, 114, 150, 153, 188, 189, 193, 195, 214, 345, 355; publishes *Ulysses*, xi–xii, 5–6, 14–20; operates Shakespeare and Company, xi, 9, 28; described, xi, xii–xiii, 6–7; and James Joyce, xii, 5, 7, 21–26; and Adrienne Monnier, 7, 8; and Maurice Darantière, 15, 16, 17, 18; distributes *Ulysses*, 20–21; and Harriet Weaver, 23; rejects manuscripts, 29–32; defends *Ulysses*, 32; and Robert McAlmon, 34, 35, 36, 42, 46, 53, 54, 56, 65–66, 68, 69, 73, 77–78, 82–83, 86, 87–91 *passim*, 92, 93, 94; and D. H. Lawrence, 140, 195, 352; and Jack Kahane, 349–350

Beadle, Charles, 375

Beardsley, Aubrey, 266

Beasley, Gertrude, 62, 65, 68; writings of: *My First Thirty Years*, 62, 65

Beaton, Cecil, 258

Beckett, Samuel, 86, 166, 276–278, 282, 296; wins poetry contest, 277; writings of: *Echo's Bones*, 322, "From the Only Poet to a Shining Whore," 282, *Whoroscope*, 276–278, 281

Bell, Clive, 273

Benet, Stephen, 12

Benét, William Rose, 85; reviews *The Making of Americans* (Stein), 70; reviews *The Portrait of a Generation* (McAlmon), 77

Bérard, Christian (Bébé), 243, 336

Berraud, Maurice: illustrates *Carmen*, 335

Berry, Walter Van Rensselaer, 178–179, 180, 181, 202; Marcel Proust's letters to, 179, 182; Henry James' letters to, 181–182

Bessie Cotter (Smith), 372, 373

Bird, Bill, 45, 51, 53, 59, 61, 64, 70, 71, 73, 92, 95–116 *passim*, 121, 150, 278; describes Robert McAlmon, 35, 93; joins Contact, 46–47, 95; founds Consolidated Press Association, 97; founds Three Mountains Press, 97; on commercial publishers, 113; sells press to Nancy Cunard, 253; writings of: *A Practical Guide to French Wines*, 97, 114, 115

Bizet, Georges, 335

Black Manikin bookshop (At the Sign of the Black Manikin), 85, 120–122

Black Manikin Press, 117–167

Black Riders (Crane), 305

Black Sun Press, 81, 150, 176–230 *passim*, 305, 321

Blackmur, R. P., 111, 112, 113

Blitzstein, Marc, 139

Bodenheim, Max, 75, 83

Bodley Head Ltd., 247

Bogouslawski, Michael, 364, 367

Boni, Albert, 66, 68

Boni, Charles, 66, 68

Boni and Liveright, 129

Booster, The (Delta), 379–380, 381

Bowles, Paul, 137, 309n

Boyle, Kay, 28, 54, 92, 136, 181, 204, 228, 296, 309n, 313, 316, 320, 321, 359, 380; and Robert McAlmon, 35, 80–82, 92–93, 226; assists Walsh, 80–81; assists Eugene Jolas, 81, 181; edits *Being Geniuses Together* (McAlmon), 92; and Harry Crosby, 181; and Hart Crane, 187, 198; and Caresse Crosby, 221, 222–223, 224, 227–228; translates *Babylon* (Crevel), 222–223; translates *Devil in the Flesh* (Radiguet), 223, 225; selects stories for McAlmon collection, 224–225; writings of: "Change of Life," 310, "In Defense of Homosexuality," 320, "Passeres' Paris," 80, *Short Stories*, 194, "Summer," 80, *Wedding Day and Other Stories*, 194, *Year Before Last*, 224

Bradley, Jenny, 369

Bradley, William Aspenwall, 235, 356, 384; agent for Gertrude Stein, 235–237, 246–252 *passim*; agent for Henry Miller, 360, 363, 364, 365, 366; and Anais Nin, 369, 370

Brancusi, Constantin, 51, 103, 136, 192–193, 258, 310

Brand, Neville, 166

Braque, Georges: and cubism, xiv, 317

Braverman, Barnet: distributes *Ulysses*, 21

Brentano, Lowell, 348, 349, 353

429

Brentano's (Paris bookshop), 24, 85, 367, 378

Breton, André, 7, 165, 166, 257, 314; writings of: *Nadja*, 229

Brewer, Joseph, 236; publishes *Useful Knowledge* (Stein), 234–235

Broca, Henri, 145; publishes *Les Souvenirs de Kiki de Montparnasse*, 145; founds *Paris-Montparnasse*, 145

Bromfield, Louis, 28

Broom, 233

Broun, Heywood, 75

Brown, Bob, 162, 210, 240, 246, 270, 281, 303–311, 313, 316; and Gertrude Stein, 304; and his Reading Machine, 304, 305, 307, 310–311; founds Roving Eye Press, 306; writings of: *Demonics*, 309, "Eyes," 303, 305, 306, *1450–1950*, 198, 200, 305, *Gems*, 307–309, *Globe-Gliding*, 307, *My Margonary*, 304, *The Readies*, 306–307, 309, 313, *Readies for Bob Brown's Machine*, 309–311, *The Remarkable Adventures of Christopher Poe*, 303, *What Happened to Mary*, 303, *Words*, 285–287, 307

Brulliard, André, 83

Bunting, Basil, 221

Buñuel, Luis, 159; works of: *L'Age d'Or*, 159, 363, *The Andalusian Dog*, 165

Burford, Roger, 380

Burke, Kenneth, 101, 103, 234

Burnett, Whit, 162n, 198, 199

Buss, Kate, 106, 108

Butts, Mary, 27, 61, 63–64, 87, 132, 134; writings of: *Ashe of Rings*, 63–64, *Imaginary Letters*, 132, 134, 167

Byron, Lord, 336–338

Cagli, Corrado, 230

Calder, Alexander, 334, 336, 343; illustrates *Fables of Aesop*, 333–334, 343

Caldwell, Erskine, 90

Callaghan, Morley, 121, 136, 150, 153–157, 167; and Robert McAlmon, 154–156; and Hemingway, 154; writings of: "A Girl with Ambition," 153, "Last Spring They Came Over," 153, *No Man's Meat*, 156–157, 164, "Now That April's Here," 156, *That Summer in Paris*, 155, *Strange Fugitive*, 154

Campbell, Roy, 263, 270, 278, 279, 377; writings of: *The Georgiad*, 279, *Poems*, 279

Camus, Albert, 229

Cannell, Kathleen, 75, 198

Cape, Jonathan, 13, 58, 194, 351, 357

Carnevali, Emanuel, 53–54, 136, 137, 217, 228, 313, 320; reviews *Explorations* (McAlmon), 37; writings of: *A Hurried Man*, 64–65

Carrefour (Anonymous Editions), 290–302, 396

Carroll, Lewis, 253, 262

Casanova, Giovanni, 280

Cather, Willa, 228

Cave, Roderick, 387n

Céline, Louis-Ferdinand, 347

Cendrars, Blaise: reviews *Tropic of Cancer* (Miller), 368

Cerf, Bennett, 227, 251, 252

Cézanne, Paul, xiii

Chamson, André, 27

Chapman, Gerald, 75

Charles I, 335

Chattopadhya, Sarojini, 267

Cheese Girl at New Bench, The (Itchwyrth), 128

Chentoff, Polia, 121, 125, 128, 139, 143, 183–184, 215; and Titus, 128–129; and the Crosbys, 183, 198; works of: *First Communion*, 183

Chicago Tribune, European Edition (Paris), 75, 106, 109, 120, 121, 123, 127, 128, 136, 152, 164, 225, 226, 312, 314, 315, 359, 361, 363

Childe Harold's Pilgrimage (Byron), 336–338

Chirico, Giorgio di, 166, 229

Chisholm, Hugh: translates *Misfortunes of the Immortals* (Ernst and Eluard), 229

Church, Ralph, 237

Claire Marie (publisher), 231–232

Clarke, Herbert, 100, 101, 169; association with Kahane, 353–354

Claudel, Paul, 8

Cleugh, James, 281

Close-Up, 78

Closerie des Lilas (café), 129

Coates, Robert, 74–76, 87, 236, 240; writings of: *The Eater of Darkness*, 69, 74–76

Cobb, Irvin, 75

Cockerell, Douglas, 284

Cocteau, Jean, 134, 198, 273, 302, 320, 321

Cody, Morrill, 3

Cohn, Louis H., 105

Colette, 222, 227

Collier, John: reviews *Contact Collection of Contemporary Writers*, 61; wins *This Quarter* poetry prize, 164

Conder, Charles, 266, 267

Connolly, Cyril, 361, 373; writings of: *Rock Pool*, 373

Constable and Company, 391; and the Seizin Press, 399, 400, 402

Contact (magazine), 38, 40–41, 45, 89, 90, 99

Contact Publishing Company, 35, 40, 45–48, 52, 54, 64, 65, 70, 80, 83, 85–86, 95, 112

Convalescent Conversations (Vara), 400

Cooper, James Fenimore, 41

Corneille, Pierre, 336

Cousins, Sheila, 384

Covici, Pascal, 111, 146

Cowley, Malcolm, 175, 186, 209, 313; writings of: *Blue Juniata*, 186

Coyle, Kathleen, 153, 167; writings of: *There Is a Door*, 157

Craig, Archibald, 136, 137

Crane, Hart, 184–188, 194, 198–199, 209, 218, 297, 313; and the Crosbys, 185–188, 198–199, 209–213; writings of: *The Bridge*, 185, 186, 187, 188, 198, 199, 209, 210–212, 213

Crane, Stephen, 305

Craven, Arthur, 49

Crawford, Nelson A., 311

Cresset Press, 28

Crevel, René, 165, 222–223, 228, 257; writings of: *Babylon* (*Mr. Knife, Miss Fork*), 222

Criterion, The, 58, 103

Crosby, Caresse, 81, 91, 143, 168–169, 171–176, 177, 178, 179, 180, 181, 182, 184, 185, 187, 188, 194, 197, 200, 202, 204–208 *passim*, 230, 286, 313; designs colophon for Black Sun Press, 171; and Joyce, 188–194; and Hart Crane, 198–199, 209–213; and D. H. Lawrence, 202–203; travels to the United States, 208–210; returns to Paris, 210; supervises publication of husband's books, 213, 217–219; and Ezra Pound, 214–217, 220–221; and T. S. Eliot, 217–218, 223–224; writes *Poems for Harry Crosby*, 219–220; operates Crosby Continental Editions, 220–228; writes "Open Letter" to Hemingway, 222; and Kay Boyle, 222–223, 224; edits *Portfolio*, 229; writings of: *Crosses of Gold*, 168–169, *Impossible Melodies*, 184, "Invited to Die," 208, *Painted Shores*, 171, *Poems for Harry Crosby*, 219–220, *The Stranger*, 171–172.

Crosby, Harry, 81, 143, 168–169, 171–176, 305, 307, 313, 321; effect of World War I on, 174–175; belief in sun worship, 175; and D. H. Lawrence, 176–178, 182–183, 195, 197, 202; and James Joyce, 188–194; buys mill at Ermenonville, 180–181; and Kay Boyle, 181; joins *transition*, 184; and Hart Crane, 185–188, 198–199, 209–213; reads *The Bridge* (Crane), 185, 187–188; death prophecies, 201, 210; learns to fly, 201–202, 207; influenced by Eugene Jolas, 204; returns to the United States, 208–210; dies, 210; writings of: *Aphrodite in Flight*, 202, 213–214, *Chariot of the Sun*, 177, 180, 183, 217, *Mad Queen*, 184, 205–207, 228, *Red Skeletons*, 171, 172–175, 228, *Shadows of the Sun*, 179, 194 (Volume II), 209, 213 (Volume III), *Sleeping Together*, 202, 204, 207, 210, 218, 228, *Sonnets for Caresse*, 169, 171, 175, *The Sun*, 198, 199–200, 202, *Torchbearer*, 218, *Transit of Venus*, 181, 194, 198, 199, 217, 218, *War Letters*, 228

Crosby Continental Editions, 91, 220–228

Cross-Country (Barber), 311

Crowder, Henry, 270, 280, 284; joins Nancy Cunard at Hours Press, 264, 268, 269; composes music for *Henry-Music*, 282

Crowley, Aleister, 334; writings of: *Memoirs*, 30

Cuala Press, 99

Cubism, xiv

Cullen, Countee, 150

Cummings, E. E., 8, 60, 75, 139, 164, 166, 181, 198, 209, 263, 310, 313; wins Aldington Poetry Prize, 163, 275; writings of: *The Enormous Room*, 148, 220

Cunard, Maud (Emerald), Lady, 256, 278, 288

Cunard, Nancy, 47, 86, 113, 116, 216, 297, 307, 309n; operates Hours Press (Réanville), xvi–xvii, 253–268, (Paris) 269–281, 287–289; and George Moore, 256–257, 258, 259, 260, 285, 287–288; in Paris, 257; and Norman Douglas, 263–265; and Henry Crowder, 264, 280–282; and Eugene Mac-Cown, 270–273; and Walter Lowenfels, 273; conducts poetry contest, 275–277; describes Samuel Beckett, 277; and Ezra Pound, 278–279; and Roy Campbell, 279; plans Negro, 284, 285; writings of: Negro, 264, 289, Outlaws, 256, Parallax, 256, 257, 273, Sublunary, 256, Two Poems, 281; mentioned, 10, 28

Curtis, Ralph, 373

Curtis Brown (publisher), 177, 374

Dahl, André, 145

Dahlberg, Edward, 137

Dali, Salvador, 165, 229

D'Annunzio, Gabriele, 152

Darantière, Maurice, 14, 42, 46, 62, 66, 67, 68, 83, 149, 168, 238, 244–245; prints Ulysses, 15–20, 23; prints A Hasty Bunch (McAlmon), 39–40; prints Some Gentlemen of the Renaissance (Van Wyck), 131; prints How to Write (Stein), 240, 241; prints Matisse, Picasso and Gertrude Stein, 246

Dark Refuge (Beadle), 375

David, Hermine, 149

Davidson, Jo, 28

Davies, Rhys, 150

Davis, Stuart, 309

Death of Madame, The (De La Fayette), 335–336

De la Mare, Walter, 10

Delisle, Françoise: translates Big Meaulnes (Alain-Fournier), 224

Demuth, Charles, 88

Devigne, Roger, 97

Dial, The, 50, 69, 70, 103, 107, 139, 163, 234, 329

Dill, Robert, 104

Dôme (café), 117, 129, 147, 148, 149, 150, 367

Doolittle, Hilda (H. D.), 43, 44, 46, 51, 53, 61, 78, 87; writings of: "Hedylus," 61, Palimpsest, 46, 69, 71–73

Dos Passos, John, 53, 60, 107, 108, 229, 313, 377; mentioned, xiii, 28

Dostoyevsky, Fyodor, 336, 338

Douglas, Norman, 61, 140, 258, 260, 273, 284; and Nancy Cunard, 263–265, 271; writings of: One Day, 264, 268, Report on the Pumice-Stone Industry of the Lipari Islands, 255, 256

Dowson, Ernest, 184, 266

Dreiser, Theodore, 127, 377

Dubliners (Joyce), 39, 40

Duchamp, Marcel, 165, 229, 302, 303, 304; and The Blindman, 303; and Henry Miller, 368; works of: "Nude Descending a Staircase," 302, 304

Duff, Charles, 311

Duhamel, Georges, 10, 28

Dunning, Ralph Cheever, 121, 122–125, 127, 139, 313; writings of: *Rococo*, 122, 124–125, *Windfalls*, 125, 143

Durrell, Lawrence, 370, 379, 383; and Henry Miller, 368–369, 375–383; contributes to *The Booster*, 379–380, 381; sponsors Villa Seurat Series, 380–381; writings of: *The Black Book*, 376, 378, 379, 381–383, *The Pied Pipers of Lovers*, 376

Earp, T. W., 279

Eastman, Max, 204, 377

Editions de la Montagne (Hugnet), 243

Egoist, The, 5

Egoist Press, 28

Einstein, Albert, 205

Eisenstein, Sergei, 344

Elegant Peccadillo, An (Rheims), 163

Eliot, T. S., 39, 41, 58, 98, 99, 165, 173–174, 217, 223, 375, 378; and Robert McAlmon, 38; writes introduction for *Transit of Venus* (Crosby), 218; writes introduction for *Bubu of Montparnasse* (Philippe), 223–224; writings of: *Ara Vus Prec*, 280, *The Waste Land*, 76; mentioned, xiii, 8

Ellerman, Sir John, 43, 45, 52, 56, 78

Ellerman, Lady, 69

Ellerman, Winifred (Bryher), 27, 37, 42, 43, 51, 53, 61, 69, 73, 78; writings of: *Civilians*, 78, *Development*, 43, *Two Selves*, 43–44

Ellis, Havelock, 61, 224, 287; writings of: *The Revaluation of Obscenity*, 287, 288

Ellmann, Richard, 193

Eluard, Paul, 165, 166, 229; writings of: *Misfortunes of the Immortals*, 229, *Thorns of Thunder*, 322

Emerson, Ralph Waldo, 182

Emile-Bécat, Paul, 195

Epilogue (Riding and Graves), 391–392, 394, 399, 400, 402, 402n

Ernst, Max, 165, 166, 222, 229; works of: *Misfortunes of the Immortals*, 229

Esquire, 368

Eton Candle, 284

Evans, Donald, 304

Evans, Walker, 209, 211

Everyman, 270, 276, 288

Exile (Pound), 111, 154

Faber and Faber, 376, 378, 379

Fables of Aesop, 333–334, 338

Fadiman, Clifton, 228

Falké, Pierre, 327–328

Fall of the House of Usher, The (Poe), 175–176

Fanfrolico Press, 28
Fargue, Léon-Paul, 8, 15, 28
Farrell, James T., 90, 162, 166, 220, 309n, 310, 313, 320; writings of: "Stud," 162
Faulkner, William, 224, 227
Faÿ, Bernard, 243, 273, 359
Fearing, Kenneth, 136
Fenton, Charles, 104
Ferber, Edna, 60
Firbank, Ronald, 10
Fitzgerald, F. Scott, xiii, 27, 60, 154, 155, 241, 296; writings of: *Tender Is the Night*, 214, *This Side of Paradise*, 357
Fitzgerald, Zelda, 155
Flanner, Janet, 27, 131, 132, 257; describes Sylvia Beach, xi–xiii, Gertrude Stein, xiii–xvi, Nancy Cunard, xvi–xvii
Foch, Marshal Ferdinand, 182
Foley, Martha, 162n
Ford, Charles Henri, 307, 309n, 320; writings of: *The Garden of Disorder*, 322, *The Young and Evil*, 357, 359
Ford, Ford Madox, 28, 55, 60, 61, 98, 106, 112, 123, 152, 235, 320, 355; relations with Gertrude Stein, 57–58; edits *Transatlantic Review*, 95, 115; comments on Three Mountains publications, 106–107; writings of: *Some Do Not*, 58, *Women and Men*, 100, 114
Forum, 197
Foujita, Tsuguhara, 144, 145, 149
Fountain Press, 350
Four Poems (Vail), 229
Fraenkel, Michael, 273, 290, 292, 294, 296, 297–298, 376, 380, 383; and Henry Miller, 294, 299, 300, 301, 302, 361, 363, 366, 368; "death" theme, 295, 298–302; writes *Hamlet* letters, 300–302; and Anaïs Nin, 370, 371; and *The Booster*, 379; writings of: *Anonymous*, 290–292, *Bastard Death*, 299, *Death in a Room*, 298–299, *Hamlet*, 295, 300–302, 368, 380, 382, 383, *Werther's Younger Brother*, 292, 294, 295, 296
Frank, Waldo, 75, 108, 187
Friend, Krebs, 58, 115, 116; writings of: *The Herdboy*, 115
Front, 311
Fry, Roger, 10
Fuller, William, 400
Furman, Lee, 235–236

Galantière, Dorothy, 13
Galantière, Louis, 13
Gale, Zona, 153
Galignani (Paris bookshop), 24, 85
Garland, Hamlin, 153
Garnett, Constance, 336

Garnett, David, 143, 263
Garnett, Edward, 351
Gascoyne, David, 380
Gaudier-Brzeska, Henri, 280
Gautier-Vignal, Edith, 368
Geddes, Virgil, 127, 128; writings of: *40 Poems*, 128, *The Frog*, 127, 128
Gemor Press, 229
Gentle Spirit, A (Dostoyevsky), 336, 338
Gershwin, George, 296
Gide, André, xiii, 8, 10, 15, 27, 198, 224, 273, 329
Gilbert, Stuart, 27, 168, 189, 204, 218, 219–220, 224, 316, 359, 371; writes preface for *Sleeping Together* (Crosby), 218–219; writes preface for *Poems for Harry Crosby*, 220
Gillespie, Link, 307, 313
Gilliam, Florence, 97
Gillie, Darsie, xii
Girodias, Marcelle Eugenie, 347
Girodias, Maurice, 360, 384
Glassco, John, 79–80, 137, 155; and Robert McAlmon, 155–156; writings of: *Memoirs of Montparnasse*, 80
Gold, Mike, 220
Goldman, Emma, 312
Goldschmidt, Karl, 393n
Gollancz, Victor, 357
Gordon, Whitold, 129
Gotham Book Mart, 28, 88, 241, 383
Gould, Wallace, 61
Grafton Press, xv, 231, 233
Grand Meaulnes (Alain-Fournier), 220, 224
Grant, Ulysses S., 250
Graves, Robert, 233, 270, 274, 279; and the Seizin Press, 385–387, 391, 393n, 394, 400, 403; associate editor of *Epilogue*, 391; writings of: *Antigua, Penny Puce*, 400, *Goodbye to All That*, 391, *Poems 1929*, 391, *Ten Poems More*, 274, 393n
Grosz, George, 229
Guevara, Alvaro: writes *St. George at Silene*, 255, 260
Guillen, Nicolas, 289

Hachette (publisher), 224, 364
Haddon Craftsmen (Camden), 343, 344
Hall, Radclyffe: and *The Well of Loneliness*, 195, 347, 359–360
Hammett, Dashiell, 88
Hamnett, Nina, 258
Hanley, James: and *Boy*, 359, 373
Harcourt, Alfred, 248, 249, 250, 251, 252; accepts *Autobiography of Alice B. Toklas* (Stein), 247–248

Harcourt Brace (publisher), 247

Harmsworth, Desmond, 356

Harper, Allanah, 178

Harper's, 204

Harper's Bazaar, 249

Harriman, Marie, 236

Harris, Frank, 32, 75, 360; writings of: *My Life and Loves*, 32, 347, 359–360

Harrison, Barbara (Mrs. Lloyd B. Wescott), 325–326, 329, 342, 343

Harrison of Paris (press), 323–344

Harrison Smith (publisher), 224

Harte, Bret: stories published (*The Wild West*), 326–328, 330, 332

Hartley, Marsden, 27, 42, 43, 61, 64, 302; writings of: *Twenty-five Poems*, 46, 48

Hayter, S. W., 322

Heap, Jane, 5, 58, 63, 66, 67, 68, 89, 108, 233

Heathen, The (Wyatt), 400

Hecht, Ben, 75

Hemingway, Ernest, xiii, 8, 15, 21, 27, 42, 44–45, 53, 55, 60, 61, 87, 93, 95, 97, 98, 115, 119, 123, 136, 149, 155, 220, 221, 307, 310, 313, 355; and James Joyce, xii; relationship with Sylvia Beach, 13–14; and Gertrude Stein, 57; subeditor of *Transatlantic*, 57, 96; comments on early writing, 104–105; writes preface for Kiki's *Memoirs*, 147–148, 149; negotiates with Caresse Crosby, 221–222; relationship with Robert McAlmon, 225, 226; writings of: *A Moveable Feast*, 13, "A Natural History of the Dead," 221, "The Battler," 107, "Big Two-Hearted River," 313, *Death in the Afternoon*, 221, *in our time*, 50, 104–108, 114, *In Our Time*, 13, 224, 227, "Indian Camp," 106, "Mr. and Mrs. Elliott," 107, "The Sea Change," 164, "Soldier's Home," 61, *The Sun Also Rises*, 76, 221, 350, *Three Stories and Ten Poems*, 46, 49–50, 104, 105, 106, 107, *Torrents of Spring*, 221–222, 223, 224, 227, "The Undefeated," 13, 138, "Up in Michigan," 107

Henderson, Wyn, 216; manages Hours Press, 281, 282, 284, 286, 287–289 *passim*; and Aquila Press, 281

Herbst, Josephine, 71, 166

Heriat, Philippe, 354

Herrmann, John, 61, 65, 90; writings of: *What Happens*, 65, 69, 71, 72

Hiler, Hilaire, 69, 83, 86, 90, 305, 309n, 318

Hogarth Press, 28, 73, 233, 273

Holliday Bookshop (New York), 28, 85

Horses (Lazzari), 229

Houghton Mifflin Publishing Company, 71, 214

Hound and the Horn, The, 87

Hours Press, 150, 216, 253–289, 307, 393, 393n

Howard, Brian, 270, 281, 284–285; writings of: *First Poems*, 285

Hubbell, Lindley, 243, 248

Huddleston, Sisley, 8, 122, 125

Huebsch, Ben, 5

Hughes, Glenn, 152

Hughes, Langston, 289

Hugnet, Georges, 243; dispute with Gertrude Stein, 243–244; writings of: *Enfances*, 243, 321

Hugo, Valentine, 166

Hunting of the Snark, The (Carroll), 253, 262

Huntington, Katharine, 128

Huser of Paris, 338, 339

Huxley, Aldous, 10, 75, 141, 195, 257, 258, 321, 376, 377; writes preface for *Devil in the Flesh* (Radiguet), 223; writings of: *Point Counter Point*, 258

Huxley, Julian, 189

Huysmans, Joris Karl, 174

Ibara, Saikaku, 84

Imagist Anthology (Ford and Hughes), 152

Imbs, Bravig, 137; on Gertrude Stein, 252

Indians in the Woods, The (Lewis), 325

Interregnum (Grosz), 229

Irish Statesman, The, 69

Jackson, Schuyler B., 389

James, Henry, 41, 164, 181–182, 250, 373

James, Norah: and *Sleeveless Errand*, 350–351, 352, 353, 354

Jewell, Kennon: reviews *Three Stories and Ten Poems* (Hemingway), 106

Jews Without Money (Gold), 220

John, Augustus, 228, 267

Jolas, Eugene, 136, 163, 164, 165, 181, 184, 185, 188, 194, 204, 210, 229, 309n, 311, 313, 314–317 *passim*, 319, 320, 321, 355; founds *transition*, 81; and the "Revolution of the Word" manifesto, 204, 205, 314, 316, 319; edits *transition* stories, 313; revives *transition* (1932), 313–316; comments on Neagoe, 321; writings of: *The Language of Night*, 314, 315–316, *Secession in Astropolis*, 204–205; mentioned, 3, 28, 89, 135, 153

Jolas, Maria, 28, 188, 317–318

Jones, John Paul, 120

Josephson, Matthew, 204

Journey to the End of the Night (Céline), 367

Joyce, James, 43, 51, 60, 61, 66, 75, 76, 86, 96, 112, 113, 119, 165, 197, 222, 277, 278, 291, 310, 316, 319, 345, 347, 349–350, 353, 365, 375, 377; described, xi–xii; and Sylvia Beach, xii, 5, 7, 21–26; publication of *Ulysses*, 5, 14–20; and Harriet Weaver, 23; and the Crosbys, 188–194; writings of: *Chamber Music*, 228, *Collected Poems of James Joyce*, 228–229, *Dubliners*, 220, "Ecce Puer," 228, *Exiles*, 220, *Finnegans Wake*, 32, 61, *Haveth Childers Everywhere*, 346, 350, 354, *The Mime of Mick, Nick and the Maggies*, 316–317, *Our Exagmination round his Factification for Incamination of Work in Progress* (various contributors), 32, 83, *Pomes Penyeach*, 32, 228,

346, 356–357, *Tales Told of Shem and Shaun*, 189, 192, *Work in Progress*, 189, 190, 316, 317
Joyce, Lucia, 317, 346, 356–357
Joyce, Nora, 349

Kafka, Franz, 222
Kahane, Jack, 32, 92, 321, 347–384 *passim*; opinion of James Joyce, 345, 346, 349; meets Joyce, 349–350; writes *To Laugh and Grow Rich*, 348; association with Babou, 348–350, 352, 354; and Sylvia Beach, 349–350; and D. H. Lawrence, 352; association with Herbert Clarke, 353–354; uses nom de plume, 353; association with M. Servant, 354, 363–364; founds Obelisk Press, 354; and Peter Neagoe, 355–356; and Henry Miller, 360, 363–368, 371, 372; and William Bradley, 364, 365; and Anais Nin, 370; and Lawrence Durrell, 376, 377, 378, 379, 381–383; dies, 384; writings of: *Daffodil*, 353, 354, 355, 364, *The Gay Intrigue*, 348, 353, *Lady, Take Heed!* 374, *To Laugh and Grow Rich*, 353, *Memoirs of a Booklegger*, 345, 347, 348, 367, 384
Kahnweiler, Daniel-Henry: describes cubism, xiv
Kamin, Martin, 88–90
Kaufman, George, 296
Keats, John, 64
Keen Edge, The (Smith), 325
Kiki (Alice Prin), 119, 121, 144–149; writings of: *Memoirs*, 145–149, 167
Kipling, Rudyard, 168
Kisling, Moise, 144, 145, 149
Knopf (publisher), 57, 58, 107
Koch, Paul, 342
Kokoschka, Oskar, 258
Komroff, Manuel, 128–130, 306, 309n; writings of: *Coronet*, 129, *The Grace of Lambs*, 129, *The Voice of Fire*, 128–130
Krell, Krauss, 221
Kreymborg, Alfred, 83, 153, 309n
Krogh, Per, 144
Krutch, Joseph Wood, 125, 164

La Rochefoucauld, Comte Armand de, 180–181
Laclos, Choderlos de, 184, 210
Laforgue, Jules, 230
Lahr, Charles, 142
Lamb, The (Heriat), 354
Lament for the Living (Parker), 224
Lane, John, 232, 234, 235, 247, 252
Lanham, Edwin, 80, 82; describes Robert McAlmon, 86–87; writings of: *Sailors Don't Care*, 83–84
Larbaud, Valéry, 8, 9, 15, 27, 51

Laurencin, Marie, 213

Lawrence, David, 97

Lawrence, D. H., 30, 31, 32, 119, 121, 139, 222, 346, 347, 352, 353, 359, 365, 372, 376; and Harry Crosby, 176–178, 182–183, 195, 197, 202; and Caresse Crosby, 202–203; writings of: "Apocalypse," 142, 143, "The Escaped Cock," 143, 197, 202–203, *Lady Chatterley's Lover*, 30, 119, 140–143, 144, 160–161, 167, 195, 308, 347, 352, 364, 367, *Love Among the Haystacks*, 143, "My Skirmish with a Jolly Roger," 141, *Pansies*, 141–142, *The Plumed Serpent*, 177, 184, 195, "Pornography and Obscenity," 140, "Sun," 142, 143, 177–178, 182–183, 195, *The Virgin and the Gypsy*, 143

Lawrence, Frieda, 141, 142–143, 195

Lawrence, T. E., 217, 385

Lazzari, Pieto, 229

Lemonnier, Leon, 151

Leonard, William Ellery, 125

Lescaret, Roger, 169, 171, 177, 179, 180, 193–194, 207, 210, 219, 228

Levy, Julian, 229

Lévy, Maurice, 115, 116, 253, 254–255, 259, 260, 262, 265, 269

Levy, Oscar, 139, 166

Lewis, Janet, 325

Lewis, Sinclair, 54, 55, 60, 125, 127, 377

Lewis, Wyndham, 46, 98, 99, 220, 257, 258, 278, 280

Lewisohn, Ludwig, 119, 121, 125, 128, 129, 139, 153, 162, 164, 167; writings of: *The Case of Mr. Crump*, 125–127, 130, 153, 167, *The Romantic*, 157–158

Liaisons Dangereuses, Les (Laclos), 184, 210

Light, Jimmy, 8

Linatie, Carlo, 55

Little Review, The, 5, 15, 50, 76, 89, 99, 104, 105, 109, 139, 215, 234, 325

Liveright, Horace, 58, 107–108 125, 211, 357

Liveright Publishing Co., 108, 211, 212

Living Frieze, The (Turbyfill), 325

Llona, Victor, 139

Loeb, Harold, 75, 107, 233

London Sporting News, 31

Loos, Anita, 147

Loria, Arturo, 152

Louis XIV, 334, 335

Love Counts Ten (Zay), 375

Loving, Pierre, 121; reviews *Rococo* (Dunning), 124

Lowell, Joan, 84

Lowenfels, Walter, 139, 270, 282, 290, 292, 295, 296, 302, 309n, 383; wins Aldington Poetry Prize, 163–164, 275; and "death" theme, 294, 297; and Henry Miller, 363; and *The Booster*, 380; writings of: *Anonymous*, 290–292, "Creed," 282, *Elegy in the Manner of a Requiem in Memory of D. H. Lawrence*, 297, *Elegy on Apollinaire*, 270, 273, 297, *Episodes and Epistles*, 292,

No More Poems, 163, *The Poem That Can't Be Stopped*, 273, *Reality Prime*, 297, *The Suicide*, 297, *U.S.A. with Music*, 292–294, 296
Lowe-Porter, H. T., 328
Loy, Mina, 27, 42, 43, 58, 61, 305; writings of: *Lunar Baedecker*, 46, 49
Loynson-Hicks, William, 142
Lucas, F. L., 217
Luhan, Mabel Dodge, 247
Lye, Len, 270, 274, 275, 280, 390n; at Seizin Press, 392–395, 396, 398, 400; works of: *No Trouble*, 392–395, 394n, 396, *Tusalava* (film), 394
Lymington, Gerald (Earl of Portsmouth), 176; writings of: *Git le Coeur*, 176, 203, *Spring Song of Iscariot*, 203–204

McAlmon, Robert, 8, 13, 17, 27, 96, 101, 103, 104, 112, 113, 132, 137, 150, 153, 194, 220, 222, 257, 309n, 313, 317; sells *Ulysses*, 15–16; described, 34–35, 37; and Sylvia Beach, 34, 35, 36, 39, 40–41, 42, 53, 54, 56, 65–66, 68, 69, 73, 77–78, 82–83, 86, 87–91 *passim*, 92; Contact Editions, 35, 45–48, 52, 59, 64, 65, 70, 80, 83, 85–86; meets T. S. Eliot, 38; arrives in Paris, 38–39; and James Joyce, 39; and Ernest Hemingway, 44–45, 225, 226; and William Carlos Williams, 51–53; travels in Spain, 53; and Emanuel Carnevali, 53–54; and Gertrude Stein, 56, 58–59, 62–63, 66–71, 73, 233; defends expatriate writers, 59–60; and Mary Butts, 63–64; separates from wife, 78; revisits the United States, 78–79; and Kay Boyle, 80–82, 224–225; travels in United States and Mexico, 87–88; returns to United States, 92; dies, 92; and Morley Callaghan, 154–156; and John Glassco, 155–156; and Taylor Graeme, 155–156; writings of: *A Companion Volume*, 42, *A Hasty Bunch*, 39–40, 42, "An Illiterate but Interesting Woman," 83, *Being Geniuses Together*, 34–35, 54, 91, 92, *Contact Collection of Contemporary Writers*, 61, "Deracinated Encounters," 79, *Distinguished Air*, 49, 64, 65, 66, 77, 82, 88, 113–114, 115, *Explorations*, 37, 38, *Family Panorama*, 73, 77–78, 82, "The Highly Prized Pajamas," 225, *The Indefinite Huntress and Other Stories*, 91, 224–226, "It's All Very Complicated," 89, 225, "The Jack Rabbit Drive," 83, "Leavetaking," 91, 313, "Mexican Interval," 90, 225, "Mr. Joyce Directs an Irish Prose Ballet," 83, *My Susceptible Friend, Adrian*, 82, "The Mystical Forest," 138, "New York Harbour," 88, 225, *North America, Continent of Conjecture*, 69, 80, 81, 83, 86, 87, *Not Alone Lost*, 92, *The Politics of Existence*, 56, 80, 82, *The Politics of Modesty*, 78, *The Portrait of a Generation*, 56, 69, 73, 76–77, 86, *Post-Adolescence*, 42, 43, "Potato Picking," 82, 83, "Spring Leaves to Consider," 61
Macauley Publishing Co., 235
McBride, Henry, 231, 240, 249
MacCarthy, Desmond, 373
MacCown, Eugene, 198, 199, 258; and Nancy Cunard, 270–273; designs exhibit catalogue, 273, 281
McGreevy, Tom, 296
Machen, Arthur, 280

McKay, Claude, 73, 150

MacLeish, Archibald, 7, 27, 181, 194, 195; writings of: *Einstein*, 194–195, 205, 214, *New Found Land*, 214

MacLeod, Norman, 87, 88, 307

Macmillan Publishing Co., 30

Macpherson, Kenneth, 78; writings of: *Gaunt Island*, 78, *Poolreflection*, 78

Maison des Amis des Livres, La (bookshop), 7

Malkine, Georges, 269

Mallarmé, Stephane, 120, 174

Man Ray. *See* Ray, Man

Manet, Edouard, 120

Manifesto for Individual Secession into World Community (King), 229–230

Manley, Edna, 126

Mann, Thomas: writes preface for *Crump* (Lewisohn), 127, 153; on the Nobel Prize, 329; writings of: *A Sketch of My Life*, 328–329, 330, 332

Mano, Guy Levis, 289

Marinetti, Filippo, 49, 320

Marks, Harry, 28, 180, 182, 197, 198, 199, 202, 203, 210, 228

Martin, Olga, 375

Martin Secker (publisher), 142, 203

Marx, Karl, 294

Mason, Walt, 75

Mathers, William Powys, 280

Matisse, Henri, xv, 229, 317

Matthews, Thomas, 400

Maugham, Somerset, 222, 368

Maurois, André, 150

Mayo, 149

Mencken, H. L., 52, 75, 107, 125, 127, 200, 304, 305, 316, 355

Mérimée, Prosper: and *Carmen*, 334–335, 336, 338, 343

Miller, Henry, 229, 299, 313, 320, 347; association with Anais Nin, 159–160, 361, 363, 364, 365, 366, 369, 370, 371–372, 382; and Michael Fraenkel, 294, 299, 300, 301, 302, 361, 363; and "death" theme, 300, 301, 302; writes *Hamlet* letters, 300–302; and the *New Review*, 320; and William Bradley, 360, 363, 365, 369; relations with Jack Kahane, 360, 364–368, 371, 372; writes D. H. Lawrence study, 365, 382; and Lawrence Durrell, 368–369, 375–383; abandons plans to publish Nin's *Diaries*, 370; contributes to *The Booster*, 379; edits Villa Seurat Series, 380–382, 383, 384; leaves France, 383; writings of: *Aller Retour*, 371, 372, *Black Spring*, 365, 368, 371–372, *Crazy Cock*, 360, 361, *Hamlet*, 295, 380, 382, *Max and the White Phagocytes*, 368, 375, 381, 382, 383, "Mlle Claude," 313, 363, *Scenario*, 370, 371, "The Sleeping Sleeper Asleep," 382, *Tropic of Cancer*, 295, 347, 360–368, 369, 371, 372, 375, 376, 378, 383, *Tropic of Capricorn*, 300, 368, 380, 382, 383, *What Are You Going to Do About Alf*, 368

Miller, June, 369

Mind Products (Duff), 311

Minet, Pierre, 151
Miró, Joan, 268
Mistake Somewhere, A (anonymous), 400
Modern Library, 248, 251
Modigliani, Amedeo, 144; works of: *Pencil Portraits*, 230
Moffit, Curtis, 258
Molière, 334
Monet, Claude, 74
Monnier, Adrienne, 27, 51, 195, 214; described, 7; operates *La Maison des Amis des Livres*, 7–8; publishes *Le Bulletin* and *Le Navire d'Argent*, 8, 13; assists Sylvia Beach, 9, 14, 15, 20; publishes "The Undefeated" (Hemingway), 13
Monroe, Harriet, 40; reviews *North America, Continent of Conjecture* (McAlmon), 86
Moon Letter (*Mah-Name*), 179, 182
Moon's No Fool, The (Matthews), 400
Moore, George, 28, 80; and Nancy Cunard, 256–257, 258, 259, 260, 285, 287–288; writings of: *Confessions of a Young Man*, 80, 156, *Peronnik the Fool*, 256, 259, 260, 264, 268, *Pure Poetry*, 256, *The Talking Pine*, 287
Moore, Marianne, 43, 70; writings of: *Marriage*, 325
Moore, Nicholas, 380
Moorhead, Ethel, 28, 55, 80, 135, 136, 137, 139, 153, 155; reviews *Portrait of a Generation* (McAlmon), 76–77; reviews *Quaint Tales of Samurais* (Sato), 84–85; castigates Pound, 136–137; sells *This Quarter*, 137
Moran, James, 387n
Morel, Auguste, 8
Morgan, Charles, 377
Morgan, J. P., 168
Morgan, Louise, 276, 285, 288; reviews *Palimpsest* (H. D.), 72–73
Morley, Christopher, 75
Morris, William, 322
Mortimer, Raymond, 273
Mortimer, Stanley, 210
Moschos, Myrsine, 21
Moss, Arthur, 75, 77
Moss, David, 88–90
Muir, Edwin, 173–174; reviews early Contact books, 47–49
Mumford, Lewis, 83
Munro, Harold, 8
Murphy, Gerald, 214
Myers, Nancy (Mrs. Lawrence Durrell), 379

Nahl, Margery, 150
Nathan, George Jean, 312
Nation, 127, 270

Neagoe, Peter, 61, 91, 309n, 312, 313, 316, 355; edits *Americans Abroad*, 312–313, 355; buys interest in *New Review*, 320; writings of: "Kaleidoscope," 321, *Storm*, 321, 355–356

Neruda, Pablo, 289

New Age, 47, 61, 99, 111

New American Caravan, 83

New Directions (Publisher), 92

New English Weekly, 91

New Republic, 70, 329

New Review (magazine), 91, 225, 312, 316, 355, 363, 379

New Review Publications, 318–322, 355

New York Herald (Paris), 198, 330

New York Times, 75, 332

New Yorker, 129, 240, 338

Nezaki, Dehzad, 179, 182

Nicholson, Ben, 400

Nin, Anaïs, 28, 167; influenced by D. H. Lawrence, 158, 160–161; relationship with Titus, 159; association with Henry Miller, 159–160, 361, 363, 364, 365–366, 369, 370, 371–372, 382; and William Bradley, 369–370; and Jack Kahane, 370; and Michael Fraenkel, 370, 371; and Lawrence Durrell, 370, 381; founds Siana, 370; and *The Booster*, 379; writings of: *D. H. Lawrence, An Unprofessional Study*, 158, *Diary*, 158, 369, 370, *House of Incest*, 369, 370, 371, *Winter of Artifice*, 370, 380, 381, 382–384

Nonesuch Press, 28

Nordstrom, Ludvig, 55

Norton, Allen, 233

Nott, Stanley, 67, 68

Nyquist, Frank, 325

Obelisk Press, 321, 345–383

Objectivists' Anthology, An (Zukofsky), 91

O'Brien, Edward J., 45, 82, 108, 162, 355; edits *Best Short Stories of 1929*, 82

Observer, 256, 270, 274, 280, 330, 338

Of Thee I Sing (Gershwin and Kaufman), 296

O'Flaherty, Liam, 139

Ogden, C. K., 189, 192

Olesha, Yurig, 320

Olson, Charles, 230

O'Neill, Eugene, 135, 199, 310

Orage, A. R., 99, 111

Orbes, 368

Orioli, Giuseppe, 28, 140, 143, 264

Ortiz, Angelès, 184

Osborn, Richard, 159; assists Henry Miller, 159, 361

Outlook, The, 70, 72

Pagany, 87, 91, 243, 244

Paideuma (Frobenius), 221

Parker, Dorothy, 224

Partridge, Eric, 351

Pasternak, Boris, 320

Pater, Walter, 158

Paul, Elliot, 28, 60, 65, 125, 127, 136, 204, 236, 313, 314, 317; reviews *Eater of Darkness* (Coates), 75; reviews *Rococo* (Dunning), 124–125; and Virgil Geddes, 127–128; describes Stein's writing, 234; writings of: *The Last Time I Saw Paris*, 128

Pegasus Press, 195, 347, 359

Perelman, S. J., 90

Peret, Benjamin, 165

Perkins, Maxwell, 153–154

Perlès, Alfred, 300, 301, 320, 361, 367, 368, 370, 371, 381, 383; edits *The Booster*, 379–380

Perse, St. J., 183

Philippe, Charles-Louis: and *Bubu of Montparnasse*, 222, 223, 227

Picabia, Francis, 49

Picasso, Pablo, 189, 192, 229, 236, 243, 310, 322, 334, 400; and cubism, xiv

Pierrots (Laforgue), 230

Pichon, Leon, 169

Pirandello, Luigi, 152

Plain Editions, 231–252

Poe, Edgar Allan, 174

Poetry, 37, 53, 76, 122

Poetry Bookshop (London), 8, 28

Poetry Review, 275

Pool Publishing Co., 78

Porel, Jacques, 220, 223

Porter, Katherine Anne, 28, 92, 225, 228, 341, 368; writings of: *Flowering Judas*, 343, *A French Song-book*, 341–342, 343, *Hacienda*, 342, 344

Portfolio, 229

Poucin, Marcel, 115

Pound, Dorothy, 10, 104, 279

Pound, Ezra, 13, 15, 34, 41, 44, 51, 60, 61, 65, 89, 92, 96, 97, 103, 105, 108, 122, 123, 126, 135, 136–137, 138, 154, 218, 225, 257, 270, 291, 309n, 312, 313, 318, 320, 321, 377; reviews *A Hasty Bunch* (McAlmon), 40; reviews *The Indefinite Huntress*, (McAlmon), 91; estimate of McAlmon, 93; edits Three Mountains publications, 95, 97–100, 106, 220; meets George Antheil, 109, 111; on publishing abroad, 112; praises Dunning's poetry, 122–123, 125, 143–144; advises Caresse Crosby, 215–217, 220–221; writes introduction for *Torchbearer* (Crosby), 219; praises Guevara's verse, 260; associate editor of *New Review*, 320–321; estimate of *Tropic of Cancer* (Miller), 367–368; writings of: "A Canto," 61, *A Draft of Sixteen Cantos*, 108, 111, 112 113, 115, *A Draft of XXX Cantos*, 278–279, *A Lume Spento*, 112, *Antheil*

Pound, Ezra (*cont.*)
and the Theory of Harmony, 96, 111, 114, 115, *Certain Noble Plays of Japan*, 99, *How to Read*, 165, *Hugh Selwyn Mauberley*, 280, *Imaginary Letters*, 214–215, *Indiscretions*, 99–100, 104, 106, 114, *Le Testament*, 111, *Noh*, 99, *The Probable Music of Beowulf*, 255, 263, *Works of Guido Cavalcanti*, 215–217
Powel, Gretchen and Peter, 213
Powys, T. F., 139
Prévost, Jean, 27
Proust, Marcel, 179, 202; writings of: *Forty-seven Unpublished Letters from Marcel Proust to Walter Berry*, 213, *Pastiches et Mélanges*, 179
Publisher's Weekly, 237
Putnam, Samuel, 149, 163, 249, 309n, 312, 313, 316, 361, 363; describes Dunning, 123; translates Kiki's *Memoirs*, 146–147, 148, 149, 163; associate editor of *This Quarter*, 146, 151, 152, 161; resigns editorship, 162; founds *New Review*, 162, 318, 319; edits *European Caravan*, 312; criticizes *transition*, 319; translates *Enfances*, 321; issues *Direction*, 321; issues and reviews *Storm* (Neagoe), 321, 355, 356

Quennell, Peter, 373
Quinn, John, 5, 18, 21, 57, 58, 115

Rabelais, 368
Racine, Jean Baptiste, 336
Radiguet, Raymond: and *Devil in the Flesh*, 222, 223, 224, 225, 227
Random House, 26, 27n, 141, 227, 237, 251, 329
Rank, Otto, 164, 370
Ransom, Will, 387, 387n; writings of: *Private Presses and Their Books*, 387n
Rascoe, Burton, 50
Ray, Man, 28, 60, 135, 144, 145, 149, 166, 258, 270, 303; makes covers for *Henry-Music* (Crowder), 282
Read, Herbert, 139
Reavy, George, 320; writings of: *Faust's Metamorphoses*, 322, *Nostradam*, 322, *Quixotic Perquisitions*, 322, *Signes d'Adieu*, 322
Reece, C. Holroyd, 359
Reeves, James, 399; writings of: *Advice to a Young Poet*, 400, *The Natural Need*, 399–400
Reid, Marjorie: reviews *in our time* (Hemingway), 106
Réjane, 220
Remarque, Erich, 295
Revue de Paris, 335
Rheims, George, 163
Richards, Grant, 56, 348
Richards, Vyvyan, 385–386
Richardson, Dorothy, 55, 61
Richardson, Hope, 368

Riding, Laura (Mrs. Schuyler B. Jackson), 233, 270, 274–275, 313; and the Seizin Press, 385–389, 390–402; comments on Gertrude Stein, 389–390; edits *Epilogue*, 391–392, 400; assists in preparation of *No Trouble* (Lye), 393; comments on, 394–395; writings of: *A Trojan Ending*, 402, *The Close Chaplet*, 386, *Collected Poems*, 387, 388n, 400, "The First Leaf" and "The Second Leaf," 400, *Four Unposted Letters to Catherine*, 270, 274, 275, 393n, *Laura and Francisca*, 395–396, 396n, 397–398, 398n, 399, "Len Lye and the Problem of Popular Films," 394n, 400, *Love as Love, Death as Death*, 386–387, 402, "Picture-Making," 402n, "Pictures," 400, 402, 402n, *Progress of Stories*, 400, *Selected Poems*, 389n, *Though Gently*, 396–397, *Twenty Poems Less*, 274, 275, 393n, *Voltaire*, 386, *The World and Ourselves*, 390, 390n, 392

Rimbaud, Arthur, 151, 169, 174, 216, 217, 266

Robert Haas (publisher), 224

Roberts, Michael: reviews *Four Unposted Letters to Catherine* (Riding), 275

Robson, Margaret, 209, 210

Rodker, John, 63, 233, 278, 279, 280; oversees publication of Egoist edition of *Ulysses*, 23; operates Ovid Press, 278, 280; and Casanova Society, 280; writings of: *Collected Poems*, 279–280, *Hymns*, 280

Rodman, Selden, 164

Rogers, W. G., 252

Rogue, 234

Rolland, Romain, 360

Romains, Jules, 8, 10, 28

Root, Waverley, 164, 166, 312, 318, 319; reviews *The Indefinite Huntress* (McAlmon), 225–226; *Lucy Church Amiably* (Stein), 240–241; *Autobiography of Alice B. Toklas*, (Stein), 249; *Requiem* (Lowenfels), 297; comments on *transition*, 315, 316; reviews *Language of Night* (Jolas), 315–316; praises Harrison of Paris publications, 330; reviews *The Young and Evil* (Ford and Tyler), 359

Rose, Francis Cyril: illustrates *Childe Harold's Pilgrimage* (Byron), 338

Rosenfeld, Paul, 83

Rothchild, Herbert L., 279

Roussy, Suzanne, 326

Roving Eye Press, 306–311

Rowse, A. L., 166

Rubinstein, Helena, 117–120, 128–129, 155

Ruskin, John, 182

Sade, Marquis de, 334

Sadoul, Georges, 269

Sage, Robert, 204, 314, 319; reviews *Eater of Darkness* (Coates), 76; edits *transition* stories, 313

Saine, UC (Hugh Saxon), 144

Saint-Exupéry, Antoine de, 220, 224, 227

Salazar, Tono, 149

Salemson, Harold J., 139, 318–319; edits *Tambour*, 318; translates *Angel Wuthercut* (Cocteau), 321

Salmon, André, 145, 317

Sanctuary (Faulkner), 224, 227

Sandburg, Carl, 65, 136, 153

Sanford, John, 88

Saroyan, William, 379

Sartre, Jean-Paul, 229

Satie, Eric, 243

Sato, Ken, 28, 73; writings of: *Quaint Tales of Samurais*, 83, 84–85

Saturday Review of Literature, 70

Saunders, Ross, 305

Schlumberger, Jean, 28

Schnitzler, Arthur: and *Der Reigen* (*Couples*), 128, 129, 130

Schwartz, Jake, 86, 88

Schwarz, Georg, 400

Schwitters, Kurt, 316

Scribner's, 154

Seabrooke, Elliot, 270

Secker and Warburg, 92

Sedgwick, Ellery, 168, 248

Seizin Press, 233, 274, 385–403

Seldes, Gilbert, 108

Select (café), 129, 155, 198

Servant, M., 100; association with Jack Kahane, 354, 363–364, 365, 374; and Vendôme Press, 354

Servire Press, 311–318

Shakespeare, William, 376

Shakespeare and Company, 3, 5, 6, 7, 9, 10–11, 27, 30, 32, 33, 37, 40, 42, 46, 65, 83, 85, 88, 108, 121, 346

Shaw, George Bernard: refuses to buy *Ulysses*, 16; mentioned, 377

Sherry, Laura, 153; writings of: *Old Prairie Du Chien*, 153

Sibthorpe, John, 216, 270, 281, 287

Sidney, Sir Philip, 74

Simenon, Georges, 227

Simon, Dick, 227

Simon, Howard, 122

Simon and Schuster, 228

Sinclair, May, 61

Sitwell, Edith, 10, 61, 217; writings of: "An Old Woman Laments in Springtime," 61, "The Drum," 61, *Wheels* (editor), 256

Sitwell, Osbert, 271

Sitwell, Sacheverell, 271

Small, Alex: reviews *Eater of Darkness* (Coates), 75–76; describes Black Manikin bookshop and Edward Titus, 120–121, 122

Smith, Eric Dorman, 106
Smith, Harrison, 83–84, 194
Smith, Maurine, 325
Smith, Wallace, 372, 373
Smith, William, 230
Smyser, William: reviews *Crump* (Lewisohn), 127
Solano, Solita, 257
Soupault, Philip, 316
Soutine, Chaim, 144
"Spain" (Auden), 289
Spear, Thelma, 126; writings of: *First Fruits*, 128
Spire, André, 151
Starborn ("Arion"), 375
Stearns, Harold, 37, 58
Steffens, Lincoln, 247
Stein, Gertrude, 10, 28, 55–56, 60, 73, 74, 75, 76, 87, 96, 188, 200, 231–236
   passim, 291, 304, 309n, 310, 312, 313, 316, 319, 321, 355, 359, 377; pur-
   chases paintings, xiii–xiv; and cubism, xiv; described, xv; and Matisse, xv; and
   Alice B. Toklas, xvi; visits Shakespeare and Company, 9; receives Stephen
   Benet and Sherwood Anderson, 12–13; and James Joyce, 13; reviews *Three
   Stories and Ten Poems* (Hemingway), 49; and Robert McAlmon, 56, 58–59,
   62–63, 66–71, 93, 233; and Ernest Hemingway, 57; and Carl Van Vechten,
   233; comments on agents, 233; and William Bradley, 235–237, 246–252
   passim; and Plain Editions, 236; feuds with Hugnet, 243–244; writes *Auto-
   biography*, 246–247; lectures in United States, 250, 252; recommends *The
   Young and Evil* (Ford and Tyler), 357; writings of: *An Acquaintance with
   Description*, 233, 389–390, 393, *The Autobiography of Alice B. Toklas*, xvi,
   57, 232, 233, 236, 246–251 *passim*, 247n, 317, 319, "Aux Galeries Lafayette,"
   233, *Before the Flowers of Friendship Faded Friendship Faded*, 242–244,
   "Blood on the Dining-Room Floor," 250, *Everybody's Autobiography*, 233,
   Four in America, 250, 251, *Four Saints in Three Acts*, 246, 317, *Geography
   and Plays*, 233, 250, *How to Write*, 240, 241, 242, 246, *Lucy Church Amia-
   bly*, 234, 235, 237–241, 242, *The Making of Americans*, xvi, 56–59, 62–63,
   65, 66–68, 93, 233, 235–236, 243, 245, 248, 249, 250, 251, *Matisse, Picasso
   and Gertrude Stein*, 245–246, *Melanctha*, 58, "Mildred's Thoughts," 235,
   Operas and Plays, 245, *Ten Portraits*, 240, 243, *Tender Buttons*, 231, 304,
   317, *Three Lives*, xv, 58, 70, 231, 232, 233, 234, 248, 251, 252, "Two
   Women," 59, 61, *Useful Knowledge*, 234–235, "Wear," 233
Stein, Leo, xiii, 334
Stein, Sarah, 317
Stella, Joseph, 186
Steloff, Frances, 241
Sterne, Laurence, 184
Stevens, Wallace, 163
Stewart, Donald Ogden, 53, 75, 107
Story, 162n

Strater, Mike, 44, 45, 108, 112
Sullivan, John, 188, 189
Surrealism (Levy), 229
Surrealists, 165, 314, 369
Sykes, Bill, 178
Symons, Arthur, 28, 265–266; writes introduction for *Usher* (Poe), 179; describes Verlaine, 266–267; writings of: *Mes Souvenirs*, 267, 268

Taggard, Genevieve, 139
Tambour, 318
Tanguy, Yves, 166, 269, 270, 273
Tate, Allen, 28, 166, 210
Tauchnitz (publisher), 220, 221, 359
Taylor, Elem du Pois, 240
Taylor, Graeme, 79–80, 137, 139, 155; and Robert McAlmon, 155–156
Tchelitchew, Pavel, 243, 322, 336, 343; illustrates *Calendar of Saints for Unbelievers* (Wescott), 339
Testimony Against Gertrude Stein, 317–318
Thayer, Scofield, 40
Theis, Otto, 90, 92, 255, 265
This Quarter: edited by Moorhead and Walsh, 55, 64, 79, 80, 114, 123, 135–137, 234, 275; purchased by Edward Titus, 135; edited by Titus, 137–140, 142, 143, 146, 150, 151, 152, 153, 155, 156, 158, 161, 162, 163, 318; closes, 166
Thoma, Richard, 166, 213, 311, 318, 359; issues *Green Chaos*, 321
Thomas, Dylan, 380
Thomson, Virgil, 28, 63; assists Georges Hugnet, 243–244; relations with Gertrude Stein, 243–244, 246
Three Mountains Press, xvi, 50–52 *passim*, 61, 69, 95–116, 121, 220, 253, 278
Through the Looking-Glass (Carroll), 262
Times (London), 338
Times (Paris), 77
Times Literary Supplement, 262, 330
Titus, Edward W., 83, 117–119, 234, 275; opens Black Manikin bookshop, 120; described, 120–122; founds Black Manikin Press, 122; plans Paris theatre, 135; publishes *This Quarter*, 135, 137–140, 318; policies of, 152; and D. H. Lawrence, 140–143, 352; publishes *Lady Chatterley's Lover*, 140–143; and Kiki, 145–149; conducts poetry contests, 150–151, 152, 153, 163–164; closes Black Manikin shop and press, 158; editorials, 164–165, 166
To Beg I Am Ashamed (Cousins), 384
Toklas, Alice B., 62, 63, 231, 236, 244, 247, 247n, 252, 317; and Gertrude Stein, xvi; editor of Plain Editions, 236, 237, 239, 240, 241
Tonny, Kristians, 243
Toomer, Jean, 75
Toronto Star, 105, 154

Transatlantic Review, 55, 57, 58, 59, 96, 106, 109, 111, 112, 115, 233
transition, 81, 89, 126, 135, 153, 164, 165, 181, 184, 188, 189, 194, 202, 204, 205, 210, 229, 233, 246, 311, 313, 314–319 *passim*, 321
Tree, Iris, 255, 263
Troubetzkoy, Princess Paul (Amélie Rives), 374, 375; writings of: *Half O'Clock in Mayfair*, 375
Turbyfill, Mark, 325
Tyler, Parker, 357, 359; writings of: *The Young and Evil*, 357, 359
Tzara, Tristan, 165, 166, 257, 289, 317

Ulysses (Joyce), 8, 12, 13, 30, 31, 33, 37, 40, 59, 72, 83, 91, 126, 150, 195, 197, 308, 319, 346, 364; publication of, xii, 6*n*, 7, 12–20 *passim*; suppressed, 5; erotic reputation, 25, 32; profits from, 25; pirated, 25; *Also see* Joyce, James and Beach, Sylvia
Ulysses Bookshop (London), 86
Uncharted Seas (Ward), 373
Utrillo, Maurice, 144

Vail, Laurence, 194, 224, 309*n*, 313; translates *Bubu of Montparnasse*, 223
Vail, Sharon, 229
Valéry, Paul, xiii, 8, 10, 27, 151, 182
Van Doren, Carl, 125
Van Krimpen, J., 339
Van Vechten, Carl, xvi, 57, 75; and Gertrude Stein, 233, 236, 252
Van Wyck, William, 121, 151, 164; writings of: *On the Terrasse*, 149–150, *Some Gentlemen of the Renaissance*, 131
Vanity Fair, 234
Vara, Madeleine, 400
Vendôme Press, 354
Venus and Adonis (Shakespeare), 326, 336
Verlaine, Paul, 120, 266–267
Villa Seurat, 292, 294, 300, 366, 370, 379
Villon, François, 74, 111
Vitrac, Roger, 151

Wadsworth, Edward, 280
Walsh, Ernest, 28, 34, 77, 79, 80, 81, 92, 122, 123, 135, 136, 137, 153, 313, 321; reviews *A Hurried Man* (Carnevali), 64–65; reviews *Distinguished Air* (McAlmon), 114; dies, 136
Ward, Eric, 373
Warren, Dorothy, 268
Wasserman, Jakob, 221
Weaver, Harriet, 5, 39, 91; and *Ulysses*, 6*n*, 14, 15; publishes second edition of *Ulysses*, 23; and Joyce, 23–24; her Egoist publications, 37
Weeks, Edward, 175–176

Wells, Kenneth McNeil, 128

Wescott, Glenway, 153, 326, 328, 329–330, 336, 343, 344; and Monroe Wheeler, 325, 326, 339, 341, 342; and Katherine Anne Porter, 341; writings of: *The Apple of the Eye*, 329, *The Babe's Bed*, 328, 329–330, 336, *The Bitterns*, 325, *Calandar of Saints for Unbelievers*, 336, 338, 339, 341, 343, *Fear and Trembling*, 339, *Goodbye Wisconsin*, 325, 329, 330, *The Grandmothers*, 329, *Images of Truth*, 329, *Like a Lover*, 325, 341, *The Pilgrim Hawk*, 341

West, Nathanael: edits *Contact*, 89; writings of: *The Dream Life of Balso Snell*, 88–89, 90, *Miss Lonelyhearts*, 90

West, Rebecca, 383

Wharton, Edith, 178

Wheeler, Monroe, 324–326, 327, 334, 335, 338, 343; and Glenway Wescott, 325, 326, 339, 341, 342; translates *The Death of Madame* (Madame De La Fayette), 335; writings of: *A Typographical Commonplace-Book*, 338–339

White, Antonia, 380

Whitman, Walt, 114, 120

Wickes, George, 247n

Wilde, Oscar, 267; writings of: *The Birthday of the Infanta*, 179, 180

Wilder, Thornton, 27

Willette, 230

William Heinemann (publisher), 372

William Jackson (bookshop), 85

Williams, Charles, 166

Williams, Flossie, 51

Williams, William Carlos, 8, 40, 41, 42–43, 48, 49, 61, 65, 88, 91, 92, 93, 98, 99, 200, 209, 217, 305, 307, 309n, 313, 377; reviews *Post-Adolescence* (McAlmon), 43; relationship with Robert McAlmon, 43, 51–53, 82; edits *Contact*, 89, 90; visits Europe, 51–53; writings of: "The Colored Girls of Passenack," 89, *Go Go*, 325, *The Great American Novel*, 51, 101, 103, 106, 107, 114, *Spring and All*, 46, 47–48, 101, 103

Wilson, Edmund, 50, 70, 105, 106, 234; reviews *in our time*, (Hemingway), 107

Windeler, B. Cyril, 98, 106; writings of: *Elimus*, 103–104, 114

Winters, Yvor, 90; writings of: *The Immobile Wind*, 325

Winzer, Charles, 12

Wolfe, Lily, 121, 128

Wolfe, Thomas, 28

Woolf, Leonard, 73, 264

Woolf, Virginia, 264

Woosley, Judge John M., 26

Wordsworth, William, 308

Wright, Wilbur, 250

Wyatt, Honor, 400

X & Y (Olson), 230

Yeats, W. B., 15, 99, 103
Yost, Walter, 55

Zarate, Ortiz de, 258
Zay, Theodor, 375
Zukofsky, Louis, 91, 263

ABOUT THE AUTHOR

H U G H F O R D , Professor of English at Trenton State College in New Jersey, is the author of several books on the expatriate period, including *The Left Bank Revisited*, *Women of Montparnasse*, and *Four Lives in Paris*, and numerous books and articles on the life and work of Nancy Cunard. The recipient of grants from the Guggenheim Foundation and the National Endowment for the Humanities, he is currently working on a biography of the late Glenway Wescott. He lives with his wife, a ceramic artist, in Lambertville, New Jersey.